100 THINGS
GAME OF THRONES
FANS
SHOULD KNOW & DO
BEFORE THEY DIE

100 THINGS
GAME OF THRONES
FANS
SHOULD KNOW & DO
BEFORE THEY DIE

Rowan Kaiser

TRIUMPH
BOOKS

This book is available in quantity at special discounts for your group or organization. For further information, contact:
   Triumph Books LLC
   814 North Franklin Street
   Chicago, Illinois 60610
   (312) 337-0747
   www.triumphbooks.com

Printed in U.S.A.
ISBN: 978-1-62937-393-5
Design by Patricia Frey
Photos courtesy of AP Images unless otherwise indicated

For *Game of Thrones* fans

Contents

1 Game of Thrones

"When you play the game of thrones, you win or you die."—Cersei Lannister

In April of 2011, HBO aired the premiere episode of *Game of Thrones*. It was watched by over 2 million people—solid ratings, but nothing to indicate that it was a major event according to simple numbers. But for fans of the book series it was based on, *A Song of Ice and Fire*, it was a huge deal. It also had the full attention of TV critics, who'd seen HBO redefine television through the 2000s but which found itself without a major hit heading into the 2010s.

The critics generally liked it, and the fans certainly supported *Game of Thrones*, but the show's meteoric rise over the next few years, to the point where it's regularly called the biggest TV show on Earth, with individual episodes earning record-breaking numbers of Emmy awards, has still been an incredible surprise.

There aren't any unicorns in *Game of Thrones*, but *Game of Thrones* itself may be a unicorn. A unique set of circumstances led to its creation and it hit television at exactly the right time as television was ready for it. There's no "next *Game of Thrones*," it is entirely unique, and when it's done, it's done for good.

So what is *Game of Thrones*? It's an adaptation, and an increasingly different one, of one of the most popular fantasy book series of all time, *A Song of Ice and Fire*, by George R.R. Martin. The changes between the books and the show have been one of the most interesting parts of seeing *Game of Thrones* air. But it's also become increasingly controversial, as the changes from page to screen became increasingly notable before the show's story passed the book's in the sixth season.

Game of Thrones is also now the pinnacle of the entire fantasy genre. From the publication of *Lord of the Rings* in the mid-20ᵗʰ century, through *Star Wars* and *The Sword of Shannara* in the 1970s, and on to Robert Jordan's *The Wheel of Time* in the 1990s, heroic fantasy was heading in a certain straightforward direction. Then *A Game of Thrones* was published and changed that direction entirely. Amazingly, the same thing happened with movies and television. After the *Lord of the Rings* film trilogy, once again *Game of Thrones* came along and dominated the genre.

But *Game of Thrones* is also a television series on HBO. There, George R.R. Martin's Westeros has been reimagined by showrunners David Benioff and D.B. Weiss. It may be a unique show in many ways, but it also comes from a tradition of the best network on television producing the most ambitious shows on television.

Daenerys Targaryen and Drogon, the most useful pet of all time. (Photo courtesy of HBO / Photofest)

Without *The Sopranos* and *The Wire, Game of Thrones* couldn't exist, and it fits in with them, as well as shows like *Breaking Bad* and *Vikings* and *Shannara Chronicles*.

Perhaps most importantly, though, *Game of Thrones* is a story. It's a fascinating, complicated story, with hundreds of characters in dozens of locations. All of them have their own histories and motivations, trying to do the best they can in the wars over the Iron Throne of the Seven Kingdoms. While *Game of Thrones* seems to start small, focusing on the Stark family and a handful of other people, it's traveled around the world to tell the stories of the woman-warrior Brienne of Tarth; the Greyjoy siblings, Yara and Theon; the Martells of Dorne; and former slaves in Slaver's Bay like Missandei and Grey Worm.

There's also a huge, complicated history behind the story of *Game of Thrones*. From the Targaryen invasion 300 years before the show begins to Robert's Rebellion just 15 before, history permeates *Game of Thrones*. Characters like Rhaegar Targaryen, Ser Duncan the Tall, and Queen Nymeria pass their influence through the series. Some of this is on-screen or in the books, and some is shown in supplemental sources, like the show's special features and books like *The World of Ice and Fire*. It's a huge world, which is one of its strengths and a source of consistent confusion.

Game of Thrones is all of these things at once. That's what makes it special. That's what made it the biggest television series on the planet. This is the magic that makes *Game of Thrones* great.

Season 1: The "They Can't Do That!" Season

"Ser Ilyn! Bring me his head!"—Joffrey Lannister-Baratheon

The first season of *Game of Thrones* is one of the great deceptions in television history. It is, like the novels it's based on, a remarkable shell game, a piece of sleight-of-hand that presents itself as one kind of story, only to reveal that it's something entirely different at the end. For much of the season, the setup is straightforward: Ned Stark tries to keep the capital stable, Dany and the Dothraki prepare to invade, and the White Walkers threaten from Beyond the Wall. Then *Game of Thrones* takes your conceptions of how stories should work and beheads them on the steps of the Sept of Baelor, then burns them at the stake for good measure.

That's not how stories are supposed to work! Sure, heroes can die—especially middle-aged ones, like Ned—but they die gloriously, not begging for their lives from a sadistic enemy. But *Game of Thrones* goes there—and TV storytelling would apparently never be the same.

The clever thing is that *Game of Thrones* worked to prepare viewers for eventualities like this long before Ser Ilyn Payne swung Ned's sword at the Sept of Baelor. The very first episode of *Game of Thrones* works similarly. It sets up grand conflicts: between the living and the dead, and between the Starks and the Lannisters. It says it's a fairly traditional fantasy story with clearly delineated good and evil, but then Bran Stark peers through a window he shouldn't have and Jaime Lannister shoves him—to his probable death—saying, "The things I do for love."

This created the model that *Game of Thrones* would consistently use for the next several years: set up a story you think is going in one direction and, with a shocking act of violence, upend it and take it in a different direction. TV doesn't just casually kill kids like that! (Bran, as we found out the next week, didn't actually die, but was permanently disabled.) What happened to Bran eventually happened to Ned, and far more permanently.

In 1996, this model of storytelling was a revelation in fantasy literature, and within five years and three books, firmly established *A Song of Ice and Fire* as the premiere (non–Young Adult) fantasy series around. *Game of Thrones* used a similar model: its initial season's ratings were fine, but a few seasons later, it was arguably the most popular show on television. In both cases, timing was essential. Fantasy novels in the 1990s were primed for a shift toward moral ambiguity and shocking violence, as discussed in the next chapter. Television was equally primed, but in a different way: *Game of Thrones* arrived at a perfect time to take advantage of the shock twist and hyperserialization (discussed in chapter 5).

It would be easy to credit *Game of Thrones* with popularizing the shock twist, but it was really a rising trend for TV when the show premiered in 2011. Its parallel genre-show-with-violence, *The Walking Dead*, premiered about six months before, while a teen soap like *The Vampire Diaries* had risen to prominence as television's "it" show based largely on its application of "surprise stabbings." The timing was perfect: HBO was in the process of adapting a novel series built on TV's hottest new trend.

And it worked: the buzz surrounding *Game of Thrones'* surprise twists helped propel it to consistently increasing ratings. Every single season finale was higher-rated than its premiere; every single premiere was higher-rated than the previous season's finale—something I've never seen with any other TV show. (This remarkable streak ended, just barely, with the Season 6 premiere being slightly lower-rated than the Season 5 finale.) If you wanted to know what everyone was talking about, you watched *Game of Thrones*. That started with the Season 1 premiere and was solidified by Ned's death.

But if you want to look at what was really revolutionary about the first season of *Game of Thrones*, you have to look closer than just "shock twists!" It was that *Game of Thrones* slowly destabilized what we expect from stories overall, by being complicated, by being inconclusive, and by killing the people who normally don't die.

One of the most shocking things about *Game of Thrones* when it debuted was how unapologetically complex it was. In many ways, this show was confusing as hell, with many early viewers feeling totally lost. HBO has done this before—*The Wire* takes about five episodes to really understand its linguistic rhythms and get what the characters actually mean, for example. But *Thrones* did this with history—there is a massive backstory to what's happening that the TV show just couldn't show. I used to describe the early seasons of the show as having about 75 percent of the conversation and action from the books, but only about 25 percent of the history and mythology—the books are just that dense.

And yet it worked. Some of this is performance-based: Peter Dinklage as Tyrion and Maisie Williams as Arya, specifically, captured the essences of their fan-favorite characters immediately, providing easy rooting interests for new fans. And the series was simply amazing to look at: superb direction, sets, locations, CGI, and costuming made it one of the most attractive shows on TV.

But the real key was the understanding that this was an already-existing story with an existing fanbase. While not every reader was enthused by the TV series, the commitment to authenticity deployed by HBO's production and marketing—like sending expensive Maester's kits to influential journalists, critics, and fans—won the bulk of fan culture to their side. Readers could function as instant experts for viewers with questions (sometimes too enthusiastically, to be fair), and a complex fandom ecosystem based on the divide between readers and non-readers sprang up. It wasn't perfect, and wars over "spoilers" continued for years, but it made certain that every time someone asked, "Wait, who's that guy again?" there was usually someone able to answer—thus allowing *Game of Thrones* to tell its complicated story with confidence.

The complication isn't just in number of names or subplots. It's also that the show doesn't tell a conventional story. *Game of Thrones* sets up a straightforward plot: Beyond the Wall, there are White Walkers, threatening us all. In Essos, the rightful heir to the throne is making deals to acquire an army to retake the kingdom. And in King's Landing, a good man heads into a swamp of moral ambiguity, seeking to save his kingdom. At a glance, these seem to correspond with evil monsters, good heroes, and a fascinating grey area in between, all headed for a giant collision.

Even halfway through the season, a conventional story still seems possible. Dany convinces Khal Drogo to bring his army across the ocean. A wight appears in Castle Black, making their threat obvious to the heroes there. And Ned Stark prepares to bypass the Lannisters by setting Robert's brother Stannis up as king, instead of the Lannister heir, Joffrey. Then it all goes wrong. Drogo is killed, partially by Dany's idealism, stranding her in Essos without an army. Ned's coup goes awry, leading to his death and apparent Lannister victory. And the White Walkers, well, they're still out there, but the show punts their investigation to a Night's Watch Ranging set for Season 2.

Even the grand mysteries of *Game of Thrones'* first season are left unresolved. Two big ones drive the early story: who poisoned Jon Arryn, and who attempted to assassinate Bran? Although the show points us toward answers—the Lannisters, in both cases—it doesn't actually conclusively resolve them. In fact, the show waits until the end of Season 4 to say who the poisoner was, and never goes back to the issue of who sent the assassin. Instead, *Game of Thrones* uses both of these to set other, bigger events in motion: Lord Arryn's death, of course, starts the entire series, while the investigation into the assassin's dagger leads Catelyn Stark to arrest Tyrion Lannister, thus starting the War of the Five Kings.

This is how the aborted fantasy stories work as well. Jon's death sets up the next phase of the story, with Ned as Hand—so Ned's death sets up the next phase, the full-on civil war of the War of the Five Kings. Likewise, Drogo's death exists not simply to prevent Dany from invading the Seven Kingdoms, but for her to find the cause of defeating slavery, build a power that's reliant on her and not her marriage, and grow into the leader she will become. Oh yeah, and *acquire goddamn dragons.*

It's also worth noting that while these resolutions don't necessarily satisfy the initial premise of the show—dragons versus zombies!—they do provide satisfying stories on their own. The first season for Daenerys is about her seizing autonomy, even when it has horrific side effects. And for poor, dear Ned Stark, the first season is about his failure to understand how power works in King's Landing, even if that leads to one son, Robb, and his daughters learning the lesson he should have in far more painful fashion.

Finally, the first season of *Game of Thrones* upends our expectations by not killing the people whom television viewers might expect to have killed. Even the most important TV shows in terms of serialization tend to rarely kill their most powerful and important characters—they usually kill off sidekicks and henchmen. *Game of Thrones* did the opposite. Not only did it kill off its hero, Ned Stark, but it also killed off the king himself, Robert Baratheon; the true heir, Viserys Targaryen; and the Khal with the military power to defeat any one of them, Drogo. They are, theoretically, the most powerful men in the world of *Game of Thrones*, and all of them are starring cast members. Yet it's the powerful, not the vulnerable, that *Game of Thrones* targets—leading to the belief that anything can happen.

And that's the model that Game of Thrones rode to becoming, a few years later, the biggest show on television. The belief that anything could happen, combined with a continuing, unapologetically deep story with a ton of existing fans, provided a solid foundation for the show. It was also a great season in and of itself.

1990s Fantasy

"The Wheel of Time turns, and Ages come and pass, leaving memories that become legend. Legend fades to myth, and even myth is long forgotten when the Age that gave it birth comes again."—Robert Jordan

If you wanna understand *Game of Thrones*, start where it came from: George R.R. Martin's 1996 novel, *A Game of Thrones*. This was the first in the initially planned trilogy, *A Song of Ice and Fire*. But, well, *Game of Thrones* is a *way* better title for the series and, uh, it's not exactly a trilogy anymore.

The reason it's not a trilogy is the same reason that *A Game of Thrones* was special when it came out in the mid-90s: it was a different kind of fantasy. Where the fantasy genre in the 1990s was straightforward and usually predictable, *A Game of Thrones* was dense, complicated, and could kill major characters at a moment's notice.

So here's how the average fantasy book looked when Martin started his series. It was "heroic fantasy," a *Lord of the Rings* or *Star Wars*–like tale of a young boy (usually) who found out about his destiny, got a group of brave companions, found magic items, and defeated an ancient evil across a trilogy of novels. At the start of the 1980s, this model had become increasingly popular, thanks to Dungeons & Dragons, *Star Wars*, and books like Terry Brooks' popular *Shannara* series.

In the 1990s, a new, incredibly popular fantasy series shook this concept up. It was Robert Jordan's *The Wheel of Time*, which engaged in the same heroic fantasy tropes, but over the course of a seemingly never-ending series. By 1996, there were six books in the series, each of which increased the complexity of the story and density of the world's history—with no end in sight, either. The series eventually concluded in 2013 after *14 books!* Jordan also tragically passed away just before the series' conclusion, leading another writer to write the ending, something many *A Song of Ice and Fire* fans are terrified might happen to George R.R. Martin.

The books were wild successes in the fantasy genre—fans loved the idea of a world with so much depth to it, and with so many different stories happening at once. Jordan's secret: he used as many different point-of-view characters as he could in order to tell every part of the story he wanted to tell. Yet it was still a very conventional, predictable fantasy, with three chosen heroes and ancient evils and so on, just told over a much larger scale of characters and pages.

A Game of Thrones would be the start of the series that would surpass *The Wheel of Time* as the biggest books in fantasy. George R.R. Martin combined several different ideas into a potent mixture: the length and density of *The Wheel of Time* combined with a subgenre called the "fantistorical." These are novels that created imaginary worlds, but didn't rely on magic to tell their stories, instead being about humans and politics. What resulted was a complicated web of interrelated characters, all with their own motives and alliances—it was like reading a popular history book, except with the most exciting story possible attached to it.

Martin's novel also managed to do the neat trick of subverting fantasy tropes, so it seemed fresh and new, while also engaging with them to feel like the story still had a point. *A Game of Thrones,* of course, feels like it's Ned Stark's story. He is the main character, and main characters of novels don't die pathetically, as Ned does at the Sept of Baelor. It was, in the novels, just as shocking and genre-defying a scene as it ended up being on the show.

But at the same time, the stories of Jon Snow and Daenerys Targaryen seemed to fit into comfortable fantasy tropes. Both of them are potentially long-lost heirs to the throne with secret destinies, forced to travel on the outskirts of civilization and into the realm of the supernatural. From the very beginning of both the books and the show, many fans have understood the endgame to be one where Dany and Jon ride the dragons, burn the White Walkers, and go home happily—this is what should happen, according to the rules of heroic fantasy, and maybe it yet will—the story is just taking the scenic route.

George R.R. Martin also created the density of his world with a variety of different point-of-view characters. Unlike Jordan, who bounced around according to who he felt like, Martin used a specific form: the prologue and epilogue of each novel were a random character to give depth to the world, like the Night's Watch deserter of the opening scene of the book/show meeting the White Walkers for the first time. But for the rest of the novel, he had a rotating group of set POV characters. In the first novel, it's the Stark family, minus Robb and Rickon, plus Daenerys and Tyrion.

The other major subversion that George R.R. Martin engaged in was this: actions, in the world of *Game of Thrones*, have consequences. This is not a happy story of gallant knights fighting evil and succeeding (or dying heroically). This is a story where good guys die horribly, because in wars people die, and everyone has to deal with that.

Stark deaths at the Sept of Baelor and at the Red Wedding are irrevocable, and the consequences that arise are unpredictable. The setup of *A Game of Thrones* is a fairly peaceful kingdom facing some potential external threats and some internal instability, for example, but *A Clash of Kings* has a full-on civil war in progress. By the time later books roll around, half of the cast has turned over, with initially minor characters like Roose Bolton and Barristan Selmy rising to become essential parts of the story.

In short, *A Song of Ice and Fire* took simple ideas of how fantasy worked and complicated them. Daenerys is the Breaker of Chains, the savior who frees the slaves—and then faces disaster when forced to deal with what happens next.

Indeed, there's a famous George R.R. Martin quote about exactly that:

"Lord of the Rings had a very medieval philosophy: that if the king was a good man, the land would prosper. We look at real history and it's not that simple. Tolkien can say that Aragorn became king and reigned for a hundred years, and he was wise and good. But Tolkien doesn't ask the question: What was Aragorn's tax policy? Did he maintain a standing army? What did he do in times of flood and famine? And what about all these orcs?"

Martin's interest in answering those questions seemed to lead him directly to Jon Snow's story as Lord Commander of the Night's Watch, in both the fifth book and season. Having won the war against the Wildlings, Jon has to win the peace. He has to keep his friends and his rivals in the right place within the Night's Watch. He has to deal with the captured King-Beyond-the-Wall, Mance Rayder, as well as the rebelling King Stannis. He has to deal with the Boltons to the south, who betrayed and murdered his brother. And he has to decide how to deal with the Wildling refugees, as well as the potential invasion of the White Walkers from the icy North. Jon fails—perhaps it was impossible. And that's Martin's point: winning the peace may be harder than winning the heroic war.

As such, the *Song of Ice and Fire* novels both critiqued and fit perfectly into 1990s fantasy. They were both a rejection of the tropes that had come to dominate the genre, and what felt like the natural evolution of them. Jon Snow is Tolkien's Aragorn and

David Eddings' Belgarion and Tad Williams' Simon and George Lucas' Luke and so many others, but he's also a version of them that has to deal with a much more complicated world than they were allowed to by their authors and fans.

You'd normally think that "like normal fantasy, but way more complicated and the heroes die" would be, at best, a cult hit. But *A Song of Ice and Fire* became a massive success in much the same fashion as *Game of Thrones* would 15 years later: it sold fairly well early, with critical acclaim and increasingly vocal fans, and became a dominant hit by the time the third novel, *A Storm of Swords*, came out. Before the HBO series even came out, it wouldn't be a stretch to call the series one of the five or 10 most important fantasy series ever.

Why? Well, some of it is that it's good. While Martin's prose is mostly workmanlike, he has a gift for dividing the narrative between characters to leave them on cliffhangers to keep people reading. Combine that with the incredible historical depth he's created for Westeros, as well as the benefits of serialization, and there's a lot to like.

But it also just hit at exactly the right time. For whatever reason, the mid-90s saw a bunch of different genres and media change drastically toward what might be called intelligent vulgarity. The violent and profane took over from the relatively staid in areas like independent film, with Tarantino's cuss-filled films supplanting quiet historical dramas in arthouse cinemas. Or video games, which moved from *Super Mario*'s intense but adorable bounciness to the cartoonishly over-the-top violence of *Doom* and *Mortal Kombat*. Fantasy, which had been dominated by the same style of story for nearly 20 years, was ripe for its own vulgar subversion.

What's amazing, though, is that *Game of Thrones* did this twice, both as novels in the mid-90s and as a TV show in 2011. It has hit exactly the right place, at the right time, twice now. Some of the reasons are the same, as on-screen fantasy fans had gotten used to the same *Lord of the Rings*–inspired tropes over the previous decade. But some of it is how television and HBO dramas worked. Regardless, *Game of Thrones* now defines the entire fantasy genre everywhere, not just novels, for better or for worse.

Season 2: The "Now What?" Season

"Power resides where men believe it resides. It's a trick, a shadow on the wall, and a very small man can cast a very large shadow."—Varys the Spider

The second season of *Game of Thrones* had one of the most difficult tasks of any season of the show. It had to maintain the momentum of the first season, where Ned's death instantly made *Game of Thrones* one of the most talked-about shows on television. But it had to do this with a story that was really part one of three, with Seasons 2–4 comprising the story of the War of the Five Kings and the rise and fall of the Lannister patriarchs, Tywin and Joffrey.

More importantly, Season 2 has to deal with the geographic divergence of its main characters. Where Season 1 had almost everyone start in the same place at the same time, Season 2 begins with almost all of them headed in different directions. Add in the introduction of major new characters and factions—Stannis at Dragonstone, the Greyjoys in the Iron Islands—and things could get confusing. Fortunately for the show, the second season successfully maintained the narrative long enough to get to its climactic episode, "Blackwater," which gave *Game of Thrones* a true hall of fame episode.

Even before the season aired, however, HBO did its very best to assure fans that the series was continuing on the right path. The "Seven Devils" trailer released before the season may well get my vote for the greatest TV trailer I've ever seen. Built on the title song from trailer music experts Florence and the Machine, "Seven Devils" more importantly opens with a slightly edited monologue from Varys, quoted above. In examining the nature of power, it says that the series will maintain its intelligence during the ensuing power struggle. But by focusing on Tyrion—making the last line of Varys' monologue about him, and showing him in full armor at the Battle of the Blackwater—*Game of Thrones* also shows that its most popular character (and Emmy-winning actor) is the main character of the season.

I don't normally consider advertising a key part of the narrative of a TV show, but in this case, this trailer was so monumentally successful at building the narrative of *Game of Thrones* as a truly intelligent, truly epic show that it's impossible not to mention.

From the premiere, Season 2 recognizes some of its difficulties. A comet streaking through the skies of Westeros serves as a connection between scenes from Winterfell to the far side of the world as Dany trudges through the Red Waste. It's a clever connection, reminding viewers that this is all part of the same story, even though it may not seem like that now.

That first episode is also notable for a turn into darkness in the end, when Joffrey orders the murder of all of Robert's bastards in King's Landing. Certainly *Game of Thrones* had portrayed plenty of violence before, but watching the Gold Cloaks knife a newborn to death screamed that things are only getting worse in the world of Westeros. This, combined with the intensity of the civil war, increasingly led to the feeling that the Seven Kingdoms were undergoing an apocalypse even before the fantastic beasts like dragons or wights showed up.

The war also drives an increase in moral ambiguity throughout the season. While the first season was obviously more complicated than the simple "Starks good, Lannisters evil" that it could have been, the second season makes that even more difficult. Joffrey Lannister-Baratheon is clearly the biggest villain of the series, but he's supported by his uncle Tyrion, one of the most likable characters in the series.

Meanwhile, as the season progresses, Joffrey's chief rival in the war shifts from being Robb Stark, bogged down in an offensive against the Lannister Westerlands, and instead becomes Stannis Baratheon.

Stannis was an important character in the world of *Game of Thrones* in the first season—he's Robert's brother, the true heir, and Jon Arryn's ally in uncovering Joffrey's true parentage. But he's also not present after Jon's death, and after Ned is named Hand, Stannis departs for Dragonstone. There he falls under the sway of the red priestess, Melisandre, who promises that he is the Chosen One who will sit on the Iron Throne and save Westeros from the darkness, but her power comes at a cost.

That cost shows up a few episodes into the season, when Stannis sails to confront his younger brother Renly, who has declared for king, leaping Stannis in the line of succession. Renly, more charismatic than his brother, negotiates a marriage alliance with the powerful House Tyrell, and also brings most of the Baratheon bannermen to his side. But Stannis has Melisandre on his side, and she works as a cheat code for the true king, birthing a shadow demon with Stannis' face who assassinates Renly. Stannis, putting the ends before the means, assumes control of the Stormland army and marches the biggest army in Westeros against King's Landing.

Fleeing the camp after the assassination are its only two witnesses: Catelyn Stark, sent by her son Robb to attempt to build an alliance with Renly, and Brienne of Tarth, a woman warrior whose success in battle got her named to Renly's Kingsguard. Cat

Stark, meanwhile, has taken on the role of Robb's chief diplomat and advisor, although he doesn't necessarily listen to her (to his detriment), as he sends Theon Greyjoy to negotiate with his father, Balon.

The rise of characters like Cat and Brienne illustrates another major theme of the second season: the role of women in Westeros as wars and intrigue take their men. Viserys is gone and Dany takes his place. Ned is dead and in addition to Robb, Cat, Arya, and Sansa take on his legacy. Robert is dead and Cersei wants to take his place—but is forced to fight Tyrion and Joffrey for that power. Daenerys, with dragons but without an army, struggles to assert her power and rights. And a new female power, Margaery Tyrell, now becomes one of the most important forces in the realm.

Even the men who remain in charge are not necessarily what would be expected from powerful men. Robb and Joffrey, both kings, still have to fight against the perception that they're children. Tyrion Lannister, the "Half-Man," has to defend himself and his disability in the face of King's Landing's bigotry. King Renly's homosexuality prevents him from fulfilling his kingly duty to impregnate his wife, leaving his cause easily dispersed upon his death—and, indeed, subverted by the Lannisters, who are able to wed the virginal Margaery to their claimant thanks to Renly's understandable failure.

The net effect of all this: Season 2 is about broken and struggling men trying to take power, as well as women trying to survive and thrive through the chaos. No scenes make this clearer than those between Tywin Lannister and Arya Stark. Tywin is, of course, the great remaining patriarch. No man alive has more of a history of power. No man more embodies the ideals of Lannister power as well. And yet he makes the time to talk to and understand the disguised Arya Stark.

The second season of *Thrones* doesn't diverge from the novels too much. It is, almost exclusively, an adaptation of *A Clash of*

Kings, the second novel in the series. But the biggest diversion is sending Arya to act as Tywin's servant in Harrenhal before the North takes over. In the novels, she serves Roose Bolton, after the Northerners take over Harrenhal thanks to her manipulation of Jaqen H'ghar. The show shifts that chronology, however, and it's a risky move.

The major advantage: the Tywin/Arya dynamic is absolutely fantastic, with the chemistry between Charles Dance and Maisie Williams sparkling throughout their scenes together. This helps add some depth to the impetuous Arya, but it also helps establish Tywin as a ruthless, although rational, villain. As the main antagonist of the third and fourth seasons, this is essential. On the other hand, it keeps Roose Bolton and the precariousness of the Northern alliance outside of the show. Instead of seeing through Arya's eyes how Roose particularly is untrustworthy, the Bolton betrayal in the third season is largely a surprise, a minor character suddenly becoming a major player. In the long run, I think this works—Tywin is absolutely essential, and Charles Dance is such a great actor you don't want to waste him. But it is a fascinating decision.

Some of the other adaptation decisions prove somewhat less successful. Two of the breakout characters, and actors, in the first season were Emilia Clarke as Daenerys Targaryen and Richard Madden as Robb Stark. Both of these characters, while important to the overall narrative as political figures, have significantly decreased roles in the second novel as characters. Dany is trapped in Qarth and manages to get away, but there isn't much tension. Robb, who isn't a point-of-view character in the novels, is largely seen through Cat's eyes—but she's negotiating with Renly or in Riverrun for most of the novel, while his army is in the Westerlands.

Instead, both of these budding stars are given bigger stories. Dany's "give me back my dragons!" story is prioritized, making her a major character throughout the latter part of the season—although it backfires somewhat, turning a three-dimensional character into an angry teenager, making constant demands of people who owe her nothing. Robb's story, on the other hand, proves more interesting. His romance with his future wife, Talisa, is given extra depth and, given their eventual fate, tragedy. Talisa challenges Robb to be a better person, and he takes that challenge with respect and eventually love, which damns him and his cause in Season 3.

Robb's story also fits with another major theme of the season: young men, suddenly thrust into positions of power, forced to decide who they are and what they stand for. Robb picks his ideals and his individual freedom over strategic logic, marrying for love instead of duty. His great rival, Joffrey, also seeks to find himself. But instead of looking to others, Joffrey turns to his own cruelty as his guiding instinct; when Tyrion sends him sex workers to perhaps relieve some of his teenaged boy tension, Joffrey instead has them abuse one another. It's one of the more controversial scenes in *Game of Thrones*, where the show takes its reputation for simplistic titillation and instead tries to make viewers uncomfortable, as Joffrey turns a sexy encounter into something disturbing and brutal.

Tyrion, too, is another of those young men forced to find themselves. The show's Tyrion isn't given a set age, perhaps because Peter Dinklage, in his forties, doesn't seem to quite fit the mid-twenties of the books' Tyrion. Still, the show does successfully portray him as the wastrel son, adrift on a sea of money and debauchery—until desperation forces him to make alliances with Bronn and the hill tribes to save his skin, and his father acknowledges his intelligence. Tywin sends Tyrion to King's Landing to be Acting Hand, where Tyrion, over the course of the season, accepts his role as one of the most important and effective politicians in the entire realm.

Two other young men in the North, however, struggle mightily with their cause. Jon Snow chafes at his role as Lord Commander

Jeor Mormont's steward, embarrassing him at Craster's Keep (even as Jon uncovers Craster's alliance with the White Walkers). Jeor seems to understand why Jon does what he does and so when the legendary ranger Qhorin Halfhand joins the Great Ranging and says he'll scout out Mance Rayder's army, Lord Commander Mormont accepts Jon's offer to join Qhorin.

Things go awry for the Stark bastard, however, when he takes a Wildling woman by the name of Ygritte prisoner. He can't bring himself to kill the (beautiful) young woman, so Qhorin leaves him to do the deed while moving ahead. What ensues is one of the odder storylines of the show, as the Jon-Ygritte relationship is portrayed as half romantic comedy, half tragic mistake for the lad. Ygritte turns the tables on Jon, and a group of Wildlings capture him and Qhorin, with the rest of the patrol dead. Qhorin forces Jon to kill him in order to gain the Wildlings' trust, secretly telling him that he can learn far more on the inside than Qhorin could alive. It's hard to tell how much Jon gets it—but he does enough to follow through, joining Mance Rayder's armies with Ygritte as his flirtatious guide.

South of the Wall, a far more successful story of a young man trying to find himself (and failing) takes place: that of Theon Greyjoy. Theon's story is, in many ways, the heart and soul of Season 2. His plot is a classic tragedy, of a single simple mistake compounding over and over to make him irredeemably doomed.

That mistake is technically Robb Stark's, at least according to his mother's warning, when she tells the Young Wolf not to send Theon to negotiate with his father, Balon Greyjoy. She's right: Theon is immediately shamed and bullied by his father, and in order to win his blood family's respect, Theon makes the fatal decision to betray Robb and join the attack on the North. But even that's not enough: he's given a tiny contingent, showing that his father still doesn't trust him.

So Theon escalates: he decides to raid far inland, pulling Stark troops from Winterfell and seizing the capital. The ploy works, although Theon, pathetically, struggles to convince Bran that he's actually betraying the Starks. He continues to make mistake after mistake, executing Rodrik Cassel, overestimating his power, and, after Bran and Rickon escape his custody, apparently having them killed (they're actually two orphan boys, but nobody else knows this). His final mistakes are not fleeing the castle and not attempting to take the black when surrounded. His men betray him and sell him to the besiegers to save their own skins.

Theon's story here is a classic prestige drama. Much of the "Golden Age" of TV is based on characters making a series of escalating mistakes, turning from clowns into vicious antagonists like Warren on *Buffy*, or sliding from antiheroes into supervillains like Walter White on *Breaking Bad*. It's also a triumphant performance by Alfie Allen, who breaks out magnificently after a first season where he was easy to see as just Robb's sidekick.

The show receives a tour de force episode at the conclusion of the season as well, with arguably the single best and most notable episode serving as its climax: "Blackwater." Most of the second half of the season is built entirely around the build-up to "Blackwater," which does make some of the mid-Season 2 episodes feel a little perfunctory.

But boy is it ever worth it, with director Neil Marshall offering both a massive action spectacle and some of the best quiet dialogue scenes the show's ever done. I go more into how "Blackwater" works in its own chapter, 54.

The episode—and season—ends with apparent Lannister victory. Having defeated Stannis, the Lannisters also find themselves allied with House Tyrell, arguably the most powerful in all the Seven Kingdoms. The status quo seems preserved in many ways, despite this: Robb remains the chief counter to the Lannisters, with his army still holding the Riverlands. Dany has dragons, but little else, as she departs Qarth. Sansa and Arya are both freed of their most pressing dangers, Joffrey and Harrenhal, respectively, but still find themselves adrift in very dangerous worlds. And Stannis has fallen almost as quickly as he rose, forced to retreat to Dragonstone to lick his wounds.

Yet with events like Robb's marriage to Talisa, Margaery Tyrell taking influence in King's Landing, and Dany realizing she cannot trust those who want to take advantage of her, the seeds for the future are planted. Season 2 is in the difficult position of being a primarily transitional season, but thanks to strong performances and the climax of "Blackwater," it's a successful transition.

5 HBO Drama

The so-called "Golden Age of Television" in the 2000s was, in many ways, HBO's age. *The Sopranos* was the defining series of the era, pioneering many of the conventions and forms used today. Chief among them: the moral ambiguity of the main characters. Tony Soprano is the premiere modern television antihero, a man whose role forced him to do bad things, but who seemed to be trying to be the best person he could. That would change over time, as Tony increasingly embraced being a villain, but it created a template followed by *Breaking Bad, Mad Men, Deadwood, Boardwalk Empire,* and *House of Cards.*

Game of Thrones didn't technically follow, as unlike most of those shows' leads, Ned Stark was actually a fundamentally decent man. But like most antihero dramas, the world wasn't one that could hold heroes. Ned Stark's execution is a shock for many reasons, but one of the most crucial ones is that it demonstrates that the world of *Game of Thrones* couldn't be viewed in black and white. Ned's replacement as Hand of the King, and star of the show? Tyrion Lannister, one of the most morally ambiguous characters in all of Westeros, whose superb work as Hand...ended up saving the kingdom for Joffrey Lannister-Baratheon. Moral ambiguity balanced on the edge of nihilism is consistently one of the antihero drama's biggest strengths, and problems, when it falls off.

The second major trait of the Golden Age HBO series is its heavy experimentation with serialization. In this, *Game of Thrones'* predecessor is less *The Sopranos* and more that other essential HBO show, *The Wire.* But to explain why, we need to take a moment to talk about the history of serialization—how episodes of a television show remember and utilize their own history.

In most primetime television, the answer was that they wouldn't. Each episode was supposed to stand alone, to invite more viewers. In fact, most TV shows were written so any viewer could get caught up in each episode after each commercial, a quirk that becomes incredibly noticeable once you start seeing it. The exception was soap operas, which had dizzyingly fast plot movement but still a core status quo; they were always in the middle of the story, never the beginning or end.

Hill Street Blues in the 1980s is the show credited with adding increasing amounts of character-based serialization to its stories. As the 1990s began, the experiments began to flourish, particularly in the realm of science fiction, fantasy, and horror. *Twin Peaks, The X-Files, Star Trek: Deep Space 9,* and especially the wildly ambitious "novel for television," *Babylon 5,* all tried to tell more complex stories across dozens or even hundreds of episodes. These experiments didn't always work: *The X-Files,* for example, famously had its "mythology" fall apart under the weight of its own complexity.

The door to sustainable serialization was unlocked not by HBO or one of its rich network brethren, but the teen-focused "netlet" the WB, with the massively influential *Buffy the Vampire Slayer. Buffy* found a sustainable mix between conventional episodes and an overarching story by adopting a "big bad" method of storytelling. Each season has a primary villain, introduced in the first few episodes, playing a more important role in several other episodes before being defeated at the season's end. Each episode could be almost totally unserialized, partially connect to the main plot, or be absolutely essential.

The "Big Bad" model became the default mode of most serialized TV quite quickly—in large part because *The Sopranos* quickly adopted it. Thanks to shorter season lengths on cable—10–13 episodes versus networks' 22-episode seasons—HBO shows took on an even more rigid form. The season slowly built up over its episodes with the bad guys increasing in power. In the second half of the season, serialization grew even tighter, before the violent climax occurred in the penultimate episode of the season. The season finale of an HBO drama would be used to examine the fallout.

While HBO's cop drama *The Wire* never had the popularity of *The Sopranos*, it may have surpassed it in critical acclaim, to the point where it's widely considered the greatest television series of all time. In some ways, it followed the HBO model perfectly: 13 episodes of increasing tension, the 12th episode is the climax, the finale the fallout. But *The Wire* didn't bother with having standalone episodes of any kind. What's more, it followed multiple plotlines in different parts of Baltimore, weaving them all together as the story of the entire city.

Game of Thrones does similar work, telling the entire story of Westeros. Dany not meeting any major characters from the rest of the series until late in Season 5 is one piece of this, but there's more. Tywin Lannister may be *Game of Thrones'* greatest villain, but he never met Robb or Ned Stark, or Jon Snow. Ramsay Bolton replaced him as lead antagonist, but Ramsay only interacted with half a dozen major characters, tops. Huge parts of *Game of Thrones'* story exist autonomously while remaining connected with one another.

The Wire's model proved influential on ambitious shows like *Game of Thrones*, but *The Wire* still had fairly distinct episodes in a way that *Game of Thrones* often doesn't. *Thrones'* best episodes contain thematic or plot links throughout, but many feel like a collection of (occasionally awesome) scenes. In this way, *Game of Thrones* is very much a show of the late 2000s and 2010s: after moving outside of "Quality TV," with episodic storytelling leading to a serialized whole, hyperserialized shows focus entirely on moving the plot forward, an hour at a time.

The ideal show of the hyperserialized era is *Breaking Bad,* with *Game of Thrones'* rival *The Walking Dead* close behind. Although *Breaking Bad* has distinct episodes with their own themes, every episode is essential for knowing what happens in the last one. *Breaking Bad* is still a constrained show, focused on its small core group of characters, so it's not like *Game of Thrones* in overall structure. But when you combine its hyperserialization with *Wire*-like diffuse serialization? You get *Game of Thrones.* and not much else, to be honest, except maybe HBO's *Boardwalk Empire* spreading to New Jersey, New York, and Chicago, and Netflix's *Sense8*, which takes place across eight locations simultaneously.

Finally, a key component of HBO's dramas is an overt focus on sex and violence. This actually predates *The Sopranos*; the network's first acclaimed drama, *Oz*, had a reputation for being unsparingly brutal in its examination of sex and violence in prison. But there were also comedies like *Dream On* and especially *Sex in the City* with direct use of nudity and, in the latter's case, frank discussion of sex. It became, in many ways, the network's brand. Even when *The Sopranos* was at its most dramatic, it still had crucial scenes in the Bada Bing strip club, utilizing a similar sort of "sexposition" that *Game of Thrones* would become famous for years later.

There would be times, however, when "sex and violence" seemed to become HBO's only brand, not depth of theme or complexity of serialization. In particular, after the end of *The Sopranos*, the network struggled to find a commensurable hit. *True Blood* got the ratings, but rarely the acclaim, while shows like *Treme* received acclaim without ratings. Even in the 2010–11 television season, *Game of Thrones* was a gamble compared to *Boardwalk Empire*, a classic gangster series from *Sopranos* vets with a pilot directed by Martin Scorcese. But while *Boardwalk* never grew to be more than a steady contributor, *Thrones* became a worldwide hit.

But even that can't last forever. With only two seasons of *Game of Thrones* remaining, HBO is struggling to find a replacement. Shows like *Vinyl* have failed to make any kind of mark on the pop culture landscape. It's the sort of situation that has lots of speculation for a spinoff series—HBO has created a monster that they now love, but that they have no replacement for. Yet the network's essential role in the last 20 years of television suggests that we'll see more great HBO dramas, inspired by *Game of Thrones*, coming soon.

6 Season 3: The Grand Tragedy

"There's a beast in every man, and it stirs when you put a sword in his hand."—Jorah Mormont

There are two kinds of scenes that *Game of Thrones* almost always nails: a grand spectacle of the sort television can almost never pull off, and two people in a room having an incredibly tense conversation. Both exist in this season, but Season 3 finds more time to just let people talk, like Robb and Talisa discussing Volantis or Jaime and Brienne in the baths of Harrenhal. Or there's the introduction of the Tully family, in a lengthy, revealing scene where Edmure attempts to light his father's pyre before the Blackfish does it. This was perhaps the greatest comic scene the show ever did, along with the new Small Council playing musical chairs to try to sit next to Tywin, which consisted of two minutes of actors silently dragging chairs around.

There are four key pillars that make Season 3 such fantastic television: Dany's march through Slaver's Bay provides the highs while Robb's slow-burning failure provides a quiet, tragic structure to the season. Jaime and Brienne's journey through the Riverlands gives the show arguably its best friendship, and the addition of Margaery and Olenna Tyrell, and Tywin Lannister, to the already potent mixture of personalities in King's Landing is a constant source of delight.

As good as Season 3 is, however, a few decisions may hold it back from being perfect. Most notably, important characters from Season 2 are still there in Season 3, just kinda...hanging out. Quite literally hanging, in the case of Theon Greyjoy, whose repetitive torture scenes were probably the only major negative for the season. But that's a small price to pay for *Game of Thrones* at its absolute best.

Season 3 begins with a speedy resolution to the cliffhanger of the second season, the White Walker attack on the Night's Watch at the Fist of the First Men. Well, "resolution" might be a strong word—it simply skips to the aftermath of the battle, with Lord Commander Jeor Mormont and the bloody survivors of the battle finding Samwell Tarly. While perhaps disappointing after the zombie army marching seen at the end of the previous season, it did match the books, only showing the result.

Things don't get better for the Watch, either. Low on morale and men, they stagger back to Craster's Keep, where the Wildling man needles the Crows viciously until, led by Karl Tanner, they snap. In the ensuing mutiny, Mormont and Craster are both killed, and Sam flees with Gilly and her newborn baby. They're attacked by a White Walker but Sam, in desperation, stabs it with a dragonglass knife from the Fist of the First Men, killing it and earning the nickname "Slayer."

After the diaspora of major characters in Season 2, the third season is also notable for having several of them come close to one another. When Sam gets to the Wall he runs into Bran Stark, who himself just helped save Jon Snow.

Jon, like Sam, has pushed his way south of the Wall. After meeting Mance Rayder and winning his trust at the start of the season by saying he didn't believe Jeor Mormont took the White Walker threat seriously, Jon was sent south with a raiding party led by Tormund Giantsbane. Jon's motives became the main question of the season, with Tormund skeptical but friendly, the warg Orell antagonistic, and Ygritte knowing that Jon hadn't truly sworn off the Crows—but trying to commit him to her.

It all comes to a head when the raiding party captures a traveler who's seen them enough to report on their whereabouts. Despite his innocence, the Wildlings decide he has to die, and they ask Jon Snow to do the deed. Forced to make a decision, Jon freezes, forcing Ygritte to kill the man for him. Then Jon makes his choice, shoving Ygritte away and fighting the Wildlings. He's aided by his brother Bran, who's hiding in a tower nearby, and who wargs into his direwolf, Summer, to help Jon. Jon kills Orell, and tells him that he was right about Jon's loyalty the whole time. The Stark bastard flees, but is hunted down by Ygritte, who, betrayed, riddles Jon with arrows, although he manages to make it back to Castle Black.

Bran Stark has spent the season moving north in order to meet Jon and Sam, because he has a destiny. Or at least that's what he's told by his new traveling companions, Jojen and Meera Reed, who meet Bran, Hodor, Osha, and Rickon on the road. Jojen, a greenseer, has already spoken to Bran in his dreams and helps Bran understand that the three-eyed raven is calling the warg north, beyond the Wall.

Osha is less than enamored both with the Reeds and this plan, explaining that she's not returning to the North, since she once lived there happily with a husband who turned into a wight and attacked her. After saving Jon, Bran realizes he can't not go farther north, but Osha can't go with him. So he decides that Osha should take little Rickon to the Umber stronghold of Last Hearth, where they'll be relatively safe. In heading north and crossing the Wall, Bran meets Sam as well, refusing his request to join him at Castle Black—but acquiring a stock of dragonglass.

Other than Bran's travels, the North, for the first time and only time, remains largely ignored in Season 3. The only significant plotline to take place in the region is the torture of Theon Greyjoy—although this takes place in an unknown location before. At the end of the season, with the Boltons' treachery revealed, it turns out to be at the Dreadfort, at the hands of Ramsay Snow.

The torture storyline is one of the least-liked in all of *Game of Thrones*, and it deserves that reputation. Even as the rest of Season 3 proved to be the show at its best, there was usually a scene involving something horrible happening to Theon Greyjoy, whose betrayal of the Starks in Season 2 made him a less-than-sympathetic figure to begin with. So seeing the Bolton men—and women—and the Bastard constantly ruining Theon is less than pleasant.

There are a few mitigating circumstances here, however. Despite Theon's betrayal, his realization that he's totally screwed up at the end of Season 2 is one of the most powerful tragedies in all of *Game of Thrones,* both on the page, and, in Alfie Allen's portrayal, on the screen as well. And in order to keep Allen, *Game of Thrones* needed to keep employing Allen—Theon may disappear entirely between books 2 and 5, but the actor needs to appear on the show. The other reason: Ramsay Snow needs an introduction.

The producers of *Game of Thrones* decided to simplify the storyline of the North in Season 2, and skipped the introduction of Ramsay, and Reek, and his corruption then betrayal of Theon in the second season. Instead, they used the core idea of introducing the series' lead villain post-Joffrey by having him free Theon, then capture him again. It's a similar story, but without connections to any of the other characters we care about, it feels much weaker.

The Ironborn invasion of the North, so important in the second season, has petered out in the third. Theon's status becomes more important, with his manhood delivered as the ultimate embarrassment to his father, Balon Greyjoy. Balon prefers to give up on Theon, but Yara decides to lead a raid on the Dreadfort to rescue her brother.

Season 3's real focus, however, is the Riverlands, with multiple plots and characters crossing paths, leading to the end of the War of the Five Kings in the south. Robb Stark's armies comprise the only serious remaining threat to the Lannisters. Since he's won every battle he's fought, the Lannisters have given up confronting Robb directly. But since they've allied with the Tyrells, and Robb has lost the support of the Freys after breaking his marriage alliance, Robb doesn't have the strength to go on the offensive.

But Robb's army is breaking apart. His sudden marriage is widely seen as a massive strategic mistake, and his mother's arguably treasonous freeing of Jaime Lannister another sign of weakness. The Young Wolf is forced into another untenable situation when Lord Rickard Karstark, whose two sons were slain by the Kingslayer, kills two Lannister boy prisoners in a fit of rage. Karstark challenges Robb's control over his army and the war, forcing Robb to decide what to do about even more direct treachery from one of his most powerful vassals.

While Robb's instinct is to imprison Karstark, he's given advice from Brynden "The Blackfish" Tully. House Tully's women, Catelyn and Lysa, have been major characters in *Game of Thrones* since the beginning, but the men arrive in the third season as well. The season opens with Hoster Tully, Cat's father, dying of old age, which has Robb return to the Tully stronghold for the funeral. The two Tully men, Hoster's son, the new Lord Edmure, and his brother, the Blackfish, are there, and are introduced in an effective scene that demonstrates the third season's superb use of pace.

The key moment of the ceremony: Hoster's "viking funeral" of being pushed out on a boat, to have it be set ablaze. His heir Edmure is supposed to shoot the fire arrow, but after missing, painfully, multiple times, Brynden—a legendary knight—seizes the bow and scores a direct hit. This is their essential relationship: Edmure is overconfident without the competence to back it up, while Brynden is brusque but usually right.

That brusqueness is seen in his advice to Robb: that Lord Karstark cannot be allowed to live. Karstark gets a few more taunts off against Robb before the King in the North takes his head off in a single blow—and loses his Karstark army. Increasingly unable to take momentum back, Robb hits upon a desperate plan: swiftly attack the Lannister home, Casterly Rock, and force Tywin into battle. But to do this, he needs men, so he forms a plan to realign with the most powerful local neutral house, the Freys. An apologetic Robb negotiates a new alliance with Black Walder and Lothar Frey: Lord Edmure Tully will wed Roslin Frey, and he and the Blackfish bully Edmure into accepting the marriage.

After House Tully, Robb's most powerful vassal is Lord Roose Bolton, who separates from his lord at the start of the season. Tywin's departure and Arya's encouraging of Jaqen H'gar's slaughter of Lannister guardsmen has pushed the Mountain out of Harrenhal, which the Northern armies take, capturing all of the Riverlands. When Robb travels to the funeral, he leaves Lord Roose behind. Jaime and Brienne, attempting to travel quietly through the war-torn lands, end up captured by the Bolton servant Locke, who, in a fit of pique, chops off Jaime's sword hand.

Once at Harrenhal, however, Roose treats Jaime with respect, and Brienne to some extent—although she's forced to wear ridiculous dresses. An ex-maester named Qyburn heals Jaime's hand, and Jaime and Brienne share one of the best scenes in the show's history when, in the Harrenhal baths, Jaime reveals that he murdered the Mad King not simply out of loyalty to his father, but in order to save King's Landing from death by Wildfire.

Jaime becomes well enough to travel as Roose prepares to leave for Edmure's wedding—he tells the seemingly gracious host to give Robb the Lannisters' regards. He and Qyburn leave for King's Landing, but Brienne is supposed to stay in the none-too-pleasant hands of Locke. Jaime Lannister, once the show's primary villain, has found himself beginning down the path of redemption thanks to his friendship with Brienne, whom he rides back to rescue.

Arya Stark, having escaped from Harrenhal herself the previous season, is also traveling through the Riverlands, when she's captured by the Brotherhood without Banners, the remnants of the group her father sent to kill Gregor Clegane way back in Season 1. She slowly loses her companions as well, with Hot Pie staying at the Inn at the Crossroads and Gendry deciding to smith for the Brotherhood. The Brotherhood then captures a familiar face: Sandor Clegane, Joffrey's former Hound, who deserted during the Battle of the Blackwater. Clegane recognizes Arya Stark, who accuses him of the murder of Mycah, the butcher's boy, way back at the start of Season 1.

Clegane engages in trial by combat with the Brotherhood's leader, another famous knight named Lord Beric Dondarrion. Beric loses, with a sword driven through his shoulder, killing him. Another member of the Brotherhood, the lapsed, cynical priest Thoros of Myr, immediately lays hands on Beric, praying until he comes back to life: the first time *Game of Thrones* shows that dead is not truly dead, at least to the Red God.

The Hound is set free, and the Brotherhood decides to ransom Arya to her brother, King Robb. First, however, they try to make money another way, when the red priestess Melisandre visits. She learns from Thoros how he performs the resurrections, but also pays for Gendry to go with her to Stannis at Dragonstone. Arya, feeling betrayed by seeing her friend sold off, runs away, only to be captured by the Hound—who decides to take her to her family to get the ransom for himself.

The major characters of the Riverlands all converge on the Frey stronghold, called the Twins, for climax of the season, "The Rains of Castamere." In *Game of Thrones'* most devastating episode, the Freys, Boltons, and Lannisters align to slaughter Robb's armies, and kill the King in the North and his wife and mother. The only characters known to survive the disaster are Arya and the Hound, who arrive too late to see her family, and the Blackfish, who went out for a piss before the rampage. The so-called "Red Wedding" was in many ways the absolute pinnacle of *Game of Thrones*, discussed in the next chapter.

Some blame for the Red Wedding may also rest with Stannis Baratheon, who spent most of the season licking his wounds after Blackwater. Davos Seaworth is rescued weeks after the battle and taken to Dragonstone, where he finds his king has let Melisandre's fundamentalism run wild. He protests and is arrested, but thanks to his friendship with Stannis' daughter Shireen, he eventually finds his way back into Stannis' good graces.

When Melisandre arrives with Gendry, she wishes to use his "king's blood" to magic Stannis back to power, and tries to overcome Stannis' and Davos' skepticism by having three leeches take Gendry's blood. They are cast into the fire with the names of the three "false kings" attached: Robb, Joffrey, and Balon. Robb and Joffrey die soon after, with Balon dying in Season 6. (In the books, word of Balon's death arrives even before the Red Wedding.)

But Davos, realizing Melisandre will burn the boy next, instead sets him free. Before he himself is executed, he uses his newfound power of literacy (thanks to Shireen) to read his king the missive from the Night's Watch that the dead have risen and Mance Rayder is attacking the Wall. Stannis and Melisandre both agree that in order for Stannis to fulfill his destiny, he must go to the Wall and fight the Long Night.

King's Landing is a little less important in the overall events of Season 3 than most other seasons, thanks to the king being securely on his throne with no threatening invaders. The powerful in King's Landing mostly spend their time moving their pieces around—quite literally, in the fantastic early scene with Tywin's first Small Council meeting, and everyone except Tyrion hurrying to sit near the new true ruler of Westeros.

Much of King's Landing's events are shown through Tyrion's eyes. The erstwhile Hand of the King has been replaced by his father, and plummeted from most powerful man in the city to yet another noble scrapping for influence. Everything starts to fall apart for Tyrion: his father refuses to grant him Casterly Rock, which should be his by right of succession with Jaime in the Kingsguard. He's given a tiny room outside of the Tower of the Hand, and demoted to Master of Coin.

His story is also intertwined with Sansa Stark's, the other point-of-view character from the novels still in King's Landing. Sansa starts the season with hope: Margaery Tyrell and her grandmother Olenna seek her out and befriend her, gain her confidence, and gain information about Joffrey's true nature. They also want to use her as a pawn in the Game of Thrones, marrying her to Ser Loras and joining the Stark family with the Tyrells. But beyond their ambition, Margaery seems to legitimately like Sansa.

It all goes wrong for both of them, however, when Littlefinger reveals the Stark-Tyrell engagement to the Lannisters. In order to steal a march on their allied rivals, Tywin orders Tyrion to marry

Sansa, and Cersei to wed Loras. The Tyrion-Sansa wedding is a disaster, with Sansa too upset to show kindness to the Imp; and Joffrey's cruel taunting drives Tyrion into a rage where he threatens to kill the king. Tyrion, out of kindness to Sansa—especially after her brother's death—never attempts to consummate the marriage. This doesn't help his relationship with Shae, who turns increasingly unhappy once the wedding is announced—although she rejects an offer from Varys to leave King's Landing.

At the end of the third season, we've seen Lannister victories in Westeros three years in a row: Ned's coup was defeated, Stannis' attack on King's Landing turned back, and Robb and his army were destroyed. Joffrey and Tywin are ascendant, with nothing standing in the Lannisters' way. People who'd read *A Storm of Swords* might have known that the Lannisters were going to get theirs—but with nine months between the end of Season 3 and the start of Season 4, *Game of Thrones* needed to do something to say that there was *some* hope, some reason to watch.

That hope came in the form of Daenerys Targaryen, who, after two years of trying to find herself, finally seized power for herself. The turning point for Dany comes in the slave city of Astapor, which Jorah convinces her to stop in so that she can buy an army of Unsullied, supposedly the greatest soldiers in the world. While there, she's also joined by Ser Barristan the Bold, the greatest living knight from the Seven Kingdoms.

Dany hatches a bold plot to gain an army from the tiny amount of gold and power she has. She strikes a deal, against her advisors' wills, to trade her largest dragon, Drogon, for all eight thousand Unsullied in Astapor (as well as the translator, Missandei.) It's a trap: as a speaker of Valyrian, she's had the advantage over the despicable trader Kraznys the entire time. In one of my favorite scenes in all of *Game of Thrones*, Dany turns revolutionary: as soon as she acquires control of the Unsullied, she orders them to "kill the masters!" Drogon, too, cannot be controlled by the pathetic

Kraznys. With her army, she frees the slaves of Astapor and takes her role as a hero, the Breaker of Chains, and not merely a claimant to the Iron Throne.

With her army and the addition of the Unsullied leader Grey Worm to her council, Dany marches through Slavers' Bay for freedom. First up is the city of Yunkai, which attempts to bribe her to leave and invade Westeros. Dany rejects them, and instead lures one of their mercenary companies, the Second Sons, to her side. Their captain, Daario, joins Jorah and Grey Worm in a sneak attack on Yunkai.

The city falls, and in the last scene of the season, *Game of Thrones* shows Daenerys as its figure of hope, called "Mhysa"—mother—by the former slaves of Yunkai and carried by them into the final credits. It's a difficult scene for a couple reasons: first, the sort of "white savior" narrative of this white woman being the saving hope for innumerable people of color fulfills a long-standing stereotype of Western fiction. But for readers of the novels, it's problematic in a different sense: George R.R. Martin is well aware of the white savior trope, and Dany's story after Yunkai is an examination of all the problems of what happens after you win the war. But *Game of Thrones* needs a hopeful scene to end on, so *Game of Thrones* gets the "Mhysa" scene.

Still, it accomplishes its goal: it gives viewers a reason to keep watching, even at the darkest point of the narrative, with Lannisters triumphant and yet another heroic Stark dead. Thanks to being a less-than-complete adaptation of a single book, Season 3 of *Game of Thrones* was theoretically at a disadvantage, but instead it turned that into a strength, crafting the most impressive season of the show's entire run.

7 The Red Wedding

"The Lannisters send their regards."—Roose Bolton

June 2, 2013, may have been the greatest day in social media history. This was the date that *Game of Thrones* aired "The Rains of Castamere," the ninth episode of the show's third season—aka the "Red Wedding." This was arguably the peak of *Game of Thrones* as a cultural phenomenon. The ratings had continued to grow, the third season was the most critically acclaimed yet, and there really wasn't any kind of backlash of the sort that started to show up in Season 4.

The Red Wedding itself is arguably the most important moment in all of *Game of Thrones* as well. Three major characters are killed all at once, but, more importantly, so is the idea of hope for a legitimate resolution to the civil war in Westeros. To have that all happen at once turned the *Game of Thrones* fans who didn't know what was coming into shrieking messes—and those who did know what was coming ready to watch the spectacle. (As a fascinating historical document, the Twitter account @redweddingtears still has several of the best reactions easily accessible.)

To quickly summarize: Robb Stark made a marriage alliance with House Frey in Season 1, but broke it to marry Talisa Maegyr in Season 2. When his armies started falling apart in Season 3, he recruited his uncle, Edmure Tully, Lord Paramount of the Riverlands, to marry into their upstart rivals, House Frey. But the Freys join with the Lannisters and Roose Bolton, Robb's chief henchman, to betray the King in the North. At the feast at the end of the wedding, the Freys attack, slaughtering most of Robb's armies and his lords in the castle hall. Talisa is killed first, then

Catelyn Stark attempts to allow her son to flee by taking Lord Frey's newest wife hostage. He rejects her demand, Roose Bolton stabs Robb, and Cat gets her throat cut. Even Robb's direwolf is killed!

It was also, for those watching, the single biggest spoiler in all of *A Song of Ice and Fire*. Once the episode's title was revealed, readers knew that "The Rains of Castamere" was going to be the episode that broke viewers' hearts. We watched with glee as Twitter and Facebook exploded with pain—partially because it was funny, but also because we were welcoming people into the club of knowing that, yes, George R.R. Martin was going to tear out your heart in this particular way. And even those of us who thought we knew what would happen had a few surprises: Robb's wife in the novels doesn't go to the Red Wedding and survives for several books. Talisa Maegyr is not so lucky.

Much like Ned Stark's death in Season 1, the key to the Red Wedding's importance is how many rules it breaks. Certainly it's possible for heroes to die, and only the most devoted Robb Stark fans might say that he's more important than Arya or Sansa, let alone Jon and Dany. But Robb represents the hope for a conventional victory. If Robb can survive and thrive, then maybe there's a way for the good guys to win through straightforward war and diplomacy.

But Robb can't. The political structures of Westeros have been so thoroughly broken that they cannot grant our heroes victory. Bran Stark has to go learn magic. Arya Stark learns to become a warrior and assassin. Sansa Stark, the political football for so long, learns subtle diplomacy and negotiating the halls of her enemies' power. And Jon Snow has to prepare to lead against the true threat, the White Walkers, instead of fighting a petty civil war.

The key crime of the Freys and Boltons who commit the Red Wedding isn't murder but, instead, the denial of guest right. Westerosi culture is built around the idea that once a guest has been offered bread and salt, they will be protected. The Freys go out of their way to do this and, as Bran explains, for this they will be damned. For Roose Bolton and Walder Frey, who take over the North and the Riverlands respectively, this seems a small price to pay—but both are dead by the sixth season's end, as is Tywin Lannister, who allied with them and helped create the plot.

So the net result isn't merely a political loss for the Starks and victory for their enemies, but an absolute disaster for nearly all of Westeros. The bad guys, so desperate to defeat the Young Wolf, destroy all norms of aristocratic interaction and, in so doing, damn themselves as much as the people they've murdered. The Red Wedding is an apocalypse, both for the Stark armies and for the hope that the civil war isn't the end of everything good in the Seven Kingdoms.

After the Red Wedding it becomes clear: Westeros can only be saved by a massive change in how it works, so that nothing like the Red Wedding can ever occur again. And for fans? It's proof that there's nothing else like *Game of Thrones* on television.

8 Season 4: The Bloody Climax

"Fuck the king."—Sandor Clegane

Game of Thrones reached its peak in its fourth season, in many ways. This was the last season with King's Landing at its center, the Lannisters in clear control, the Starks as simple underdogs; likewise, it was the last season based on an unambiguously strong novel, the last third of *A Storm of Swords*. It also lives in the shadow of the Red Wedding, an event so monumental and culturally defining that *Game of Thrones* has tried, with only partial success, to regain that level of media attention. As such, the fourth season of *Game of Thrones* is the most explosively violent of the series, an orgy of death with over half a dozen major characters dying over the course of the season.

While some of this is the show attempting to raise the stakes as often as possible, much of it comes from the structure of the books it's adapted from. The final third of *A Storm of Swords,* starting with the Red Wedding, is, in many ways, the climax of the entire story up to this point. All the surviving major characters up to this point have built up their tension to an intolerable level, and it snaps brutally over the course of the end of that novel, which provides the backbone of the season.

The middle seasons of any television series are also typically amongst their best. The show has been on long enough that everyone involved knows exactly what they're doing when they put it together, but it's still reasonably fresh. This shows in the fourth season, with perhaps the highest number of incredibly strong individual episodes of any season of the show (episodes 1–2 and 6–10 all have a ton to recommend them by my rating).

Yet Season 4 is also the season where the story starts to most strongly diverge from the novels. As ever in the early seasons, it's in Jaime and Brienne's story, accelerated to give these two superb characters more to do. It works for Brienne, whose confrontation with the Hound gives a strong climax to both characters' stories that was partially lacking in the novels. But for Jaime, it leads to massive controversy: his sexual encounter with Cersei next to Joffrey's body, portrayed as consensual in the books, read as rape on the screen, seeming to ruin Jaime's carefully presented redemption from Season 3.

This is, in a sense, the core tension of Season 4: it creates a set of dazzling climaxes to the most important storylines in *Game of Thrones*, but in its rush it might not quite do justice to all of them.

At the start of the season, Joffrey Lannister-Baratheon seems to be the dominant force in all of Westeros. With the destruction of the Stark armies at the end of Season 3, nothing apparently is stopping the Lannisters from achieving victory. As such, the entire focus of the fourth season shifts to King's Landing, in particular the marriage of Joffrey and Margaery, which should solidify Lannister control of the Seven Kingdoms for good.

But that swiftly falls apart in the Lannisters' own "Purple Wedding," where Joffrey, at the peak of his power, is poisoned, and the once-proud king chokes pathetically, calling for his mommy. In an instant, Lannister power is shattered—the new king, Tommen, is an easily manipulable boy, and the chief suspect, Tyrion, is a member of Joffrey's own family.

After Joffrey's death, *Game of Thrones* aired one of its most controversial scenes in the third episode of the season, "Breaker of Chains." At the end of the episode, Jaime Lannister appears to rape his sister Cersei. The scene was written as apparently consensual in the novels, but on the show, Cersei rejects Jaime's advances and never gives any indication of changing her mind. Fuel was added to the fire when director Alex Graves claimed that the scene was supposed to be consensual, despite almost every context clue saying otherwise.

There were two major reasons that this became such a controversy. First, it was a departure from the novels, which put readers of the books on edge, especially because there were multiple other changes in the previous seasons that seemed to add more objectification of women and more sexual assault. Second, Jaime Lannister's path toward redemption is widely considered one of the best stories of the show, particularly his scenes with Brienne in the third season. That redemption came when he tried to prevent Brienne's rape at the hands of Locke and the Bolton men—to have him turn around and engage in that same behavior seemed to go against Jaime's evolving characterization.

The argument over this scene eventually ended up changing how *Game of Thrones* was perceived. After the success of the third season, when the show seemed to put it all together, now there was a constant debate over whether the show was too abusive toward women, as well as whether it was deviating too much from the novels. Although the show's ratings have continued to generally improve, after this scene, *Game of Thrones'* critical reception varied wildly.

After Joffrey's death, Lannister power is also threatened by the arrival of Oberyn Martell of Dorne, the first major appearance by the last of the Seven Kingdoms to take a role in the War of the Five Kings. The famously hotheaded Oberyn initially seems like he's there to integrate Dorne into the new establishment after they'd been shut out by King Robert after supporting the Targaryens in Robert's Rebellion. But Oberyn swiftly reveals his true purpose: to find and punish the Lannisters responsible for the death of his sister Elia in Tywin's sack of King's Landing.

Tyrion takes the blame for Joffrey's death, as he had previously threatened the boy king, and was the last person to pour his drink. His wife, Sansa, too takes the blame—although she flees with Littlefinger in the chaos. Tyrion is put on trial, with Cersei pushing for him to take the blame, and Tywin providing no protection for his son whatsoever. They even dig up Tyrion's lover Shae, who had been sent away against her will, and whose bitterness turns her against Tyrion, leaving no chance for him to win the trial conventionally. In a blistering final monologue, Tyrion lambasts his family and the entirety of King's Landing for not giving him the credit he deserved for saving the city, and for putting him on trial for being a dwarf. Instead of confessing to the murder of King Joffrey, he wishes he'd done it—and demands trial by combat.

The "trial by combat" ploy that worked so well for Tyrion in the first season, however, doesn't have quite the same strength it did then. His bodyguard, Bronn, has been promised a lordship and doesn't want to fight the Mountain, Cersei's champion. Jaime is no longer capable, even if he could go against his sister. But the Red Viper, Oberyn Martell, sees the opportunity to take revenge on his sister's murderer, Gregor Clegane, and becomes Tyrion's champion.

In one of the most impressive duels in television history, Oberyn talks and fights the Mountain into a corner, stabbing him and severing his tendons, leaving him broken on the ground. But instead of simply finishing the deed, Oberyn postures to get the Mountain to finger Tywin for his murders. He slips up—quite literally—as the Mountain grabs his ankle and pulls him to the ground. Clegane confesses to the murders, but only as he kills Oberyn, winning the trial for Cersei and Tywin.

Yet Tyrion still has allies. Varys and Jaime find a way to free him from his cell before his execution, and the Imp heads to the Tower of the Hand to exact his revenge. There he finds Shae in Tywin's bed, in the cruelest betrayal yet. She attacks him and he strangles her with the necklace he gave her. He then grabs his crossbow and finds his father, shooting him in the privy, killing *Game of Thrones'* most powerful and human villain. Tywin dies, and Tyrion flees the city with Varys.

Although Sansa has finally left King's Landing after two-plus seasons of abuse at the hands of King Joffrey, hiding in disguise in the Vale proves to be no safer for her. Although she manages to befriend the fragile Lord Robin Arryn, her relationship with Littlefinger—including him kissing her in the snow—causes Littlefinger's new wife Lysa to grow jealous of her niece. This culminates in a mad Lysa threatening to push Sansa out of the Moon Door—and revealing that she had poisoned Jon Arryn at Littlefinger's behest as well. Lord Baelish steps in and seems to calm Lysa down, telling her that he only had love for one woman—before telling her that it was her sister, Cat, and pushing Lysa out the Moon Door himself.

At the end of the season, a group of Vale lords approach to find out what happened to Lysa. Sansa, with Littlefinger's fate in her hands, reveals her true name and lies to protect Baelish, putting him in her debt. At the end of the season, Sansa, now with her own agency instead of being forced into subservience to survive, steps out in an imposing black dress, ready to play the game of thrones for herself.

Sansa's sister Arya also ends the season with her own major changes. Arya has one of the best scenes of the season premiere. When the Lannister power seems to be unbeatable, she manipulates the Hound into taking her inside an inn with Lannister soldiers, some of whom are on her list. The Hound offers a powerful note of resistance—"Fuck the king"—and the two combine to kill the Lannister soldiers, with Arya retrieving Needle in the process.

Although Clegane is on Arya's list, the two form an unsteady alliance and mentorship. His plan is now to ransom her to her aunt Lysa in the Vale, so they must traverse the war-torn and occupied Riverlands, stealing and fighting all the way. They arrive at the Vale just after Lysa's murder, a fact that sends Arya into hysterical laughter. As they head back into the Riverlands, the two have a surprise meeting with Brienne of Tarth.

After spending some awkward time in King's Landing, Brienne is given a new quest. Jaime Lannister, remembering his promise to Catelyn Stark, assigns her his job of finding and keeping the Stark girls safe. He also gives her a new Valyrian steel sword, Oathkeeper, reforged from Ned Stark's Ice, as well as Tyrion's former squire, Podrick Payne.

The two seek Sansa Stark with no luck until they come to the Inn at the Crossroads, where Hot Pie reveals that the long-missing Arya Stark is alive. Brienne seeks her out, correctly guessing with Pod that she might have gone to the Vale and her aunt. In a chance encounter, Arya meets Brienne and is initially impressed with the woman fighter. But the Hound recognizes that Brienne has a Lannister sword and starts a fight with the Maid of Tarth for Arya.

This is a major departure from the novels, where the Hound fights a group of his brother's men from Harrenhal in the third book, while Brienne fights a different set of Harrenhal mercenaries in the fourth. In bypassing the fights with Lannister men, the show cleverly forces its best characters into a dramatic confrontation, which turns into a brutal, bloody test of strength. Brienne eventually wins, with the Hound falling down a cliff. She loses Arya, though, who finds the apparently dying Clegane. Rather than give him the gift of mercy, as he demands, she steals his coin and leaves him on the road. Her money isn't enough to take her north to her brother—but finding out her captain is Braavosi, Arya shows him the coin Jaqen gave her, with the words "Valar Morghulis." The last shot of the season is Arya Stark on the boat, leaving the war-torn Seven Kingdoms.

In the North, Roose Bolton attempts to consolidate his power as the new Warden. He orders his son Ramsay to help retake the lands from the Ironborn invaders, particularly Moat Cailin, which stands between his armies in the Riverlands and Winterfell. Roose is upset that Ramsay has damaged Theon too much, but the Bastard of Bolton reveals that Theon told him that he didn't kill the Stark boys. The Boltons send Locke to the Wall to see if Jon Snow is sheltering the Starks.

Yara Greyjoy raids the Dreadfort, but finds her brother cowering in the kennels. When he refuses to leave, and Ramsay starts to kill the Ironborn, she retreats. Ramsay, pleased with his Reek's loyalty, decides to use him to recapture Moat Cailin by playing the role of Theon Greyjoy and ordering the Ironborn to surrender. Theon succeeds—and Ramsay kills the Ironborn anyway. For his success, Roose Bolton rewards Ramsay with an order from King Tommen, legitimizing him and making him House Bolton's heir.

Locke's arrival at the Wall comes during a chaotic time for the Night's Watch. Jon Snow has warned the brothers that Mance's army is coming, and Tormund's raiding party is causing refugees to flee to Castle Black. Jon's old rival, Ser Alliser Thorne, is Acting Commander, and he doesn't trust Jon—or fully heed his warnings. Jon realizes, however, that the information he gave Mance inflating the Watch's numbers can be refuted by the deserters at Craster's Keep, so he leads a small group to kill them. Locke goes along after overhearing Sam tell Jon that Bran is beyond the Wall.

The raiding party finds a scene of gothic horror, with Karl Tanner and the other deserters apparently having spent their months in Craster's Keep in an orgy of rape and feasting. Coming so soon after the controversial Jaime-Cersei rape scene, this only reinforced the controversy about *Game of Thrones*. Nevertheless, Craster's wives do get some revenge. As the battle rages, Jon finds Karl Tanner in the burning keep. With the aid of one of the women, he gruesomely kills Tanner, and Craster's women enjoy the burning of their former nightmare of a home.

Bran Stark and his party are captured by Tanner's men right before the raid, which disrupts Tanner's interrogation and potential torture. Locke, in the midst of the battle, seeks Bran Stark and seems to capture him. But Bran skinchanges into Hodor's body and slaughters Locke. Despite another near-meeting with Jon, Bran again turns north to find the Three-Eyed Raven.

Bran finds a giant tree, the object of his quest, when he's attacked by the undead. Although Meera, Hodor, and Summer fight the skeletons off, one of them finds and stabs Jojen Reed to death. One of the Children of the Forest, the legendary, long-lost original inhabitants of Westeros, arrives and calls fire down on the skeletons, allowing Bran to meet the Raven, who promises to train the Stark boy. The battle at the weirwood tree also proved divisive among fans, with the overt use of magic and Harryhausen-like skeletons giving *Game of Thrones* the feel of a much more traditional fantasy—although this seems like the direction the novels are heading anyway.

Back at the Wall, the Watch and the Wildlings both prepare for a monumental battle. The ninth episode of the season, "The Watchers on the Wall," is exclusively devoted to that fight, just as "Blackwater" was for that battle in the second season. But this was a bigger risk for *Game of Thrones*—unlike the fight for King's Landing, the battle at the Wall involved only a tiny number of major characters: Jon, Sam, Ygritte, Alliser, Tormund, and Mance. Despite this, the episode is a monumental achievement. (See chapter 75 for more.)

While Mance's army attacks the Wall directly, Tormund's raiders hit Castle Black from behind. Ser Alliser is wounded in single combat with Tormund, giving Jon command of the siege. He heads down into the courtyard to meet them, facing Styr, the Magnar of Thenn, and defeating him in combat. Jon is faced by Ygritte, with a bow trained on his heart, but she hesitates and is killed by Olly, a refugee boy whose village was wiped out by Tormund and Ygritte's raiders. Castle Black holds for the night.

Jon Snow decides that the only way the castle can survive is if Mance Rayder is killed, and his alliance of clans falls apart. Jon travels to Mance's camp to parley, but Mance realizes Jon's intention. Before the King-Beyond-the-Wall can do anything, a surprise charge from the knights of Stannis Baratheon's army routs the Wildlings, capturing their king.

Stannis has been plotting this move the whole season, though largely off screen, keeping it a surprise. He got the coin to hire the ships to transport his army from the Iron Bank of Braavos, where Davos Seaworth's inspired monologue convinces the bankers to support his claim. From the far North, Stannis now plans to reclaim the North and attack the Lannisters.

Finally, across the world in Slaver's Bay, Dany's revolutionary war effort continues—at least initially. With Astapor and Yunkai taken, her army moves to Meereen, which refuses to yield, crucifying 163 slave children along her march. She sends Grey Worm into the city to initiate a slave revolt. The ensuing riot kills many of the city's Great Masters and opens the gates for the Breaker of Chains. As revenge for the murder of the slave children, Dany crucifies 163 members of the Great Masters' families.

But in Meereen, the revolution begins to stall. News arrives that both Astapor and Yunkai have slid back—the former with a brutal Emperor named Cleon, and the latter becoming a slave state again. Having found that revolution needs to be solidified lest it be lost, she decides to stay in Meereen to learn how to rule.

It doesn't go so well. The Masters are a constant thorn in her side, demanding old privileges. Even some former slaves, who had been comfortable in their former lives, asked to return to slavery. Her more steadfast ally, Jorah Mormont, is revealed to have spied on her for King Robert, and he's sent into exile. But worst of all, she finds out that her increasingly large dragons have begun killing humans. Although the largest, Drogon, is still free, Dany decides to chain the two other dragons up in a pit beneath the city.

The end of the fourth season sees utter chaos for the Seven Kingdoms. The stories that had driven the previous few seasons—Tywin's consolidation of power, Dany's march to freedom, Mance's invasion—have resolved. In the fifth season, the characters are forced to confront the wreckage that Season 4 left for them.

9 A Song of Ice and Fire

"Such a splendid fantistorical! I read my eyes out."—Anne McCaffrey

Reading the novels upon which *Game of Thrones* is based can feel like stepping into an entirely different world at times, especially deeper in the series. This isn't just based on the changes from book to screen—although there are plenty. Rather, the difference comes from *how* the story is told. There are three key formal differences between the books and the show, and they help explain a ton about how the show became what it is: point-of-view; the unreliability of information; and character and historical density

A Song of Ice and Fire uses a rigid point-of-view, putting the reader in a specific set of characters' heads and only showing what they think and see. Each book also has a prologue and an epilogue with a one-off character who usually dies in some creepy supernatural fashion. The initial batch of POV characters is the core Stark family minus Rickon and, oddly, Robb, plus Tyrion and Dany. As the series expands in scope, point-of-view characters are added to tell the most important parts of the story across the world—with the War of the Five Kings starting to rage in the second book, for example, Davos and Theon are added so that we can see what happens with Stannis' armies and the Ironborn invasion of the North.

This has a few effects on readers. For one thing, it gets us attached to the characters whom we spend time with. A friend who only watched the show, without reading, asked me to name my favorite characters. All but one was a POV character—unlike the show, where Margaery and Tywin and Jorah and Littlefinger feel roughly equally important as the Starks and the rest. But this can backfire: after sticking with the same core with only partial changes through the first three novels, George R.R. Martin went a totally different direction in the fourth, *A Feast for Crows*. That book didn't have Jon, Dany, Tyrion, or Bran, but it did add multiple new POV characters showing the politics of the Iron Islands and Dorne. Because it veers into entirely new territory, with characters we have, in a few cases, never even heard of, *Feast* is probably the least-liked novel in the series.

Martin decided to add these Greyjoys and Martells to the narrative because he had to in order to show what was happening in all the far-reaching parts of the world. A major byproduct of only telling the story through specific characters' eyes is that those eyes have to be in the part of the world where the story is happening. Without Catelyn Stark's journey to Renly's camp in the second book, for example, we wouldn't see his death. As the novels have gotten more ambitious, growing from telling the story of the Starks to encompassing the entire political drama of Westeros, Martin has found himself adding new points of view to show diverse parts of the world.

For example, because he had no one in Meereen after the Sons of the Harpy attack in Daznak's Pit (Tyrion not having met Dany in the books yet), he added the still-living Barristan Selmy as a POV character for a few chapters.

Limiting our knowledge of Westeros to the minds and eyes of a handful of characters also means that readers can only get the information that these characters receive. This means that news, rumor, and innuendo play powerful roles in the books, whereas on the show, what we see is treated as the objective truth. As a simple example: Theon Greyjoy's last chapter in the second novel has him receiving a head injury that, for all we know, is fatal. For the next two novels, Theon's fate is uncertain. Roose Bolton presents the Starks with a piece of skin he tells them has been flayed from Theon before the Red Wedding, while at the Iron Islands, the Kingsmoot proceeds with most present unsure if Theon is alive or dead.

Because of this, the characters—and by extension, the readers—are desperate for scraps of information that become essential for understanding the world. In *A Feast for Crows*, the characters in the Riverlands constantly hear stories of the Hound going on a violent rampage through villages—even though we last saw him through Arya's eyes as he lay apparently dying. The question of whether the Hound is dead or not isn't just that we didn't actually see his body, as it was for two seasons of the show before his reappearance.

As the novels progress, Martin gets better at using these rumors, and cleverly starts to weave them through different points of view. In *A Storm of Swords*, several of the characters in the Riverlands start encountering the word "Tansy." Lord Hoster Tully, on his death-bed, keeps repeating it, though Catelyn Stark doesn't understand what he means. Arya runs into an innkeep named Tansy, and it gets confused with the continuing rumor-based search for the mother of Jon Snow. It's finally revealed that it was an abortion-inducing herb given to Lysa Tully after Littlefinger impregnated her when they were young, in order to cause an abortion—thus tying together the storylines of Catelyn, Arya, and Sansa in *A Storm of Swords*.

The show just doesn't have the time or space to be able to do that. All of the speculation about Jon's mother, whether she's Ashara Dayne, or a serving woman, is just gone. "Tansy" becomes just a name on the show, given to one of Ramsay Bolton's lovers, the one he murders with his dogs at the start of Season 4.

On the other hand, because the show isn't limited to point-of-view characters, we can see far more of what's happening and be sure of its truth and value. *Game of Thrones* has used this especially well in fleshing out characters like Littlefinger and Varys, both of whom have several excellent scenes with each other on the show that we never see on the page.

Margaery Tyrell in particular is massively changed for the show: in the books, she's a cypher, someone who seems friendly and charming to everyone she meets, and they judge her for that (Sansa positively, Cersei negatively). On the show, Cersei's perception of Margaery as a wildly ambitious young woman using every means to gain power is largely correct, and Margaery's an impressive character on her own because of this, instead of merely being an interesting part of Cersei's story.

The final major difference between the books and the show, and the one a reader will probably notice first, is just how *dense* the books are. On the show, we see the dialogue and the action, and this creates a complex enough story. But in the books, every single character has a history, and their house has a history, and these things all interact with one another.

For example, the Tournament of the Hand, in the middle of the first season, only has the semi-finals of its joust shown, with the Clegane brothers, Loras, and Jaime taking part. But on the page, it's a multi-part affair, with many of the great knights of the realm being introduced. Sansa's friend Jeyne Poole gets a crush on a dashing young knight named Beric Dondarrion; an archer named Anguy wins a shooting contest; and Thoros of Myr's flaming sword makes waves in the tourney melee. These characters eventually become the backbone of the Brotherhood without Banners—all set up early on.

Likewise, someone like Roose Bolton starts out in the first novel as one of many moderately powerful Northern lords, and only slowly rises to prominence over the course of the next few books, which makes his betrayal at the Red Wedding both more shocking and seemingly more inevitable in retrospect.

Because the show doesn't have this dense foundation of potentially important characters, it relies on merging the major characters we care about and having them be in more places, taking more action. Often this works, with Brienne meeting the Hound in

Season 4, as opposed to both of them fighting different groups of roving mercenaries or guardsmen. Sometimes it doesn't, as with Jaime and Bronn going to Dorne, instead of Arys Oakhart.

This tendency is also the one that tends to create the biggest changes from the page to the screen. *Game of Thrones* focuses on a couple dozen characters, where *A Song of Ice and Fire* has hundreds with their own motivations and agency. Over time, this has led to the books feeling like they're an entirely different method for telling a similar story as the show—which to me is a good thing, as it means the two aren't in conflict, and both novels and television series can be enjoyed as their own thing.

10 Season 5: In Which Things Get Dark

"I'm going to break the wheel."—Daenerys Targaryen

The fifth season of *Game of Thrones* hit both some of the series' highest highs as well as its lowest lows. Ratings continued to improve, with its streak of every premiere rated higher than the previous season's finale continuing, if only barely. Perhaps more importantly, Thrones finally captured its first Emmy victory for Outstanding Drama Series, traditional mark of "best show on television."

On the other hand, Season 5 proved to be one of the most controversial with both fandom and critics. The season in general was considered to be far too dark and nihilistic, while specifically the scene where Sansa Stark is married to and then sexually assaulted by Ramsay Bolton marked a major turning point, with some websites even refusing to continue covering the show. That storyline was one of many disliked by fans of the books for major changes from the novels.

Those changes are part of what made Season 5 unique. Where every other season adapted a single novel, or less, the fifth season adapted the fourth *and* fifth books, *A Feast for Crows* and *A Dance with Dragons*. So in addition to all the escalating adaptation changes from the previous four years, Season 5 adapted roughly 2,000 pages. (The most pages adapted prior to this, with the third book split up across Seasons 3 and 4, was Season 2 portraying the nearly 800 pages of *A Clash of Kings*.) In a few critical cases, the fifth season also, finally, passed the books, particularly in the North with Stannis' attack on Winterfell.

With that said, many of the problems in Season 5 do exist in those two novels—both of them came under a lot of criticism for extraneous side plots like Dorne, not much happening in plotlines like Arya's, a general nihilistic tone, and, for the first time in the series, a major reliance on cliffhangers like Jon Snow's death.

The biggest change in the season, and perhaps in the show as a whole, is that for the first time since Ned rode into town in the third episode of Season 1, King's Landing isn't the center of the story. The end of the fourth season saw many of the major players leave the capital behind: Littlefinger and Sansa departed first, after the Purple Wedding; Brienne and Pod departed on their search for the Stark girls; Oberyn Martell was killed; and finally, Tyrion Lannister killed his father Tywin and lover Shae and fled the city with Lord Varys.

The net result of this is that King's Landing, once the narratively vibrant home to representatives of almost every major faction in the novels, becomes simply the battleground for control of the weak-willed King Tommen between the Lannisters and Tyrells, with the High Sparrow manipulating matters in the middle.

Narrative focus shifts far to the north and east instead. At the Wall, Jon Snow is elected Lord Commander of the Night's Watch, while King Stannis plots his attack on the Boltons at Winterfell. To the east, finally—finally!—Daenerys Targaryen meets a major character from the rest of the story, as Tyrion Lannister arrives in Meereen just as the rebellion against Dany's rule boils over. This shift in focus goes along with the overall trend toward conventional fantasy narrative: the show works to set Jon and Dany up as the main characters of the series by the end of the fifth season.

In the meantime, the main character of the fifth season is instead arguably Stannis Baratheon, whose decision to attack Winterfell drives both his story and the narratives of several other major characters: Jon and Sam at the Wall; Davos, Shireen, and Melisandre with his army; and Ramsay, Sansa, and Brienne in Winterfell.

Stannis starts the season at the Wall, having just defeated Mance Rayder's army and attempting to recruit more men for his army—Mance and his Wildlings first, then Jon Snow and the lords of the North via his royal ability to legitimize bastards, although these attempts fail. Stannis also grants Sam Tarly true respect in a scene where he describes how fine a warleader Sam's dad Randyll Tarly is—the only man to defeat Robert in the civil war fifteen years before. But instead of comparing Sam to his abusive father, Stannis notes that Sam's skills are in research, and provides encouragement.

Scenes like that one are what centers Stannis as the key figure of the season. He's set up as both a good father figure and a good king—a man worthy of the hope invested in him as the only good contender for the Iron Throne to actually be in Westeros.

All this makes the end of Stannis' campaign even more bitterly devastating. His army is trapped in the early snows on its way to Winterfell. In desperation, he listens to Melisandre's advice: that he should burn his daughter Shireen, with her blood of kings, to gain the power of the Red God. The move succeeds in making the snow melt, but his mercenaries desert, his wife commits suicide, Melisandre leaves (with Davos having left before the execution), and Stannis' tiny army fights a desultory battle against Ramsay

Bolton's forces in front of Winterfell. Stannis himself, wounded and beaten, is executed by Brienne of Tarth, gaining vengeance, three seasons later, for the assassination of her lord, Renly.

Stannis' transition from legitimate king to pathetic child-killer is emblematic of Season 5's overall darkness. In almost every part of Westeros, stories that begin with hope for a better world are shattered by violence and betrayal. Even more than with Stannis, this is apparent at the Wall he leaves behind.

Jon Snow, the newly elected Lord Commander of the Night's Watch, is attempting to do the best he can to be a great leader. The core problem with almost every leader in *Game of Thrones* is that they work only in the short-term, winning the battle that's in front of them, or surviving their enemies. But Jon knows the enemy facing the Seven Kingdoms when winter comes and wants to work to fight the invasion of the White Walkers.

To this end, he joins forces with Tormund Giantsbane to recruit the remnants of Mance's army at the Wildling village of Hardhome. He gets part of the way through the process when, in one of the most stunning episodes of the entire series, Hardhome is ambushed by the forces of the Night's King. Jon manages to rally some of the survivors, but most of the Wildlings are killed and then resurrected to join the army of the undead. When Jon returns, he sends Samwell Tarly to Oldtown to become a maester and replace the dead Aemon Targaryen.

Yet despite Jon's heroism and attempts to prepare for the winter, his brothers in the Night's Watch are unhappy with his attempts to forge peace with the Wildlings, the Watch's enemies for centuries. Ser Alliser Thorne, Olly, and several others assassinate Jon, saying "For the Watch!" as they do. The last sight of the season is Jon Snow, bleeding and dying on the ground, as if to say "So much for hope."

As distressing as this was, it didn't feel like the end of Jon's story. With the two previous major Stark deaths, Ned's execution and Rob and Cat's assassinations at the Red Wedding, the show depicted them in the ninth episode of the season, not the tenth. It then used that final hour to have the rest of the characters react to the deaths, to make them real. Robb Stark takes the crown after his father's death in Season 1, for example, while the third season finale has the rest of the world learn of and discuss Robb's death. Jon, however, was dying as an end-of-season cliffhanger—not something the series (or books) did before this point. For this reason, Jon's potential return to the series was a major point of discussion between seasons, and his eventual resurrection less of a surprise.

This wasn't the only cliffhanger, either. Sansa Stark's season ended almost literally on a cliff. The elder Stark daughter ended Season 4 on a high point when, after years of abuse in King's Landing at the hands of the Lannisters, she stepped out of the role of "victim" and seemed to take control of her own destiny. Season 5, however, said otherwise, with Sansa being taken north by Littlefinger and given to Ramsay Bolton in marriage.

Sansa is then maritally raped by Ramsay in one of the most disturbing and controversial scenes in the series. For one thing, this didn't happen in the novels—the woman who married Ramsay was a northern girl trained to pretend to be Arya Stark. Thus the show's producers made the specific decision to use Sansa for this disturbing storyline. Sansa herself (as I discuss in her chapter) is in many ways the most hopeful character in Westeros for surviving the worst abuse possible and rising above it. But instead, she's given over to Ramsay, arguably the only character in the entire story more reprehensible than Sansa's previous fiancé, Joffrey.

Game of Thrones had faced criticism for its depictions of sexual assault before, most notably in Season 4's Jaime-Cersei scene, but this one was a bridge too far for some people. The show generally, and this season specifically, seemed to be an unrelenting march of pain and death. There were other examples in Season 5 as well, like the Night's Watch members trying to attack Gilly, or Meryn

Trant's predilection for young girls in the season finale. This debate, perhaps more than anything else, defined critical perception of the fifth season—and helps explain why, in response, Season 6 was so hopeful.

After her marriage, Sansa attempts to find an ally in Theon Greyjoy, the man who betrayed her family, but has been broken by Ramsay into becoming the apparently loyal servant Reek. Initially Theon continues to serve Ramsay, but he eventually turns toward Sansa. Sansa tries to find Brienne of Tarth, but when she doesn't reply, Theon kills Ramsay's lover Myranda, and the two leap off the walls of Winterfell before they are recaptured—another cliffhanger.

Brienne, with Podrick Payne in tow, was last seen hunting Arya in the Riverlands. She is in the North because she'd previously met Sansa Stark and Littlefinger. Seeing the chance to fulfill her oath to Catelyn Stark, Brienne attempted to join with Sansa, but was rejected in favor of Littlefinger. So she followed the Stark woman to Winterfell, where she waited for a sign that her rescue was needed. Yet after waiting for weeks, Brienne turned away from her watch when Stannis attacked, seeking revenge on the man who killed her king, Renly. In yet another bitter irony in Season 5, Brienne may have succeeded in her push for violent revenge, but at the cost of being missing when Sansa most needs her aid.

Further south, the Riverlands are skipped once again, so the story of the Tullys and the Freys is pushed to Season 6.

King's Landing may be less important in the fifth season than prior, but it's still one of the chief focuses. The War of the Five Kings may be over, but two queens, Cersei Lannister and Margaery Tyrell, battle politically for influence over King Tommen. With Tywin dead, and Margaery able to use her intelligence and sensuality on her new husband, Cersei finds herself increasingly shut out. Cersei's story is also given motivation by the show's first-ever flashback, in which a teenaged Cersei is given a prophecy that her children will die and she herself will be supplanted by a younger, more beautiful queen, which Cersei believes is Margaery.

So the Queen Mother turns to the most important new character of the show in its later seasons, Jonathan Pryce's High Sparrow. He plays a religious leader for the disaffected in King's Landing. One of the things that *Game of Thrones* sacrificed in adapting the story from the page to the screen is that the stories of the regular people are almost entirely untold—we've heard almost nothing of the people of King's Landing since the riot of the second season at this point, but now there are so many that they comprise a major political force.

This is a problem that occurs in the Sons of the Harpy storyline in Meereen as well—in both cases, the people in lands torn apart by war are suddenly rebelling, but because they've been unexamined on the show, their motivations are entirely overshadowed by how their rebellions threaten the stars.

Despite this, Pryce's performance makes the Sparrow storyline work well. He plays the religious leader with a superb combination of overt humility and ruthless political acumen. Initially allied with Cersei, he attacks Margaery through her gay brother, Ser Loras, trapping her in perjury. But when his erstwhile ally Cersei comes to reinforce her victory, the High Sparrow lays a similar trap, luring her in with his apparently genuine care, then hitting her with her crimes.

The arrested queens, imprisoned by the army of the Faith Militant, leave Tommen helpless. The only escape is confession, which Cersei attempts to take, acknowledging the least worst of her crimes. For this, she's allowed to leave the Sept of Baelor if she participates in the Walk of Atonement, traveling naked through the streets, accosted by the citizens who despise her, with "Shame!" ringing in her ears.

Cersei returns to the Red Keep to her family, only to discover that Tommen has replaced her with her uncle, Ser Kevan Lannister, and the Small Council is shutting her out. The only good news: Maester Qyburn reveals that he's successfully reanimated the dying Ser Gregor Clegane, giving her a champion for her potential trial by combat.

Jaime Lannister isn't present for his sister's crisis because he's been sent to Dorne, where, alongside Lannister retainer Bronn of the Blackwater, he's supposed to rescue Princess Myrcella from the threat of the Sand Snakes: Oberyn Martell's daughters, seeking revenge for their father's death in Season 4. This is a huge change for the Dorne plot from the novels, which had an entirely new set of characters apart from Myrcella. Here Bronn, Jaime, and Ellaria Sand are all familiar faces. For this reason the Dorne storyline in the novels can feel like a distraction—why are we learning about these new characters instead of the people we care about? Adding known characters was a great opportunity for the show to do better than the books.

And...it failed. The Dorne storyline is widely considered among the worst things the show ever did, both among fans and critics. Ellaria and the Sand Snakes are cartoon villains, murdering Myrcella and manipulating Jaime and Bronn predictably. Jaime and Bronn don't have anything interesting to do after an initial fight sequence, and the new characters—Doran Martell, his son Trystane, and their guard, Areo Hotah—do little more than introduce themselves. It's no wonder that the sixth season premiere murderously dispenses with the storyline entirely.

The fifth season is also notable for shifting the focus to the continent of Essos more than previous seasons. Across the Narrow Sea, Arya Stark has found her way to Braavos, where she takes part in a storyline almost totally detached from the rest of the world. Arya finds and joins the Faceless Men at the House of Black of White, where Jaqen H'ghar, the assassin she helped and manipulated in Season 2, returns to train her. She also has a rival student, a girl known only as "the Waif."

Arya goes through a training montage with the Faceless Men until a delegation from King's Landing arrives, seeking coin from the Iron Bank of Braavos. Led by Mace Tyrell, the Kingsguard Ser Meryn Trant—a name on Arya's list, for killing Syrio Forel—is there as a guard. In perhaps the darkest scene of the entire series, Arya finds out that Meryn's weakness is getting pleasure from brutally beating young girls. She adopts that as a disguise, reveals herself, and stabs Meryn to death. For this, the Faceless Men steal her eyesight, another cliffhanger for the end of the season.

Not too far from Braavos, the fifth season also took us back to the city of Pentos, home of Targaryen supporter Illyrio Mopatis, for the first time since the very first episode of the series. Varys has brought Tyrion here to convince him to join in support of Daenerys—but Tyrion just wants to drown himself in drink, having killed his lover and father after his sister demanded he be executed.

Still, Tyrion travels along until he's kidnapped by Ser Jorah Mormont, who has the same goal of taking the dwarf to Dany. Along the way, Tyrion sees a dragon—the image used as the promotional poster for the season—while Jorah contracts the disease of greyscale. Both are captured by slavers and taken to the fighting pits near Meereen.

The fighting pits are re-opened because Daenerys Targaryen, facing the popular revolt of the Sons of the Harpy against her radical anti-slavery rule, is attempting to assuage the people of Meereen. Active campaigns of repression have already led to the death of Ser Barristan, so she takes the advice of Hizdahr zo Loraq, the young Meereenese nobleman who attempts to steer her toward compromise. Hizdahr, a frustratingly one-dimensional character in the novels, is played with charm and energy by Joel Fry, making Dany's decision to marry him to help Meereen actually make sense.

One of his pieces of advice: reopen the fighting pits, leading to an extravagant holiday at the giant arena called Daznak's Pit. The fighters in smaller arenas are competing for a chance to participate there, which Dany is supposed to watch. Ser Jorah wins his fight and reveals his gift to his queen, Tyrion. The Lannister is, eventually, welcomed into Dany's inner circle, but he advises her to exile Jorah again.

Jorah is not a man to take no for an answer, and fights his way into the pits again. After Jorah's victory, the Sons of the Harpy attack, with Jorah saving Dany's life initially, although Hizdahr—previously suspected by Daario (and many readers) as the Harpy's leader—is murdered by the Meereenese nationalists. As the fight continues, the heroes are surrounded by Harpies, but Dany's black dragon, Drogon, arrives, nearly full grown, killing dozens of Harpies before Dany flies off on his back, driven from her seat of power.

Yet even that image, of the rightful queen and anti-slavery crusader finally able to ride a dragon, is arguably the happiest ending of any major character's all of Season 5. Jon died trying to make the world a better place, Stannis sold his soul to win a battle he lost anyway, Brienne sacrificed her honor for revenge, Sansa's abuse became so intolerable even she had to flee, Margaery and Cersei saw their dignity degraded, Jaime had his daughter die in his arms, Arya turned into a cold-blooded killer, Tyrion found a cause only to immediately lose it, and Dany's best intentions still led to a mass rebellion. Season 5 of *Game of Thrones* may be the peak of the show's popularity—but it's also the most difficult chapter in the series.

11 The Winds of Winter

George R.R. Martin has released several sample chapters from his as-yet-unfinished sixth novel in *A Song of Ice and Fire*, called *The Winds of Winter*. The collection illustrates just how far the stories of the TV show have diverged from the novels.

Let's take a quick look: Theon Greyjoy has fled Winterfell with Ramsay's bride, "Arya Stark"—a girl who is actually Sansa's friend Jeyne Poole. They've been captured by Stannis' forces, who have made their camp in the snow, near Winterfell. Meanwhile, Sansa Stark is still in the Vale, preparing for a marriage of her own to Lord Robert Arryn's heir, Harrold (Lord Robert had his name changed to Robin in the show, but the character is roughly the same.) She's also still in disguise as "Alayne"—her seizing of power at the end of Season 4 has yet to happen in the novels.

Point-of-view characters for the sixth book include Aeron and Victarion Greyjoy—two brothers of Balon and Euron who were removed from the series. Aeron is still with Euron, who is fast becoming a Ramsay-level villain, while Victarion is sailing to meet Dany in the massive collision in Meereen known as the Battle of Fire. There, the still-alive Barristan the Bold has a point-of-view chapter leading the defense, while Tyrion, who's yet to meet Dany, attempts to sway the mercenaries who've enslaved him to join the Mother of Dragons—a far more complicated mess than the Meereenese versus slavers fight in "The Battle of the Bastards."

Yet even these are still connected to the story we've seen on the show, enough so that even a viewer-only can make sense of the plot summary. That's not the case with Arianne Martell, a point-of-view character introduced in the fourth novel, who was removed entirely from the show. In the books, it's Doran Martell's daughter who rebels against him attempting to kidnap Princess Myrcella. Doran and Myrcella still live, Arianne has reconciled with her father, and now goes to meet the most important character removed from the books—the man called Young Griff (see Chapter 79).

There is one chapter that has been adapted mostly intact: that of Arya Stark, playing an actress named "Mercy." In this chapter, Arya Stark, training with the Faceless, sees a man from her list and kills him on her own. This has been transferred relatively intact to the show: the man is the Lannister guard Raff the Sweetling instead of Ser Meryn Trant, and the theater background involving Lady Stork became Lady Crane in Season 6. Despite those slight changes, its appearance on the show feels like a close adaptation—the only part that feels that way out of all of these.

The delay in publishing *The Winds of Winter* has created several controversies for *Game of Thrones* and *A Song of Ice and Fire* fans. The first three novels in the series were released every other year: 1996, 1998, and 2000. Since then, however, the pace has slowed dramatically: *A Feast for Crows* in 2005, *A Dance with Dragons* in 2011, and, as of the end of 2016, still no *Winds of Winter*.

The first of these controversies is how much responsibility—or blame—George R.R. Martin deserves for the increasing delays, as well as the show passing the book in every storyline except possibly one at this point. Many fans are incredibly frustrated with Martin, to the point where any time he makes a public appearance or writes something that's not about *Game of Thrones,* the mocking cry of "Why aren't you writing?" comes up. It's become so predictable that, at the 2014 Emmys, a performance by Weird Al adding lyrics to TV shows' theme songs involved the performer—who didn't know anything about Martin—demanding "We need more scripts!"

Yet many other fans, and especially other writers, push back on blaming Martin for the delays. The most famous came from fantasy novelist and comic writer Neil Gaiman, who in 2009 wrote a blog post declaring *"George R.R. Martin is not your bitch."* As a writer with his own struggles with deadlines (aka, a writer) I can certainly sympathize. Writing isn't a process where you just sit down and the words come out in good shape.

On the other hand, George R.R. Martin became rich and famous *because* he created the sort of dense, complicated, highly serialized story that gathers huge fanbases these days. We've seen it with novels like *The Wheel of Time* and TV series like *The X-Files* and *Lost*. Martin rode that tiger to success, and now he has a story that's too dense and too complicated for him to deal with quickly.

The question becomes more complicated now that the series has progressed beyond the books in the sixth season, which, thanks to a finale called "The Winds of Winter," we can assume the sixth season largely covered that story. Jon Snow's story—his resurrection, his parentage, his crowning—are all new revelations, and for people who prefer the books to the show, seeing it "spoiled" was upsetting.

Many blame Martin for selling the rights to the show before he'd finished the series, which seems fair. Yet Martin has, in various blog posts, consistently expressed confidence that he'd resolved the issues that were slowing him down, primarily the famous Meereenese Knot (see Chapter 80). He's also said that, with his point-of-view characters running into one another, he can cut down on the narrative complexity of the story (i.e., kill several of them off.) So with *A Dance with Dragons* almost done (it would be published in 2011, just after the end of the first season of the show) and his difficult plot threads seemingly resolved, Martin may have thought he was in shape to get the last two books done in the next six years. As happened to so many of his characters, George R.R. Martin's best-laid plans backfired.

Are these disappointed fans wrong to be unhappy that Season 6 came out before *The Winds of Winter*? On the one hand, Season 6 acts like a traditional fantasy series, where a ragtag band of heroes join together to defeat the evil threatening their land. Its simplified morality is a far cry from the complex politicking of the story at its peak. This may be how the story is going in the books as well, but it's hard to reconcile with the gritty, complicated fantasy of Martin's writing style.

And yet, while the grand sweep of who gets which crown may be there, the stories are moving in totally different directions. The books' focus on seemingly minor characters gathering increasing power makes us interested in the stories of Aurane Waters or the Shavepate, which gives them power. But the more manageable simplicity of the shows makes great moments more likely, like Brienne's duel with the Hound, instead of each of them fighting some random mercenaries at different times. No matter how Martin resolves the Ramsay-Jon battle in his books, it's unlikely they'll have a moment as striking as Davos uncovering Shireen's pyre at dawn in "The Battle of the Bastards."

There is still one important similarity between the books and show: they still have to achieve the seemingly impossible goal of creating a satisfying ending to one of the most morally, narratively, and thematically complex stories of our age. Whatever release date for *The Winds of Winter* makes this outcome most likely is probably the one we should be cheering for.

12 Season 6: Brings Hope Back

"I choose violence."—Cersei Lannister

It takes about ten minutes for the sixth season of *Game of Thrones* to adopt a totally different tone from the grim, controversial Season 5. After scenes at the Wall and Winterfell, we join Theon and Sansa, who've fallen into a snowdrift and are being chased by a gang of Boltons. Exhausted and freezing, they're forced to stop. The Bolton men catch them and make cruel threats against Theon—when Brienne of Tarth and Podrick Payne arrive. With help from Theon, they kill the Bolton soldiers.

Then, one of the most inspiring scenes in the entire series takes place. Sansa Stark, a child and a prisoner for almost the entire series before this point, accepts Brienne's oath of service, just as her mother did four seasons before. Pod and Brienne are two of the most purely heroic characters in the series, meeting with Sansa, who embodies the potential for a better Westeros, and Theon, the character most working toward redemption. Together, this crew of misfits forms the start of a rebellion of hope that the good guys might actually win; that there might be a happy ending at the end of all this death and despair.

For this, the sixth season was one of the most instantly beloved in the show's history. The ratings also continued to improve, although the show's streak of every premiere being rated higher than the previous season's finale finally broke, by a little bit. On the other hand, some critics—particularly readers of the novels—felt that the season's positivity was a little too superficial and worked against the themes of the story from earlier.

The season was also noteworthy for placing the show's women at its center. While it had been moving in this direction since the first season killed off so many of the world's patriarchs, the sixth season fully committed to having women be wielders of power. In addition to Cersei, Dany, and Margaery, Sansa, Yara, Ellaria, and Olenna all took major roles in the War of the Queens.

Season 6 is the first season to take place almost entirely based on events that haven't occurred in the novels. Only Jaime Lannister's story at the siege of Riverrun and the Ironborn's Kingsmoot were things that had happened in the novels that hadn't on-screen. The rest was, for the first time, entirely new to everyone watching the show, whether they'd been reading or not.

The result was a season that felt like everything *Game of Thrones* could possibly be in terms of grand spectacle and the emotional catharsis of the show at its best, but at the cost of oversimplification of complex people and issues. It's exciting and inspiring to see *Game of Thrones* shift toward the victory of the good guys, but the complexity that made it great in the first place is somewhat lacking.

Season 5 ended with major cliffhangers, a rare occurrence in *Game of Thrones'* history (the biggest previous example: the White Walkers attacking the Night's Watch at the end of Season 2). The Sansa-Theon escape was, as noted above, resolved with a rescue from Brienne of Tarth. But the bigger one was Jon Snow's apparent murder at the hands of the Night's Watch, which ended both the season and the last released novel, *A Dance with Dragons*.

Fans of both the novels and the show were therefore desperate to learn whether Jon was actually dead or not, a subject that dominated the discourse. On the one hand, killing a major Stark every odd-numbered season (or book) seemed to work well for the plot, with Ned and Robb's deaths being arguably the story's biggest selling points. On the other hand, Jon was too much the chosen hero, with too much investment, to just die like that—especially with a priestess of the Red God, who's shown resurrection potential before, right there.

George R.R. Martin played coy about it, even telling distraught fans that the death might not have been as it appeared, but show-runners Benioff and Weiss were more direct about it, saying that in the world of *Game of Thrones*, "dead is dead." (There are a lot more resurrections or pseudo-deaths in the novels, making that claim almost laughable.) This lasted just a couple months, before photographs of Kit Harington in costume filming leaked online. It's a good thing, too, for the sixth season was Jon Snow's season, in many ways.

Season 6 opens where Season 5 ended, with Jon's body in the courtyard of Castle Black. He's discovered by Davos Seaworth, who recognizes the political power of the body as Alliser Thorne attempts to consolidate his power. Davos and the remaining loyalists gather to defend Jon's body. Why, exactly, Davos was so willing to risk everything for a corpse is unclear, but he was a loyal man, and he did know a sorceress, with Melisandre returning from Stannis' defeat. He begs her to help, and though she's lost faith in herself since Stannis' defeat, she says the words like Thoros of Myr told her he did to resurrect Lord Beric. Eventually, it works.

The revived Jon Snow first takes revenge, rallying the Night's Watch to overthrow Thorne. He executes the traitors himself, then tosses the Lord Commander's cloak to Dolorous Edd, stating "now my watch is ended," which is a pretty baller move for the show's most conventional hero, it must be said. Jon's bitterness and helplessness at being murdered for doing the right thing as Lord Commander motivates him through the season.

After fleeing Winterfell, Brienne, Sansa, and Podrick come to Castle Black (Theon having left for the Iron Islands). For the first time since the first season, two of the Stark children reunite, another essential moment of uplift in a story that had almost forgotten how. Then, Sansa and a letter from Ramsay Bolton work to convince Jon to join his sister in overthrowing the Boltons and retaking Winterfell. With Tormund, Davos, and Melisandre, they set about the North, recruiting.

Despite the apparent strength of their position, the Boltons have their own issues. When Walda Frey bears Lord Roose a son, Ramsay, despite being assured he was still the heir, murders his father and brutally kills Walda and the baby by feeding them to his dogs. He then cements his power in the North by aligning with two of the most powerful Houses remaining. The Karstarks, still angry at the Starks over the execution of their lord, join happily, while Smalljon Umber decides to offer proof of his loyalty: Rickon Stark, Osha, and the head of Rickon's direwolf, Shaggydog. Osha attempts to seduce her way out of trouble, but Ramsay's heard of this tactic from Theon, and murders her.

Recruitment for the Stark armies does not go well. Sansa and Jon's ragtag band of misfits succeed with Tormund and the Wildlings, as well as the scene-stealing child ruler Lyanna Mormont, but it's not enough.

Sansa has her own options, however. She secretly meets with Littlefinger, who, in Season 5, acquired a mandate from the Lannisters to attack the Boltons for their betrayal in marrying Sansa. He manipulates Robin Arryn into convincing the warrior Bronze Yohn Royce to join Sansa's side with their armies. Lord Baelish offers her an alliance with the Vale, but Sansa, stung by his role in selling her to the vile Ramsay Bolton, rejects him outright. Littlefinger claims to understand, and offers a piece of information: Sansa's great-uncle, Brynden "The Blackfish" Tully, has retaken Riverrun. Sansa sends Brienne to attempt to recruit him.

As the tiny Stark army moves on Winterfell out of necessity, Jon and Sansa fight over what could have been done to actually give them a chance. Jon asks Sansa if she has any better ideas. She demurs—but secretly sends a letter to Littlefinger. The Stark armies camp at Stannis' ill-fated site from the year before, and

Davos uncovers evidence that Shireen was burned at Melisandre's bidding.

What ensues is "The Battle of the Bastards," one of the highest-rated and regarded episodes of Game of Thrones' run. (See chapter 77 for more.)

When the battle begins, the Starks have a plan to lure the Boltons into range of their archers. But Ramsay sends Rickon Stark running toward the Stark lines, if he can dodge Ramsay's arrows. Jon attempts to meet his brother halfway, but fails. The Stark plan is also ruined, as Davos tells the army to charge to save the now-stranded Jon Snow. The Boltons gain the upper hand, surrounding and attempting to crush the Starks, when the Knights of the Vale arrive and rout the Bolton armies. Ramsay is captured and Sansa Stark leaves him to his starving hounds, killing one of the show's greatest villains.

Davos confronts Jon with evidence that Melisandre had Shireen killed, and Jon exiles the red priestess. The remaining Northern lords and the men of the Vale gather in Winterfell, where Lyanna Mormont leads them in declaring Jon Snow King in the North. Littlefinger has attempted to recruit Sansa to be his queen on the Iron Throne. She demurs, politely, but he exchanges an ominous look with Sansa as everyone else in the room cheers their new king.

But that's not the only Jon Snow–centered revelation of the season, although only one person knows the other. Bran Stark, after skipping the fifth season, makes his return. His training with Bloodraven continues, as Bran sees elements of the past, filling in some of the most important gaps in Westerosi history, for himself and for viewers.

First, he sees the Children of the Forest create the first White Walker, shoving an obsidian dagger into a man's chest. The First Men were on the verge of genocide against the Children, who resorted to desperate measures. Bran then attempts to use a vision on his own, but encounters the Night's King, who marks him—and reveals his army outside Bloodraven's cave. The wights attack, killing Bloodraven, the Children, Bran's direwolf Summer, and finally Hodor, all of whom sacrifice themselves for Bran and Meera's escape. Hodor's origin is finally revealed as well, with Bran warging into the big man's body. Being so powerful it transmits to Hodor from an earlier time in Bran's visions—his name, "Hodor," was a reference to Bran and Meera's desperate need for him to "hold the door."

Meera isn't strong enough to carry Bran like Hodor did, leaving the two in desperate straits Beyond the Wall. But their rescue solves one of *Game of Thrones'* oldest mysteries. Benjen Stark of the Night's Watch, missing since the first season, returns as the part-wight "Coldhands" and helps bring them south.

The season ends with Bran resolving arguably *Game of Thrones'* biggest mystery: Jon Snow's parentage. He returns to a vision of his father fighting the Kingsguard at the Tower of Joy. He'd visited it earlier and seen the death of Ser Arthur Dayne, in one of the show's best action scenes. At the end of the season, Bran returns, and sees Ned Stark find his sister, dying in childbirth. With her last breath, she gives the baby to Ned and forces him to promise her he won't reveal his true parentage, as Robert will almost certainly kill him for being a Targaryen. That baby is Jon Snow, Ned Stark's nephew, not his bastard son—and an heir to the Iron Throne.

Meanwhile, Brienne's expedition to the Riverlands doesn't go quite as well as she or Sansa had hoped. She meets with Jaime Lannister, just arrived from the capital to lead the Lannister armies. Out of respect, he gives her a day to convince the Blackfish to surrender the castle. The season had largely been building to a collection of heroic misfits in the North saving the day, but the Blackfish refuses to join, preferring to fight for his home. Jaime launches his plan at nightfall, sending Lord Edmure Tully, imprisoned since the Red Wedding, to convince Riverrun to surrender in exchange for partial freedom. Edmure agrees—the keep falls, the Blackfish fights to the death, and Brienne flees.

This isn't all that happened in the Riverlands, either. In the show's first use of a cold open before the credits that wasn't in a season premiere, it's revealed that the Hound is still alive, and helping Ian McShane's Septon Ray rebuild. But Brotherhood deserters slaughter the hopeful community, sending Sandor Clegane on a spiral of vengeance. Lord Beric attempts to recruit the superb fighter to join them in heading north for the impending fight against the Night's King, but Clegane isn't ready to commit just yet.

One more major act takes place in the Riverlands, but it takes a while to get there. Arya Stark, blinded in Braavos, is continually bullied by her fellow trainee, the Waif. Arya is sent to kill an actress named Lady Crane, but she befriends the older woman instead. The Waif treats this as proof of Arya's betrayal of the Faceless Men, and is given leave to kill Arya. She wounds the Stark girl, kills Lady Crane, and eventually corners Arya in a dark room. Arya, with no chances left, cuts the light to the room, and seemingly uses the darkness to kill the Waif. She returns to the Faceless Men, who allow her to depart, with faces. Arya returns to Westeros, disguises herself as a serving girl, and kills Lord Walder Frey as well as his sons Lothar and Black Walder, the architects of the Red Wedding.

Jaime had gone to the Riverlands after a failed ploy to defeat the Sparrows in King's Landing. At the start of the season he returns from Dorne to discover Cersei humiliated by the High Sparrow, and has to bring her the news of Myrcella's death. In an attempt to break the Sparrows' power, Jaime and the Tyrells bring their forces to the Sept of Baelor, but they're undercut by Margaery Tyrell joining with the High Sparrow. Queen Margaery has recruited King Tommen to the side of the Sparrows in exchange for her freedom. The Tyrells are embarrassed, and Jaime is forced to leave the capital to finish the war.

The High Sparrow's ascendance continues with Tommen's decision to disallow trial by combat, which Cersei had planned to use the Mountain for. The season builds to the triple trials of Loras, Margaery, and Cersei, and Cersei finds herself apparently powerless. Loras gives in to the Sparrows, leaving the Tyrells heirless. But as Margaery's trial is set to begin, she realizes that Cersei isn't there—and what that means.

The trial scene is one of *Game of Thrones'* most memorable. The show slows down, letting the music, costumes, and actors tell the story. It slowly builds dread, as Cersei prevents Tommen from attending, Margaery realizes something's wrong, and Lancel goes to investigate a suspicious child. What he discovers is a massive stock of wildfire, directly under the castle. He's stabbed before he can do anything about it. Cersei's ally Qyburn likewise has Grand Maester Pycelle murdered by his army of orphan children. The Sept of Baelor explodes, Margaery's wisdom going unheeded. In this strike, Cersei manages to kill almost all of her enemies: the High Sparrow, Margaery, Loras, and Mace Tyrell, Pycelle and Lancel, and Ser Kevan Lannister.

Cersei's last child, Tommen, seeing and understanding the havoc his mother has wrought, commits suicide. With nobody else holding any significant power anywhere else in the realm, Cersei is free to take the throne herself. Her brother Jaime, who's already killed one mad ruler for attempting to slaughter innocents with wildfire, watches helplessly as Qyburn crowns her Queen Cersei Lannister, first of her name.

The Tyrells, having lost their entire family save Lady Olenna, seek an alliance with another House seeking vengeance against the Lannisters. The end of the season sees her negotiating with Ellaria Sand, apparent ruler of Dorne. She seized Dorne in the season premiere when she and the Sand Snakes murdered Doran and Trystane...then disappeared for the rest of the season, indicating the show's realization that the Dorne storyline wasn't working. There, the two vengeance-seeking women meet with Lord Varys, who tells them that they can achieve it, alongside Daenerys Targaryen. (Meanwhile, Samwell Tarly finally made his way to the Tyrell homeland of The Reach, attempting to become a maester.)

They weren't the first powers to seek Dany from the Seven Kingdoms, either. After leaving Sansa, Theon returns to his home. His father has been murdered by his brother Euron, and the Ironborn meet for a Kingsmoot to choose their next ruler. Theon, broken and unable to produce an heir, tells Yara she has his support. She seems to win over the Ironborn before Euron Greyjoy comes and promises to take Daenerys Targaryen and her dragons and use them to make the Iron Islands ascendant. Theon and Yara take the Greyjoy fleet and flee to Essos to meet with Dany.

At the start of Season 6 Daenerys Stormborn finds herself captured by Dothraki, who want to take her and imprison her with the rest of the Khals' widows in Vaes Dothrak. Daario and Jorah find her trail and follow her there, where Dany has recruited fellow widows to her plan. She traps the Khals in a room and burns them, where her Targaryen immunity to flame allows her to survive. With a new khalasar, Daenerys returns to Meereen. Jorah is sent on a quest to cure his greyscale.

The city needs her desperately. With Dany gone, Tyrion takes command. He attempts to pacify the city with religion, inviting in priestesses of the Red God, and also to remove support for the Sons of the Harpy by compromising with the slavers. The latter fails spectacularly when, after a short period of peace, the slavers besiege the city. Tyrion attempts to free Dany's dragons, but he cannot control them. Dany, however, returns on Drogon, with a khalasar, and counterattacks. The Dothraki kill the Sons of the Harpy in the city, and the dragons burn the slavers' ships, leaving Daenerys triumphant.

At the peak of the battle, Dany is ready to burn all who oppose her, reminiscent of the Mad King, but Tyrion talks her down. For his service, he's raised to Hand of the Queen. The queen also breaks up with Daario, leaving him in charge of the Bay of Dragons to allow it to transition to self-rule. She negotiates an alliance with Yara Greyjoy (who hits on Dany, naturally), taking the Ironborn's fleet in exchange for the freedom of the Iron Islands. And with that, the heir to the throne finally sails for Westeros, with an army of dragons, Dothraki, Ironborn, Unsullied, Tyrells, and Martells.

After years of increasing violence and moral ambiguity, the sixth season of *Game of Thrones* was one filled with moral clarity. Over the course of the ten episodes, heroes were finally allowed to be heroic, villains showed their true colors, and those in between either died like the Tyrells, or joined with heroes like Ellaria Sand. Only Littlefinger remains to complicate matters, seemingly, and Jon and Dany prepare to war against Cersei and the Night's King. But this is *Game of Thrones*, and there are two seasons left.

13 George R.R. Martin

"Some writers enjoy writing, I am told. Not me. I enjoy having written."—George R.R. Martin

In the "Golden Age of Television," most of the great shows have had one or two particular creators take their places as the auteurs behind the greatness. This is usually the showrunner—the lead writer and producer, as well as usually the person who pitched the series initially, like David Simon for *The Wire* or Joss Whedon for *Buffy*. Occasionally, a defining star can put him or herself on near-equal footing, like James Gandolfini for *The Sopranos*, Amy Poehler for *Parks and Recreation*, or Timothy Olyphant for *Justified*.

But *Game of Thrones* doesn't quite have that. Its ensemble cast and diffused serialization mean that no single actor could possibly define the entire series. Its showrunners, David Benioff and D.B. Weiss, don't have the big personalities or media-friendly quirks of a Whedon or *Mad Men's* Matt Weiner. So the role of the "face of the franchise" has fallen on a man who isn't even directly involved with the day-to-day production of the show: the author of the *A Song of Ice and Fire* novels, George R.R. Martin.

Now, this isn't to say that Martin (or GRRM, to many fans) isn't involved in *Game of Thrones* at all. At a famous meeting, when Benioff and Weiss pitched him on the show, Martin gave them a final test, asking this: "Who is Jon Snow's mother?" The two passed, presumably by saying it was Lyanna Stark based on all the clues in the novels, and Martin hasn't ever said a negative thing about them since.

He's even participated directly in writing a few episodes of the series, including two of its most-acclaimed hours: "Blackwater," the climax of the second season, and "The Lion and the Rose," the royal wedding episode at the start of the fourth season. In later seasons, Martin has stepped back from this role, ostensibly to finish the sixth book in the series, *The Winds of Winter*.

As the show has increasingly diverged from the novels, fans have looked to Martin to speak out against the changes, but he's continually supported the show. For example, in one of the biggest controversies surrounding changes from the novels, Jaime's apparent rape of Cersei in Season 4, Martin explained the situation by saying that because Jaime was present for his son's death on the show, but not in the books, that would understandably change his behavior. And he's consistently described the differences between the show and the books as taking different routes to get the same location.

If you saw this picture and immediately screamed "START WRITING!" you might be a Game of Thrones *fan.* (Photo courtesy of Matt Sayles/Invision/AP Images)

Martin is also, as an executive producer, a regular presence for *Game of Thrones* at awards shows, and is a very public presence in that respect. He looks unique in the room, too, fairly short and round, with a massive beard, all of which tend to stand out in Hollywood. The author very much seems to be enjoying and utilizing his fame, although that has caused him to come in for some criticism from demanding fans waiting for the next book.

GRRM has several notable quirks in his biography as well. He was born in New Jersey, and maintains a strong rooting interest in the current or former New Jersey sports teams like the Jets and the Giants. The giant Wun Wun, for example, is named after the jersey of Giants great Phil Simms, who wore number eleven—one one—during his playing days.

He's also famous for his deliberately old-fashioned writing style: Martin uses a 1990s DOS computer and word processor, disconnected from the Internet, and only a half-step away from being a typewriter. Many writers try to disconnect themselves from the Internet in order to focus entirely on the work, but Martin takes it above and beyond.

But if you truly want to understand who GRRM is and how he created the novel series that redefined fantasy and dominated television, the most important thing to understand is this: George R.R. Martin is a committed member of science fiction fandom, a crucial member of the network of fans, editors, and fans who defined the genre for decades before the Internet, and continue to be key members of that community even after the Internet reshaped it.

Martin began his time in fandom as a teenager in the 1960s, even getting letters published in early issues of the *Fantastic Four*, the comic that reshaped that industry. By his early twenties in the 1970s, he was publishing stories in major magazines, and by the end of that decade, he was getting nominated for major awards.

His early work very much fits in with the form of the genre of the 1970s. Like Ursula K. Le Guin or Anne McCaffrey, his writing fits in the mode of "science fantasy"—stories that are technically set in a future on other planets, but with the tropes of fantasy (the most famous of these today would be *Star Wars*, with its knight-wizards waving magic swords around). In the 1980s, he was publishing fairly well-reviewed novels, but poor sales pushed him in a different direction.

Martin turned to Hollywood, where he worked as a writer for the rebooted *Twilight Zone*, *Max Headroom*, and, most importantly, the 1980s *Beauty and the Beast*. This scriptwriting experience no doubt helped him when it came time to write episodes of *Game of Thrones*—his episodes are generally very good, and display no particular difficulties functioning as television instead of merely adapted novels. After the end of *Beauty and the*

Beast, Martin returned to writing literature, leading directly to *A Game of Thrones*.

Despite his success with the main *A Song of Ice and Fire* series, GRRM has continued to write in the somewhat old-fashioned formats of the genre. The Daenerys chapters of *A Game of Thrones*, for example, were published as a novella in *Locus* magazine in order to engage with that readership. Other *Thrones* spinoffs, like the *Dunk and Egg* series or the description of the early Targaryen civil war called the "Dance of the Dragons" were published in anthology series collecting the best and most famous fantasy authors of their time.

The *Wild Cards* series is Martin's attempt to create a platform for others to write in. He works as editor for these occasional anthologies, which depict a superhero-like post-World War II world where people are gifted or cursed with powers. Over the course of 23 different books, the series has produced stories by dozens of different authors. With Martin's rise to prominence, *Wild Cards* has gotten new life, and in 2016, Martin announced a new crop of rising science fiction and fantasy authors would be joining the next installments.

One of the ways that George R.R. Martin shows his full engagement with the science fiction and fantasy communities (often abbreviated as SF/F) is his commitment to the Hugo Awards, one of the premiere awards in speculative fiction.

The Hugos are one of the most fascinating major cultural awards because they're voted on by fans. It's not a total free-for-all like, say, the MTV Teen Choice Awards, but instead it's voted on by the members of World Science Fiction Society, with the winners announced as a key part of Worldcon, the largest literary-focused SF convention. That may sound complicated, but it's not: the Hugos are nominated and voted on by thousands of the most dedicated fans of science fiction, fantasy, and horror. And they're announced at SF/F's biggest party.

The Hugos are divided into literary form: novels, novellas, novellettes, short stories, graphic stories, and several other categories for fans and publishers. There are also Best Dramatic Presentation awards for film and television. Winners are generally well worth seeking out and reading or viewing—they tend to be the works that define the genre for years to come—at a far better rate than the Oscars or the Grammys do for film or music. *Game of Thrones* has won three Hugos, for the first season as a whole, and the episodes "Blackwater" and "The Rains of Castamere."

George R.R. Martin has won five Hugos for his writing. Four were for shorter works of his during the 1970s, and one was for a novella called "Blood of the Dragon" published in 1996—basically the Daenerys chapters of *A Game of Thrones*. (Both *A Feast for Crows* and *A Dance with Dragons* were nominated, as well.) But Martin's possibly most famous for *losing* a Hugo. After being nominated in 1976, and not winning, he and fellow losing author Gardner Dozois were drowning their sorrows and decided to throw a party for all the fellow losers. It became a tradition, even an official part of the convention.

In 2015, the Hugos, Martin, and the party he'd started became part of the culture wars. A group of reactionary science fiction authors and fans in two semi-aligned groups called the "Sad Puppies" and "Rabid Puppies" decided to fight back against what they saw as the Hugos becoming too liberal, and so nominated slates of what they decided counted as "real SF" (also, works written by them and their friends). The nominations were almost totally hijacked by this process, with Puppy works taking over almost every category.

George R.R. Martin took to his "Not A Blog" to decry this hijacking. He lambasted the core assumptions of the Puppy groups—that conservatives were being excluded, primarily—and went deep into the history of the books and people who've been nominated and won. The voting fans, at Worldcon, chose "No

Award" in almost every category for that year, which stopped the Puppies from taking over the process, but ended up leaving an almost blank set of awards.

So Martin, using his cachet as the biggest name in SF/F, and the originator of the Hugo Losers party, took further action. He reclaimed the Hugo Losers party and turned it into a celebration of the authors who'd been erased by the political machinations of the Puppies.

The most blatant way he did this was by giving out "Alfie Awards"—named after Alfred Bester, the author who won the first Hugo. Using the now-public ballots, Martin gave these awards to the authors who would have won, had the process not been hijacked, as well as two who had the integrity to pull out of the running when they saw they'd been the beneficiaries of unethical ballot-stuffing.

It can be easy to see *Game of Thrones* as some sort of special story, so popular that it's become separate from the rest of science fiction and fantasy. But *Game of Thrones* comes from that world, just as its original author is part of that world, as George R.R. Martin's relationship with the Hugo Awards shows.

The big question for George R.R. Martin continues to be "When will he finish?" At this point, it's all but guaranteed that *Game of Thrones* will finish before *A Song of Ice and Fire*—it's even possible that it'll finish before the sixth book comes out, let alone the seventh. But regardless, Martin's legacy is already in great shape. He's become the face of one of the most popular television series in history, has redefined the fantasy genre, and has become an elder statesman of the science fiction and fantasy community.

14 Season 7: The Beginning of the End

Game of Thrones has followed a pretty rigid structure for its six seasons thus far. Premiere in April (except for Season 3, which started March 31). Run for ten episodes, across ten straight weeks, maybe taking Memorial Day weekend off. Air the finale in June. Easy. Straightforward. And...not the case at all for Season 7.

From the beginning, the producers of *Game of Thrones* said they were aiming for seven seasons, to match the supposed seven books. But there were two pressures on that goal: first there's a ton of story, with a bunch of characters, which means there's plenty of story to tell even as we hurtle toward the ending. Second, *Game of Thrones* is incredibly popular, so of course, HBO wants more of it.

The result? A compromise: the final seasons of *Game of Thrones* will be split into two parts. Season 7 airs in 2017, with seven episodes, and the final eighth season presumably a similar size—the showrunners had said they had 13 episodes left, so six episodes in 2018 is entirely possible.

This may sound strange, but it's become normal in the world of prestige television. *The Sopranos, Mad Men,* and *Breaking Bad* all split their final seasons into two halves. Fans and critics divide these differently: *The Sopranos'* last two parts are usually called Season 6a and Season 6b, while *Breaking Bad* often gets simply split into Season 5 and Season 6. For *Game of Thrones* it looks like it's going to be Seasons 7 and 8, clearly delineated.

Part of the reason for the shorter season is also that *Game of Thrones* is getting bigger and badder as it moves to an explosive climax. Showrunner D.B. Weiss compared it to a "mid-range movie" in terms of production.

After all, we have Dany's massive invasion with her increasingly large dragons, as well as whatever the Night King and the White Walkers have planned. There's also the ends of the stories of characters both major and minor—a lot more needs to happen than just dragons versus zombies, but we're also probably going to see a lot more of the dragons and the zombies.

The season is also not going to debut in April, like all the others—it'll air on July 16. The main reason for that: winter has come. In order to be able to film more in natural snow and ice conditions, *Game of Thrones* pushed back its production schedule to actually be on location in the winter. Usually, they started filming in late summer and wrapped in early December, with winter reserved for editing. So a two- or three-month delay in order to have characters who aren't in the Night's Watch frolicking in the snow makes sense.

We'll see if it's all worth it come summer 2017.

15 Daenerys Targaryen

Once upon a time there was a beautiful princess, exiled from her homeland to live with her brother across the ocean. Her desperate brother married her off to a cruel warlord, trying to get his army, but the warlord killed her brother, then died himself. But the princess found some magical eggs and somehow made them hatch, becoming the only person in the world to have dragons. The princess gathered an army and traveled across the ocean to reclaim her rightful kingdom from the people who stole it from her family.

It's a nice story, right? And a pretty conventional one, when told like that. Long-lost heirs to thrones retaking their kingdoms from usurpers using a party of ragtag misfits and some discovered magic is what fantasy is all about, a lot of the time!

That just doesn't seem like the story of Daenerys Targaryen that we've actually seen. Her brother, after all, was the villain of the early part of her story, not her husband, Khal Drogo. Drogo's death was caused by Dany's mistakes, and certainly not what she wanted. And the years intervening, where she acquired her dragons and army, have not been a simple rise to power. At every point the story of the long-lost princess has been made complicated, even if it seems like a regular old fantasy story in broad strokes.

But there is one way in which Dany's story is conventional fantasy: it's all about growing up. Lots of heroic fantasy is about a child becoming an adult, a palace servant becoming a king, or a farm boy becoming a Jedi Knight. Dany starts as a naive teenage girl, and at the end of Season 6 departs Essos as the steely leader of a massive, diverse alliance of factions, having both crushed all opposition to her rule and freed thousands of slaves. How did this happen? Simple. Daenerys Stormborn grew up.

In the first season, Dany's growth is the clearest. Emilia Clarke plays the last Targaryen woman with a wide-eyed curiosity that easily shifts to fear initially. She comes across in the first few episodes as a skittish cat, curious about the Dothraki, but terrified if they do the wrong thing. That terror is justified by the abuse she's suffered—at her brother's hands, not just her uncommunicative new husband. Viserys Targaryen, believing himself the Last Dragon, is willing to do anything to regain his crown, and he isn't shy about abusing his sister both verbally and physically to attempt to prove it.

Meanwhile, Dany's new husband, Khal Drogo, is not treating her well. When the pilot and first few episodes of *Game of Thrones* aired, this was one of the most controversial aspects, because it certainly looks like on their wedding nights, Dany doesn't give Drogo any kind of consent before he has sex with her. (This is in opposition to the novels, where they overcome her fear on that night—but she makes it clear that he doesn't care in post-marriage sexual encounters.)

But Dany, in a culture with no concept of "marital rape," instead decides to win her over husband. She goes to her hand-maidens for training in Dothraki language, as well as learning what works in the bedroom (or the Dothraki variation thereof). Drogo quickly develops a respect for his wife, eventually turning into a strange sort of love. Daenerys moves past the terrified teenager part of her life when Viserys, insulting her and Dothraki customs, demands his crown from Drogo. With Daenerys' blessing, Drogo gives him a molten "Golden Crown," killing the Targaryen heir. He was no dragon.

The new, confident Daenerys, secure in her alliance with Drogo and now pregnant with his child, seems to be on the path back to her crown. An attempted assassination—foiled by her Westerosi bodyguard, Ser Jorah Mormont—finally motivates Drogo to declare his intent to invade the Seven Kingdoms. First, however, his khalasar invades the neighboring lands of the Lamb People to get the booty and slaves to sell for ships for the crossing.

Daenerys, still kind-hearted, witnesses one woman being raped by Dothraki and demands that she be freed. Drogo agrees, anger-ing some of his warriors who've been less than impressed with his apparent weakness for his wife. One of them duels Drogo, wound-ing him. The woman Dany rescued with the best of the intentions, Mirri Maz Duur, claims to be a healer, and says she's going to take care of the Khal.

The lesson that Dany learns next is perhaps the cruelest, and the one that separates *Game of Thrones*' coming-of-age story from the kind that normally exists: the best intentions can often create the worst results. In this case: Mirri Maz Duur has no love for

Daenerys, and vengeance in her heart from the Dothraki who destroyed her home, murdered her people, and raped her multiple times before Daenerys witnessed and intervened.

The sorceress makes Drogo's wound fester, and when he collapses, she tells Daenerys that she can keep him alive with dark magic. Dany, still unaware of Mirri Maz Duur's true motives, agrees to the black magic ritual, which requires life for life. Dany believes this means Drogo's horse; a huge deal for the nomadic Dothraki on its own, and one which leads to a violent attack against the tent where the ritual takes place.

Jorah and Dany's Dothraki allies fight the attack off, but when the dust settles, Mirri Maz Duur's revenge is complete. Drogo is alive, but a vegetable, and the life required to save the Khal was not the horse, but the unborn child Rhaego, who becomes a stillborn monster. Only a pathetically small remnant of the khalasar remains, with Drogo's army scattering without its leader.

At the end of the first season, Daenerys Stormborn learns Mirri Maz Duur's lesson: nothing comes without a price. She mercy kills Drogo and then burns his corpse. Alongside him, she places her dragon eggs and the still-living Mirri Maz Duur. As the fire burns, the Targaryen heir walks into it. The girl is burned away, as is Drogo, as is Mirri, and the dragon eggs. In their place, a woman: the Mother of Dragons.

The education of Daenerys Targaryen continues in the second season, although it's not quite as explicit. Dany, her infant dragons, and her tiny khalasar flee into the brutal desert called the Red Waste, when they're rescued by the discovery of the city of Qarth. The wealthy merchant Xaro Xhoan Daxos initially offers Dany a safe haven, but when she rejects his marriage offers in favor of continuing her attempts to get to Westeros, he betrays her, stealing her dragons and murdering much of her khalasar.

Xaro and his allies, the warlocks of Qarth, underestimate Daenerys and her dragons. She commands her largest dragon,

Drogon, to burn the warlock leader, Pyat Pree, and then punishes Xaro Xhoan Daxos for his treachery by sealing him in a vault and ransacking his house. It's enough to buy a ship, which takes Daenerys to Slaver's Bay.

There Dany puts the lessons she learned from Qarth into action—although exactly which lessons those are isn't quite clear. Never trust powerful men? Attack them before they take advantage of you? The ends justify the means? All are plausible, as Dany makes a shocking deal with the slaver Kraznys in Astapor: she sells him Drogon in exchange for a small army of elite Unsullied soldiers. Dany does this without taking any kind of advice from her two advisors, Jorah Mormont, and the new arrival, the venerable knight Ser Barristan the Bold. She even shuts the two men down, telling them never to question her in public.

When it comes time to make the deal, Dany betrays Kraznys, ordering her new army of Unsullied to "kill the Masters" of Astapor, as Drogon continues to follow her lead, killing the slaver attempting to control him. It's one of *Game of Thrones'* most impressive and inspiring scenes, the formerly scared girl becoming the symbol of freedom in Slaver's Bay. It's also an incredibly dishonorable act, and something Dany would be unlikely to do without having been betrayed similarly in Qarth.

With a new nickname—Breaker of Chains—the Targaryen woman leads her army on a brutal conquest of Slaver's Bay. She recruits a mercenary, Daario Naharis, and takes Yunkai, ending the third season with its former slaves calling her "Mhysa" or "mother." It's an odd scene—it ends the third season with a bunch of dark-skinned slaves praising a lily-white rescuer, and came under criticism for that. But it's also another example of *Game of Thrones* telling a cliché story, that of the white savior, and then complicating it—except we don't see the complication until Seasons 4 and 5.

Meanwhile, Daenerys' triumphant army moves onto Meereen, the most powerful and proudest city of Slaver's Bay. It, too, falls before her, seemingly completing her conquest in the name of liberation. That's when the complications arise, and quickly: Astapor and Yunkai have fallen into oppression again, and oppose her. Her trusted advisor, Ser Jorah, is revealed to have been a spy, for which she exiles him. And her increasingly large—and uncontrollable—dragons have started killing humans, apparently, which causes her to imprison the two she can find, while Drogon remains at large. War in the name of freedom, as idealistic as it may seem, has its complications at the political level, just as freeing Mirri Maz Duur in Season 1 did at the individual level. Realizing this, Dany decides to stay in Meereen, to learn to rule in addition to learning to conquer.

With the start of Season 5, the backlash to Dany's war for liberation takes a specific form: the Sons of the Harpy, a Meereenese insurrection against her rule. Dany is presented with two options. She initially picks violent, Targaryen-style counter-insurgency, the preferred option of Daario, her new lover. When that fails—costing the life of Ser Barristan—she takes a different, kinder route. She even marries a Meereenese aristocrat, Hizdahr zo Loraq, who has tried to push her toward compromise.

Hizdahr's first push for compromise is to reopen the famous Meereenese fighting pits for gladiatorial combat, leading to a grand spectacle at the Great Pit of Daznak. First, they go and view some of the qualification matches, which Ser Jorah is attempting to infiltrate. He brings along a gift: Tyrion Lannister, son of the man who killed much of Dany's family in the sack of King's Landing. Tyrion, however, is an enemy to his father, and an ally to Dany. He joins her service, although he advises keeping Jorah out.

At the Great Pit of Daznak, however, disaster strikes. The Sons of the Harpy attack at the height of the pit combat, with Ser Jorah once again entering the games and seeming to win. He helps save Daenerys' life, however, although Hizdahr is killed by the Harpy. As the insurrection surrounds Dany and her inner circle, Drogon appears, saving her life and she rides him to safety, far away from Meereen, ending the fifth season.

In Season 6, Dany finds herself far away from the sources of her power, so carefully cultivated over the past several seasons. Her armies and most of her retainers are in Meereen, and Drogon is too wounded by his battle in Meereen to help her. She finds herself captured by the Dothraki, although she leaves a clue for her retainers to find her.

In a full circle, Dany is taken back to Vaes Dothrak, the Dothraki capital, with the apparent intention of placing her in the home of widowed khaleesis for the rest of her days. That's not really Dany's style, and recruiting another woman, she makes a plan to free herself and take revenge on the abusive khals. Ser Jorah and Daario find her with their own rescue plan, but end up aiding her in hers anyway. The Mother of Dragons locks all the Dothraki khals in a building with her, then she sets it alight, using her Targaryen blood to survive yet another fire. The Dothraki horde kneels to her and joins her in returning to Meereen.

Meereen, under command of Tyrion Lannister, is besieged by the armies of Yunkai and Astapor. But Dany's dragons and the Dothraki arrive just in time, destroying the slavers' navy and killing the Sons of the Harpy, apparently freeing Slaver's Bay—now the Bay of Dragons—from slavers forever.

After the victory, Dany is joined by several Westerosi forces. Yara and Theon Greyjoy, in exchange for independence, give her the Ironborn navy. And as the army sets sail, they're joined by the Martells of Dorne and the Tyrells of Highgarden, seeking revenge for Lannister violence. The army of Dothraki, Unsullied, Westerosi, and dragons approaches the Seven Kingdoms, finally, after six seasons of buildup.

But what did Dany learn in the last few seasons? That's less clear, for the first time in a while. The accelerated pace of the storytelling has led to the end of the story. Dany has her army and navy and is preparing her invasion—taking precedence over all else. What did she do right in Meereen, and what did she do wrong? It's impossible to tell now, but perhaps when Daenerys Stormborn attempts to assert her right to the Iron Throne in Season 7, we'll find out for certain.

16 Jon Snow

"You know nothing, Jon Snow."—Ygritte

After the sixth season, it's become clear that Jon Snow is the hero of *Game of Thrones*. I don't just mean "hero" as in the main character who's also a good guy, although that's possibly true as well. It's more Jon Snow is the traditional fantasy hero in a story that's not supposed to be traditional fantasy—*Game of Thrones* breaks the rules, but Jon Snow follows them.

These rules were called the "Hero's Journey" by the literary critic Joseph Campbell, who argued that similarities in major myths across different cultures could be fit into a story type. Campbell may have been wrong about the history, and he definitely over-simplified, but his work proved popular, particularly with George Lucas, who used it as a source for the original *Star Wars*. Luke Skywalker's story became incredibly popular in the 1980s and '90s when fantasy started booming, and this was the model that George R.R. Martin set out to deconstruct.

So let's take a look at the conventional traits of the Hero's Journey, as seen through Luke, Jon, and any number of popular heroes. They start out boys or young men (occasionally, but rarely, young women) in humble positions: a farmer, or a bastard. They dream of adventure, but something shoves them into a far more dangerous and supernatural world than they expect. They acquire friends, allies, and magical swords. The hero often dies or comes to the brink of death, and is brought back by his friends, growing from boy into man. In the end, they defeat a great evil and fulfill their destiny, often having discovered they are the heir to a great legacy.

Game of Thrones has toyed with audience expectations before, particularly with Jon's family members, Ned and Robb, who were each set up as worthy heroes before they were suddenly killed for their poor decisions. But Jon is following this role almost perfectly.

To everyone in the world except Ned Stark and Howland Reed, Jon Snow's origins are a mystery. Ned Stark returned from Robert's Rebellion with a baby he called his own bastard, and a refusal to speak of the mother. Only Bran Stark's vision of the Tower of Joy revealed the truth of Jon's parentage to viewers—it's still unknown to Westeros at large that Jon Snow is the son of Ned's sister Lyanna (see the next chapter for why this is important).

Ned's unwillingness to talk about Jon's mother led to strife in the Stark household. He tried to raise Jon alongside his legitimate children, but his wife, Catelyn Tully, resented Jon and made sure he never quite felt like he belonged—in the books, in order to be accepted by the Wildlings later, Jon tells the story about the grand Stark feast when King Robert arrived, and how he was at a table at the far end of the room as his siblings sat with royalty.

But Jon became an honorable lad regardless, and when the time came, he followed his uncle Benjen Stark into the Night's Watch—the surest place for a misfit to have a life of service. Almost everyone attempts to dissuade the teenager from making a dramatic decision before experiencing life, but only Tyrion Lannister, who joins Jon on the trek to the Wall, actually tells him that the honor he seeks will be with new brothers who are rapists, thieves, murderers, and bullies. Jon initially wants to treat these boys and men as their superior—but advice from Tyrion, and the arrival of future best friend Samwell Tarly, convinces Jon to work with his cohorts instead of rejecting them. This is his first step toward becoming a leader, but it earns him the enmity of the Watch's drill sergeant, Ser Alliser Thorne.

When Jon is sworn in as a brother of the Night's Watch, he's disappointed to learn that he's been placed in the role of the steward, instead of becoming a ranger like his uncle. Sam Tarly, however, sees what's really happened: Jon has been named squire to the Lord Commander, Jeor Mormont, because Mormont wants to groom Snow to be his successor. Even still, Jon very nearly deserts when he discovers that Robb Stark has called the banners of the North to rescue Ned from the Lannisters. He's pulled back by the friendship of his fellow recruits—not the first time Jon is tempted by the political world south of the Wall.

When Jon returns, he finds himself in the supernatural world pressuring Westeros, when the body of a Night's Watchman rises and attacks the Lord Commander. Jon, thinking quickly, throws a torch at the corpse. For this, he's rewarded with the Mormont's sword, Longclaw—one of the few Valyrian steel blades in Westeros. Mormont, for his part, decides that an attack of the walking dead is enough to call a Ranging, where the bulk of the Night's Watch travels north of the Wall to find the missing Benjen Stark and discover what's happening with the risen dead.

In the first season, Snow's actor, Kit Harington, fit the role perfectly. Harington played handsome, honest, self-righteous, and kinda dense—Jon Snow's early defining traits—perfectly. But in the second season, Jon was called upon to do more. Initially, he pushed the story forward by investigating the Wildling Craster's children, and discovering a White Walker. But he eventually meets the legendary Night's Watch ranger Qhorin Halfhand and volunteers to scout Mance's army.

Along the way, Jon captures a young Wildling woman, Ygritte (Rose Leslie), who tries to use her sexuality to distract, demean, and recruit him ("You know nothing, Jon Snow!"). This is a struggle for both the show and Harington. Leslie gives it her all, but romantic comedy just isn't a genre that comes easily to *Game of Thrones*, and Harington's denseness becomes frustrating.

For example, when the tables get turned, and the Wildlings capture Jon and the Halfhand, Qhorin tells Jon that a spy in Mance's camp will be worth more to the Watch than a patrol of rangers, if he makes the right choices—meaning killing Qhorin in a duel in order to ingratiate himself with the Wildlings. Jon does what he's supposed to, but there's never a clear indication on Harington's face that he gets why.

In the third season, though, Kit Harington and the writers find a better niche for him. His relationship with Ygritte dominates the season and calmed down as it turned into something gentle and sweet. The show played it up, ending one episode with Jon and Ygritte, having climbed the Wall with a Wildling raiding party, looking at the southlands, which are drawn up like a watercolor of hope, and they kiss. It's probably the most romantic moment of the entire show. A few episodes later, they violently break up because, after all, this is *Game of Thrones*.

While Jon was tempted by his time with the Free Folk, he couldn't stick with it—they were fighting a war, and the raiding party called upon the fundamentally decent Stark bastard to execute a prisoner. Jon couldn't do it and, aided surreptitiously by his brother Bran, who's warged into his wolves, he makes a getaway. (The scene is also famous for being arguably the only time *Game of Thrones'* vaunted special effects don't work, when Jon is attacked by a Wildling warged into a ridiculous eagle.) Ygritte hunts Jon down and puts some arrows in his back, but he makes it back to Castle Black with a warning of Mance's attack.

In the fourth season, Kit Harington comes into his own with the show finding a great new role for him: action hero. The Night's Watch, not in good shape to begin with, has been demolished by the Great Ranging being attacked by the White Walkers, and the mutineers killing Lord Commander Jeor Mormont. Jon, after convincing the officers of the Watch that's he's still loyal, realizes the mutineers at Craster's Keep could tell Mance just how weak the Crows have become, and they have to be killed.

This is a sequence entirely invented for the show—in fact, much of the buildup to Mance's attack is embellished a great deal in order to prioritize the big battle at the end of the season. The mutineers, led by "fookin" legend Karl Tanner, are ridiculously cruel, apparently having been feasting and raping at Craster's Keep for weeks, or months, since they took the keep over in the third season. Jon duels Karl, resulting in one of the show's most gruesome deaths when the bastard's sword shockingly emerges from Tanner's mouth, having been shoved through the back of his head. It was a great action sequence to finish off a dubious storyline— and it ensured that Harington would be well-prepared to take on the role of action hero in the big battle episodes of the next three seasons.

Another major boost for Harington is the increasing prominence of his old rival, Ser Alliser Thorne, played by Owen Teale. Teale managed to imbue the potentially cartoonishly cruel Thorne with a sense that he was a man trying to do his best in a world that had passed him by. Which makes the grudging respect that he comes to grant Jon over the course of the season, preparing for the battle, all the more impressive. Perhaps because Teale was so effective at working with Harington, the show gave him a much larger role on the screen than in the novels.

When the battle comes, it has a full episode to itself: "The Watchers on the Wall." Tormund's raiders attack Castle Black from the south, while Mance's main army attacks the Wall directly. Harington does his best work as Jon Snow here, quietly discussing the battle with Thorne, then starring in the fighting when it kicks into gear. The battle, directed by Neil Marshall, is a technical marvel, and Harington's in the center of much of the best of it: he kicks off a 360-degree shot that may be the most awe-inspiring of the series, wounding and capturing Tormund Giantsbane, taking over leadership when Thorne is wounded, and killing the Thenn in single combat. He also meets Ygritte on the battlefield. Both of them freeze, and a boy named Olly, recruited into the Watch after Tormund's raiders killed his village, shoots and kills Jon's Wildling love.

Despite beating the raiders back, the battle isn't won. Jon hits upon an idea to disintegrate the Wildling army by assassinating Mance Rayder. He heads out to negotiate, but Mance sees through his plan when Jon's eye falls on a knife. Right then, Stannis Baratheon attacks, and the Wildlings are routed, with the King-Beyond-the-Wall captured.

In Season 5, Jon's role as traditional hero really gets going. "Kill the boy, and let the man be born" is the advice Maester Aemon gives Jon, a line that also serves as one that defines what a chosen hero needs to do in order to achieve success.

Jon needs that advice because he's entered the political battle of *Game of Thrones*, instead of merely having his adventures in growing up. Stannis quickly realizes that Jon is worthy of respect and sends him to negotiate a surrender from Mance Rayder. Mance refuses to bend the knee, and is set to be executed by fire, a death he's terrified of. As the flames start, Jon shoots the erstwhile King-Beyond-The-Wall, preventing a cruel death.

Despite this, King Stannis offers Jon a tempting prize: he will legitimize the bastard in order to have a Stark ally in the war for the North. Jon rejects the offer out of loyalty to the Watch, which is rewarded when he shockingly wins the election to become the new Lord Commander.

Game of Thrones is continuing to subvert the ideas of heroic fantasy in this moment—one of the key moments in the Hero's Journey is that the inevitable hero "refuses the call to adventure" in a supernatural world—like needing to stay home to do chores, instead of seeing the universe, or not stopping a mugger despite superpowers because it's none of your business. Jon refuses the call to head south three times before accepting: first, when he joins the Watch despite being told he should live a little beforehand; second, when he initially tries to desert to join Robb's army after Ned's death but loyalty to his brothers brings him back; and third, with Stannis.

But by refusing the call, Jon had the sorts of adventures the chosen hero is supposed to have! He fought the dead, traveled to the most exotic parts of the world, fell in love with a free woman, won an impossible battle, and became a leader of men. From the time he fought the wight in Castle Black on, Jon tried to stay in the realm of the supernatural, beyond the Wall. The "call" he refused for over five seasons was the call of responsibility in the world of men and their grubby politics, subverting Campbell's Hero's Journey.

As Lord Commander, Jon managed both his responsibilities and his sense of adventure. His chief problem: what to do about the Wildlings' defeated army. With the White Walkers threatening in the North, Jon Snow made the decision to recruit and integrate the Free Folk, a decision that was both moral in the short term and practical in the long term—he'd need an army, after all. There were two major short-term practical problems, though: the Wildlings had retreated to the village of Hardhome, far to the North, and Jon's brothers in the Watch had been fighting Wildlings for thousands of years and just a few weeks back, making them rather unhappy about aiding their sworn enemies.

So, in the eighth and best episode of the fifth season, "Hardhome," Jon and a few loyal brothers joined Tormund in sailing to Hardhome and attempting to convince the Free Folk to join. The episode builds tension brilliantly, with Tormund using violence, then Jon using diplomacy, to recruit a decent amount of Wildlings. But suddenly the weather turns freezing, and an army of wights, led by a White Walker, attacks the village.

It's the first major pitched battle between the living and the dead. The Wildlings and Crows fight bravely, but are slowly overwhelmed at the walls. The leaders are attacked by a White Walker, who seems invincible, shattering every blade until it confronts Jon, whose Valyrian steel sword is able to destroy the Walker. Jon gathers as many survivors as he can onto the boats and sets sail, but as they leave, he sees the Night's King arrive, raise his arms, and all the corpses remaining in Hardhome rise.

Things don't get better from there. When Jon returns, his steward, Olly, tells him that his long-lost uncle Benjen has returned. Jon heads to the courtyard where Olly, Ser Alliser, and many of his sworn brothers take turn stabbing the Lord Commander, saying "For the Watch!" with each blow.

But when the sixth season starts, it becomes clear that Maester Aemon's advice to "kill the boy" was meant literally. Jon's allies, led by Ser Davos, who's returned from Stannis' defeat, take his body to defend it. Davos recruits the red priestess Melisandre to do anything she can to raise Jon from the dead—and she succeeds, letting the new man be born. Jon arrests and executes his murderers, then tosses his cloak to his surviving friend, Dolorous Edd, declaring that his Watch is ended.

The fourth call to come south arrives soon after, when Jon's sister Sansa arrives at Castle Black, having fled Ramsay Bolton and Winterfell. She implores Jon to help her fight Ramsay, and when a letter from the Bastard of Bolton arrives, threatening Sansa, Jon, and the Wildlings, Jon commits to freeing the North.

With his motley collection of Sansa, Tormund, and Davos, Jon negotiates with the Wildlings and the lords of the North to build an army. He succeeds wildly with breakout star Lyanna Mormont and gets most of the Wildlings, but a full army eludes him. Despite this, he and Sansa attack Winterfell. They set a defensive plan for Ramsay Bolton, but Ramsay lures the Starks into a trap, using the youngest brother, Rickon, to pull Jon out—and Rickon dies anyway. Jon finds himself at the center of the battle, and Kit Harington once again rises to the occasion as an action hero in the midst of a brutal, chaotic mess.

The Boltons surround Jon's army and slowly grind them into a pile of corpses, with Jon trapped beneath. But he breaks free, reaching his arm to the sky, and Sansa, who's secretly negotiated for aid from Littlefinger and the knights of the Vale, arrives and wins the day. Jon beats and captures Ramsay, who's executed by Sansa.

In the aftermath of the battle, Jon finds himself in the uncomfortable position of holding true power. Davos confronts Jon with proof that Melisandre had Stannis' daughter Shireen killed. Melisandre argues that her power will be needed when the Long Night begins, which causes Jon to exile her. Then, in a council with the lords of the North and the Vale, Lyanna Mormont calls for Jon to be named King in the North, to general approval. Jon, as ever, looks blank, as he's put in the position of being the true hero of Westeros.

But there's one final piece required to being a chosen hero: having a secret destiny. In its sixth season finale, *Game of Thrones* finally revealed Jon's: he's the son of Lyanna Stark, Ned's sister. For why that's important, read on....

 R+L=J

"Promise me, Ned."—Lyanna Stark

There's a famous story about *Game of Thrones* showrunners David Benioff and D.B. Weiss' meeting with George R.R. Martin, when they made their pitch to have him give the rights to the story to them for their TV show. The critical moment, they say, was this: Martin asked them who they thought Jon Snow's parents were. Their answer got them the rights.

The question of Jon Snow's parentage is probably the greatest mystery in the novels, hanging over the story, demanding an answer. The most popular theory became known as "R+L=J," an acronym whose simplicity served to make it very easy to write on message boards, and whose abstractness makes it disguised from people who don't want to be spoiled, a group whose numbers swelled when the show moved to HBO. There's a moment in the pilot, when Jon leans against a pillar that has "R+L" carved into it, that suggests this was Benioff and Weiss' answer—and the reveal of Jon's mother in the Season 6 finale confirmed it.

R+L=J means this: Rhaegar Targaryen and Lyanna Stark are Jon's Snow's parents. Robert's Rebellion is, in many ways, predicated on Rhaegar and Lyanna's relationship. The opening act of it is Rhaegar kidnapping Lyanna, who was Robert Baratheon's fiancée. Ned's father and older brother go to confront the Mad King, who has them publicly tortured and killed, causing Robert and Ned to raise their banners in rebellion. They win, with Robert defeating Rhaegar in single combat, and then, after the war is over, Ned travels to the Tower of Joy, where he kills Ser Arthur Dayne of the Kingsguard and meets the dying Lyanna in the events we saw in the sixth season finale.

This is a huge deal for several reasons. First, it means that Jon is a Targaryen, with the blood of the dragon in his veins. Jon, arguably, is the true heir to the Iron Throne, according to the rigid laws of primogeniture—the Targaryens fought a civil war, The Dance of the Dragons, over whether a woman could inherit the throne, and it was inconclusive. Regardless of whether Jon would have a better claim than his aunt, Daenerys, he would almost certainly be her heir, since Dany is barren after Mirri Maz Duur's curse. But the blood of the Targaryens is also apparently necessary to tame dragons, and Dany can only ride one at a time, after all.

The second major thing is that it suggests that everything the characters think they know about the history of the Seven Kingdoms is wrong. Rhaegar was always assumed to have kidnapped Lyanna, but the famously strong-willed Stark woman may well have gone on her own, possibly to escape the overbearing Robert, or possibly just because she loved Rhaegar. And this means Rhaegar, treated as a villain by so many, may have just been a lovestruck fool.

Finally, it also sets Jon up as having a secret destiny, which is a critical component of him being a traditional fantasy hero in a series that often seems like it's anything but traditional fantasy.

Thanks to *Game of Thrones'* avoidance of flashbacks, readers always had an advantage in understanding this. Most of what we saw at the Tower of Joy took place in the first season, as Ned, recovering from his wound in the dungeons of King's Landing, has a fever dream where he flashes back to the war.

Most everything seen in the sixth season finale takes place there, with all the necessary clues: Ned meets the Kingsguard, led by Arthur Dayne, and wonders why they weren't at any of the battles where the ruling family died. Dayne says that Rhaegar wanted him in Dorne, at the Tower, suggesting that the ruling family needed guards there. And when Ned fights his way into the

Tower, he discovers Lyanna on a bed, in a pool of her own blood, saying "Promise me, Ned."

There are two key additions to the show's version. In Ned's flashback, Lyanna doesn't actually offer a baby on the page, but the way she's described strongly implies death in childbirth, and Ned arrives home from the wars with a babe that nobody else ever saw. On the show, Lyanna also makes it more clear what Ned's promise has to be: that Robert would kill the baby if he found out. Given the King's bloodlust against all Targaryens, it's reasonable to assume she's saying the baby has their blood. (Although nothing she says proves that it's Rhaegar's baby, it's far more likely, at every level, that it's his and not the Mad King's—the only other adult Targaryen male at the time. Well, except for Maester Aemon at the Wall, but I think we can rule him out.)

Still, this evidence was strong enough that R+L=J was the default theory for most readers, to the point where some believed that the strongest evidence against it was that it was *too* obvious. The books occasionally tried to toss up alternate theories, like a servant girl named Willa that other lords believed was Ned's mistress, but it always came back to Lyanna.

The novels also offer two other prophecies that show why this is so important. In the books, when Daenerys visits the House of the Undying in Qarth, she receives a prophecy suggesting "the dragon has three heads." For most fans interpreting this prophecy, it means that three characters will ride on Daenerys' three dragons. Dany is one, of course, and R+L=J means that Jon is almost certainly the second. (The third is a matter of no small debate—see chapters on Tyrion, Bran, and Young Griff for the most likely candidates.)

But there's another part to the prophecy, both in the House of the Undying and referred to by several other characters: "the prince that was promised," or Azor Ahai (see chapter 83). This prophecy indicates that there is a chosen hero in the world of *Game of Thrones,* and with the characters who believed themselves to be such—Rhaegar and Stannis—already dead, the suggestion is that Jon Snow is the man who will fulfill these prophecies.

18 Tyrion Lannister

It's not exactly a secret that much of *Game of Thrones'* popularity comes from its archetypes. There are certain kinds of characters that people really like seeing in their stories, and *Thrones* has these types while also complicating them, turning them three dimensions. For example, *Game of Thrones* has not one but two woman warriors, one an adult in her prime, Brienne of Tarth, and the other a girl growing in her power, Arya Stark. That's a damn powerful archetype, and it's no surprise that they're two of *Thrones'* biggest fan favorites.

The most popular archetype may be the trickster: the character who stands between the sides of good and evil, or of law and chaos, and balances them with a sense of both humor and morality. On television, these are characters like Omar from *The Wire* or Spike from *Buffy*. It's also a common mythological archetype: the coyote in some Native American myths, the Monkey King in Chinese lore, and Han Solo in *Star Wars*.

Game of Thrones' Tyrion Lannister may add his name to that list of legendary pop culture tricksters once all is said and done. He is arguably *Game of Thrones'* most popular character, and is played by its most-decorated actor, Peter Dinklage, who's won two Emmys for the role. Dinklage is fantastic, and he's also written with many of the best lines and scenes in the show. But all this goes in with the trickster archetype (the Imp!), and that's the key to what makes Tyrion so great.

Tyrion and Sansa's dreadfully unhappy marriage is probably still the most successful on the show. (Photo courtesy of HBO / Photofest)

The most important thing about the trickster is that they operate between two worlds. Think of Loki from Norse mythology, the child of giants, but adopted and raised by their enemies, the gods. While Marvel's version of Loki is primarily a villain, Norse mythology has him constantly straddling both lines, helping and hurting the gods according to his whims (until he cracks and triggers Ragnarok.)

Tyrion stands between two worlds because on the one hand, he is the son of arguably the most powerful man of his generation, Tywin Lannister, Hand to three different kings, and the winner of two of Westeros' greatest civil wars. Tyrion can never escape his name, and always finds himself drawn back into the circles of power, whether it be against his will, as when Cat Stark arrests him to start the civil war, or according to his sense of duty, as when he refuses to flee King's Landing alongside Shae.

But Tyrion is also not allowed to fully engage with that world because of his physique. On the show, he is simply a dwarf, while in the novels, he's written as ugly and misshapen. This prevents him from ever being a true knight, the peak of masculine ideals (although he is a surprisingly successful warrior, see: Blackwater). He's also despised by his father and sister for having killed his mother during his birth. Hence Tyrion finds himself more at home with the world's misfits: the "cripples, bastards, and broken things" of *Game of Thrones'* fourth episode, as well as the sex workers he can pay for affection.

This leaves Tyrion both alienated and empathetic. Because he never fits in, he gets bitter and petulant, like when he attempts to demand Casterly Rock from his father, or righteously angry, as in his devastating monologue at the end of his trial, where he lambasts the entire royal court for turning on him.

But the empathy leads him to genuine kindness, which he demonstrates often to his family's supposed rivals, the Starks. Early in the first season, he plans a saddle that the paralyzed Bran Stark can utilize to ride a horse once again. When he becomes Hand, he protects Sansa Stark from the depredations of her fiancé, King Joffrey—a kindness he attempts to continue when he's forced to wed the girl, but refuses to bed her until she desires it.

The empathy and anger can get Tyrion in trouble as well, as illustrated in his relationship with Shae, a prostitute he finds in the Lannister camp and hires permanently as his paramour. Tyrion has fallen in love with a sex worker before, when an ill-fated ploy by his brother Jaime to help Tyrion lose his virginity ends up with Tyrion wedding the prostitute Jaime picked out—until his father Tywin punishes his youngest son by forcing him to watch, then join, as all the men of the guard take their turns with the girl.

Tyrion falls for Shae again, and *Game of Thrones* makes it seem like a great romance. This is a departure from the novels, where Shae is given much less of a personality and a romantic subplot. But with acclaimed German actress (and ex-porn star) Sibel Kekilli, the *Thrones* producers struck gold. They couldn't not play up her chemistry with Dinklage to add to both characters' depth.

But when it came time for Shae to betray Tyrion, and ruin his chance of surviving his trial—leading to him murdering her— *Game of Thrones* was in trouble. It was one thing for the books to have Tyrion kill someone who betrayed his trust, but another for him to kill someone depicted as his lady love. The show's solution? An incredibly bad breakup, with the marriage to Sansa permanently driving a wedge in their relationship, despite Tyrion's best attempts to be honorable. Shae also attacks Tyrion as soon as she sees him, making the killing one of self-defense as much as revenge—although I'm not entirely certain it was enough.

Whether it was this murder, or a change of scenery for Tyrion, he seems a very different character in the fifth and sixth seasons. The trickster who had attempted to flit through life, drunk on wine and sex, is replaced by a far more serious character who drinks and fucks to forget, at first, and then becomes Daenerys' lead advisor, finding meaning in life. He's also, well, a little more boring, though that might be just be because the story moves so quickly in Meereen once he arrives.

It's also possible that he's just hanging out with more boring characters. Well, that's not entirely fair: Dany and her crew are filled with strong personalities and interesting stories. But they're not clever like Tyrion and his sparring partners. Indeed, throughout the first four seasons, Tyrion is defined by his current sparring partner.

In the first few episodes, this is the Night's Watchmen Yoren as well as Jon Snow, to whom he gives some important advice for survival amongst people who hate him. But it really kicks into gear when he's arrested by Catelyn Stark for attempting to have her son

Bran murdered. Tyrion didn't do it, and in a series of dialogues, seems to create doubt in Cat's mind—in addition to saving her life when her party is ambushed.

He also befriends one of his most constant companions, the sellsword-become-knight Bronn. Bronn, a relatively smaller role in the novels, becomes far more prominent on *Game of Thrones*. This is largely thanks to his larger-than-life personality and Peter Dinklage's chemistry with his actor, former one-hit-wonder pop star Jerome Flynn. Flynn constantly keeps pace with Dinklage, creating a sparkling set of one-liners.

When he returns to King's Landing in the second season, Tyrion again meets perhaps his very best starring partner: his sister Cersei. Their scenes, especially in the second season as they struggle for power with each other and King Joffrey, as well as planning to defend the city against Stannis, are consistently the very best of the season. Dinklage also brings out the best in Lena Headey, who had rarely shown three dimensions in the first season. But this combination of actors, and the show putting Cersei in a room with someone who truly knows but does not like her, gives her the chance to shine.

Tyrion also meets his best friend (that he's not paying) in *Game of Thrones*: Varys the Spider, the eunuch spymaster of the Iron Throne. Nobody trusts Varys, or even really likes him. But Tyrion discovers that the spymaster may well be the most honorable man in King's Landing, in his own way. And the two of them together help develop the plan that delays Stannis long enough to win the Battle of Blackwater for the Lannisters.

A few other characters benefit from their time with the Imp. Podrick Payne, initially a minor character and a joke, is built up by Tyrion to the point where he's one of the show's heroes in later seasons. Oberyn Martell develops enough of a friendship with and respect for Tyrion that he becomes the Imp's champion in the trial by combat, albeit with disastrous results. And, in a similar manner as had happened with Cat Stark, Tyrion befriends his skeptical captor in the fifth season, Ser Jorah Mormont—and later saves Jorah's life.

Still, perhaps the most important relationship in his life is one with a man that Tyrion cannot spar with: his father, Tywin. Like Cersei and Jaime, Tyrion can only manage a few lines of defiance before Lord Tywin reasserts his dominance, making the Imp (and everyone else) look like a chastened schoolchild.

But in joining with Cersei to accuse and convict Tyrion of the murder of King Joffrey, Tywin overplays his hand. He underestimates Tyrion's relationships with the powerbrokers of King's Landing, most notably Varys. He also underestimates Tyrion's relationship with his brother Jaime, the Lord Commander of the Kingsguard. Those two break Tyrion out of prison before his execution. And Tywin has also underestimated Tyrion's drive for revenge. Instead of merely seeking his freedom, Tyrion seeks his father, and fires a crossbow bolt into Daddy's belly.

With his father gone, Tyrion is allowed to seek a new goal in life. While his initial impulse is alcoholism, first Varys, then Jorah, convince the Imp to seek out Daenerys Targaryen. Tyrion does, and swiftly rises to the top of her advisors. When the Mother of Dragons arrives to discover her city under siege, she initially flies into a rage, threatening to burn all her enemies' cities in vengeance. But Tyrion talks her down from being the next Mad King, one child of a horrible father to another.

For this rise to respectability and balance, Daenerys pins the symbol of the Hand on Tyrion's chest, making him the second-most powerful person in her army. And perhaps with this, Daenerys has killed the Imp, finally pushed Tyrion from his youthful trickstery into serving a cause greater than himself. But hey, he's still played by Peter Dinklage, he's still heading home to meet his brother and sister again: Tyrion will almost certainly still be a fantastic character in the end, even if he's outgrown his initial archetype.

19 Sansa Stark

"Your words will disappear. Your house will disappear. Your name will disappear. All memory of you will disappear."—Sansa Stark

In the world of *Game of Thrones*, Sansa Stark represents hope. She's not just hope for a happy ending, like Dany saving the day on her dragons, Jon being the chosen hero, or even Faceless Arya murdering everyone on her list. Sansa represents the hope that people got Westeros into the mess it's in, and people can get them out of it.

Of the major heroes—the four main Stark kids, Tyrion, and Dany—Sansa is the only one who hasn't had significant interaction with the supernatural. She's always been navigating the world of politics, not zombies or dragons. Even her direwolf was killed before it could become more than a fairly large puppy.

Yet Sansa has also successfully navigated the minefield that is Westerosi politics. Starting as a naive young girl, she learns politics from the most powerful players in the game of thrones: her father Ned, Queen Cersei, Margaery and Olenna Tyrell, Tyrion Lannister, and Petyr "Littlefinger" Baelish. And those lessons are learned as Sansa becomes a major player in the Starks taking the North back, despite the years of abuse and pain she faced as a hostage.

It is for this reason that *Game of Thrones* faced its biggest backlash when, in the fifth season, Sansa was married to Ramsay Bolton, who rapes and abuses her. Sansa Stark's character before this point was a clear line of a foolish but fundamentally good person who learns lessons from villains while retaining her morality, and this brings her power. But when she was forced to face another season of abuse, it seemed to remove all that progress for more pain (in a storyline that was written in the novels for another character, no less). But happily, the show righted itself and placed Sansa at the center of Season 6, and at its end, with her alliances to Jon Snow and Littlefinger, she is one of the most powerful people in Westeros.

In the original pitch for *Game of Thrones*, Sansa isn't a major character at all. She ends up married to Joffrey, bearing his babies, and only later realizing that something has gone wrong, while Arya, Jon, and Bran become heroes. Aspects of this Sansa can be seen in how she starts the story. Sansa Stark at Winterfell is superficial and flighty, cruel to Arya and dismissive of Jon. She dreams of courtly love, and when she's set to be engaged to the prince, it's a dream come true.

The dream, to the young Sansa, is so appealing that when Joffrey and Arya fight, and Arya's direwolf attacks the future king, Sansa claims that she couldn't tell who did what. Perhaps it was a teenager's attempt to navigate a politically fraught situation with the least damage, perhaps it was being unwilling to break up her perfect romance, or perhaps it was truthful confusion about the events. Regardless, the situation earns Sansa her sisters' hatred as Arya's friend is killed, and Sansa's direwolf is executed by her father as a stand-in for Arya's lost pup.

Sansa's naiveté continues through events of the first season, even as characters like Littlefinger and the Hound question her faith in chivalry. After Ned Stark's fall from grace, Sansa is called upon by the queen and the Small Council to write a letter to her family as an attempt to prevent them from rebellion, which she does—although its dishonesty is easily seen through by her family, who march south anyway. (In the novels, Sansa's crime is more explicit: she tells the queen of Ned's plan to send her away, which clues Cersei in to Ned's plans for a coup.) It's this Sansa who became one of the most hated characters in certain sections of fandom. But Sansa is a survivor, and tries to find her way to redemption.

The Stark daughter pleads to her fiancé and the entire court for mercy for her father if he confesses his crimes, which Joffrey says he will grant. But despite Ned's confession, Joffrey's mercy is an illusion—he demands Ned's immediate execution, to the shock of everyone present, especially Sansa.

With no reason to pretend toward her anymore, Joffrey demonstrates his sadism to Sansa. In her most essential scene of the first season, the new king forces her to look at her father's decapitated head. It's here that Sansa's character evolves from the pathetic girl she started as, as Sansa demonstrates her inner strength in looking at the head, talking back to Joffrey, and even pondering pushing him to his death. Joffrey has her beaten by a Kingsguard (although not Sandor Clegane, who demonstrates some measure of kindness toward the "little bird").

The scene is essential not merely for Sansa, but also her actress, Sophie Turner. Her acting is subtle and mature, showing grief, resolve, and the ability to go through the motions, all at the same time. It was also apparently the scene used for auditions for Sansa Stark. Its complexity, and Turner's ability to manifest it, make her one of the most superb casting choices in all of *Game of Thrones*. (It's also launched her career, as she recently landed another massive franchise role: Jean Grey in the *X-Men* movies.)

For the next two seasons, Sansa is forced to navigate the lion's den of her enemies in Lannister-controlled King's Landing. She shows an increasing deftness in surviving, although thanks to Joffrey's viciousness, it isn't enough to keep her sane. For that she has allies: Queen Cersei, who oddly seems to take a liking to Sansa, mentoring her in what it's like to be a queen; Tyrion Lannister, who wishes to defend the weak generally and understands her importance specifically; and Littlefinger, whose motives appear genuine, but given his teenaged love for her mother, who Sansa resembles, is also rather creepy.

This peaks in "Blackwater," where Sansa may have the best moments in arguably *Thrones'* greatest episode. The women of the court are locked in a room in the Red Keep along with Cersei, who has no interest in calming or leading them. The increasingly drunk Cersei's interactions with Sansa are a delight. Lena Headey gives no fucks, and Sophie Turner plays Sansa's realization of this—that she's the only adult in the room—marvelously. When Cersei deserts the room, it's Sansa who leads the terrified women in a hymn to calm them. Even still, she's convinced to flee and return to her room as well by her handmaiden Shae.

There she meets the Hound, who, after fleeing the fiery battle, has decided to desert the Lannisters. He offers to take a terrified Sansa with him, but she declines, apparently out of fear of Joffrey's dog. (This is fair on the show; in the novels their relationship is significantly more complex, to the point where Sansa even remembers a kiss.) But Stannis' army doesn't win—it's the Lannisters who've allied with the Tyrells who do, and the key to that alliance is a marriage contract between Joffrey and Margaery. Joffrey feigns wishing to stay engaged to Sansa in front of the court, but he allows himself to be convinced to break the betrothal. Sansa initially celebrates, but Littlefinger finds her and tells her that Joffrey doesn't give up his toys so easily.

In Season 3, Sansa's ambiguous status makes her more of a political prize, although it's unclear exactly how much she realizes this. She befriends Margaery and Olenna Tyrell, who seem to honestly sympathize with her, but also need her to give information on Joffrey's personality. "He's a monster," Sansa blurts out.

With Bran and Rickon's disappearance, Sansa is Robb Stark's heir, and therefore the key to the North. Littlefinger plans to steal her away, but Varys finds out and encourages an alliance with her and the Tyrells. When Margaery informs her that she's to wed the dashing knight out of her stories, Ser Loras, Sophie Turner somehow manages to get rainbow stars in her eyes at the prospect of marrying Loras. She seems firmly unaware that he's gay, although does seem to note that he doesn't seem at all interested in the bridal aspect of marriage.

But before Sansa can be betrayed by the vagaries of sexual orientation, she's betrayed by Littlefinger, who finds out about the engagement and informs Lord Tywin, in order to have Sansa for himself. Tywin quickly arranges a marriage between Tyrion and Sansa, which turns into a disaster—Sansa refuses to help Tyrion and embarrasses him, Joffrey taunts both the bride and the groom, Tyrion responds violently, and the marriage passes without violence, barely (a rarity in *Game of Thrones* in the third and fourth seasons.)

Sansa is crushed by the marriage. The Imp is no Knight of Flowers in her chivalry-addled eyes, and the Lannisters have attempted to destroy her family for two seasons now. Tyrion does try to show her kindness, and never consummates the marriage.

In the fourth season, the Lannisters seem to have triumphed over all enemies, with Sansa's brother and mother murdered by Tywin's plans at the Red Wedding. Sansa, naturally, is crushed, but she still goes through the motions at the royal wedding. She is an unwitting pawn in Joffrey's poisoning: Littlefinger's agent, Ser Dontos, gives her a piece of jewelry to wear, which Olenna Tyrell swipes and drops in Joffrey's wine, killing him in minutes. In the chaos Sansa flees with Ser Dontos, who is killed by Littlefinger, swiftly ending Sansa's belief in Dontos as a chivalric hero. (Sansa is also implicated, incorrectly, in the claim that Tyrion killed Joffrey, and is considered a traitor to the crown for it.)

At the Eyrie, Sansa quickly discovers she's traded one nightmare hostage scenario for another. The Lord of the Eyrie, Robin Arryn, is a small, sickly child with a propensity for having anyone he dislikes executed. His mother Lysa, Sansa's aunt, is devoted to Littlefinger and (rightly) distrusting of his relationship with Sansa. When she sees Littlefinger kiss Sansa on the mouth she flies into a rage, threatening Sansa with death, until Littlefinger pushes Lysa out the Eyrie's Moon Door to her death.

When the Lords of the Eyrie come to investigate Lysa's death, Sansa finally, after four seasons of carefully surviving politics, finally takes agency for herself. She blows her cover, revealing herself as Sansa Stark, and lies to protect Littlefinger—but she does so in such a way that he becomes indebted to her. The end of the season shows Sansa in a new raven cloak, leading Robin and Littlefinger into the Eyrie, finally asserting her power as the only Stark capable of navigating the game. (It also pushes Sansa past her place in the books, where she's still disguised in the Vale, and her story in the fourth book ends disappointingly with Littlefinger planning to marry her to Robin's heir.)

Yet the fifth season seems to take a step back, returning Sansa to being dominated by more powerful players, and facing abuse for it. First, Brienne of Tarth finally meets one of the Stark daughters, only to be mocked by Littlefinger and sent away by Sansa. The meeting takes place on the road, where Littlefinger has a plan to marry Sansa to Ramsay Bolton. This is one of the most debated decisions in all of *Game of Thrones*. First, it's way off the books, where Ramsay's wife is a Northern girl pretending to be Arya Stark. Second, it seems incredibly dubious that Sansa would ever marry into the family that murdered her brother. The show does try to explain this, and Turner and Aiden Gillen (Littlefinger) try to sell the hell out of it, but it always seems like a stretch.

Sansa's arrival at Winterfell does do good things for the show in that it gives depth to the Boltons, who, before her arrival, had only interacted with one another. When Ramsay Bolton attempts to torment Sansa emotionally at a dinner, for example, he's reined in by his father Roose's power. Ramsay is at his most interesting in this moment—the sadist forced to disguise himself. It doesn't last: after the marriage, Ramsay sexually assaults Sansa, making his torment more direct.

The Stark woman is not helpless in the situation. When Brienne of Tarth, who has followed her to Winterfell, sneaks word into Sansa she'll aid in any escape, Sansa attempts to recruit Theon Greyjoy to her cause. Theon initially betrays her, but as the situation spirals out of control and Stannis' army attacks, he changes his mind and joins her escape. Yet they choose to flee the one time Brienne isn't watching for their signal, as she's seeking Stannis for revenge. Instead, Theon and Sansa jump off the walls of Winterfell, ending Sansa's dismal season on a freezing cliffhanger.

But in the sixth season, Sansa turns everything around. Fleeing with Theon, she wants to die free rather than return to the Boltons. It looks like she won't have the choice, when Brienne arrives and swears fealty to the Stark woman in one of the show's most inspiring scenes. Finally, the heroes are on the same side, and it's Sansa Stark who's leading them.

Sansa heads to Winterfell to see Jon, who she believes is Lord Commander, but has just been assassinated and resurrected, which he treats as being freed from his vows. She attempts to recruit him to crush the Boltons, and Jon is hesitant, since he spent the fifth season trying to lead and died for his efforts. But when Ramsay Bolton sends a taunting, threatening letter, Jon joins the cause.

He and Sansa spend their time trying to recruit the beaten Northern lords to rebel once again. They are only partially successful, and when Littlefinger arrives to offer a meeting, Sansa accepts. He offers her an alliance with the Vale, but she rejects him. In a cathartic scene for her and viewers, she lambasts him for selling her to the sadistic Ramsay Bolton, saying "If you didn't know, you're an idiot; if you did, you're my enemy." Littlefinger acts understanding and provides her with information: her great-uncle Brynden Tully has reassembled the army of the Riverlands, who may join her. Sansa sends Brienne to recruit the Blackfish.

The Stark army marches on Winterfell despite being outnumbered, and Sansa warns Jon, as he plans the battle, that Ramsay is cunning and will trick him into making the wrong move. Jon asks if she has a better idea, and Sansa is silent.

That trickery comes with Ramsay using the youngest Stark brother, Rickon, as bait to lure Jon, then his army, out of their defensive position. Rickon is killed, and the Stark army is surrounded by the overwhelming forces of the Bolton army. But when all seems lost, Sansa arrives alongside Littlefinger at the head of the Knights of the Vale, who charge into battle, routing the Bolton forces. Jon beats and captures Ramsay Bolton, leaving him to Sansa's revenge—which she takes by having him fed to his beloved man-eating hounds.

The Stark victory is undercut by Sansa's deception, however. Exactly why she let Jon fight a battle he'd inevitably lose, instead of telling him about her allies in the Vale, is unclear. The best possible explanation is that she needed Ramsay to grow overconfident by seeing Jon use a small army's battle plan, the worst is that she was too scared to tell him, thus costing the lives of half his army. (Or perhaps even worse, that it was poor writing to create extra dramatic tension). In the aftermath of the highly rated "Battle of the Bastards," Sansa's motives were the key point of debate.

She does apologize to Jon at the end of the season, and they decide that they need to trust one another. But a possibility for that trust to be broken comes when Littlefinger arrives and makes an offer: join him on his quest to take the Iron Throne, as his queen. She very subtly rejects him, but shortly after, in the great hall of Winterfell, both are present when Jon Snow is crowned King in the North, with no apparent credit given to Sansa for her role in retaking the North. The season ends with her locking eyes ambiguously with Littlefinger, two of the only people in the room not celebrating.

It has been a long road for Sansa Stark, but through her, hope remains. That someone can suffer the abuses of the Lannisters, Lord Baelish, and the Boltons, and turn out to be a major player on the side of good is one of *Game of Thrones'* greatest story achievements—with a ton of credit to Sophie Turner's acting as well. Just one question: instead of a king, shouldn't there be a Queen in the North?

20 Arya Stark

"I see a darkness in you. And in that darkness, eyes staring back at me. Brown eyes, blue eyes, green eyes...eyes you'll shut forever. We will meet again."—Melisandre to Arya Stark

In terms of the grand, overarching story of the game of thrones, Arya Stark may be the least important of the Starks. But to *Game of Thrones* as a show, Arya may be the most important Stark. Here's what I mean: Arya hasn't been engaged to any kings, or led rebellions, or uncovered the magical secret history of Westeros. She hasn't even been an essential part of a major battle, like poor, doomed Rickon. She's done two things in the grand geopolitical sense: helped the North take Harrenhal (an achievement downplayed on the show compared to the books anyway), and killed Walder Frey at the end of Season 6.

But Arya's also one of *Game of Thrones'* most popular characters, arguably its moral center, and her story has consistently been one of the most compelling for the show. Think back to the very first episode of the show, when everything was new and confusing, filled with dense history and characters with unclear motives and names. There was Arya Stark—not actually *doing* much, but being present, an energetic force with big wide eyes, arriving late to the official greeting party, wearing a Stark helmet over her gown.

Arya's story initially is a fairly traditional one: the tomboy princess, oppressed by patriarchy, pushes back on society's norms. This, combined with Maisie Williams' instant charisma in the role, provided an easy emotional gateway for viewers. Arya's difficult—but loving—relationship with her father and sister was one of the most humanizing elements of the first season.

The younger Stark daughter also provided a straightforward moral clarity to the story from the beginning. While almost every other character makes excuses for Joffrey and Cersei Lannister, on account of them being the heir and the queen, Arya understands them to be her enemies. Her attempts to directly confront them don't go well—on the Kingsroad, her fight with Joffrey causes her friend Mycah's death, as well as that of Sansa's direwolf—and Arya's wolf is driven into the wild. It's thanks to Arya that we recognize Joffrey and Cersei as irredeemable villains, even as the rest of the characters, particularly Ned, underestimate their ruthlessness.

Arya's a girl of action, not politics, which is the trait that largely removes her from the game of thrones. Her heroes, after all, are warrior women like Queen Nymeria of Dorne, after whom she names her direwolf, or Visenya Targaryen, Aegon the Conqueror's dragon-riding sister, which Arya knows destroyed Harrenhal.

So Arya provides a critical physical counterbalance to a story that increasingly takes place in meeting rooms and tense dialogues. She also has a strange set of teachers along this path. Her brother, Jon Snow, supports her martial training by giving her the sword Needle. Ned Stark, while he wants her to be a good daughter of a lord, sees his wild sister Lyanna in Arya, and hires a Braavosi water dancer named Syrio Forel to train her in a combat style worthy of her slight build.

But when things go bad at King's Landing, only the Stark daughters manage to survive from the original entourage. Sansa is pushed into a world of politicized abuse, treated as nothing more than a name and body for marriage as she learns how to seize power. Arya goes on an opposite journey, fleeing the chaos of the battle, seeing Syrio get killed, and even killing a venal stable boy on her way out—a shocking act for a pre-teen girl.

Arya ends the first season with even more trauma: she's present in the crowd for her father's shock execution. Ned's quick thinking in spotting her and telling the Night's Watch recruiter Yoren where she is spares her witnessing the actual beheading, and Yoren has a plan to get her out of the city and up the Kingsroad to her family.

As the second season begins, Yoren becomes another mentor for Arya, helping her through her recent trauma by giving her a specific piece of advice: list the people she wants to see dead. This tic becomes one of Arya's trademarks. She also befriends a few of

Game of Thrones' best buddy tragedy, Sandor Clegane and Arya Stark.
(Photo courtesy of HBO / Photofest)

the younger recruits, King Robert's bastard son Gendry, and two boys named Hot Pie and Lommy. An act of kindness toward a charming, supposedly dangerous man chained in a cage also earns Arya the respect of Jaqen H'ghar.

A Lannister attack ends in the deaths of Yoren and Lommy, adding some enemy names to Arya's list. The rest of the crew is captured and put in a pen to be tortured by Ser Gregor Clegane's men. This ends with Tywin Lannister's arrival—who also sees through Arya's disguise as a boy, and makes her his servant during his time at Harrenhal.

Arya manages to free Jaqen H'ghar, winning his loyalty and a gift: three names, three lives for him to take. The theoretically moral Stark girl has a choice to make here: whether to name names for death or not. But she doesn't treat it as much of a moral dilemma. Her family is at war, and she and her friends are in danger. First on the list: the Tickler, the torturer who threatened to kill her, Gendry, and Hot Pie. Next: Ser Amory Lorch, the Lannister loyalist who discovers her potential treachery, and is killed by Jaqen right as he threatens to tell Tywin.

Arya shows her true potential with her last "wish," though. In order to escape Harrenhal, she orders Jaqen to help her or the name she gives him is...his own. "A girl lacks honor," he says, and she shrugs. Honor has nothing on survival—something she learned that her father Ned and brother Robb failed to. Jaqen helps, and reveals himself to be a Faceless Man—and gives her a coin that can make her one too.

In the next two seasons, Arya hits her peak as a character. In Season 3, her friends seek and find some stability in the Riverlands, with Hot Pie joining an inn and Gendry the Brotherhood without Banners. But the Brotherhood sells Gendry out, and for that, Arya flees, into the arms of Sandor Clegane, the Hound, one of her supposed greatest enemies.

But Clegane instead becomes her fascinating relationship. Out of supposed cynicism, he promises to take her to her family for ransom money. But especially after seeing the aftermath of the Red Wedding, the two begin to form a bizarre bond: they're both enemies of the Lannisters, both too bitter to actually join or trust anyone else. The breaking point for Arya comes when they arrive at the Vale—only to discover that her aunt Lysa, like Arya's brother and mother before her, has died just before they arrive. Arya breaks into hysterical laughter, and the two move on.

They're confronted shortly after by Brienne of Tarth, who recognizes Arya as one of the Stark girls she's pursuing. Arya is initially tempted by the promise of a woman warrior as a new mentor, until the Hound arrives and notices that Brienne is wearing Lannister weapons. Both Arya and the Hound are far too paranoid about the Lannisters to hear Brienne out. The Hound fights, and Arya flees. She later returns to find the defeated Hound, who asks for the mercy of death. But he is still on her enemies list, so the girl without honor steals his purse and leaves him to die. At the end of the fourth season, Arya finally takes advantage of Jaqen's offer, and purchases a trip to Braavos and the Faceless Men.

The next two seasons see Arya attempting to train under the Faceless, under Jaqen, or at least someone with his face, and with a rival known only as "the Waif." Arya is physically and spiritually gifted in terms of becoming a Faceless, but she struggles mentally with losing her "self" and her face in order to become the perfect assassin. At the end of the fifth season, this means that she diverts from her mission in order to kill Ser Meryn Trant, a man on her list and fully deserving of her wrath. But he's not the man on her list from the Faceless, and for this they take her eyesight.

Arya continues to train, and, at least apparently, goes through the motions of being a good assassin despite the Waif's bullying, and is eventually given her sight back. She's ordered to kill an actress, Lady Crane, but once again goes against her orders and tells

Crane that she's a target. Arya goes on the run against the Faceless, but the Waif finds and stabs her—it should be fatal, but either the show doesn't care, or there's something special about Arya that helps her survive multiple stabs to the torso that nobody else on the show has survived.

The Waif kills Lady Crane, and corners Arya in a tiny room. But Arya, realizing she's trained for this, snuffs the room's candle and fights the Waif in the dark. While some have theorized that the wounded Arya couldn't possibly have killed the Waif, who takes the Stark girl's face, the show seems to indicate the opposite. Arya, who's trained in the dark, has the advantage over the Waif, and kills her Braavosi rival.

When Arya returns to Jaqen and the Faceless, he tries to tell her that she's passed his tests and truly "become no one"—lost her identity. Instead, Arya reasserts that she is a Stark. And she proves it by assassinating Walder Frey, the man most responsible for the deaths of her brother and mother.

But Arya's in a weird role now. She has become the bringer of death, the perfect assassin for her family. This is tinged with the Stark sense of justice, but is it enough? How much of Arya is built for revenge, and how much of her is the strongly moral girl who started the series? We'll see—and we'll see how much it matters—as *Game of Thrones* heads to its conclusion.

21 The War of the Five Kings

"The War of the Five Kings" is the name given to the civil war that kicks off in the first season of *Game of Thrones*. Ned Stark getting his head chopped off and the Lannisters throwing all their support to King Joffrey triggers a multi-way battle for Westeros, with brother literally fighting brother as one of the first major confrontations of the war.

The five kings, only a few of whom have leeches associated with them by the sorceress Melisandre, are these: the supposed legal heir **Joffrey Lannister-Baratheon**, with the Lannisters and much of the Crownlands behind him; **Stannis Baratheon**, the true legal heir with Joffrey a child of incest, though with only a few houses in the Crownlands behind him; **Renly Baratheon**, leaping his older brother Stannis in succession by virtue of the fact that people actually like him and uniting the Stormlands and Highgarden via his marriage to Margaery Tyrell. Fighting for the independence of the North and the Riverlands is **Robb Stark**, the King in the North; and **Balon Greyjoy**, attempting to seize independence for the Iron Islands by stabbing King Robb in the back. The Eyrie and Dorne remain neutral throughout.

The events of the war comprise much of the first four seasons of *Game of Thrones,* so in broad strokes we've already discussed what happens. Still, the military and geographic aspects of the civil war are a little confusing, so it's worth focusing on them specifically.

The instigating event of the War of the Five Kings is Catelyn Tully's arrest of Tyrion Lannister for the supposed attack on her son, Bran Stark. Cat and Tyrion go on a ride to the Eyrie, leading to one of *Game of Thrones'* first great buddy comedy combinations. Tyrion's father, Lord Tywin, has a rather uncomedic response, sending the Mountain to raid House Tully's lands, killing peasants and burning crops. Ned Stark, the Hand of the King, sends Ser Beric Dondarrion and a hundred men to bring Clegane to justice—a group that will eventually become the "Brotherhood Without Banners" and meet up with the Hound and Arya Stark.

This, combined with King Robert's death, leads to an escalation in hostilities. Lord Tywin invades the Riverlands with two armies, one commanded by Jaime Lannister, who besieges the seat of House Tully, Riverrun. Robb Stark raises his banners and begins to march south, while Renly Baratheon, unable to make a deal with Ned Stark, flees King's Landing and forms an alliance with House Tyrell. Ned's capture and execution lights a match on this pile of gasoline, triggering Robb's counterattack in the Riverlands—one which requires a marriage alliance with House Frey.

Robb divides his army into two as well. The smaller one, under Roose Bolton, intentionally loses to Tywin and Tyrion's army, while Robb's own ambushes Jaime Lannister and, at the Battle of Whispering Wood, captures the Kingslayer, lifts House Tully's siege, and essentially destroys the second Lannister army. For this, he's crowned King in the North, as the Starks and Tullys fight for independence, ending the first season.

In the second season, the focus of the war shifts south, to the Baratheon brothers. Renly's massive army is marching up from the Stormlands on the road to King's Landing, which is barely defended, as Tywin Lannister has to keep an eye on Robb Stark. Stannis, stubborn non-bastard that he is, decides to invade the Stormlands, his by law, and force its lords to return to him. He and Renly won't deal with one another, so using a magical shadow assassin (because why not) Melisandre kills Renly. One king down! The lords sworn to the Baratheons join Stannis, while the Tyrells seemingly go home—though they actually join the Lannisters, thanks to some deft negotiating by Littlefinger to convince Margaery to marry Joffrey.

As all this is going on, Robb Stark is invading the Lannisters' Westerlands. In the novels, he's doing this to pull Lord Tywin's army away from King's Landing so that Renly or Stannis can take the capital from his big enemies, though the show doesn't make this clear. However, Robb betrays his alliance with the Freys by marrying Talisa Maegyr. Robb himself is betrayed by Theon Greyjoy, who joins his father Balon in attacking the North, and seizes Winterfell. Robb keeps winning battles, but he's totally cut off from his support at this point.

At the end of the second season, Stannis attacks King's Landing with a huge army, and very nearly takes it, but genius strategizing by Tyrion Lannister holds the city long enough for Tywin and the Tyrells to attack and defeat Stannis. On the other hand, Arya Stark, somewhat accidentally, captures the castle of Harrenhal for the Starks—a key strategic position. Robb unwisely positions Roose Bolton there. The Boltons have already begun to take the North for themselves when Roose sends his son Ramsay to retake Winterfell from Theon.

In the third season, the Lannisters seem totally in control. Robb may win battles, but he keeps losing allies, being forced to kill Lord Karstark after he murders Lannister hostages. In order to bring his army back up to snuff, he tries to rebuild his alliance with House Frey by offering his uncle, Edmure Tully, in marriage to a Frey daughter.

In order to celebrate the marriage, Robb and his army travel to The Twins, home of the Freys, where a conspiracy of Lannisters, Freys, and Boltons has him killed (two kings down) and his army destroyed. The Boltons officially take over the North and the Freys receive the Riverlands. The third season seems to end with the Lannisters triumphant almost everywhere.

Still, there's resistance: the Brotherhood Without Banners, in the name of King Robert, keeps fighting in the Riverlands and the Crownlands. So too does Brynden Tully, the Blackfish. The Greyjoy invasion stalls out, and the Boltons, with the help of the tortured and abused Theon Greyjoy, consolidate the North. The sociopathic King Joffrey is assassinated by the Tyrells and Littlefinger (three kings dead!), and replaced by the much calmer King Tommen.

Stannis, under advisement from Davos and Melisandre, decides to shift north, where he helps the Night's Watch defeat Mance

Rayder and his army of Wildlings (a sixth king!). At the end of the fourth season, Stannis seems to be the only major counter to the Lannister-Tyrell alliance. But in the sad last act of the War of the Five Kings, Stannis leads his army south against the Boltons, only to be caught by a snowstorm. He sacrifices his daughter, Shireen, to get out of it—but that triggers the desertion of most of his forces. King Stannis is easily defeated and is killed by Brienne of Tarth. With the assassination of Balon Greyjoy soon after, the War of the Five Kings comes to its end. But in its place: several queens arise.

22 The War of the Queens

When all the kings die, it's the queens who rule. The women of *Game of Thrones* were important throughout the entire series, but as the War of the Five Kings ended, they became obviously the most important figures in Westerosi politics. But who are the queens continuing the fight?

Three of them are obvious. First is **Daenerys Targaryen**, who at the end of the sixth season, is finally ready to begin her invasion of Westeros. Then there are the two queens in King's Landing: **Cersei Lannister**, the Queen Mother, and **Margaery Tyrell**, wife of the king. They battle for influence and control over the weak, easily influenced King Tommen. Those are the obvious ones.

But there are a few more potential queens in the discussion. **Sansa Stark** did not take the title of Queen in the North, but with the world believing Bran and Rickon Stark to be dead, she would have been both the legal and practical person to do so...if she so desired. Either way, she behaved like a ruler, forming alliances and winning wars to regain her home. Likewise, **Yara Greyjoy** declared for queen, and was only thwarted by the criminal acts and lies of her uncle, Euron Greyjoy. She is still acting and negotiating as a queen, delivering a fleet to Daenerys in exchange for independence later.

A sixth queen is more complicated. **Ellaria Sand**'s title is never mentioned on *Game of Thrones*, though she is clearly ruling Dorne in the sixth season finale. However, she's largely a replacement for a character from the novels, Arianne Martell, who *is* attempting to take a crown for herself. (See Chapter 79 on "Young Griff.") She's also negotiating with a metaphorical queen: Lady **Olenna Tyrell**, the Queen of Thorns. So, the seven possible queens: Cersei, Margaery, Sansa, Dany, Yara/Asha, Ellaria/Arianne, and Olenna.

The death of Tywin was the key event that shifted the focus of power onto the women of Westeros. Without him at the center of power in King's Landing, the battle for power was a battle over who would be able to manipulate the weak King Tommen: his mother or his wife. Although Tywin's death means the proposed marriage of Cersei to Loras Tyrell never occurs, Cersei quickly sees her power slipping away toward the charismatic new queen, Margaery. In order to try to stop the Tyrells from regaining power, Cersei empowers the religious fanatics known as the "Sparrows," who imprisoned Ser Loras for his homosexuality. Margaery, defending her brother, is imprisoned soon after, apparently giving Cersei free reign over the capital.

Meanwhile, Petyr Baelish, attempting to consolidate his alliances, marries Sansa Stark off to Ramsay Bolton, despite the Boltons betraying the Starks at the Red Wedding. When Stannis attacks Winterfell, in the last act of the War of the Five Kings, Sansa seizes agency and escapes, gaining a loyal retainer in Brienne of Tarth, then enlists her brother, Jon Snow, in a campaign to retake the North for the Starks.

Far to the south, Ellaria Sand, seeking revenge for her lover Oberyn Martell's death at the hands of Lannister henchman Gregor

Clegane, launches an attack on Myrcella Lannister-Baratheon. This fails, but she and Oberyn's daughters, the Sand Snakes, manage to poison Myrcella, win their freedom, and launch an attack on House Martell, taking power in Dorne.

Far to the east, Daenerys Targaryen has carved out a seat of power for herself in Slaver's Bay. Using her dragons and a bit of treachery, she gains an army of Unsullied and takes the cities of Astapor, Yunkai, and Meereen. But she finds holding them more difficult than conquering them, so instead of pushing onto Westeros, Dany stays in Meereen, to learn how to rule. It doesn't go so well: Astapor and Yunkai's slavers retake control of those cities, while a rebellion of the "Sons of the Harpy" threatens Meereen.

At her low point, the Mother of Dragons flees the city on the back of Drogon, the largest of her "children," in order to escape the Harpy's most vicious coup. Her newest supporters from Westeros, Tyrion Lannister and Lord Varys, join with Missandei and Grey Worm to rule the city. Tyrion, ever the pragmatist, pushes for a truce from the slavers, which they use to attack the city. Daenerys, however, has, through sheer force of will, regained a Dothraki khalasar, and with her dragons, she retakes the city, crushing the slavers.

Joining the story here is the last of our queens, Yara Greyjoy. The murder of her father Balon leaves the throne of the Iron Island up for grabs in a Kingsmoot. Her brother Theon, broken in body and spirit, is unwilling to support his own claim and instead supports hers—which seems to give her the crown until their uncle, Euron, murderer of Balon, appears and sways the vote with ambitious promises to marry Daenerys and use her dragons to allow the Ironborn to conquer Westeros. Yara, recognizing that Euron would have her killed, flees with the Iron Islands' fleet—in order to forge her own alliance with Dany.

In the North, Sansa Stark joins with her brother, Jon Snow, to rally the former Stark vassals against Ramsay Bolton, who has murdered his father to take Winterfell for himself. The Starks struggle to form a decent army, but with the ragtag army of former Stannis and Robb supporters, as well as Jon's aligned Wildlings, they attack anyway. They're likely doomed until a surprise attack from the knights of the Vale, thanks to an alliance between Sansa Stark and Littlefinger—arguably the most powerful male remaining in Westeros.

Littlefinger proposes putting himself on the Iron Throne with Sansa as his queen. She demurs, but immediately after, Stark allies declare Jon Snow the new King in the North, leaving Sansa and Littlefinger looking ominously at one another.

In the south, the standoff in King's Landing reaches an explosive finale after Margaery enlists Tommen to join the High Sparrow, putting Cersei in a corner. At the Sept of Baelor, where the trials of Loras, Margaery, and Cersei are set to occur, all the great lords and ladies of the Tyrell-Lannister families are present....and Cersei skips it, and nukes them wildfire, killing the High Sparrow, Margaery Tyrell, Kevan Lannister, Grand Maester Pycelle, and all her enemies. King Tommen, seeing his wife's death and realizing his mother is responsible, takes his own life, leaving Cersei to take the crown for herself.

Olenna Tyrell, last of her family, is recruited by Varys and Ellaria Sand to join Daenerys Targaryen. Dany has also forged an alliance with Yara Greyjoy, promising her a free and independent Iron Islands in exchange for the Ironborn fleet and promises to stop raiding the Seven Kingdoms. The combined Targaryen-Tyrell-Martell-Greyjoy fleet sets sail for the Seven Kingdoms, with the War of the Queens set for a final conflict between Cersei and Daenerys for the Iron Throne. Yet Sansa, Littlefinger, and Jon Snow—now known to be the son of a Stark and a Targaryen himself—wait in the North, and the Night's King lies Beyond the Wall.

23 Glossary of *Thrones*

Game of Thrones fans use a lot of jargon to describe certain scenes in the books and show. There are often incredibly important events that they don't want to spoil new readers or viewers on but still want to refer to (like the Red Wedding, chapter 7), or they're theories about what's going to happen that are accepted enough to be argued over consistently (like R+L=J, in chapter 17). Here are some of the most commonly used terms, and what they've meant.

Secret Targ: A character having direct Targaryen blood, unbeknownst to the audience and probably the character as well. Jon Snow is the obvious model for this thanks to it always being likely that he was the son of Rhaegar and Lyanna. There are a few other characters with various theories attached, however.

Mance Rayder's lack of a satisfying background story has made him a common suggestion. We know that he was a member of the Night's Watch at one point before deserting, and that's about it. This, combined with the fact that he played music in disguise at the initial Stark feast, has led to some speculation that he might be Rhaegar Targaryen, who somehow survived the Trident and fled north. Mance's unceremonious death on the show (he's still alive in the novels) has largely rendered this speculation moot.

Three-Headed Dragon: There's a reason for the "Secret Targ" theories: Dany has three dragons, only Targaryens seem to be able to ride dragons, and she and Jon make for just two Targs. I think there are other options (see chapter 62) but this is still fertile ground for speculation.

The Purple Wedding: There are two hugely eventful weddings in the middle seasons of *Game of Thrones*: the Red Wedding, where Robb and Cat Stark are murdered, and the wedding of Joffrey and

Margaery, where the Lannister king is poisoned. The former gets a nickname that's used in the story just after it happens. The latter doesn't—but fans applied their own color. Joffrey's poisoning is thus known as "The Purple Wedding" for the color of royalty. Also Joffrey's face as he chokes to death.

The Battles of Ice and Fire: As *A Dance with Dragons* concludes, it ends on cliffhangers for two major, apparently simultaneous battles: the slavers' attempts to reconquer Meereen, and Stannis' march through the snow on Winterfell. The parallel stories have led fans to dub them the Battles of Ice and Fire, after the title of the novel series.

In the fifth season, the show passed the books in terms of the Battle of Ice, actually depicting Stannis' defeat, which is mentioned but unclear in the novels. It also separated that battle from the Battle of Fire in Slaver's Bay—but "The Battle of the Bastards" episode did have parallel fights in the ice and filled with fire, as Jon and Sansa's army attacked Winterfell a second time during Dany's defense of Meereen.

The Pink Letter/The Bastard Letter: The letter Ramsay Bolton sends to Jon Snow at the Wall following Stannis' defeat. On the show this is just a pile of threats against Jon and Sansa. In the novels, the Pink Letter has taken on a different role, because we don't actually see The Battle of Ice. Only the letter exists, declaring that Ramsay has surprisingly defeated and killed Stannis. Jon, hearing this, decides to rally the Wildlings and march south—for this, he's murdered by his brethren.

Due to the shocking claim of Bolton victory, and some inconsistencies in how the letter is portrayed, it's become the subject of several fan theories that someone else may have written it in order to get Jon and/or the Wildlings headed toward Winterfell. The clear depiction of Stannis' crushing defeat on the show, however, renders most of those theories irrelevant.

For the Watch!: Many of these terms, you may have noticed, are ways for people who've read the novels to talk about shocking events without spoiling them. The biggest twist in the fifth novel and season of *Game of Thrones* was the death of Jon Snow at the hands of mutinous Night's Watchmen. As they cry "For the Watch!" they stab him; that became the shorthand for mentioning the spoiler without spoiling it.

Tansy: By the third novel in the series, Martin's characters were so far-flung that it was hard to connect them—but he'd learned how to do it through mysteries and themes. One of these is "Tansy," introduced in *A Storm of Swords* as Hoster Tully's muttered final words, to his daughter Catelyn.

Over the course of the book, characters in the Riverlands keep encountering the term—possibly it's Jon Snow's mother, or an innkeeper has the same name. The ending revelation: it's the herb that Hoster Tully forced his daughter Lysa to drink to abort her bastard child with Littlefinger.

"Tansy" shows up in *Game of Thrones* as one of Ramsay's lovers, alongside Myranda. When he hunts and kills her in the fourth season, he repeats her name in a sing-song voice—a reference the fans might get, though one that's hard to get too excited about.

Cleganebowl: At the end of the fourth season/third book, both Clegane brothers appear dead: the Hound from battle and infection, and the Mountain from Oberyn Martell's poisoned spear. The novels showed the possibility that both were alive, but unlike the show, hasn't yet confirmed that they are. (It's a lot easier to keep a secret the size of Gregor Clegane on the page than on the screen). Meanwhile, Cersei's conflict with the High Sparrow seems to be leading to a trial by combat.

The fan theory for the idea that the two brothers would finally face off to the death in that trial by combat has taken the name "Cleganebowl." The theory may have taken some hits in the sixth season of the show, when Tommen outlawed Trial by Combat and Cersei found her freedom another way. But the brothers are still (mostly) alive, so the possibility that the Hound might get justice remains.

Bad Pussy: This one's show-only. At the end of the fifth season, Tyene Sand whispers to Bronn "You want a good girl, but you need the bad pussy." It was the least-liked line in the least-liked plotline of all of *Game of Thrones*, and so has come to represent the biggest mistakes of the series, particularly to fans who prefer the novels.

Frey Pies: In *A Dance with Dragons*, the Bolton-controlled Winterfell is a gothic nightmare, with Ramsay torturing both Theon and his bride, members of the Frey family being murdered or disappearing, and Stannis' army coming closer and closer. Lord Wyman Manderly has promised Davos that he will turn on the Boltons when Stannis attacks, and he seems to subvert morale as much as he can.

In particular, he serves meat pies to the Boltons specifically, while referencing the betrayal of "guest right" that the Freys and Boltons committed at the Red Wedding. All of the evidence suggests that Manderly had three Freys killed, cooked into the pies, and fed to their allies.

Most of the horror of Winterfell-before-the-attack was removed from the show, but a reference to "Frey Pies" did make it into *Game of Thrones*, when the disguised Arya Stark fed Lord Walder Frey his sons Lothar and Black Walder before killing him at the end of the sixth season.

24 Cersei Lannister

Cersei Lannister is the queen of short-term planning, as well as Westeros. Her motives are always evident on the surface: she acts to protect herself and her family. And yet, Cersei consistently wins. As she tells her public ally/secret rival Littlefinger, in the Season 2 premiere after he tries to weasel out of her wrath: "Power is power." Cersei is never subtle, but she goes up against people who either pride themselves on subtlety above all else, or people who can't defend against the sledgehammers she wields. And so Cersei Lannister ends up on top of King's Landing, winning her greatest dream—at the cost of almost everyone she loves and any kind of stability in Westeros. But that's Cersei's way: she had to save herself.

Cersei's career is almost entirely one of survival. Born a powerful, ambitious woman in a rigidly patriarchal society, Cersei always chafed against the limits of her power as a woman. In her early life, she was used as a political pawn: her father Lord Tywin attempted to wed her to Prince Rhaegar Targaryen and was rejected, but successfully wed her to a king when Robert Baratheon took the crown.

But Cersei had a secret: ever since she was a child, she'd been hiding an incestuous relationship with her twin Jaime. Given this, the marriage to Robert was always on shaky ground. She tells Ned Stark that she was in love with Robert initially, but his continued love for Lyanna Stark, as well his alcohol and domestic abuse, ended that in a hurry.

Cersei bears Robert an heir—a boy with coal-black hair—who dies quickly. This is a story she tells Catelyn Stark in a moment of seeming vulnerability. In the novels, Cersei aborts a child of Robert's, and given the cruelty of the queen on the show, it's easy to make the assumption that Cersei either killed or allowed her son by the hated Robert to die.

Regardless, the three children who do survive infancy are all blonde-haired, blue-eyed products of Lannister incest: Joffrey, Myrcella, and Tommen. This hair coloring eventually raises the suspicions of the king's brother, Stannis, and the Hand, Jon Arryn, who examined the history books and discovered that Baratheon children always had black hair. For this secret, Jon Arryn was killed, and Stannis fled the capital.

It's here that *Game of Thrones* begins, with Jon Arryn dead, and the Lannisters' old rivals, particularly the Starks, believing the worst of the family. Cersei, Jaime, and especially Joffrey don't make any friends with their public behavior in Winterfell, but their biggest misstep occurs in private, when a secret liaison between Jaime and Cersei is overseen by Bran Stark. Jaime pushes him out the window, and the game begins.

Game of Thrones plays a clever little trick early on. By having Jaime push Bran out the window, and Cersei console Catelyn about her dead son, the show makes it seem like she's not the villain. Indeed, its shifting portrayals of the complicated Cersei continue throughout the series, making it hard to treat her as pure stereotype. But by the end of the second episode, Cersei, in spitefully demanding the death of Sansa's innocent direpuppy Lady, firmly establishes herself as *Thrones*' lead villain.

Cersei defends herself with her particular form of vicious cunning throughout the season, as Ned Stark gains influence and knowledge. In pushing forward in his investigation Ned discovers Cersei's incestual secret. But he foolishly confronts her about it before acting, and Cersei does what she does best: she defends her status and her family. She manipulates her side piece, her cousin Lancel (she has a type...) and has him give Robert undiluted wine on his hunt, making him staggeringly drunk and leading to death at the tusks of a boar. Robert attempts to entrust Ned with his kingdom, but when Ned tries to enforce this, Cersei tears up his legal document, trampling on the rule of law for her personal gain, and with the aid of an alliance with Littlefinger, arrests Ned.

While successful overall in maintaining her life and her family's position, Cersei's success does backfire for her ambitions briefly. While she becomes the most powerful person in the realm briefly when Ned is arrested, her psychopathic son Joffrey usurps that role when he has Ned beheaded, escalating the civil war to the point of no return and making it clear that she cannot control her oldest son.

For the next few seasons, Cersei is forced to take a back seat to her son the king, her hated brother Tyrion as Acting Hand, and then her father Tywin. Each of these three become the new center of power in King's Landing, and each believe they've outplayed Cersei. Joffrey thinks his power is sufficient to bypass his mother. Tyrion refuses to let himself be beaten by Ned Stark and does the opposite of his predecessor. And Tywin asserts what he believes is his natural dominance, and doesn't let his children get in the way of that.

So for the middle seasons of *Game of Thrones*, Cersei appears somewhat sidelined. Consider what she does during the Battle of Blackwater at the climax of Season 2. Cersei, helpless to affect the battle, sits in a room full of scared women, gets wasted, tries to teach Sansa Stark whatever bitter wisdom she can, and prepares to kill herself and Prince Tommen when Stannis breaks through. It's a fairly passive role for the show's supposed biggest villain, but it's one that humanizes Cersei. She can fight the Lannister men in her life even if she can't beat them, and she's willing to die rather than lose the autonomy she's gained.

With the Lannisters having control of most of the southlands, and her respected father instead of her hated brother acting as Hand, the third season should be better for Cersei. But it's not. She still has to wrestle with Tyrion for influence, and neither

The passing of the torch from King's Landing's greatest villain to his successor.
(Photo courtesy of HBO / Photofest)

Tywin nor Joffrey see her as powerful in her own right—the latter situation exacerbated when Margaery Tyrell, Joffrey's new fiancee, demonstrates skill in manipulating the previously headstrong ruler.

Cersei takes action, trying to turn Tywin against the Tyrell-Lannister alliance. Tywin doesn't entirely believe her, but does give her the chance to find proof, which, via Littlefinger, she does: they plan to wed Sansa Stark to their heir, Loras. But once again Cersei's short-term success backfires. She stops the Stark-Tyrell marriage, and she even gets her famously lecherous brother Tyrion married to Sansa as well—but Tywin arranges a marriage between her and Loras instead, theoretically solidifying the Lannister-Tyrell alliance she's worked so hard to undermine.

But in the fourth season, the King's Landing power structures begin to collapse in ways that bring Cersei back into power. Joffrey is murdered at his wedding and Tyrion takes the blame, knocking out two of Cersei's rivals—although Joffrey's death does represent a tragedy for her and her family, it doesn't stop Cersei from taking advantage. Margaery's skill in manipulating the king is pushed into the background until she can get to Tommen, but Tommen, far less stubborn than his brother, is equally under the sway of his mother Cersei and grandfather Tywin.

More of King's Landing's powers disappear. Littlefinger has departed, Tyrion has been arrested, and the rest of the council collapses after Tyrion's trial by combat and escape from prison, which kills Lord Tywin, and sees Varys and Tyrion flee the city.

Season 5, therefore, begins with Cersei examining Tywin's murder scene, and realizing that the power vacuum seems to have left her in charge. Although there's a complication: Season 5 actually begins, both on the show and equivalently in the novels, with a flashback to Cersei's past, where she meets a hedge witch as a teenager, who tells her that Cersei will earn everything she's ever dreamed of, only to have it taken away by a younger, more beautiful queen.

Cersei interprets Maggy the Frog's prophecy to mean Margaery Tyrell, who has certainly supplanted Cersei as queen, is certainly younger, and is more beautiful by certain standards. This background information drives Cersei for the fifth and sixth seasons, and she does whatever she can to stop Margaery from taking over.

Despite Tywin's death, a new royal wedding gives Margaery the simplest, least devious form of control over the new king possible: Tommen is a teenager, and his queen is attractive and interested in sex. It's enough to make Margaery confident in mocking Cersei when she visits, which triggers Cersei's instincts for survival and ambition.

Again, Cersei focuses on her short-term gains: pushed away from conventional sources of power by Margaery and Tommen as the queen and king, she takes control of the Small Council. Kevan Lannister, her uncle and the leading lord in the Westerlands, opposes her. He leaves after she appoints her new favorite, Qyburn, as Varys' replacement, and she doesn't manage to present proof of the king actually supporting her actions.

Cersei's attempts to remove the Tyrells from power lead to her aligning with a new group in King's Landing: the Sparrows. This is a fanatic religious group, composed primarily of refugees from the wars in the Riverlands and the Crownlands. They're led by the "High Sparrow," whom Cersei invests with power in exchange for him going after the sexually decadent Tyrells. On the show, they attack Loras' homosexuality, in the novels, they attack Margaery's promiscuity. The end result in both cases: Tyrell power is curbed, and Cersei, with the help of the Sparrows, once again reigns supreme.

But once again, Cersei's short-term brilliance is undercut by the long-term effects of her plans. The puritanical Sparrows, once empowered, turn on the publicly amoral queen, accusing her of adultery, incest, and regicide. Cersei, like Loras and Margaery, is imprisoned, leaving only the Sparrows and the weak king Tommen in King's Landing.

Cersei survives, though. She finds a loophole: if she undergoes a walk of penance—naked, through the streets of King's Landing, confronting all the hate the common people have for her—she can be free, or at least live in the Red Keep on bail until her trial. The end of her demeaning march has several pieces of news: Kevan Lannister has returned, taking control of the Small Council, while Qyburn has resurrected Ser Gregor Clegane to act as Cersei's bodyguard and champion. No matter what she lacks in political power from this point, Cersei is given physical power.

In the sixth season, she uses it. Attempts by Jaime and the Tyrells to wrest control of King's Landing from the High Sparrow fail after Margaery convinces King Tommen to join them and support the Sparrows. This move also sets Cersei at odds with her one surviving child, after Myrcella is killed by Dornish poison.

Removed from every source of power she had previously, Cersei ends up accepting Littlefinger's "knowledge is power" ideology, and she uses that to cast one last roll of the dice. As her trial begins, Ser Gregor keeps her remaining child, King Tommen, from attending. Qyburn, having successfully adopted Varys' "little birds"—the orphans of King's Landing—directs them to join their cause, even killing Grand Maester Pycelle. And with their collective knowledge, Cersei sabotages the Sept of Baelor with dozens of barrels of wildfire. Setting them off kills all her remaining enemies: the High Sparrow, Margaery and the rest of the Tyrells, and Kevan Lannister. Tommen, realizing the full magnitude of his mother's crimes, commits suicide.

With nobody left in her way, Cersei is able to crown herself Queen Cersei Lannister, first of her name. Her lover and brother, Jaime, seems horrified at this result, but Cersei, despite having risen to the top at the cost of nearly her entire family, is now sitting on the Iron Throne, the true successor to Tywin and Joffrey—if not the Mad King himself.

But Queen Cersei has always succeeded by putting the short-term needs of herself first and her loved ones second, above everyone else. Why should this time be any different? Apart from the fact that a younger, more beautiful queen is directly moving on her works in order to supplant her. Perhaps Margaery was not the true rival Cersei's prophecy foretold....

25 Petyr "Littlefinger" Baelish

"Chaos isn't a pit. Chaos is a ladder."—Petyr "Littlefinger" Baelish

There aren't many self-made men in Westeros. It's a feudal system, after all, with only the vaguest manifestations of the sort of capitalism that would allow a man to work from nothing to become one of the most powerful in the realm. And yet one of *Game of Thrones'* most powerful characters, Petyr "Littlefinger" Baelish, is very nearly a self-made man, against all odds—and he wants more.

Let's take a look at where Littlefinger is, as of the end of the sixth season. He is regent of the Vale, which has been essentially untouched by civil war and is now one of the most powerful of the Seven Kingdoms. Its lords have just declared Jon Snow the King in the North, joining their forces to his—which would make Baelish the second-most powerful man in that kingdom, if he wanted to stay. But he still has bigger goals, as he tells Sansa Stark: he dreams of sitting on the Iron Throne, with her by his side. And he's the only man in the room not cheering when Jon is crowned.

Now let's see where he came from. Littlefinger came from as close to nothing as any member of the Westerosi nobility possibly could. His great-grandfather was a Braavosi sellsword who attached himself to the medium-sized Vale house, House Corbray, and was knighted. His son managed to gain a lordship and a tiny keep in the Fingers, a set of thin peninsulas that reach into the Narrow Sea, and which are generally regarded as some of the worst land in the Seven Kingdoms. The Baelish lands are on the smallest of the Fingers, no less, hence the (hated) nickname "Littlefinger."

The Baelish keep is a pathetically small tower, and their lands are a few acres surrounded with only a handful of tiny villages to support it. When the War of the Ninepenny Kings began, the next Baelish lord, Petyr's father, joined the Targaryen army and managed to befriend Lord Hoster Tully of Riverrun, father of Catelyn, Lysa, and Edmure. This friendship led to Petyr being fostered in Riverrun, surely an honor for such a minor House, alongside the Tully sisters. And it is from this point that Littlefinger launched his entire political career.

Why, exactly, Littlefinger has been such a successful politician despite being of such meager means is something of a mystery. There is nothing in his family's history to suggest high levels of ambition or intelligence, either culturally or genetically. He's just a wildcard.

There is, perhaps, a clue as to how he gained his ambition in his life at Riverrun: resentment of the powerful. Littlefinger had romantic intent for both of the Tully girls. His true affections were for Cat, who didn't reciprocate, but Lysa truly desired him, and he was happy to oblige. Still, his love for Cat continued, and when she was engaged to Brandon Stark (Ned's older brother, killed by the Mad King soon after), Baelish challenged him to a duel. Brandon didn't want to kill the boy, but Littlefinger didn't quit, and was scarred both physically and emotionally by his defeat.

From that point on, Littlefinger had a focus for his resentment: the Starks, of course, the family that embarrassed him, led the charge, and he got revenge when he betrayed Ned Stark to Cersei Lannister. He also came to hate those with more physical power, and decided to use money and intelligence to gain power—and had no love for chivalric ideals, a point of view he spends much of his early time trying to convince Sansa to join. Finally, he resents the people with bigger names than his. Like the Starks, they're not smarter or better, just older and more powerful. But when you resent and wish to supplant everyone like that, well, the Iron Throne is the only conceivable goal.

The first indicator of this skill came after his time at Riverrun. Jon Arryn, Lord of the Vale and husband to Baelish's old flame

Lysa, gave him a role in charge of customs at Gulltown, the Vale's main port. Baelish apparently increased revenues tenfold, which led Arryn, when he became Hand, to bring Baelish along.

Once in King's Landing, Littlefinger began to play the game of thrones. The odd thing about Littlefinger is that, despite starting from the lowest rung, more than any other player of the game, he's successful in making a plan, sticking to it, and having it work for him. He became Master of Coin, and managed to ingratiate himself with the Lannisters as well as Lord Arryn. He also formed a cordial rivalry with Lord Varys, the other master player.

Baelish gains a reputation as a magician with money, although when he's replaced by Tyrion Lannister, Tyrion discovers the truth: that he just always had money because he constantly borrowed it. Baelish also ran the most expensive brothel in King's Landing, which gave him both influence with, and power over, the richest and most powerful clientele in the capital.

When *Game of Thrones* starts, it's actually Littlefinger who kicks off the chaos that leads to civil war. When Jon Arryn discovers the truth about Joffrey's parentage, Littlefinger convinces Lysa to poison the Hand, then send a letter to her sister blaming the Lannisters. It's unclear what his exact goal is but it helps in three ways: his Lannister patrons remain in power, it creates chaos by setting the Starks and Lannisters against one another, and it brings his enemy Ned Stark to King's Landing.

All of these work marvelously well for Baelish—the Lannisters give him greater and greater rewards as he proves useful through the civil war, including the castle of Harrenhal and the hand of Lysa Arryn in marriage. And he takes advantage of Ned's naiveté to have him killed.

But there are some complications for Littlefinger, involving arguably his greatest flaw: his inability to control the urges foisted upon him by his, ah, little finger. His love for Cat is his greatest weakness, and his support for the Lannisters helps lead to her death (and turns him against the ruling family.) He also, rather creepily, transfers that love onto Catelyn's daughter, Sansa Stark.

While initially Baelish acts as Sansa's patron, including murdering King Joffrey and fleeing the city, then murdering Lysa Arryn in order to save Sansa's life from Lysa's jealous rage, those tables get turned. Sansa has learned from him, and Cersei, and everyone else she's had to deal with to survive King's Landing as a Stark. She lies for Littlefinger when the Lords Declarant of the Vale question him about Lysa's death, putting him in her debt, and coming out as a power in her own right.

Sansa's rise to power takes a detour in the fifth season, however, when Littlefinger controversially has her married to the abusive Ramsay Bolton. Littlefinger, too, is forced to go out of his way to make a decision as to whose side he's on. He makes an arrangement with Cersei to destroy the Stark-Bolton marriage (which he neglects to mention was his idea), but then turns and betrays Cersei to Olenna Tyrell, his former partner in assassinating Joffrey. It's a seemingly smart move: he attaches himself to every power in King's Landing—the Arryns, the Lannisters, the Starks, the Tyrells—then deserts them when it suits his needs. Cersei is imprisoned, and Littlefinger remains free to intrigue in the North—and has free reign to take his army to Winterfell.

Sansa, however, has survived Ramsay Bolton. When she joins forces with her brother Jon, she demonstrates the power she holds over Lord Baelish. Littlefinger offers her an alliance. Sansa, however, has none of it: she chastises Lord Baelish in a way that nobody else manages to, telling him that he's either evil or foolish for not knowing who Ramsay Bolton was. It is, arguably, the only plan he's made in the six seasons of *Game of Thrones* to not obviously succeed.

Yet eventually Sansa relents, needing the Knights of the Vale in order to defeat the Bolton army. Littlefinger joins the northern cause, although he immediately turns to Sansa and asks for her help in taking the Iron Throne for himself. Whether this represents a good thing for Baelish or not is unclear, but I wouldn't bet against him. Chaos is a ladder, after all, and a new Stark King in the North adds to the chaos of a civil war long thought to be over. While most of the great villains of the Seven Kingdoms are gone, Petyr Baelish remains—and he's with people who don't yet know how villainous he truly is.

Things may start to get chaotic in Winterfell, as the self-made man has a few steps left to climb on his ladder.

26 Lord Varys, the Spider

If anyone can make the claim to serving the realm effectively, it's Varys. He served the crown for decades, being arguably the only person to hold power consistently through the reign of both Aerys II and King Robert. Either the Mad King pushed them out (like Lord Tywin), or Robert kept them away (like the Tyrells and Martells). Varys, however, remained.

Ironically, this may have been a mistake, as Varys may have remained more truly loyal to the Targaryens than anyone. In the first season, Arya Stark sees the Spider and his trusted ally (and overt Targaryen supporter), Illyrio Mopatis, having a secret meeting in the basement of the Red Keep where they discuss the realm's impending collapse into chaos and the potential Targaryen restoration.

But Varys is also an expert at providing advice and help to his new rulers, regardless of his true motives. He always looks the part of the loyal councilor, even if nobody entirely trusts him. When Robert wants Daenerys dead, Varys argues for it, in such a transparently cynical fashion that it seems impossible to believe he'd actually oppose it. But he also apparently warns Jorah Mormont, who saves Dany's life.

Sometimes, though, he does seem to selflessly serve the realm. When Stannis Baratheon prepares to attack in the second season, Varys fully commits to aiding Tyrion. The two half-men have become friends, but Varys also recognizes an intelligence and commitment to justice in Tyrion that he believes could serve the realm. In the case of Blackwater, this means preventing Stannis and his rigid, violent religion of the Red God from taking control of King's Landing. Varys never makes it clear whether stopping Melisandre is his only goal, or if he also believes that Stannis might be strong enough to defeat a Targaryen invasion while the Lannisters are not. Since the plan works, we never have to find out.

The dual nature of the Spider also rears its head again in the fourth season. In the Small Council, Tywin Lannister begins to work against Dany and her increasing power in Slaver's Bay. He asks Varys if the eunuch can get a spy to Meereen, and Varys says yes. Shortly after, Ser Barristan is given proof that Jorah Mormont had been a spy for the Iron Throne against Daenerys, a plot which deprives Dany of one of her most trusted advisors, and which required Varys' help to succeed.

When Joffrey is assassinated, Varys also testifies against Tyrion at the Imp's trial. Tyrion, feeling betrayed at his supposed friend's turn against him, demands to know if the Spider remembers the compliments he'd paid Tyrion in the past, particularly about his little-known heroism at the Battle of Blackwater. Varys says he never forgets, with an expression that seems to say he had no desire to testify against his friend.

The Spider proves this in the fourth season finale, when he takes the biggest risk of his political life: working with Jaime Lannister to free Tyrion and send him to Essos. Tyrion takes a detour in the process, however, killing his ex-paramour Shae and his father Tywin. Varys, realizing what Tyrion has done, decides to join him on his journey across the Narrow Sea.

At this point, the show's Varys starts to diverge wildly from the book's Varys, with interesting effects for the idea that he truly serves the realm. On the show, Varys stays with Tyrion, convincing him to join him in seeking the true and just ruler of Westeros: Daenerys Targaryen.

Varys initially joins Tyrion on this journey, although Tyrion's kidnapping by Jorah Mormont disrupts his plans somewhat. The Spider manages to arrive after the battle at the Great Pit, but he joins Tyrion in ruling the city. Varys' work helps keep Meereen seemingly stable, and he leaves for parts unknown before the slavers make their true move, and before Dany successfully returns (meaning he still hasn't met the woman he's working for). The Spider's secret plan is a negotiated alliance between the vengeance-seeking Ellaria Sand and Olenna Tyrell, joining the power of Dorne and the Reach to Dany's army. The last shot of the season shows him finally at his queen's side, sailing to Westeros.

But that's not the way Varys' story goes in the books. Instead of going with Tyrion, he stays behind in King's Landing, living secretly in the secret passages only he knows about. Varys becomes something of a bogeyman for Cersei, with his and Tyrion's plots seen behind anything that goes wrong for the increasingly paranoid queen. And it's he who ends up killing Grand Maester Pycelle and Kevan Lannister, with the stated goal of maintaining the chaotic Cersei's power to keep the realm primed for his true ruler's invasion.

That invasion takes a very different form, however, arguably the biggest change from the show to the books, as Tyrion discovers over the course of *A Dance with Dragons*. It's both fairly complicated and potentially something that still could affect the show, so I've separated it into its own chapter, 79. But the net effect is that Varys looks like a political genius, working on a plot for decades instead of attaching himself to Dany once she's established herself as a legitimate claimant. It also embodies Varys' political philosophy that the realm is best served by a ruler dedicated to and trained for public service. It also shows a much darker side to the Spider, who on *Game of Thrones* can appear downright cuddly.

Is that enough to change who Varys is, and his role as one of the best players of the game of thrones? Perhaps—but now that he's met Dany, and now that he's made his true intent clear on the return to Westeros, we'll see even more of the Spider's truly heartfelt actions.

27 Who are *Game of Thrones'* Writers?

The bulk of *Game of Thrones* has been written by three men: the two showrunners, David Benioff and D.B. Weiss as a team, and Bryan Cogman, the show's story editor. Benioff and Weiss—often called D&D by fans—are the series' creators, showrunners, and most common writers: seven out of ten episodes per season are credited to Benioff and Weiss.

David Benioff is the more prolific of the two, with several notable projects to his name, including the novel *The 25th Hour*, which was turned into an acclaimed Spike Lee film in 2002. He was also the screenwriter for *Troy*, the 2004 epic starring Brad Pitt (and Sean Bean as Odysseus). Although as a film *Troy* received mixed reviews, its focus on human conflict instead of magical deities served as a kind of dry run for *Game of Thrones'* political "fantistorical" genre.

D.B. Weiss has a published novel, *Lucky Wander Boy*, and has worked on several notable scripts that didn't make it to the screen, like *Halo* and an original take on *Ender's Game*. But many of his projects were in conjunction with Benioff, making the two a team by the time they pitched HBO and George R.R. Martin.

Bryan Cogman has one of the more interesting jobs on the show: the "keeper of the mythos." He's the person whose job is taking Martin's massive, complicated original story and distilling it for the people working on the series. As such, he's responsible for many of the major adaptation choices. This shows in some of his episodes: in his first credit, "Cripples, Bastards, and Broken Things" the series really comes into its own, with a non-book scene involving Robert, Barristan, and Jaime discussing their first kill. In the second season, he gets the episode that really introduces Margaery Tyrell, "What is Dead May Never Die," which directly examines Margaery's, Loras', and Renly's sexuality in ways that the books only hinted at.

But as the adaptation has diverged from the novels, Cogman has come in for some controversy. Most notably, he was the writer of Season 5's "Unbowed, Unbent, Unbroken," which changed the story that Sansa Stark marries—and is sexually abused by—Ramsay Bolton. While many of the adaptation choices made by Cogman and the showrunners have borne fruit, he's also become a scapegoat for the ones that didn't.

Four of the show's most important episodes were written by the man who knows even more about the story than those three: **George R.R. Martin.** This can seem odd to many people in fandom who see the books and the show as antagonistic toward one another, but Martin has always been publicly supportive. His episodes are some of the show's best, too: "The Pointy End" and "The Bear and the Maiden Fair" are essential setup for the endgames of Seasons 1 and 3, respectively. His other two comprise two of the biggest events in Westeros: Stannis' attack on King's Landing in "Blackwater" and the so-called "Purple Wedding" between Joffrey and Margaery in "The Lion and the Rose."

Before Season 5, however, Martin announced that he wouldn't be writing an episode that season due to his focus on finishing *The Winds of Winter*, which, still not being finished, means that Martin's hasn't been credited since early Season 4. (Some fans have speculated that this is evidence that Martin is annoyed at the changes to the story on the show, but there's no real evidence for a rift outside this.)

Fans of genre television sometimes do a double take on seeing **Jane Espenson**'s name in the listings for the teleplay of Season 1's "The Golden Crown." Espenson made her name on *Buffy the Vampire Slayer*, as one of the cult hit's most consistent writers, especially comedically. From there she moved on to *Battlestar Galactica* and *Caprica*, and currently works on ABC's *Once Upon A Time*—all conventional episodic television, unlike *Game of Thrones*' diffused form of hyperserialization. Espenson's credit is a reminder that while *Game of Thrones* may be a unique television series, it's still a television series.

The only other woman with a writing credit on the show is **Vanessa Taylor**, who wrote three episodes in Seasons 2 and 3. Taylor is another longtime television writing veteran, although with a quieter rep than Espenson. She left the show to pursue feature film writing, including 2014's *Divergent*.

After Taylor's last episode at the start of Season 3, almost every episode of the show has been written by Benioff and Weiss, Cogman, or Martin. The only exceptions are two episodes by **Dave Hill**, who had been a production assistant on the show until he made a story suggestion: that Olly, the orphan in Season 4, should stay on with the Night's Watch. This made so much sense to Benioff and Weiss that Hill was invited to join the writer's room. No news has yet come out of any new writers for the seventh or eighth seasons.

28 Who are *Game of Thrones'* Directors?

Thrones' grand cinematic scope relies on some excellent directors, many of whom have worked on several HBO series before. But oddly, despite using several of the best directors on television, *Game of Thrones* hasn't ever really found any consistency with its directorial choices. No director has been credited with more than six episodes total, nor has any director worked on episodes in more than three seasons of the show. (Showrunners Benioff and Weiss have directed a handful of episodes.)

Despite that, several of the directors have left strong marks at least on their episodes. Here are some of the biggest and more important names.

The pilot and second episode of the series were directed by **Tim Van Patten**, an HBO veteran famous for working on several *Sopranos* episodes, including "Long Term Parking," widely cited as the series' best episode. As the pilot's director, Van Patten was essential in setting the tone for the entire series, but after those two episodes, he left to serve as an executive producer and director for HBO's other ambitious early-2010s drama, *Boardwalk Empire*.

Perhaps the most important director of the first two seasons was **Alan Taylor**, another HBO vet and an Emmy winner for *The Sopranos*. Taylor directed the final two episodes of the first season, including the famously shocking "Baelor" and four episodes at the start and end of Season 2. Most all of these episodes have centered on the pomp and pageantry of King's Landing, like Ned's execution, or Margaery's introduction to Joffrey. Taylor, after a four-season hiatus from *Thrones*, has been invited back for the seventh season.

The late-Season 2 episode that Taylor didn't direct was directed by **Neil Marshall**, who, with just two episodes, still became possibly the most important director in all of *Game of Thrones*. That's because Marshall's two episodes are unique in *Game of Thrones*: they're "Blackwater" and "The Watchers on the Wall." These are the two episodes that center exclusively on specific battles, the former in King's Landing, and the latter, obviously, at the Wall. Marshall's an accomplished film director, winning acclaim for one of the best horror films in recent years, 2005's *The Descent*. "Blackwater" is a sensational combination of quiet, tense character-building and escalating action. "Watchers" is a technical marvel, a high-quality war movie compressed into a single television hour.

David Nutter started directing the *Game of Thrones* series in its second season and became one of the show's most prominent directors. Nutter is famous for directing pilots, with almost all of his pilots going to series (most famously, *The X-Files*). With *Thrones*, Nutter got the nod to direct the last two episodes of both the third and fifth seasons. As these are arguably the most depressing of the seasonal endings, it's fairly clear what *Thrones* thinks Nutter is good at. And he proved worthy of that trust with "The Rains of Castamere"—arguably the show's single most important hour, the Red Wedding.

In the third season, *Game of Thrones* added two famous directors who'd won acclaim outside of HBO shows. **Michelle MacLaren** rose to prominence as one of *Breaking Bad's* most dependably excellent directors, including the episode "One Minute," the episode that kickstarted the AMC show's rocket up to prominence as one of the all-time greats. MacLaren's prominence became such that she was even attached to DC's *Wonder Woman* film, before departing. As with *Breaking Bad*, MacLaren's *Thrones* episodes hinge on her ability to disorient viewers—she highlights power imbalances with different camera heights and placements. While her mid-third season episodes were excellent, she oddly got the short end of the stick with her fourth season episodes (the fourth and fifth), arguably the weakest of that season, and she hasn't returned to the show.

Alex Graves followed a similar trajectory, directing some of the most acclaimed episodes of the third season, as well as more controversial episodes in the fourth. Graves was famous primarily for his work on *The West Wing*, one of the most acclaimed shows of the early 2000s, for which he received a few Emmy nominations. His work in the middle *Game of Thrones* seasons was likewise acclaimed, directing a few all-time classics like "The Lion and the Rose," "The Mountain and the Viper," and my sneaky pick for the series' best episode, Season 3's "Kissed by Fire" (most famous for the Brienne/Jaime scene in Harrenhal's baths).

Graves' strength is his ability to build tension via formality and informality. At the Purple Wedding, for example, the supposedly happy celebration combined with Joffrey's bullying build to the surprise poisoning. But this skill also led to one of the show's—and Graves'—biggest controversies. In the episode immediately after Joffrey's death, Jaime appears to rape Cersei—a scene that wasn't portrayed as assault in the novels. While most of the world saw the scene as nonconsensual—and the showrunners gave interviews agreeing—Graves said he shot it as representative of Jaime and Cersei's kinky sexualities, fueling the fires of controversy. He hasn't returned since Season 4.

The hottest *Game of Thrones* director for the fifth and sixth seasons was **Miguel Sapochnik**, who quickly rose to Emmy-winning star status after directing two of the show's most popular and acclaimed episodes, "Hardhome" and "The Battle of the Bastards." Sapochnik had previously directed a generally disliked film, *Repo Men*, and was a television journeyman. But his work on "Hardhome"—turning in a superb episode almost immediately after *Thrones'* critical nadir with the Sansa-Ramsay marriage—set his reputation and promoted him to the role of director of Season 6's most essential episodes.

Sapochnik isn't quite the battle director that Marshall is— neither "Hardhome" nor "Bastards" present themselves as coherent tactically as "Blackwater" or "Watchers." That said, Sapochnik has a clear gift for presenting indelible moments. Think of Dany's "I'm going to break the wheel" in "Hardhome," Davos discovering Shireen's pyre, or Jon breaking free of the pile of bodies in "The Battle of the Bastards." His aesthetic and *Game of Thrones'* have perfectly combined in the last few seasons. Which makes it odd that he isn't scheduled for the seventh season, although he has said he's available for the eighth and final season.

With all these talented directors, it seems a little odd that *Thrones* hasn't picked a reliable, go-to director for crucial episodes. As it heads into its last batch of episodes, perhaps we'll see someone get the nod as *Game of Thrones'* star director. Or perhaps we won't, and the show will remain a showcase for a wide diversity of television directorial power.

29 The Continent of Westeros

Westeros is, roughly, a north-south oriented rectangle, with the water on both sides squeezing a "Neck" that divides the continent into northern and southern halves. To the west is the Sunset Sea, a massive ocean that has never been crossed. To the southeast is the Narrow Sea, which separates Westeros from *Game of Thrones'* other major continent, Essos. The Free Cities of Essos sit facing the southeastern part of Westeros. The ocean to the northeast of the continent is called the Shivering Sea.

Despite being called the "Seven Kingdoms," there are ten major regions of Westeros. The furthest north lies Beyond the Wall, an untamed arctic wilderness filled with Wildlings, as well as White Walkers, giants, and the Children of the Forest. It is the only region of Westeros free of the Iron Throne's control.

The Wall is the northern border of the Seven Kingdoms. Beneath it lies the North, home of Houses Stark of Winterfell, Bolton of the Dreadfort, Mormont, and Reed. The North is a massive region, nearly the size of the entire southern half of Westeros, although harsh and sparsely populated compared to the other kingdoms.

Between the North and the southlands, the oceans squeeze the continent. From the east, connected to the Shivering Sea, is the bay called The Bite, which divides the North from the Vale. From the West and the Sunset Sea is Ironman's Bay, which divides the North from the Westerlands.

Ironman's Bay is, naturally, the location of the Iron Islands, home of House Greyjoy of Pyke and the Ironborn (whole lot of iron going on here). From here, the reavers of the Iron Islands can easy attack the coastlines of the North, Westerlands, and Riverlands.

Between the Bite and Ironman's Bay is the Neck, the thinner land bridge between the two halves of the continent. House Frey's castle, the Twins, sits at the major rivers of the Neck, which is why Robb Stark had to negotiate his army's way through in Season 1. The northern part of the Neck is guarded by Moat Cailin, the keep Theon helped Ramsay Snow capture in Season 4.

The Neck is mostly considered part of the Riverlands, the north-central region of the southern part of the continent. Home to House Tully of Riverrun, the Riverlands have, both historically and during *Game of Thrones,* been the battleground for the kings of Westeros. It's also where Arya's and Brienne's adventures in the middle seasons took place.

To the east of the Riverlands lies the Vale, home of House Arryn, House Baelish, and the hill tribes Tyrion befriended in the first season. The Vale is a famously mountainous region, and its capital, the Eyrie, uses its imposing elevation for both prisons and executions.

On the western side of the Riverlands are the cleverly named Westerlands, home to House Lannister, from their seat in Casterly Rock. The Westerlands have barely been shown on the show (just Robb's battles in Season 2), but are known for their gold mines—although Tywin has revealed that they've run out.

To the south of the Westerlands lies the Reach, home of House Tyrell and House Tarly. The Reach may be the most powerful region in Westeros, with a strong economy and large population—whoever House Tyrell of Highgarden allies with suddenly becomes the favorite in the civil war. It's also the home of Oldtown, Westeros' largest city, and the location of the Citadel, where maesters are trained—the Reach made its first appearance in *Game of Thrones* when Sam was sent to the Citadel in Season 6.

The Stormlands, home of House Baratheon of Storm's End, sits to the east of the Reach. We haven't seen much of the Stormlands—only the conflict between Renly and Stannis in early Season 2—but House Baratheon is obviously one of the most important players in *Game of Thrones*, and the Stormlands one of the most powerful regions.

A small but essential region sits on the eastern coast of Westeros: the Crownlands, location of the capital King's Landing. The Stormlands border this region to the south, the Reach to the southwest, the Riverlands to the northwest, the Vale to the North, and the Narrow Sea to the east. The Narrow Sea also spills into Blackwater Bay leading to the capital, with the island of Dragonstone straddling both bodies of water.

The last of the Seven Kingdoms is Dorne, which sits at the far southeastern part of the continent. The desert region is the home of House Martell, with a capital in Sunspear. The Water Gardens of Sunspear have been the home of most of the action to take place in Dorne.

A final essential part of Westeros is the Kingsroad, which traverses most of the continent and is also where much of the series is set. It starts at the Wall in the North, passes through Winterfell, goes through the Neck via Moat Cailin, connects with other major roads at the Inn at the Crossroads, passes near Harrenhal, connects to King's Landing, ending at Storm's End. Chances are decent that if *Game of Thrones* has had a scene on a major road in these regions, that's been the Kingsroad.

30 The North

"Welcome home, Lady Stark. The North remembers."—Sansa Stark's maid

Game of Thrones starts in the North, and for all we know it'll end in the North. The region has varied in significance since then quite a bit, however, but from the fifth season on, it's been the focal point of the series.

The first we see of the North is a windswept knoll where Ned Stark and his retainers execute a deserter of the Night's Watch. Although it's green, it seems like a harsh land, with all the men wearing heavy furs, violently maintaining their honor. This remains true throughout the series, especially when, as per House Stark's words, winter comes.

The North is the largest of the Seven Kingdoms, a northern half of the continent roughly as big as the southern half. It extends from the Wall bordering the lands of the Free Folk, south to the Neck, where the Riverlands begin. In the southeast, a gulf known as the Bite exists between the North and the Vale, while to the southwest are the Iron Islands, which are nominally under the aegis of the Starks and the North, but have declared independence (and thus get their own chapter).

There aren't any major cities in the North, although White Harbor, on The Bite, is the largest. Instead, the relatively small population tends to live near the region's castles. Winterfell, home of House Stark and a consistent presence in the series, is the largest. To the south, on the border of the Neck, is Moat Cailin, the strategically important gateway to the region—it's shown up in a few episodes, when Theon Greyjoy retakes it for Ramsay Bolton in Season 4. The Dreadfort, further east, is the home of House Bolton, and was where Theon was taken and tortured in Season 3 (although we weren't told what it was until the end of that season).

Running right through the middle of the region is the Kingsroad, which goes from Castle Black in the far north, to Winterfell, through Moat Cailin and the Neck, all the way to King's Landing. There are also two major islands in the far northeast and northwest: Skagos, which rumor has it is home to cannibals; and Bear Island, home of the small-in-size, huge-in-prowess House Mormont.

The North is considered one of the wildest and harshest regions in Westeros, and its denizens are honest, direct, and strong. In pragmatic terms, this means that the North is neither the richest nor the most populous, but its armies tend to be the best, as Robb Stark proved in never losing a battle.

Houses Stark and Bolton are the two most important in the North, but several others have played minor or major roles on the series. House Mormont may be the most geographically diverse on the series, thanks to Jeor Mormont serving as Lord Commander of the Night's Watch and dying Beyond-the-Wall, his son Jorah traveling with Daenerys Targaryen all around Essos, and his grand-daughter Lyanna joining Jon Snow's army in recapturing Winterfell (and becoming the breakout new star of Season 6).

There's also House Karstark, whose Lord Rickard joined Robb's army in Season 2 and 3, and was executed for betrayal in the act that broke Robb's armies. The surviving Karstarks, still unhappy with House Stark, join with House Bolton in the sixth season. Likewise, House Umber initially joins Robb's armies enthusiastically, and are so famously loyal that Osha takes Rickon Stark to hide in their keep. But when their lord the Greatjon dies, his son, the Smalljon, joins the Boltons in order to fight Jon's army of Wildings.

Several other northern houses show up at least briefly: House Glover and House Manderly both reject Jon and Sansa's pleas in Season 6, before joining him in the finale. There's also House Forrester, a relatively minor House that's barely mentioned in either the books or the show, but are used successfully in the Telltale *Game of Thrones* game (see Chapter 96).

Historically the land was settled by the First Men, and resisted the Andal invasion soon after. This means that the citizens are both ethnically and religiously separate from the rest of the Seven Kingdoms—although it's hard to tell an Andal from a First Man in *Game of Thrones*, the Northerners worship the Old Gods, while the southerners worship the Seven.

After the legendary Long Night, when the White Walkers invaded and were defeated, House Stark rose to prominence in the North, becoming the Kings in the North, or Kings of Winter. Their bitter rivals were House Bolton, famed for flaying their enemies, making the whole thing seem like a good versus evil affair. Roughly a thousand years before the events of *Game of Thrones*, the Boltons finally swore allegiance to the Starks, although apparently they were just biding their time.

When the Targaryens invaded, the Starks prepared an army to march against them, but, seeing what happened to the southern kings at the Field of Fire, Torrhen Stark surrendered, becoming the King who Knelt. The North was largely removed from the civil wars of the Targaryen era, with the only major battle in those 300 years on Northern soil a Wildling invasion, decades before the events of the show.

On the show, we saw the North almost exclusively at and around Winterfell in the first two seasons. In Season 1, the North is relatively dormant until Robb raises the banners and marches his men south. But once the War of the Five Kings is engaged, Balon Greyjoy raids the eastern coasts, seizing the critical castles of Moat Cailin and Deepwood Motte—and, when Theon Greyjoy strikes out on his own, Winterfell itself. A Bolton force under Ramsay Snow retakes the castle, but they burn it to the ground, destroying the Stark headquarters in preparation for their eventual total betrayal.

The third and fourth seasons are the quietest for the region. In Season 3, the Greyjoys remain in control of the coasts, and the Starks are totally detached from their home. Bran's party travels to Castle Black through generic scenery, while Theon is tortured in the Dreadfort. Following the Red Wedding, the Boltons reveal their true loyalties. Yara Greyjoy raids the Dreadfort and is turned back. Ramsay Snow moves to consolidate power in the North, using Theon to drive the Ironborn out of Moat Cailin and allow Bolton armies to return to their homeland—but in a new home, when they take over Winterfell.

In the fifth season, the North and Winterfell become the focus of the story. The Boltons attempt to hold on to their power, with Ramsay wedding Sansa Stark at Winterfell. Meanwhile, Stannis Baratheon marches south, attempting to take the region and add its forces to his to aid his claim on the Iron Throne. The onset of winter hits his armies, though, and after selling his soul by murdering his daughter for the magic to break free, Stannis' troops desert him and he loses pathetically.

But the war for the North has only just started. Sansa Stark has fled Winterfell, and recruits her brother Jon Snow to help re-conquer the North, starting with the child Lady Lyanna Mormont and her remembered note to Stannis, "Bear Island knows no king but the King in the North, whose name is Stark." They meet with as many lords of the North as they can, and acquire a small army. It's insufficient to defeat Ramsay Bolton—but it holds him off until Sansa's allies from the Vale show up and win the day. Jon Snow is proclaimed King in the North...but winter has come.

Almost all the scenes in the North are filmed in Northern Ireland near Belfast. Many of them are on private property, so they're hard to visit, but there are enough accessible to the public that there are several *Game of Thrones* tours out of Belfast.

31 House Stark and Winterfell

Game of Thrones is centered in the North. The first scene we see with regular characters is of Ned Stark, his sons, and his retainers watching him execute a man. The implication there, and through most of the series, is this: the North is a harsh but honorable realm, and House Stark are harsh but honorable people.

The Starks are an ancient House, descending from the First Men, and largely holding off the Andal invasion. As such, they are the only Great House to still worship the Old Gods instead of the Seven, something largely accepted by the rest of the realm, and they hold the cultural cachet of being more First Men than Andal. This makes them seem more barbaric to the rest of Westeros, but they, and the Northmen, are also arguably Westeros' greatest warriors.

House Stark claims descent from the legendary Bran the Builder, a legendary figure from the Age of Heroes, and supposed descendant of Garth Greenhand, father of the Gardeners of the Reach. Bran the Builder is generally credited with having built the Wall to prevent another attack from the White Walkers after the Long Night, as well as the Stark home of Winterfell. Legend also has it that the ur-architect also built Storm's End, home of the Baratheons, and Hightower in Oldtown.

Regardless of the truth of their founding legends, House Stark did become one of the dominant houses of the North. Their great rivals were House Bolton, with whom they battled for the North for millennia before finally becoming clear winners a thousand years before *Game of Thrones*—although obviously some in House Bolton still harbored resentment.

The Starks became the Kings in the North, or the Kings of Winter. Most of their energy in the pre-Targaryen era was spent subduing the local lords, like the Reeds of the Neck or the Manderlys of White Harbor.

Their greatest war was against the Arryns of the Vale over the Three Sisters, a set of islands in the Bite that divides the North from the southlands on the eastern side of the Neck. While initially a bloody, brutal war, eventually the Northerners lost interest, leaving the islands to House Arryn.

House Stark, thanks to its location, also allied regularly with the Night's Watch. Several Lords Commander of the Night's Watch were Starks, and on the rare occasions when a King-Beyond-the-Wall managed to invade, it was usually the combined forces of the Starks and the Watch that turned the Wildlings back.

The Starks' distance from the rest of the Seven Kingdoms has usually been a major issue with their ability to engage in the politics of the realm. During Aegon's Conquest, the Starks did raise their armies, with the potential to fight against the Targaryens. But they arrived after the Field of Fire, and seeing that if even the combined

Sean Bean, on-screen fantasy's most consistent purveyor of tragic deaths.
(Photo courtesy of Handout/MCT/Newscom)

Lannister-Gardener host couldn't defeat Aegon, King Torrhen Stark surrendered.

Likewise, House Stark did not have a major role to play in the Dance of the Dragons until the very end. Once the war was largely won, Cregane Stark invaded the southlands and, in the "Hour of the Wolf," took control of the Iron Throne long enough to ruthlessly "win the peace." Cregane left almost immediately after, but the remnants of his armies sowed disorder through the south for years after the supposed end of the war.

Finally, the Starks had a huge political influence over Robert's Rebellion, though a slow military one. It was their daughter, Lyanna, who was kidnapped by Rhaegar Targaryen, and their lord and heir, Rickon and Brandon, who attempted to obtain justice from the Mad King, only to be executed. When the war started, Ned immediately joined with his friend Robert, but had to raise his armies. He made the dangerous crossing of the Bite, gathered his armies, and eventually saved Robert at the Battle of the Bells—and took King's Landing for him after the war was won.

House Stark is based out of Winterfell, a powerful citadel in the heart of the North, supposedly built by Bran the Builder. Winterfell is built upon a region of hot springs, which run the walls of the castle throughout, providing heat and warm baths to its inhabitants.

Winterfell is one of the key locations in *Game of Thrones*, appearing in every single credit sequence regardless of whether it appears in the episode. It's also so important in the eyes of northern lords that when House Bolton is given the North following the Red Wedding, they move to Winterfell to solidify their legitimacy.

Most of the North and Winterfell's scenes are filmed in Northern Ireland, in and around Belfast. They tend to be on private lands, however, so it may be difficult to visit "Winterfell" itself.

32 King's Landing and the Crownlands

Beyond just being the capital and second-largest city of the Seven Kingdoms, King's Landing is crucial to *Game of Thrones* as the home of the show's political story. A high fantasy like *Thrones* usually starts with the story of young people going on adventures and finding themselves. The show certainly has that with Jon and Dany, arguably its two most important characters, as well as Arya, Robb, Theon, and, later, Sansa and Tyrion. But the plot's increasing focus on the political machinations of its adult characters are what set it apart from most other fantasy stories, and that's centered on King's Landing, where Cersei and Littlefinger and Tywin and Margaery and Varys have played their games.

King's Landing is a relatively new city in the Seven Kingdoms. It was founded by Aegon Targaryen after he landed his armies (and his dragons) there in the first step of Aegon's Conquest and, due to being the new seat of power for the Seven Kingdoms, quickly grew to become the second-largest city in Westeros (Oldtown, in the Reach, is the largest).

Although the city itself is most important, King's Landing sits in a region of Westeros known as the Crownlands. It's not one of the Seven Kingdoms, which is kind of a misnomer—the Crownlands, along with the Iron Islands and Beyond-the-Wall, are one of the ten most important regions of Westeros. The Crownlands sit in the center-east part of the southern half of the continent, with the Vale to the north, the Stormlands to the south, and the Reach to the southwest.

The Crownlands' main border, however, is with the Riverlands, the center of the continent and focus of the War of the Five Kings. There's no major geographical barrier between the two regions, which is what made Robb's victories so threatening to the capital. Without Tywin's armies in Harrenhal, Robb could easily have struck the capital—like King Robert did fifteen years before when he took King's Landing after winning the Battle of the Trident not far from the border. It also meant that refugees fleeing the war tended to turn to King's Landing, leading to both the riots in Season 2 and the rise of the Sparrows in Season 5.

The mainland part of the Crownlands hasn't been shown on *Game of Thrones* often, except for bits and pieces of the Kingsroad, which heads north from King's Landing into the Riverlands, and south into the Stormlands. On the water is a different story: King's Landing lies at the end of the huge Blackwater Bay, which became famous on the show in the episode "Blackwater," when Stannis attacks King's Landing and Lannister forces barely push him back.

Stannis attacked from the other major feature of the Crownlands, the island of Dragonstone, which sits on the eastern edge of Blackwater Bay, with the Narrow Sea on the other side. Dragonstone was the former home of the Targaryens, where they landed after fleeing the impending Doom of Valyria, bringing their dragons to Westeros. There they stayed for over a century before launching Aegon's Conquest, and turned the island into the home of the dragons, covering it in statues.

After the Conquest, Dragonstone became the traditional seat of the Targaryen heir. This didn't always have advantages. First, they had to live on Dragonstone, and second, if there was a disputed succession, the heir may not have been present. That was the case with the civil war called the Dance of the Dragons, when Rhaenyra Targaryen was on Dragonstone when her father died, allowing her younger brother Aegon II's allies in the capital to crown him. Much like the civil war between Stannis and his supposed nephew Joffrey on the show, this set up a civil war of Dragonstone versus King's Landing. More recently, Dragonstone was where the Mad King sent his family during that civil war, and where Daenerys "Stormborn" acquired her very first nickname before the Targaryens fled across the Narrow Sea.

There are several minor houses in the Crownlands, although the television show has ignored the bulk of them thus far. These include Houses Rosby, Kettleblack, Velaryon, Blount, Bywater, Stokeworth, and Massey. Most of the mainland houses remained loyal to the Lannisters, while those on the islands in Blackwater Bay tended to remain loyal to Stannis. The bastard name in the Crownlands is "Waters," hence Robert's son Gendry's legal name is Gendry Waters.

As the Targaryen capital, and the city that was their home for almost all of its existence, King's Landing itself is dominated by Targaryen monuments. The city itself is framed between two of them in particular: the Red Keep, started by Aegon Targaryen and finished by his son King Maegor the Cruel; and the Sept of Baelor, named after the mid-period Targaryen king, Baelor the Blessed. The importance of the two was shown in the climax of Cersei's story in Season 5, when she is forced to walk naked in front of the jeering crowds from the Sept to the Keep.

Most of *Game of Thrones*' King's Landing scenes have taken place in or around the Red Keep, for the simple reason that that's where the king and his court reside. The Sept of Baelor has, however, housed two of the most memorable scenes of the show: the execution of Ned Stark in Season 1, and Cersei's destruction of the entire Sept with wildfire in Season 6.

There are a few other consistently used, if relatively minor, locations in King's Landing. There are the docks, of course, a key part of any port city. Littlefinger's brothel has shown up regularly, in part to deliver consistent sexuality, and also to stand in for the upscale seediness of the city. And the neighborhood of "Flea Bottom" seems to serve as a stand-in for every slum in Westeros. The show has explicitly visited it a few times, but it also serves as the origin of some of its non-aristocratic characters, like Davos Seaworth, Gendry Waters, and Karl Tanner.

If you want to travel to the locations used for King's Landing, it's arguably the most straightforward location of any in the show: every season after the first has filmed the goings-on of the capital in Dubrovnik, Croatia. Many of the sites are open to the public when filming isn't going on, which has allowed a cottage industry of *Game of Thrones* tours to grow in the city. (The first season of *Game of Thrones* filmed its King's Landing scenes in Malta, which is noticeable when you're looking for it: Dubrovnik has much crisper whites and greys, while the Maltese locations are warmer oranges and browns.)

King's Landing has been by far the most important location in *Game of Thrones* almost from the beginning of the series. The pilot includes a hushed conversation between Jaime and Cersei by Jon Arryn's body, but it's the arrival of Ned Stark in the capital in the third episode that kicks the first season into gear. From then on, there's a King's Landing scene in virtually every episode, with the exceptions being the climactic ninth event episodes of seasons three through six (and, oddly, the mid-fifth season episode "Kill the Boy"). Not only can no major location match that, but most everywhere else disappears almost entirely for full seasons: the Wall in Season 2, Winterfell in Seasons 3–4, and the Riverlands in Season 5.

The story of King's Landing is centered on the Lannisters, who've had control of the Iron Throne for essentially the entire run of the series. Specifically Cersei Lannister, who, apart from the journey to Winterfell at the very start of the series, hasn't left the city. Tywin, Tyrion, Joffrey, Tommen, and Jaime have all come and gone, as have Littlefinger, Varys, Margaery, Renly, and Sansa—but Cersei is always present. And now she's running the joint!

How did we get there? King's Landing started under the ostensible control of King Robert Baratheon, but his Hand, Jon Arryn, and brother Stannis largely ruled in his stead. When Jon died due to poison at the start of the series, Stannis fled the capital, leaving a power vacuum. The new Hand, Ned Stark, attempts to fill it, but his push to give Robert a spine helps lead the Lannisters to have Robert killed. As Robert lays dying, Ned is given several choices. Robert's youngest brother, Renly, offers to help him seize the city if Ned supports Renly as king over his elder brother Stannis, which Ned declines. But Ned also makes the unfortunate decision to trust the Master of Coin, Petyr Baelish, and his plan of bribing King's Landing's police—the Gold Cloaks—turns to disaster, as Baelish reveals his true alliance with the Lannisters. The newly crowned King Joffrey executes Ned, establishing total Lannister control over the capital.

Joffrey names his grandfather Tywin his new Hand, but as Tywin is directing the war against the Starks, he instead sends his son Tyrion to rule as Acting Hand for the second season. Tyrion is determined to not make the same mistakes Ned did. But before Tyrion can take control, King Joffrey attempts petty revenge against his (legal) father, King Robert, by ordering the Gold Cloaks to kill all of Robert's known bastards—even infants. Having the police kill babies, it turns out, is a bad way to get the people on your good side, and Tyrion is forced to clean up the mess.

Tyrion aligns with Lord Varys instead of Littlefinger, and also immediately has Janos Slynt, leader of the Gold Cloaks, sent to the Wall. It's not enough—the pressure of the war on the city, plus Joffrey's missteps, trigger a riot that threatens the entire royal family. They survive, but King's Landing as a city is treated as dangerous ground by the Lannisters from this point on. Tyrion leads the city's defenses against the armies of Stannis Baratheon at the end of the second season, holding them off long enough to allow the battle to be won, but his father Tywin and his new allies, the Tyrells, take all the credit for the victory.

Lord Tywin and the Tyrells become the new dominant forces in King's Landing in the third and fourth seasons, pushing Tyrion to the side and jockeying for influence over the king. Margaery's ability to gain the love of the common folk of King's Landing through charitable works impresses King Joffrey—which scares Cersei. She escalates the rivalry by revealing to Tywin that they plan to wed Sansa Stark to Loras Tyrell, thus aligning two powerful houses. Tywin's response is to have Sansa wed Tyrion (which happens) and Loras wed Cersei (which really, really doesn't). After the Red Wedding ends the third season, the Lannister forces seem to have consolidated the Seven Kingdoms under their rule, making King's Landing safe—although Stannis still lurks at Dragonstone (he soon departs for the North).

In the fourth season, the focus of King's Landing turns even more to the expensive and extravagant royal wedding, where the differences between Margaery and Cersei are made clear by the former wanting the leftover food given to the poor, and the latter trying to stop that. The wedding ends in disaster when Joffrey is poisoned, and the entire focus of the King's Landing story turns to the question of who did it—with Littlefinger and Olenna Tyrell revealing that it was them, even as Tyrion takes the fall for it.

Tyrion is found guilty after his champion, Oberyn Martell, loses a trial by combat, but his brother Jaime and Lord Varys set him free. He exacts revenge against his father Tywin, murdering him and fleeing the city alongside Varys, leaving a power vacuum in the capital as the fifth season begins.

The new king, Tommen, is weak and easily manipulable. Another royal wedding—less ostentatious, and also less murdery—gives the new Queen, Margaery, more power than the now–Queen Mother Cersei. Seeking allies, Cersei turns to a rising power in the city: a religious movement called the Sparrows. In the novels, the rise of the Sparrows is given more detail: refugees from the war have been streaming into King's Landing, and flocking to a militant preacher called the High Sparrow. Their numbers intimidate the voters for the next High Septon, and the High Sparrow is chosen, who then negotiates with Cersei. On the show it's simpler: Cersei gives him the power to become High Septon, and then allows him to reinstate a private army for the Faith of the Seven, called the Faith Militant.

The newly empowered fundamentalists are turned against sexual deviance in King's Landing, arresting the gay Ser Loras Tyrell and smashing Littlefinger's brothel. Cersei's plan initially seems to work when Loras' arrest causes Margaery to perjure herself and join him in the dungeons. But it backfires spectacularly when Cersei finds herself arrested for her crimes of incest, adultery, and regicide. She's beaten and starved, but is given the opportunity to do a Walk of Penance, nude through the near-riotous streets of King's Landing, as her bail. She agrees, and returns to the Red Keep only to discover that the Small Council has been taken over by her familial rival, Ser Kevan Lannister, leaving her seemingly powerless.

In the sixth season, the High Sparrow is the dominant power in King's Landing. His private army controls the streets, and holding Queen Margaery hostage paralyzes King Tommen. The Lannisters and Tyrells outside of his grasp—Jaime and Olenna, primarily—make an alliance to bully him into releasing the queen. But they arrive to find that Margaery has sidestepped them, apparently converting to the Sparrows' form of fundamentalism, and bringing Tommen into the fold with her. Tommen immediately bans trial by combat, eliminating Cersei's best opportunity to get out of her trial, and seeming to lead toward doom for Cersei and Loras (though perhaps not Margaery, whose supposed crimes were far lesser).

The peak of the High Sparrow's power in King's Landing is the three-part trial of Loras, Margaery, and Cersei in the Sept of Baelor. The entire court attends and witnesses Loras' disinheritance and swearing in to the Faith Militant, apparently ending the Tyrell line. But when Cersei's trial begins, she isn't there (nor is her son, King

Tommen). Only Margaery realizes that this is because Cersei has something planned: a massive wildfire attack that incinerates the entire Sept, killing her, the High Sparrow, Loras and Mace Tyrell, Ser Kevan, and anyone who could possibly challenge her. The season ends with Cersei finally taking the throne for herself. And although four of her seven kingdoms are in open rebellion against her, Queen Cersei finally has full control over King's Landing.

33 House Targaryen

The story of House Targaryen begins in Valyria, a peninsula in Essos whose inhabitants discovered and tamed the dragons, which they used to create an empire. Over 400 years before *Game of Thrones*, Daenys, the daughter of Lord Aenar Targaryen, had a prophetic dream that Valyria would fall. Aenar believed her, and moved his family to Dragonstone, at the far end of the Valyrian empire. Shortly after, the mysterious Doom of Valyria destroyed the entire empire, with the Targaryens the only surviving dragonriders.

A hundred years later, the proud young Aegon Targaryen began his conquest of the Seven Kingdoms. Alongside his sisters Rhaenys and Visenya, he invaded the mainland of Westeros, building a fortress on the site that would become King's Landing.

The story of Aegon's Conquest is a fairly simple one, but the defining act of House Targaryen. He landed with a small force of men and, with his dragons, gained some local loyalty. One by one and two by two, the houses of Westeros attacked him and were defeated primarily by dragons. First, the Crownlands' houses of Darklyn and Mooton attacked, and were forced to surrender, granting the Conqueror the bulk of the Crownlands.

Aegon next turned on the Riverlands, then ruled by the Ironborn of House Hoare, who had just completed their magnificent castle at Harrenhal. The Ironborn were not well-loved by the Riverlanders, who, led by House Tully, joined their strength to the Targaryens. Aegon burned King Harren Hoare and his castle at Harrenhal, taking the Riverlands. At the same time, Aegon's sister Rhaenys and army commander Orys Baratheon defeated the armies of the Stormlands, with Orys wedding the last Storm Queen and having his House named Lords Paramount of that region.

The next conflict was the greatest and last of the major battles. House Lannister of the Westerlands and House Gardener of the Reach joined forces and marched against Aegon. At the Field of Fire, Aegon and his sisters on all three dragons burned the attacking host, destroying House Gardener and forcing the surrender of the Lannisters. The melted swords from the battle were shaped into Aegon's Iron Throne, the symbol of power of Westeros from then on. The North and the Vale swiftly surrendered after this.

Only Dorne held out against the Targaryens, for the simple reason that they refused to fight. They presented the Targaryens no armies, and left their castles undefended. When Aegon invaded, the Dornish only fought guerrilla battles. Aegon "conquered" the region, only to have it swiftly rebel when he departed. For the next hundred and fifty years, the Targaryens attempted to take and hold Dorne.

In the first hundred years of Targaryen rule, the dragonriders' main political rival was often the Faith of the Seven. The Faith's uneasy alliance with the Iron Throne was complicated by two factors: the conflict between church and state, and the Targaryen's marriage habits. The Faith preached that incest was a crime, but the Targaryens consistently wed brother to sister.

This led to a major uprising in the time of Aegon's grandson, Maegor. The Faith of the Seven in those times was allowed to have its own loyal armies, the Faith Militant, the Poor Fellows, and the

Warrior's Sons. They rebelled, and Maegor, riding Aegon's dragon Balerion, brutally beat the uprising down, earning the name "The Cruel." He died shortly after, and his heir Jaeherys negotiated a peace treaty, disbanding the militant orders—a law later foolishly revoked by Cersei for the High Sparrow's benefit.

Targaryen rule continued relatively peacefully for the next half century as Westeros became acclimated to their rule, and their capital at King's Landing continued to grow—the Aegonfort having been replaced by the Red Keep, home of the Iron Throne. But by the end of their first century in charge, the Seven Kingdoms faced a full-blown succession crisis.

The problem was this: King Viserys I, for most of his life, had one surviving child, Princess Rhaenyra, who was treated as his heir. Later in life, he remarried and had more children, the eldest male child being Aegon II. Although no woman had ever inherited the Iron Throne, Rhaenyra had an entire political faction around her claim and took control of Dragonstone, traditionally the seat of the Targaryen heir.

This proved to be a political mistake. When Viserys died, Aegon and his supporters in King's Landing swiftly moved to crown him as king. This triggered the civil war known as the "Dance of the Dragons." With the Iron Throne, Aegon had enough strength to go toe-to-toe with Rhaenyra, and so Westeros' most brutal civil war until *Game of Thrones* began. (Much of the history of the "Dance" is told in a novella by George R.R. Martin called "The Princess and the Queen," released as part of the 2013 anthology *Dangerous Women*.)

Dragons were the key to Targaryen power, but in the Dance, both sides had roughly equivalent numbers. So they fought and killed one another in the skies, as the armies clashed below. The war also hurt the common people enough that a riot in King's Landing attacked the Dragonpit, where several dragons were killed by the mob. So many dragons were slain in the Dance that they could not maintain their numbers and went extinct just a few decades later, damaging Targaryen power for good.

Both Rhaenyra and Aegon died over the course of the Dance, leaving Rhaenyra's son, Aegon III the Younger, the nominal winner of the war. But with the realm shattered and the Targaryens losing most of their dragons, it took some time to restore stability. The Dance also established the general precedent that for the Targaryens, men come before women in the succession—something that may become relevant once Daenerys arrives on the shores of Westeros.

Within the next few decades, however, Targaryen power was reestablished. This wasn't done with dragons, but with legends. Several of their most famous kings reigned in the middle of their second century: King Daeron, the Young Dragon, led a conquest of Dorne as a teenager, seeming to do without dragons what Aegon the Conqueror could do with them. The Dornish rebelled again, eventually killing Daeron and pushing the Iron Throne out, but Daeron had established a foothold militarily that the next few kings exploited via other means.

Daeron's successor was his brother, the zealous king Baelor the Blessed—who gives his name to the Sept of Baelor, home of the Seven in King's Landing. Baelor worked to piously mend the scars of the Dornish invasion, including walking across a pit of vipers to rescue his captured cousin, the legendary Dragonknight Aemon Targaryen. He also negotiated several marriage alliances with the Dornish. While successful there, his zealousness was a liability in King's Landing, where he tried to outlaw prostitution, amongst other things, and eventually died young, possibly poisoned. His faith also prevented Baelor from consummating his marriage to his sister Daena, which helped lead to the next great succession crisis.

The Blackfyre Rebellions were triggered by possibly the worst Targaryen king before Mad King Aerys, Aegon IV, cousin to Daeron and Baelor, and brother to Aemon, the famed Dragonknight. On his deathbed, the womanizing Aegon legitimized all of his bastards.

The most powerful of them, Daemon Blackfyre, started a series of Blackfyre Rebellions that threatened the Targaryens for decades. (See Chapter 35.)

Yet Aegon's son, King Daeron II, survived these rebellions. He also fulfilled the marriage alliances with Dorne negotiated by Baelor the Blessed and, using those, finally added Dorne to the Seven Kingdoms under the Iron Throne, nearly 200 years after Aegon's Conquest.

The next great crisis for the Targaryens occurred after the death of Daeron II's son, King Maekar. The Targaryen reliance on incest was finally manifesting, with several children of the ruling house being stillborn, insane, simple-minded, or sickly. At a Great Council to decide who should succeed Maekar, the choice came to his two youngest sons, both of whom connect to *Game of Thrones*. Aemon Targaryen was the elder and better-liked by the lords of Westeros, but he had sworn a vow to become a maester, and refused the crown—eventually heading to the Wall and becoming a mentor to Jon Snow and Samwell Tarly.

Instead the crown passed to Aegon V, also known as "Egg." Egg is the subject of the stories that are the most likely *Game of Thrones* spinoff, the "Tales of Dunk & Egg" about the wandering life of him and his future Kingsguard, Ser Duncan the Tall (see Chapter 87). This era is well-documented in the most detailed canonical stories about Westeros outside of *Game of Thrones*. Dunk and Egg led Westeros wisely and fairly, the last time the land was generally peaceful and prosperous. But in the mysterious Tragedy at Summerhall, Aegon, Duncan, and much of the court perished in an apparent attempt to bring back the dragons.

What remained for the Targaryens was tragedy. Aegon's children married for love, both with or without the crown's blessing, in ways that removed them from the succession (dying young also didn't help in most cases). One of his daughters, Rhaelle, was wed to House Baratheon, and became the grandmother of Robert,

Stannis, and Renly. But the rest of the Targaryens had been trimmed to just a single family line.

The show and the books diverge a bit here, because at one point Maester Aemon, talking about his family, seems to skip over Jaeherys Targeryen and says that the Mad King was Aemon's nephew, while the books have Aemon as King Aerys' great-uncle. Regardless, just a few decades before, the only Targaryens left outside the long-forgotten Maester Aemon were the Mad King Aerys, his sister and wife Rhaella, his son and heir Rhaegar, and his younger son Viserys. Three babies were known added by the time of Robert's Rebellion. Rhaegar had a son and a daughter with Princess Elia Martell, and Daenerys Targaryen was born at Dragonstone after the death of her father and brother—and costing the life of her mother.

House Targaryen had battled against the manifestations of their incest for decades, but with the line trimmed down to just Aerys and his family, they had no choice but to crown him. Aerys II Targaryen was prone to mood swings and whims early on, but with his friend Tywin Lannister as his Hand, he mostly managed to keep it together.

But eventually he drove Tywin away and his madness became more and more apparent. Everything came to a head fifteen years before *Game of Thrones*, when the supposedly sane and wise Rhaegar Targaryen kidnapped Lyanna Stark, betrothed of Robert Baratheon, who through his grandmother, Rhaella, had a claim to the throne. The Mad King burned the Starks who protested in King's Landing, making his madness impossible to ignore and triggering the War of the Usurper.

Robert's forces eventually won the war, with Robert slaying Rhaegar at the Battle of the Trident. Tywin Lannister, previously neutral, tricked his way into King's Landing and sacked the city, leaving Aerys and Rhaegar's children dead, and Targaryen rule over the Seven Kingdoms ended.

House Targaryen was left in ruins, with Viserys and Daenerys surviving in the Free Cities, eventually beginning to push their claim when Viserys came to adulthood. He failed generally, earning the derisive nickname "the Beggar King" for his troubles. But they survived with the help of loyalists like Varys the Spider and the merchant Illyrio Mopatis. Eventually Daenerys wed the Dothraki Khal Drogo, supposedly to give Viserys an army, but events would see both men dead, and no army for the Targaryens.

Daenerys has, however, managed to resurrect the initial sources of Targaryen power: dragons. With them she has gained herself a new army, and the excesses of Lannister-Baratheon rule have pushed Dorne and the Reach into her armies. She now sails for Westeros, attempting to regain Targaryen power.

But unbeknownst to anyone but Bran Stark, a Targaryen has already regained power in Westeros. Jon Snow, the unwitting bastard of Rhaegar and Lyanna, has been crowned King in the North. The fate of Westeros once again rests in the hands of the Targaryens.

34 Robert's Rebellion

One of the things that makes *Game of Thrones* so special is that it's steeped in history. All of its characters' motivations are informed by the events of the near and distant past, which makes them feel like real people, and the politics of the realm feel authentic. No historical event casts a longer shadow over the early seasons of *Game of Thrones* than Robert's Rebellion, the War of the Usurper, a great civil war that took place just fifteen years before *Game of Thrones*.

Robert's Rebellion ended nearly 300 years of Targaryen control of Westeros, and put him on the throne for the start of the series. It also set up many of the marriages, alliances, and rivalries that dominate the Seven Kingdoms when the show starts. Yet the show never sits down and explains exactly what happened, which led to significant confusion for new viewers when *Game of Thrones* began. (I thought they should have aired an animated mini-episode, but it was not to be—at least, not until the DVD extras.) Eventually enough explanations were given both in the show and outside of it that it became less essential to grasp *Game of Thrones*, but it's still a key piece of history.

The antagonist of Robert's Rebellion is the Mad King, Aerys II, who, born of generations of Targaryen incest, was unsuited to sit on the throne. He was propped up for most of his reign by his Hand, Tywin Lannister, and later by his son, Rhaegar Targaryen, who was supposedly the perfect prince: wise, powerful, and kind.

As Aerys' madness became less controllable and he pushed Tywin away, several lords started to see if he could be replaced. The Tournament at Harrenhal, the grandest of its generation, was perhaps supposed to be the focus of a conspiracy to replace Aerys with his son Rhaegar. But Aerys surprisingly attended, and instead the events of the tourney tore the realm apart. Aerys made Jaime Lannister a knight of the Kingsguard, deepening the divide between him and his erstwhile ally Lord Tywin, who wanted Jaime as his heir.

But the biggest crisis appeared when Prince Rhaegar won the tournament, and instead of crowning his wife Elia Martell as the "Queen of Love and Beauty," he gave the crown to the wild and beautiful Lyanna Stark (who may have competed in the tourney in disguise as the Knight of the Laughing Tree, a story Meera tells Bran on *Game of Thrones*). Lyanna was also betrothed to Robert Baratheon, Rhaegar's future archrival.

A year later, Rhaegar's symbolic faux pas turned into a national crisis, when he kidnapped—or eloped with—Lyanna Stark. Lord

Rickard Stark and his eldest son Brandon went to King's Landing to demand redress for this crime. Instead, the Mad King had them publicly humiliated and executed in front of the entire court, Rickard by wildfire, and Brandon by strangulation.

Aerys sent a demand to Jon Arryn, Lord of the Vale, to execute his two wards who might also cause trouble. They were Lord Robert Baratheon, Lyanna's betrothed, and Ned Stark, the new Lord of Winterfell. Instead, the three raised their banners in rebellion, the biggest threat to Targaryen power since the Blackfyre Rebellions.

If you look at a map of the Seven Kingdoms, however, you might see a slight problem with this rebellion. All three of its realms are separated from one another; the Vale from the North by water, and from the Stormlands by the Crownlands in between. All three realms, however, border the Riverlands—for this reason, the traditional battlefield of the Seven Kingdoms. So the rebels aligned themselves with the honorable Lord Hoster Tully of the Riverlands, with Lords Stark and Arryn wedding the two Tully daughters, Catelyn and Lysa.

While four of the Seven Kingdoms had joined the rebels, the loyalists swayed two to the Targaryen cause: House Martell of Dorne, joined by marriage to the Targaryens, and the consistent loyalists of House Tyrell. House Lannister remained neutral, as did several smaller houses, waiting to see how the war would unfold.

The rebellion lords cast their lot in with Robert, as he had the strongest claim on the Iron Throne due to his grandmother being a Targaryen. Much of the early focus of the war centered on Targaryen forces attempting to capture Robert and thus end the rebellion, while the lords farther north gathered their forces.

Robert won battles and evaded capture until two battles nearly cost him the war. At the Battle of Ashford, Tyrell forces under Lord Randyll Tarly defeated Robert's small Stormlands army and sent the future king retreating north, leaving the Stormlands open to the Tyrell armies. Stannis Baratheon, upon meeting Randyll's son

Samwell Tarly, notes that Randyll is the only man who defeated Robert in battle. But the Tarly and Tyrell forces didn't follow Robert. Instead they besieged Storm's End, which was held for months by Stannis, with aid from Davos Seaworth.

The Targaryen armies, led by Aerys' Hand, Jon Connington, trapped Robert's army in the Stoney Sept, deep in the Riverlands. There Robert managed to hide and hold out until the Tully and Stark forces finally joined him, defeating Connington. Aerys realized that revolt was getting out of hand at this point, and exiled Connington (this ended his part in the show's narrative, but the books tell a different story—see Chapter 79). In his place he assigned Rhaegar Targaryen, removing him from Lyanna's side at the Tower of Joy in Dorne.

With Robert now in possession of the bulk of his armies, and Rhaegar taking command of the full Targaryen forces, the stage was set for a final battle. Robert marched on King's Landing, and Rhaegar met him at the Battle of the Trident. The battle raged inconclusively as several lords and knights became heroes or died, but in the end, it was decided by a single fight. Robert Baratheon met Rhaegar Targaryen in a ford of the Trident rivers, and with a blow of his warhammer, crushed his breastplate. The rubies that scattered from the blow gave the location the nickname the "ruby ford," which caused Westerosi like Arya Stark in the first season to seek the rubies that might still be found.

Rhaegar's death effectively won the war for Robert, but there was still significant and painful cleanup to do. In King's Landing, Aerys, now nearly totally insane, refused to give up—although he did wisely send his pregnant wife and remaining son Viserys to Dragonstone. Aerys seeded King's Landing with wildfire, threatening to send the whole city up in flames and be reborn as a dragon if attacked.

The attack came from an unexpected source. Tywin Lannister finally moved his armies and managed to beat Robert's forces to

King's Landing. He claimed to come to reinforce the city, which Aerys believed, opening the gates. Instead, the Lannisters began to sack the city. Aerys attempted to set his wildfire plan into motion, but Jaime Lannister, his last remaining Kingsguard, killed Aerys and sacrificed his honor to save the people of King's Landing.

Lannister forces, led by Gregor Clegane, killed Elia Martell and Rhaegar's two children, a cruel and destructive act that nevertheless was cited as helping preserve the realm. Robert could not, as a potential king, kill two babies, but neither could he leave the Targaryen heirs alive. Tywin doing that for him allowed him the victory while maintaining his honor. Tywin also gave Robert more power: the new king married Cersei Lannister to create a rigid alliance between the two most powerful houses of the realm.

With King's Landing taken, the war wound down everywhere else. At Dragonstone, Rhaella Targaryen gave birth to a daughter, Daenerys, during an epic storm that gave Dany the nickname "Stormborn." Before Robert's forces could capture them, Targaryen loyalists smuggled Viserys and Dany across the Narrow Sea.

With Aerys gone, the Tyrell forces broke the siege of Storm's End—successfully held by Stannis for months—and bent the knee to Robert. So too did Dorne, although both realms found themselves largely frozen out of the politics of King's Landing by the vengeful Robert, only returning to the capital after his death.

Dorne was also the scene for the last act of the war, when Ned Stark and a group of Northern nobles headed to the Tower of Joy, where Rhaegar took Lyanna. There they encounter Ser Arthur Dayne, the greatest knight in Westeros, and other members of the Kingsguard, protecting Lyanna for some unknown reason. They refuse to let Ned by to see his sister, and a battle ensues. Dayne kills most of the northmen, and is on the verge of slaying the young Ned Stark, when Howland Reed backstabs him and wins the day.

Ned climbs the stairs to discover his sister dying from childbirth. She hands him her son, and whispers "Promise me, Ned."

The promise is that Ned will not reveal to the vengeful Robert her boy's true identity: Jon Snow, the son of Lyanna Stark and Rhaegar Targaryen. Ned keeps the promise: he raises the lad as his own bastard son, at the cost of great friction to his relationship with his wife, Catelyn Tully.

That's just one of the ways that Robert's Rebellion defines the entire political and personal situation in Westeros at the start of *Game of Thrones*. Every Great House, most marriages, and the Stark-Lannister rivalry come from this. And Robert's inability to solidify his victory leads directly to his assassination and the civil war that comes from his death.

35 The Blackfyre Rebellions

The story of the second half of the rule of the Targaryens is, in many ways, the story of the Blackfyre Rebellions. A single, misguided act by one Targaryen king on his deathbed set into motion five different rebellions, lasting nearly sixty years, and spanning from a century before the events of *Game of Thrones* into the start of the career of Ser Barristan the Bold.

After the devastating Dance of the Dragons, the Targaryens had lost much of their power along with their dragons. But a series of legendary rulers and knights maintained their power. The Young Dragon, Daeron I, finally conquered Dorne, and his brother, Baelor the Blessed, integrated it into the Seven Kingdoms. Both died young, however, and the crown fell on Viserys II Targaryen, who reigned for just a year. Viserys was the father of two of the most famous Targaryens: Aegon IV, the Unworthy, and Prince Aemon the Dragonknight (a Lancelot-like figure).

Aegon IV was widely regarded as a bad person and worse king, fathering several bastards with a variety of different mistresses. His sister and wife, Naerys, was not one of his beloveds, and rumor always had it that she was in love with Aemon, the perfect knight—and her son was theirs. These rumors would lead to many believing Aegon and Naerys' heir, Daeron, was illegitimate.

Matters only got worse when Aegon IV, on his deathbed, decided to use his royal powers to legitimize all of his bastards. The one with the strongest claim to the throne was Daemon, who created House Blackfyre, named after the traditional sword of the leader of House Targaryen—but which had been given by Aegon IV to the bastard Daemon instead of Prince Daeron.

Two of Aegon's other children—known as the Great Bastards—played a major role in the ensuing crises. Aegor Rivers, nicknamed Bittersteel (because he was a real goddamned jerk), joined with Blackfyre's faction, and essentially acted as their Hand. His greatest rival was his half-brother Brynden, a Targaryen loyalist known as Bloodraven, who became the Hand of the King.

Blackfyre was viewed by many as an ideal king, reminding people of Aegon the Conqueror. He was a mighty warrior whose skill in battle contrasted sharply with King Daeron, who was kind of a nerd. In this way, Daemon initially found it easy to raise an army and threaten the crown.

At the Battle of the Redgrass Field, Daemon proved his personal skill in battle, killing several great knights. But Bloodraven proved the better general, positioning a unit of elite archers where they could rain arrows on Blackfyre, killing him and two of his sons, ending the First Blackfyre Rebellion.

Bittersteel went into exile in the Free Cities. There, he founded the Golden Company, an elite mercenary unit of exiled knights who would provide the backbone of the Blackfyre Rebellions from this point on—they're around in the time of *Game of Thrones*, 100 years later, and play an important part in the novels, but haven't appeared in the show.

In the next several decades, a pattern emerged: Bittersteel would launch an invasion with or for one of Daemon's successors, and Bloodraven would either stop it before it started, or defeat it in battle. Bloodraven, the Hand of the King, gained a reputation as a ruthless, near-magical figure who single-handedly kept the crown safe for the Targaryens.

This ruthlessness cost Bloodraven his honor during a succession crisis after the death of Daeron's grandson, King Maekar. A grand council was held to determine who was supposed to be king, and the latest Blackfyre claimant asked to attend. Bloodraven agreed, then had the Blackfyre murdered anyway. The council selected Aegon V as king—Maester Aemon's brother, and "Egg" of Dunk & Egg as well as the name Aemon mutters as he dies. Aegon V gave Bloodraven the chance to avoid death by taking the black.

Bloodraven rose to become Lord Commander of the Night's Watch, but disappeared while Beyond the Wall. In the novels, the Three-Eyed Raven that Bran discovers is Bloodraven himself—a complicated story that *Game of Thrones* the show ignores, sadly.

The final act of the Blackfyre Rebellion occurred after Aegon V's death. The last Blackfyre, known as Maelys the Monstrous, aligned with nine other powerful lords in the Free Cities, all promising to help one another. After achieving some success in Essos, they invaded the Stepstones, the islands between Essos and Westeros.

Several major characters in *Game of Thrones* fought in the battles against the Ninepenny Kings, including Tywin Lannister, the future Mad King Aerys, Brynden "Blackfish" Tully, and Barristan Selmy. Selmy eventually won the war, defeating Maelys in single combat, and earning a place in the Kingsguard on his way to becoming the greatest knight in the realm.

The Blackfyre Rebellions are usually considered a disaster for the Targaryens, sapping their strength in a series of minor wars and intrigues that eventually weakened them for Robert's Rebellion. But it could also be argued that they helped save the Targaryens in a way; that after the dragons' departure, there were no longer any guarantees that the Targs could survive as kings. By setting up decades of internal Targaryen politics as the dominating force in Westeros, Aegon the Unworthy accidentally helped prop up his line.

Regardless, the Blackfyre Rebellions were the last major threat to the Iron Throne until Robert's Rebellion, and the events that directly led to *Game of Thrones*.

36 House Lannister and the Westerlands

Game of Thrones presents itself as the story of the Starks, following the four children as they become adults. But the political story is that of the Starks' greatest rivals: House Lannister of Casterly Rock. Led by Lord Tywin Lannister, his children Cersei, Jaime, and Tyrion are also close to the reins of power, if not holding them directly.

The Lannisters rule the Westerlands, a mountainous region in, obviously, the west of the Seven Kingdoms. Its major bordering regions are the Riverlands to the east, and the Reach to the south. The Iron Islands are not far to the north as well. The seat of power is Casterly Rock, a never-captured stronghold carved into a hill above the thriving city of Lannisport. The most famous trait of the Westerlands is their gold mines, which have turned House Lannister into the richest family in Westeros.

Oddly, that's about it for details about the Westerlands. Despite House Lannister's obvious importance to the story, the location itself is only shown a handful of times on *Game of Thrones*, when King Robb takes the offensive against the Lannisters in Season 2 and he meets Talisa Maegyr. You may have missed that these battles took place in the Westerlands, as the show doesn't make a big deal out of it, and every scene takes place in a fairly generic army camp. With the Reach finally making an appearance in the sixth season, it's easy to argue that the Westerlands as a setting are the least important on the show.

The Lannisters trace their heritage back to a legend of Westeros, Lann the Clever. This golden-haired trickster god was supposed to have swindled his way into Casterly Rock and took it from House Casterly, leaving a blond-haired brood of Lannisters in its place. With an origin story like this, praising charisma and scheming, the Lannisters were opposites and natural rivals for the straightforward, honest Starks of Winterfell, something seen from the beginning of *Game of Thrones* in Ned's honor opposing Jaime's sly smirk.

House Lannister ruled as Kings of the Rock for millennia, before joining the Kings of the Reach to attack Aegon Targaryen after the Conqueror had settled at King's Landing. At the Field of Fire, Aegon and his sisters unleashed all three dragons against the assembled host, destroying it and capturing the last Lannister king, Loren, who surrendered and became Warden of the West.

The Lannisters were one of the most powerful Houses in the kingdoms, and played major roles throughout the Targaryen era, fighting in the civil war called the Dance of the Dragons, and helping put down the Blackfyre Rebellions. But their peak would be right before the events of the show, in the reign of the Mad King.

Lord Tywin Lannister came of age when his father, Tytos, had squandered Lannister money and power. Tywin set about regaining it, brutally suppressing the revolt of the ambitious House Reyne of Castamere. Tywin destroyed them so devastatingly that the song "The Rains of Castamere," about his success, became the Lannister anthem. Tywin is also a friend to King Aerys II Targaryen, who had him named Hand.

The first Lannister children were born to Tywin and Joanna Lannister in his time as Hand. Joanna, a Lannister cousin, was a gentle and believed balance to Tywin's ruthlessness, but she died giving birth to the dwarf, Tyrion, something for which neither Tywin nor Cersei ever forgave Tyrion.

Tywin's time as Hand of the King ended as Aerys Targaryen descended further into paranoia, turning him against the man who ruled the Seven Kingdoms in his name. Aerys rejected a betrothal of Cersei to Prince Rhaegar, and raised Jaime Lannister to the Kingsguard, removing him from consideration to be the heir to Casterly Rock, which Tywin took as a personal affront. (There were also rumors that Aerys pursued Joanna Lannister, giving rise to speculation about Tyrion's true parentage.)

The Lannisters nursed their grudge from the Westerlands, as Aerys appointed weaker Hands and descended further into madness. When the Mad King's cruelty triggered Robert's Rebellion, the Lannisters were the only Great House to remain neutral, despite Tywin's previous bonds to Aerys. After the Battle of the Trident, when Targaryen forces were defeated, Tywin's army arrived at King's Landing. Aerys, believing his old friend had come to reinforce the capital, let them in.

But Tywin instead unleashed his army on the capital, particularly his two lead henchmen, Ser Gregor Clegane and Ser Amory Lorch, to rape and pillage and murder the Targaryen heirs, thus proving their loyalty to the future King Robert. King Aerys planned to set the city ablaze with wildfire, but Jaime Lannister, sworn Kingsguard, stabbed his ruler in the back to prevent it, becoming the Kingslayer.

In order to shore up his support, Robert wed Cersei Lannister, a marriage of alliance and nothing more. Cersei despised Robert for remaining in love with the now-dead Lyanna Stark, and for abusing her in drunken rages. She continued an incestuous affair with her twin Jaime, and bore him three children, Joffrey, Tommen, and Myrcella. She had first had one of Robert's children, but it died shortly after birth. (In the novels, Cersei deliberately aborts the child; it's unclear if the death was intentional on the show.)

When *Game of Thrones* starts, the parentage of Cersei's children becomes the driver of the plot. Bran Stark catches Cersei and Jaime screwing, and is thrown out the window—the investigation leads Catelyn Stark to arrest Tyrion Lannister, for which Tywin starts the War of the Five Kings. Meanwhile, in King's Landing, Ned Stark investigates his predecessor Jon Arryn's murder and, following in his footsteps, discovers that Joffrey and the other children are born of incest.

Cersei, feeling the walls pressing in on her, reacts with violence: she helps Robert to his death by having his squire, her cousin Lancel Lannister, give him undiluted wine. Then she, with Lord Petyr Baelish's help, puts down Ned's coup against Joffrey. Joffrey, who increasingly shows himself to be an uncontrollable sadist, has Ned executed, leaving King's Landing under Lannister control.

The Lannister armies, however, do not fare so well. Robb Stark deceives Tywin, and sneak attacks Jaime's army, capturing the Kingslayer. With one Lannister army defeated, and Kings Stannis and Renly raising their armies to attack King's Landing, Tywin is forced onto the defensive in Harrenhal. Because the decision to execute Ned was such a disaster, Tywin sends his son Tyrion to King's Landing as Acting Hand.

Tyrion's time in King's Landing is largely spent preparing for the attack of Stannis Baratheon, in the Battle of Blackwater. Tyrion's wildfire trap severely damages Stannis' fleet, and Joffrey proves a coward, forcing Tyrion to lead the defenders, which he does, before being wounded.

But another plot of Tyrion's ends up, accidentally, saving the capital and winning two wars. He sends Lord Baelish to Renly's camp to find Catelyn Stark and offer her daughters in exchange for the Kingslayer. She rejects the proposal, but knows it exists, and Baelish finds himself in the camp after Renly's death, where he offers an alliance to Margaery Tyrell that will let her be queen. This is to join the Lannister armies, smash Stannis' attack, and wed King Joffrey—which happens, when Tywin and the Tyrells arrive in the nick of time at Blackwater.

The third season sees the Lannisters at the height of their power. All of them are in King's Landing, the south is largely free of civil war with Stannis licking his wounds at Dragonstone, Robb's army diminished by his betrayal of the marriage contract with the Freys, and Theon Greyjoy's seizure of Winterfell in the North.

Tyrion's ploy has also succeeded with Catelyn Stark: she secretly frees Jaime Lannister and sends him to King's Landing, escorted by Brienne of Tarth. This act sows discord in the Stark camp, eventually resulting in Robb executing Lord Karstark, one of his most powerful vassals. Desperate for reinforcements, Robb attempts to reunite with House Frey when Tywin's trap is sprung. The Hand, having spent the entire third season writing letters, finally has his communication revealed when the Freys and the Northern House Bolton betray Robb, murdering him, his wife, his mother, and most of his armies, essentially winning the War of the Five Kings.

In King's Landing, however, things go less well. Both of his children in the capital chafe under Lord Tywin's heavy-handedness, with Tyrion unhappy that he isn't being given Casterly Rock, to which he should be the legal heir, and Cersei unhappy at Margaery's increasing control over Joffrey. Still, there's some happy news as Jaime and Brienne arrive at the capital, although the Kingslayer has lost his sword hand. With them comes the disgraced former maester Qyburn, who'd healed Jaime's hand, and who ingratiates himself in the court, particularly with Cersei.

At the start of the fourth season, the Lannisters appear to have won the war, with their victories having been the climaxes of all three seasons. It doesn't last: at the royal wedding, Joffrey Lannister-Baratheon is poisoned. Tyrion is the most likely culprit, and he's imprisoned, although it's revealed that the culprits were Olenna Tyrell, seeking to save her granddaughter from the sadistic Joffrey, and Petyr Baelish, attempting to sow chaos and continue his alliance with the Tyrells.

Tyrion's trial breaks the power of the Lannisters. His sister and father manipulate the proceedings against him, but Tyrion fights back, revealing their hypocrisies. He demands trial by combat, and Tywin's henchman, the giant Mountain, Ser Gregor Clegane, frightens away any of Tyrion's sympathizers—except for Prince Oberyn Martell, Elia's brother, who is in King's Landing to take revenge against the Lannisters for their murder of his sister so many years before.

Oberyn defeats the Mountain in combat, but before striking the final blow, attempts to shame Lord Tywin by having the Mountain confess that the Lannisters ordered Elia's murder. But the poisoned, dying Clegane is just alive enough to grab Oberyn and kill him. Tyrion loses his trial and is sentenced to death.

Tyrion has allies in the court who don't want him to die, however. His brother Jaime and Lord Varys free the youngest Lannister, who goes to take revenge, shooting and killing his father Tywin before fleeing the city.

With Tywin dead, a power vacuum takes hold in the capital in the fifth season, to be filled by whoever can manipulate the good-natured, weak-willed King Tommen. Margaery Tyrell, once she marries him, gains the upper hand and taunts Cersei about it. Cersei also finds herself increasingly out of favor even with her own family, as Kevan Lannister, Tywin's brother, refuses to serve on the Small Council she's set up as her own, without Tommen's input.

Cersei, however, is not the sort to suffer abuse, and hatches a plan to remove the Tyrells. Like most of Cersei's plans, it's initially clever, but incredibly short-sighted. She recruits a religious leader among the poor of King's Landing called the High Sparrow and empowers him to make an army of believers called the Faith Militant. She points them at Margaery's brother Loras, who is arrested for his homosexuality. Margaery is implicated as well, for committing perjury to cover for her brother.

But Cersei grows overconfident and, visiting the High Sparrow, finds herself arrested for her crimes of adultery and incest. She is imprisoned and tortured, until given the opportunity to conduct a Walk of Atonement, where her hair is shaved, she's stripped naked, and she's forced to walk in front of the jeering crowds to return to the Red Keep. There she discovers that her familial rivals have taken power, with Ser Kevan acting as Hand of the King with Pycelle's support. The one bit of good news: Qyburn has apparently succeeded in reanimating Ser Gregor Clegane, now appointed to the Kingsguard.

Jaime isn't present for this since he's been sent to Dorne to recover the other child, Myrcella, engaged to Prince Trystane Martell and threatened by Ellaria Sand, Oberyn's paramour. The less said about the Dorne journey the better, but it ends with Myrcella's death by poison. Tyrion, meanwhile, is on a journey across the Narrow Sea to Essos, where he ends up as an adviser to Daenerys Targaryen.

In the sixth season, Cersei, Jaime, and Olenna Tyrell hatch a plan to threaten the Sparrows and free King's Landing from their influence. They're outmaneuvered by Margaery, who brings King Tommen into the High Sparrow's influence. Jaime is sent away from King's Landing to the Lannister armies in the Riverlands, and Tommen also removes Cersei's best option for winning her trial when he bans trial by combat.

Cersei is forced to resort to desperate measures. In the season finale, she launches a decapitation strike, working with Qyburn to plant wildfire under the Sept of Baelor. She skips her trial, and only Margaery realizes what is happening. Before the young queen can convince the High Sparrow to evacuate, the plan goes off, the building is destroyed, and all Cersei's enemies—the Sparrows, the Tyrells, Kevan Lannister, Grand Maester Pycelle—are killed. Although she prevented Tommen from attending, he realizes what has happened and commits suicide.

Jaime Lannister, having succeeded with his task in retaking the Riverlands, rides into King's Landing to discover that Cersei, having killed literally everyone else in her way, is being crowned Queen of the Seven Kingdoms, with Qyburn as her Hand.

Cersei is, however, not the only Lannister to get a promotion. Tyrion becomes the leader of Meereen in Dany's absence, and though his attempts at making peace in Slaver's Bay fail, his loyalty and counsel when Dany returns gains her confidence, and she names him her Hand. He now sails with her army against his sister, Queen Cersei Lannister, First of Her Name.

37 The Vale

The Vale, home of House Arryn, was one of the least important regions in *Game of Thrones* in its first five seasons. Their leaders remained assiduously neutral, and the region itself was primarily a stopping point for characters on larger journeys—Cat Stark and Tyrion Lannister in Season 1, and Sansa Stark in Season 4. But in the sixth season, the Knights of the Vale join with Jon and Sansa's northern army, and the quietest of the Seven Kingdoms has finally entered the wars.

The Vale is the northeastern part of the southern half of Westeros, and is one of the continent's most isolated regions. It is located in the Mountains of the Moon, and as such is filled with rocky hills and valleys. As such, it's one of the least populated of the Seven Kingdoms. Its power comes from its defensive locations, not huge armies or wealth. The Vale is, however, known for the quality of its knights, if not the size of its armies—their addition to Jon Snow's armies is a major alliance.

Its isolated nature means that, although it is technically bordered by the Crownlands to the south and the Riverlands to the west, the Vale is still easily shut off from them. The chief road in and out of the Vale is the High Road, which goes from east to west and meets the Kingsroad at the Inn at the Crossroads in the Riverlands. This road has provided almost all of the action to take place in the Vale itself: Cat and Tyrion are attacked by the mountain clans here; Brienne runs into Arya and the Hound; and Sansa and Littlefinger journey through this road on their way to meet the Boltons.

The mountain clans are a notable part of Vale culture in *Game of Thrones*: these supposed savages are descendants of the First Men who have remained free in the Mountains of the Moon for centuries. Their heritage, violence, and egalitarianism makes them somewhat related to the Wildlings beyond the Wall. Tyrion Lannister recruits some of their clans to aid the Lannisters and himself personally in the first season, but, along with jokes about feeding manhood to goats, they fade into the background as the series progresses. (They play a slightly larger part in the novels, and are specifically paid off by Tywin to leave and lower his son's influence, but the trajectory is basically the same.)

The mountain clans being descendants of the First Men is one of the interesting historical quirks of the Vale. In Westerosi history, it is most famous for being the landing point for the Andals in their successful invasion. (The Andals are perhaps best thought of as the Saxons to the First Men's Britons, a successful invasion that eventually merged with the conquered subjects.) House Royce led the fight against the Andal invasion, but House Arryn eventually won, building the impregnable mountain stronghold known as the Eyrie.

After this, the Vale was never conquered, with the Arryns only surrendering to the Targaryens when they landed a dragon in their citadel, the Eyrie. It was largely spared the depredations of the occasional Targaryen civil war, although its lords did take sides.

House Arryn are the Lords Paramount of the Vale. The death of their Lord, Jon Arryn, starts the story of *Game of Thrones*. He's succeeded by his son Robin (Robert in the novels, although nicknamed "Sweetrobin") whose mother, Lysa, rules in his stead. That's pretty much it for House Arryn.

The only other house to appear are House Baelish, a new, tiny lordship in the Fingers, the worst location in the Vale, but with arguably the cleverest Lord in the Seven Kingdoms, Petyr "Littlefinger" Baelish. He marries, then murders, Lysa Arryn and takes control of the Vale. His sudden ascent is opposed by the traditional lords of the Vale. These "Lords Declarant" challenge Littlefinger, but find themselves outmaneuvered by Sansa Stark. One of them, Bronze Yohn Royce, head of one of the most traditionally powerful houses of the Vale, becomes a recurring character—hosting Robin Arryn and helping defeat the Bolton army at the end of Season 6. With the lords of the Vale swearing allegiance to the King in the North, the region will likely become far more active in the final seasons of the show.

Like much of *Game of Thrones*, the Vale's scenes are usually shot in Northern Ireland; however, a few cliff scenes have been shot in Iceland as well. The region has not had many iconic outdoor scenes, however, making them difficult to specifically tour.

38 House Arryn and the Eyrie

Of all the Great Houses of Westeros, House Arryn is in the worst shape at the start of *Game of Thrones*. The Lords Paramount of the Vale traditional Wardens of the East were one of the most powerful Houses in Westeros, and their power may have peaked just before the start of the story, with Jon Arryn essentially ruling as King Robert's Hand. But it's Lord Arryn's murder that starts the game of thrones and removes House Arryn from the center of power. The Vale remains a potential sleeping giant, however, making it increasingly important after every other land has been shattered by war.

Unlike many of the Great Houses of Westeros, the Arryns have a documented historical origin. The Vale is the closest region to Essos, so when the Andals migrated, they landed there first. An Andal knight, Ser Artys Arryn, unified the Andals and confronted King Robar Royce in the Battle of Seven Stars, killing the king and taking over the Vale. From there, the Andals and their Faith of the Seven spread across the southern half of Westeros, and the Arryns ruled as the Kings of Mountain and Vale.

The Arryns ruled for thousands of years, until the Targaryen invasion. A naval battle destroyed the Targaryen fleet. Although their dragons struck back and destroyed the Arryn fleet, it made any water invasion impossible. As the lords of the Vale gathered their armies below, Aegon the Conqueror's sister Visenya Targaryen flew her dragon to the Eyrie and took the boy king Ronnel Arryn hostage, which caused the Arryns to surrender.

The Arryns became major players in Iron Throne politics in the Targaryen era, even including a rare marriage of a non-Targaryen to a Targaryen, which made them blood relatives and allies of Rhaenyra Targaryen, one of the claimants in the brutal civil war called the Dance of the Dragons. They remained loyal to the crown after that, but that would soon change.

House Arryn's loyalty was one of the key questions of Robert's Rebellion. Jon Arryn was fostering Robert Baratheon and Eddard Stark when Rhaegar kidnapped Robert's betrothed, Lyanna Stark, and murdered the other Starks, leaving Ned Lord of Winterfell. Aerys demanded that Ned and Robert be surrendered, but instead, the three men launched the rebellion that would end Targaryen claims for good. Jon Arryn and Ned Stark formed a marriage alliance with the Riverlands, marrying Lysa and Catelyn Tully, respectively. These four lands would win the rebellion, and Jon Arryn would become Robert's Hand.

Robert proved disinterested in his kingly responsibilities, so Jon and Robert's brother Stannis essentially ruled the kingdom. They also grew suspicious of the parentage of Robert's children, beginning an investigation into Robert's bastards and Baratheon genealogy that showed that the king's very blond children couldn't possibly be his. Lord Arryn was poisoned for this, with the strong implication that it was Queen Cersei who did it—although late in Season 4, Jon's wife Lysa lets slip that she poisoned the Hand, at the request of Littlefinger, seeking to sow chaos for his own advancement.

Following Jon's death, both Lysa and Stannis departed the capital. Lysa took her son, the sickly Robin Arryn, back to the Eyrie, the capital of the Vale. The Eyrie is one of the most fantastic locations in Westeros, a beautiful castle atop a mountain, extremely difficult to get in and out of. Its most notable feature is the Moon Door, a circular opening in the floor of the Eyrie's throne room, used for capital punishment.

We first see the Moon Door in action when Catelyn Stark brings her prisoner Tyrion Lannister to the Eyrie, thinking it a safe place after kidnapping the Imp. What she finds, though, is that her sister Lysa is increasingly unstable, coddling her pathetic son Robin and refusing to engage with the world. Tyrion recruits the sellsword Bronn, who wins his trial by combat by kicking Ser Vardis Egan through the Moon Door.

House Arryn remains neutral in the War of the Five Kings until, as a reward for bringing the Tyrells into the fold, Tywin Lannister allows Petyr "Littlefinger" Baelish to seek the hand of Lysa Arryn. The two were old lovers from their time as youths at Riverrun, and Littlefinger has no difficulty marrying Lysa. He also brings Sansa Stark, who's fled King's Landing, and who is the true object of his affections. When Lysa sees them kiss, she flies into a rage, and when she threatens Sansa, Littlefinger pushes her out the Moon Door, declaring that he only ever loved her sister and Sansa's mother, Catelyn. At this point, Lord Baelish becomes the speaker for House Arryn, assuming Robin Arryn's regency—a regency that may never end, given Robin's sickliness.

A group of powerful nobles of the Vale come to investigate Lysa's death and Littlefinger's now-total power over the Vale. They're called the Lords Declarant in the novels, though this is never stated on the show. In the novels, Littlefinger wins them to his side with a clever ploy, but the show takes a different stance, having Sansa Stark reveal her true identity and save Littlefinger from their accusations (while putting him in her debt). Baelish also publicly declares his plan to try to seize power for Robin Arryn instead of remaining loyal to one of the remaining kings.

When the fifth season begins, Lord Baelish puts down dissent from Lord Yohn Royce by demonstrating his control over the increasingly violent and unstable Lord Robin. He then takes Sansa Stark to wed Ramsay Bolton, attempting to create a new alliance. Cersei Lannister, threatened by the Sparrows, calls him back to King's Landing, where he tells her of the apparent Stark-Bolton alliance (omitting his part in arranging it, of course). He offers to lead the Knights of the Vale to Winterfell to defeat the Boltons or Stannis and be named Warden of the North.

Instead he turns and offers his army to Sansa, who has escaped Ramsay Bolton's clutches. She rejects him for selling her to the cruelest man in Westeros, but when she realizes that Jon's army just isn't strong enough to win, she calls Littlefinger in. The Knights of the Vale arrive at Winterfell just in time to win the Battle of the Bastards.

Lord Baelish attempts to woo Sansa to his side when he sits on the Iron Throne, although she rejects him. But when the lords of the North declare Jon Snow to be their king, the lords of the Vale present, like Yohn Royce, join in. Littlefinger, however, is less than enthusiastic. Nor is it clear where Robin Arryn is, and whether he would join with King Jon. At the end of the sixth season, House Arryn itself may be largely powerless, but the power they once wielded is now influencing the entire realm.

39 The Riverlands

The Riverlands lie at the heart of Westeros. Apart from the massive North, they're the only one of the Seven Kingdoms to border the seas on both sides of the continent, and the land that leads between the Southlands and the North, The Neck, is part of this domain. They're also bordered by every other kingdom except Dorne, with the Iron Islands not far to the northeast. They're flat, with only the rivers that give them their name—Blackwater Rush, and the three rivers that comprise the Trident—providing strategic defenses.

For this reason, the Riverlands are often the battleground of the other kingdoms, like Robb Stark's first victory over Jaime Lannister at the Battle of Whispering Wood, and King Robert's defeat of Rhaegar Targaryen at the Trident. Indeed, most of *Game of Thrones'* scenes that take place in the war zone in the first four seasons are in the Riverlands.

The Lords Paramount of the Riverlands are House Tully, seated in Riverrun, discussed in Chapter 40.

The second most important house in the Riverlands is House Frey, whose castle, The Twins, sits on The Neck at a strategically essential bridge. The Freys were a relatively new, tiny house, but parlayed their geographical importance into money and power—though they still lacked respect.

On *Game of Thrones*, the lord of House Frey, Walder, is introduced in the first season when Catelyn Stark negotiates passage across the river for her son Robb. Walder's sons, Black Walder and Lothar, appear in the third season to negotiate the Red Wedding with the Starks and Tullys, while his daughters, Roslin and Walda, marry Edmure Tully and Roose Bolton. (Several more Freys, including Walder's heir Ser Stavros and the adolescent bullies Big and Little Walder, appear in the novels but not the show.)

Other notable Houses in the Riverlands include House Darry, Mallister, Blackwood, Whent, and Bracken, though none of these play a notable role on the show, and only minor roles in the novels.

The Riverlands' central location has given them one of the most chaotic histories of any of the Seven Kingdoms, most notably being the only kingdom to be conquered by others before the Targaryen conquest. Centuries before Aegon's Conquest, Storm King Arlan III Durrandon conquered the Riverlands and added them to his possessions in the Stormlands. Three hundred years later, the Ironborn under King Harwyn Hoare invaded the Riverlands and Haryn was named King of the Isles and the Rivers.

Harwyn's grandson, Harren the Black, was a cruel, vain man who drained the Riverlands in order to build his grand castle, Harrenhal, which was completed when Aegon Targaryen landed on Westeros. While Harren was fighting Aegon's armies, the lords of the Riverlands rebelled against him and joined the Targaryens. Harren took refuge in his supposedly invincible stronghold, but it wasn't enough. Aegon's dragons burned it, and him, and Aegon raised Edmyn Tully, one of the rebelling lords, to Lord Paramount of the Riverlands.

In Robert's Rebellion, House Tully negotiated marriage alliances with the Starks and Arryns quickly, adding their armies to the rebellion, along with most of the Riverlands—except for House Frey. The Freys also demonstrated their slippery nature in the civil war, as Lord Walder remained assiduously neutral throughout the war. (How the Stark armies marched south without Frey help is unclear.)

When the final battle at the Trident was inevitable, Walder finally decided to march and showed up after Robert's victory, claiming he intended to join the new king the whole time. Not many believed him, and for this he earned the nickname "The Late Lord Frey" and a reputation for untrustworthiness.

The Riverlands are one of the major locations in *Game of Thrones*, with much of Robb Stark's theater of war taking place there, as well as Brienne and Arya's storylines in the middle seasons.

When the War of the Five Kings breaks out, the Tullys in the Riverlands take the first hit. After Catelyn Stark abducts Tyrion Lannister, Lord Tywin sends raiders under the Mountain to punish the Tullys for the crimes of their daughter. Both Houses also raise their armies, while Ned Stark, as Hand of the King, sends a hundred men under Beric Dondarrion to capture Ser Gregor. The Lannister armies smash the Tullys, and Jaime's army besieges Riverrun.

Meanwhile, Robb Stark, upon hearing that his father has been imprisoned, raises his banners and marches south. In order to gain passage at the Twins, his mother Catelyn negotiates a marriage for him and his sister Arya with the Freys, whose troops join his army. Robb deceives Tywin, sending a small force to distract his army, while the main Stark force ambushes and captures Jaime Lannister, with the Tullys joining the northern army.

Much of this political action takes place in generic Stark camps. But the Riverlands have actually been seen before, primarily at the Inn at the Crossroads, a major stopping point on the Kingsroad between Riverrun and King's Landing. This Inn is where Robert's procession stops by the river, where Arya and Joffrey fight, leading to Sansa's direwolf being killed. Later, Catelyn runs into Tyrion there and abducts him. Later on, it's the inn where the Hound and Arya fight the Lannister men.

The television series doesn't make it clear that it's the same location for all of these events, and it may not even be the same set. But the novels do, and the Inn at the Crossroads is used to depict how brutal the war has been in the Riverlands. In one of the most potent metaphors of the books, the innkeeper met at the start of the books is killed by the Lannisters, and the state of her rotting head on a pike matches the increasing destruction of the Riverlands.

We see some of this throughout the show, particularly Brienne and Jaime's journey to King's Landing in the third season (the dead women's corpses and signs saying "they lay with lions" being the most notable example), and the Hound's community being massacred in the sixth. If anything, it's worse in the novels, which make the location of Brienne's journeys seem downright post-apocalyptic.

The war rages on in the second season, though on the show, it seems quieter. Robb invades the Westerlands, while Tywin sits in the castle of Harrenhal, with his army between Robb and King's Landing. Tywin and the Lannisters are keen on finding a group of bandits known as the Brotherhood, although viewers aren't told who they are. But as Stannis approaches the capital, Tywin takes his army to defeat Stannis'. Arya Stark, with Jaqen H'ghar's help, kills the Lannisters inside, allowing Roose Bolton and the Northerners to take the castle.

In the third season, the Riverlands are arguably the most important location in the show apart from King's Landing. The Tully seat of Riverrun finally becomes a major location, included in the credits. Here, Robb and the newly introduced Tullys plot the next phase of the war. Robb is angry with Edmure Tully for messing up a trap he'd set for Ser Gregor Clegane, putting Edmure in his debt. (In the novels, Edmure's failure is significantly worse: he was supposed to act to keep Tywin pinned and away from King's Landing, and his mistake allowed the Lannisters to defeat King Stannis.)

Despite consistently winning battles, Robb finds he's losing the war: the Ironborn attack on the North has cut him off from his home, his marriage to Talisa Maegyr cost him his alliance with the Freys, and his mother's freeing of Jaime Lannister cost him the support of the Karstarks. So Robb develops a new plan: win the Freys back by negotiating a new marriage, involving his uncle Edmure. With his reinforced army, Robb plans on capturing the Lannister home of Casterley Rock.

Lothar and Black Walder Frey negotiate with Robb, eventually seeming to agree to his terms. The Stark and Tully armies depart to The Twins, where Walder Frey and Roose Bolton (who'd married Walder's daughter) betray the King in the North. At the Red Wedding, Robb, Catelyn, and Talisa are all killed, Edmure is captured, and Brynden flees. For this, the Lannisters reward the Freys with both Riverrun and the Riverlands, while Roose Bolton is made Warden of the North and granted Winterfell.

Several other characters spend much of the season in the Riverlands as well. Arya Stark, having fled Harrenhal, eventually finally meets the Brotherhood and their leader, Beric Dondarrion. The Brotherhood without Banners are the remnants of Ned Stark's expedition to kill the Mountain, continuing to fight against King Robert's enemies. They also now worship the Lord of Light, thanks to Thoros of Myr's ability to resurrect Ser Beric, which is demonstrated after he's killed by the captured Hound in single combat.

Finally, Brienne and Jaime continue their journey to King's Landing, seeing much of the worst of the Riverlands. They're captured by Roose Bolton's men and taken to Harrenhal. Lord Roose frees Jaime, an early indication of his planned betrayal. Jaime takes Brienne with him to King's Landing. The Boltons flip Harrenhal to Lannister control after the Red Wedding, with Petyr Baelish having been given the castle earlier, although he never actually takes up residence in his new home.

After the Red Wedding, the Riverlands lose almost all importance for the show for a few seasons. The Freys, Tullys, and Brotherhood don't appear at all in Season 4 or 5, nor does Harrenhal or Riverrun. The region is only shown in Arya's and Brienne's stories in Season 4. Arya and the Hound traverse the Riverlands to reach Arya's aunt Lysa Arryn in the Vale. Brienne attempts to find the Stark girls and runs into Arya's friend Hot Pie (possibly at the Inn at the Crossroads), who puts her on Arya's track. This eventually leads to the confrontation between The Hound and the Maid of Tarth.

In Season 5, the Riverlands aren't shown at all, except perhaps for Brienne's chance meeting with Sansa Stark on her way to Winterfell. This was treated as odd at the time, since that season adapted *A Feast for Crows*, which had a significant amount of story in the Riverlands in Brienne and Jaime's chapters. But Brienne's story in that book had mostly moved to Season 4, while Jaime's got pushed into Season 6. Another critical element, Lady Stoneheart and the Brotherhood without Banners, was ignored completely by the show. (See Chapter 60 for more on why Lady Stoneheart is so important.)

It's Jaime's story in Season 6 that brings the Riverlands back to prominence. On the show, the Blackfish has returned to Riverrun with Tully troops and retaken the castle (in the novels, he never left). Jaime is sent by the Lannisters to end the war in the

Riverlands by capturing the Tully stronghold. The Freys are there besieging the castle, attempting to demoralize the defenders by parading the captured Lord Edmure Tully in front of the castle. Brienne arrives to recruit the Blackfish to join his great-niece Sansa Stark in the North, but he rejects her offer, preferring to defend his family home.

Jaime takes a different tactic and threatens and bribes Edmure Tully to betray and surrender the castle, which he does, over the Blackfish's objections. Brienne escapes, trying to take the Blackfish with her, but Brynden Tully instead prefers to fight and die in the castle. (In the novels, a similar ploy succeeds for Jaime, but it's the Blackfish who escapes on the river, making his apparent off-screen death on the show somewhat suspicious.)

But just when it seems that the Riverlands are secure under the Lannisters and the Freys, Arya Stark arrives and assassinates Lord Walder Frey and his sons Lothar and Black Walder, getting revenge for her mother and brother. As with most of the lands of Westeros at the end of the sixth season, the Riverlands are leaderless and broken. But since they're between Cersei in the Crownlands, Jon in the North, and Euron in the Iron Islands, it's reasonable to assume that they will be Westeros' battleground once again.

40 House Tully and Riverrun

At the start of *Game of Thrones*, the Riverlands are ruled by House Tully of Riverrun. The Tully sigil is leaping fish, and their words are "Family, Duty, Honor." House Tully is led by the aged Lord Hoster Tully at the start of the story, though he never appears alive on-screen. Lord Hoster dies at the start of the third season and his heir, Edmure, and younger brother, Brynden "the Blackfish" Tully, are introduced at Hoster's funeral. (The Tully men play a larger role in the novels, and all are introduced in *A Game of Thrones.*) Hoster's daughters, Catelyn Stark and Lysa Arryn, play larger roles, and show up earlier in the first season.

House Tully is seated in Riverrun, a powerful castle in the west of the Riverlands, located at the junction of two major rivers, making it extremely difficult to besiege effectively. Riverrun has been a major location twice in *Game of Thrones*, during Season 3 after Robb arrives for Lord Tully's funeral, and Season 6 when Brienne heads there to recruit the besieged Blackfish. Gosford Castle in Northern Ireland was used for filming outdoor scenes at Riverrun.

The Riverlands were one of the more chaotic of the Seven Kingdoms before the Targaryens arrived, with multiple houses seizing power from one another and, prior to the Targaryen attack, successful invasions from the Stormlands, then the Iron Islands. The Ironborn House Hoare ruled poorly, so several lords, led by House Tully, rebelled against them and joined Aegon Targaryen's armies. After the destruction of the Hoares at Harrenhal, Aegon raised the Tullys to Lords Paramount of the Riverlands.

During the reign of the Targaryens, the Tullys were a Great House of Westeros, but are not considered one of the strongest Houses. Neither their armies, their economy, or their reputation is ever described as top-tier. They did, however, consistently pick the winning side in every civil war until the War of the Five Kings, indicating their primary strength was diplomatic.

That diplomatic ability was on display in Robert's Rebellion, fifteen years before the start of the series. When Brandon Stark, the heir to Winterfell, was burned by the Mad King, his fiancée was Catelyn Tully. Hoster Tully negotiated her marriage to the new Lord Stark, Eddard, and married his younger daughter, Lysa, to Robert and Ned's mentor, Lord Jon Arryn of the Vale. In doing this, the Tullys instantly allied themselves with two of the most powerful Houses in Westeros, and added a fourth kingdom's armies to the eventually successful rebellion.

Hoster Tully's diplomacy had less luck with his brother, the Blackfish, whose refusal to marry led to a rift in the family (and Brynden's rebellion led to his nickname). The two were only reunited when Hoster was on his deathbed. Likewise, Edmure Tully is less than keen to wed, though while Brynden's motives are a mystery, Edmure wants to maintain his playboy lifestyle.

Riverrun was also the location of the fostering of Petyr Baelish, who became friends with Hoster's daughters, Lysa and Catelyn. Lysa grew infatuated with Littlefinger, who preferred Catelyn but led the younger sister on. When Catelyn was engaged to Brandon Stark, an upset Littlefinger challenged the Northern noble to a duel, which he lost, embarrassingly.

The Tullys are the early focus of the War of the Five Kings after Catelyn arrests Tyrion. Tywin Lannister sends his armies to raid her family's lands in return, and when war fully breaks out, Jaime besieges Riverrun. Robb Stark, in his first great victory, distracts Tywin and ambushes Jaime, capturing the Kingslayer and adding Tully strength to his own. When he is declared King in the North, House Tully declares the Riverlands for him as well.

Although the Tullys are part of Robb's forces from the end of the first season on, the male members of the family aren't shown on-screen until Season 3. That's not the case in the novels, where the Blackfish joins Catelyn when she leaves the Vale and then joins Robb, Edmure becomes a notable character after Riverrun is freed, and the infirm Lord Hoster is visited by Cat a few times.

In the second season, although offscreen, House Tully still plays a role in the wars. Robb Stark sets a trap for the Mountain, which Edmure ruins. (In the novels, the trap is meant to prevent Tywin from reaching King's Landing during Stannis' attack, which is far more consequential.) Regardless, Edmure's failure puts him in Robb's debt.

When Hoster Tully finally passes away at the start of Season 3, Robb takes his troops to Riverrun for the funeral. There his armies start to fall apart, leading to the execution of Lord Karstark. Robb's new plan, to regain an alliance with the Freys involves a new marriage: Edmure Tully's. Although resistant, Edmure eventually concedes to Robb's plan.

He probably shouldn't have, as his marriage becomes the "Red Wedding." If your wedding has a nickname in *Game of Thrones*, that means it probably went badly. Robb and Catelyn are killed, Edmure is imprisoned, and the Blackfish only survives by virtue of a well-timed piss.

House Tully disappears from the show for the next two seasons. (One possible reason for this: Tobias Menzies, who plays Edmure Tully, got a major starring role in the show *Outlander*.) House Frey is given Riverrun, and the show's focus shifts to King's Landing and the North instead of the Riverlands. But they all come back in Season 6, where it's revealed that Brynden Tully has rallied the Tully troops and recaptured Riverrun. The Freys attempt to besiege the citadel with no success, until Jaime Lannister arrives to finish the war at the same time Brienne of Tarth arrives seeking allies for Sansa.

Jaime grants Brienne a day to attempt to convince the Blackfish to take his men north. She fails, and Jaime launches his plan. The Freys have been parading Edmure Tully in front of Riverrun in order to break the defenders' resolve, with no luck. Jaime instead browbeats and bribes Edmure into taking the castle for him. He demands entry as Lord Tully and, over the Blackfish's objections, the defenders let him in. The now-pathetic Edmure immediately surrenders the castle. Brienne escapes and attempts to take the Blackfish with her, but he prefers to stay and die. Neither Brynden's death nor his body are shown on-screen, and we aren't given any reason to believe that he survived, although it may be possible.

If not, then Edmure Tully is the last surviving member of House Tully, firmly under Lannister control. Tully blood does run in the veins of Robin Arryn and the surviving children of Ned and Cat Stark, so the family may control Riverrun again as the series heads to its close, but the Tully name seems dead as a major power in Westeros.

41 House Greyjoy and the Iron Islands

The Iron Islands and its inhabitants are perhaps the strangest region in Westeros. Although not technically one of the Seven Kingdoms, the Iron Islands have long been an independent power—or tried to be. But beyond that, the Ironborn have their own unique religion and customs, which puts them at odds with much of the mainland.

In many ways, the Ironborn seem to fit in the roles of the Vikings to Westeros' England-style setup. Their culture is built on reaving, violently taking the riches of the mainland for themselves while sailing on longship-like vessels, and striking fear in the coastal regions near their location (the "green lands"). They also have kingsmoots to elect their rulers. But the specifics of their culture—and the application of Viking-like looks and berserker rages to Wildlings like Tormund Giantsbane—make the Ironborn more than just fantasy Vikings.

The Ironborn are the only culture in Westeros to worship the Drowned God, a cruel religion based around drowning and resurrection. When Theon Greyjoy returns to the Iron Islands and joins with his father, he's "baptized" by a priest of the Drowned God by having his head wholly immersed in water, as is Euron Greyjoy when he's crowned in the sixth season.

Exactly what the Drowned God is is somewhat unclear. It's spoken of ominously enough by some characters (particularly in the novels) to suggest that it is some kind of ancient evil—a Lovecraftian horror, perhaps the opposite of the Red God, R'hllor. Some external texts, like *A World of Ice and Fire*, even have fictional Maesters theorizing about where the Drowned God religion came from, even to the point of believing in a half-human race called the Deep Ones that left scattered pieces of their culture around Westeros, particularly the Iron Islands—or perhaps that they came from the other side of the Sunset Sea, the ocean to the West of Westeros. It's unclear if any of this might be relevant to the HBO series or the novels, but it all serves to reinforce the fact that the Ironborn are *weird* compared to the rest of the Seven Kingdoms.

The culture of the Ironborn involves choosing to keep, or reject, the "Old Way" of reaving and raiding. The "Old Way" is the idea that only physical prowess and violence should be rewarded—riches and salt wives acquired via raiding (aka "paying the iron price"), castles conquered by storming the walls instead of sieges, and so forth. The drive to reclaim the Old Way after being forced away from it by the Iron Throne has led to the Ironborn's drive for independence.

The Iron Islands themselves lie in the western part of Westeros, in Ironman's Bay, a body of water that helps create the Neck which divides the northern and southern parts of the continent. Because of this, the islands lie roughly equidistant from the Westerlands to the south, the Riverlands to the East, and the North to, uh, the north.

The capital of the Iron Islands is the citadel of Pyke, home of House Greyjoy, on the island of the same name. The largest of the islands is Great Wyk, followed by Harlaw. Several days' journey to the northwest is a small cluster of islands called the Lonely Lights, which are the westernmost lands in the known world.

House Greyjoy is the current ruling house of the Iron Islands, having taken over from House Hoare, who themselves displaced House Greyiron thousands of years before. Before that, kings were chosen by Kingsmoot, with the crown passed from family to family.

It's unclear where exactly the Ironborn came from. While most theories have them as First Men who simply traveled across the sea and started their own religion, their unique culture has led to theories like the Deep Ones, or that they came from the other side of the Sunset Sea. Once the Ironborn unified under a king and started attacking the mainland, they conquered several coastal regions and islands up and down the western side of Westeros. The coming of the Andals, who could build competitive ships and stronger fortifications, ended this era.

Not long before the Targaryen invasion, the kings of House Hoare even invaded the Riverlands, seizing it from the Storm Kings and declaring themselves the Kings of the Isles and the Rivers, a pretty excellent title.

However, the Hoares proved to be less than excellent rulers. They focused their time on the Riverlands, alienating the Ironborn, and oppressed the Riverlanders, leaving them open to rebellion. King Harren the Black attempted to create a massive fortress—Harrenhal—but he built it just as the Targaryens invaded, whose dragons rendered the castle's defenses irrelevant. The Riverlands rebelled, and King Harren and his sons were killed, ending House Hoare. Aegon invaded shortly after, ending Ironborn independence in exchange for allowing them to choose their new rulers: House Greyjoy.

The Greyjoys had a generally nervous alliance with the Iron Throne, with the Targaryens giving the religious and cultural independence in exchange for the Ironborn not raiding the Seven Kingdoms—instead they sailed to Essos. The major exception to this took place in the civil war called the Dance of the Dragons, when the Ironborn took advantage of the chaos to raid the Westerlands. In exchange, Lady Joanna Lannister counter-invaded and attempted to modernize the Ironborn, including reintroducing the Faith of the Seven. This ambitious plan failed, but was a reminder of House Greyjoy's relative weakness. The Greyjoys stayed loyal to the Targaryens during the Blackfyre Rebellions.

During Robert's Rebellion, the moderate and cautious Lord Quellon Greyjoy wished to remain neutral, but his sons, including his heir Balon, convinced him to join the war later on. Quellon was killed in a skirmish against Tyrell forces, leaving his son Balon, an aggressive reactionary, in charge.

Believing King Robert was weak following him taking the throne, Balon rebelled a few years later, disastrously. His navy was beaten, his castle stormed, and his adult sons killed. His remaining heir, the boy Theon Greyjoy, was taken as hostage and ward by Ned Stark.

But as *Game of Thrones* begins, Balon still wants independence for the Iron Islands. When war breaks out, he declares independence again, gaining the nickname "Twice-Crowned." Robb Stark sends the now-grown Theon Greyjoy to negotiate with Balon, offering an alliance against the Lannisters with both gaining their independence. But Balon, committed to the Old Way, feels he needs to pay the iron price for his crown, and instead attacks the coastal holdings of the King in the North.

Theon, desperate to prove his worth to his father and rejoin the culture of his heritage, launches an aggressive, doomed raid against Winterfell. His sister Yara, seemingly Balon's perfect heir, refuses to reinforce him, leaving him to hold Winterfell almost alone against an entire Bolton army. Instead he's captured and humiliated, and Winterfell is sacked.

When Robb Stark is murdered at the Red Wedding, seemingly ending the war in the North, the new Wardens of the North,

House Bolton, move to kick the Ironborn out of their castles. Ramsay Bolton uses his abused and brainwashed captive Theon Greyjoy to win back the most important of those castles, Moat Cailin. Balon and the rest of the Ironborn fall out of the narrative at this point until Season 6.

In the sixth season, Balon's brother Euron Greyjoy, a famous pirate, returns from his time in exile. He murders Balon and seizes the crown at the Kingsmoot from an alliance between Yara and Theon. They realize just how dangerous Euron is and flee, taking much of the Ironborn fleet, before he can kill them. The Greyjoy siblings go to Dany and negotiate an alliance: Yara will provide Daenerys with the fleet she needs to take her army to Westeros, and in exchange, the Iron Islands will have their independence so long as they do not reave the Seven Kingdoms.

Euron, meanwhile, seems to be well on his way to becoming Westeros' next big supervillain, perhaps even at Ramsay or Cersei levels. Both the novels and the show portray his rise in different ways, but both point at his nastiness. The novels, for example, don't have him killing Balon directly—it's unclear what killed the king exactly. But the show doesn't have Euron's crew showing off their magical artifacts, including Valyrian steel armor and a horn said to be able to control dragons. Euron also abuses his two brothers, both cut from the series, manipulating the warrior Victarion into trying to get Dany's dragons, and binding the priest Aeron Greyjoy to the prow of one of his boats as it sails.

Exactly what role Euron, Theon, Yara, the Ironborn, and the Drowned God have to play in the conclusion of *Game of Thrones* is unclear, but they're on the verge of being a key part in the massive confrontation to come.

42 House Baratheon and the Stormlands

Technically, the most important house in the War of the Five Kings is House Baratheon. The king whose death starts the war, as well as three of the kings in the civil war, and one of their successors, are legally part of House Baratheon. That's King Robert, his brothers Stannis and Renly, and his supposed sons Joffrey and Tommen. It's just that, oddly enough, we almost never see where the Baratheons are from, or hear them treated as a power in the way that "the Lannisters" or "the Starks" are.

Of course, the show, the characters, and fans treat Joffrey and Tommen as Lannisters, while Stannis and Renly battle over the Baratheon troops, with the leaders being given the titles—Stannis' navy, or Renly's army. So viewers may see House Baratheon less as a Westerosi superpower (which it is!) and more as a name attached to some important characters. But there's a lot of significance attached to House Baratheon, and the home in the Stormlands.

The Stormlands are one of the most important locations in Westeros, sitting in the center-east of the southern half of the continent. They're bordered by Dorne to the south, the Reach to the southwest, the Riverlands to the northwest, and the Crownlands to the north. The central location gives the region strategic value, and the Stormland armies are traditionally one of the strongest in Westeros—perhaps the strongest apart from the men of the North.

Game of Thrones has spent almost no time in the Stormlands. The only exception to this is early in the second season, when Stannis went to attack Renly's camp along the southern end of the Kingsroad. The scenes were shot in Northern Ireland, and successfully looked windswept and stormy, although no castles were shown. The capital of the Stormlands is the keep called Storm's End, which also serves as the southern end of the Kingsroad that leads all the way to the Wall.

The only major geographic feature of the region mentioned in *Game of Thrones* is the island of Tarth, the Sapphire Isle. Jaime Lannister uses this nickname to deceive the Bolton henchman Locke into believing Brienne's family is incredibly wealthy—but the sapphires refer only to the color of the water around the island, not the gemstones.

In addition to the Baratheons, three minor houses of the region play notable roles. House Tarth, of course, sends its daughter Brienne to become one of the show's most important characters. House Dondarrion's lord, Beric, is one of the best knights in the Seven Kingdoms, and the leader of the Brotherhood without Banners, which was seen most in Season 3. The greatest knight of the Seven Kingdoms, though, is Barristan the Bold of House Selmy, which hails from the region.

Other minor houses of the region include Connington, Estermont, Swann, and Penrose, though their members haven't made notable appearances on the show. The bastard surname for the region is the obvious choice "Storm." No characters on *Game of Thrones* are Storms, although in the novels, one of King Robert's sons, Edric, is taken by Stannis. Edric Storm's role as potential power source for Melisandre thanks to his king's blood is given to Gendry on the show, however.

Traditionally, the Southlands were ruled by House Durrandon, as the Storm Kings. The Storm Kings were one of the most aggressive houses in Westeros prior to the arrival of the Targaryens, conquering the Riverlands to create possibly the most powerful kingdom in Westeros—until the Ironborn took the Riverlands from them a few generations before Aegon's Conquest. The Storm Kings were still powerful but were defeated, and their last king, Argilac the Arrogant, was killed by the founder of House Baratheon.

The Baratheons are one of the youngest major houses in Westeros. Some of the Great Houses, like the Lannisters and Starks, led their lands for generations. Others, like the Tullys and Tyrells, were smaller houses that stepped up after the Targaryen conquest. But the Baratheons were new.

During the Targaryen invasion, Orys Baratheon was one of Aegon the Conqueror's chief generals and friends—and, eventually, his Hand. It was Orys who killed King Argilac, then wed the dead king's daughter, combining his line with the Durrandons. Orys was rumored to be a Targaryen bastard, although he had Baratheon black hair instead of Targaryen silver—but this all helped House Baratheon become considered one of the closest allies of the Targaryens.

In the Dance of the Dragons, the Baratheons chose the side of the seeming winner, Aegon II, but they were careful throughout, as Lord Borros Baratheon refused to fight dragons. He committed to the war at its very end, but his defeat led to Aegon II's death and the end of the civil war. The Baratheons also stayed loyal to the crown during the Blackfyre Rebellions.

House Baratheon played a crucial role in the succession crises that damaged the Targaryens a few generations before *Game of Thrones.* A daughter of the house was arranged to marry Prince Duncan, the heir to the throne. Instead Duncan married a common woman, Jenny of Oldstones, and removed himself from the succession. Lord Lyonel Baratheon was so angered by this that he declared independence before being killed. In order to make peace, King Aegon V arranged for his daughter Rhaelle to wed the new Baratheon lord, Ormund.

This decision was the last time a Targaryen wed outside the family and had children, which had a huge effect on the Seven Kingdoms—it gave the heirs of House Baratheon a claim on the throne, which Rhaelle and Ormund's grandson, King Robert, would eventually use.

Their son, and the father of Robert, Stannis, and Renly, was Lord Steffon, who became a member of the Mad King's Small Council. He and his wife were sent to Essos to find a wife for Prince Rhaegar Targaryen, but a storm destroyed their ship on their return to King's Landing, leaving the three young Baratheon sons orphaned. The new lord, Robert, was fostered with Lord Jon Arryn in the Vale alongside Ned Stark, who would become his best friend. Robert was also engaged to Ned's sister, Lyanna Stark.

When Lyanna was kidnapped by Prince Rhaegar, the Mad King executed her father and brother, leaving Ned the Stark lord. King Aerys demanded that Jon Arryn execute her brother Ned and fiancé Robert, but instead the three men raised their banners. A marriage alliance added House Tully to the group, and this group won Robert's Rebellion, with House Lannister joining at the end. Robert led the armies gloriously, but Stannis won an impressive victory as well, holding Storm's End safe from besieging Tyrell armies.

With Lyanna dead, Robert ended up marrying Lord Tywin Lannister's daughter, Cersei, an abusive and spite-filled marriage that nonetheless "held the kingdom together," at least for fifteen years. Robert showed very little interest in ruling, so his middle brother Stannis and Jon Arryn largely led the Seven Kingdoms in his name. Eventually his youngest brother, Renly, would also join the Small Council. Stannis was also given the old Targaryen citadel of Dragonstone, while Renly was made lord of Storm's End— which Stannis considered a slight.

Robert's marriage with Cersei would eventually produce three Baratheon children: Joffrey, Tommen, and Myrcella. However, the three were actually all born of the incestuous relationship between Cersei and her brother Jaime, making Stannis' daughter Shireen the only continuation of the true Baratheon line. Jon Arryn and Stannis Baratheon's discovery of this truth leads to Jon's death, and the start of the story of *Game of Thrones*.

House Baratheon has been arguably the biggest loser in the game of thrones, with disaster after disaster occurring in almost every season of the series. In the first, Ned's investigation into Jon Arryn's death leads to Cersei manipulating Robert to his death. Renly prepares to declare for the throne, leapfrogging his less likeable older brother, but Ned stays loyal to the law and Stannis—which leads to his execution.

In the second season, three of the claimants in the War of the Five Kings are Baratheons: Joffrey, although he is publicly accused of being product of incest, Stannis, and Renly. Thanks to his ownership of the Stormlands and a marriage with House Tyrell, Renly has the most powerful army in the realm. But he is assassinated by Stannis' sorceress, Melisandre, and Stannis takes most of the power of the Stormlands into his new army, though it is still defeated at the Battle of the Blackwater.

Joffrey is murdered during his marriage to Renly's former wife Margaery, who then marries King Tommen. Stannis takes his army north, saving the Night's Watch from a Wildling army and attacking the Lannister stooges of House Bolton to win back Ned's old lands. Trapped in the snow, he allows Melisandre to burn his daughter Shireen, which breaks the weather, but costs him so much of his army that he is easily defeated and killed—the end of the true Baratheon line. Myrcella and Tommen both follow him, the former murdered by vengeful Dornish, the later committing suicide after Cersei kills the entire court, including his wife.

What happens to the Stormlands during all this is unclear during the show. In the novels, many Stormland lords swear allegiance to Joffrey after the Battle of Blackwater, and Tyrell armies work to reclaim the land for the crown. The only holdout is Storm's End, still under siege even as Stannis' armies are far to the north.

Stannis is also still alive in the novels, so the Stormlands technically still have their liege lord. However, with his death, the Baratheons are legally extinct, and it's unclear who would actually become the new Lord Paramount. King Robert left behind many bastards in the novels, and at least Gendry on the show, so House Baratheon does still exist at some level—even if Gendry hasn't been seen in three seasons and is presumably still rowing the boat Ser Davos gave him. Either way, House Baratheon's glory years appear to be over for good.

43 House Tyrell and the Reach

The Reach is the southwestern region of Westeros and the home to House Tyrell. It is the most fertile and populous of the Seven Kingdoms and has the largest city in the land, Oldtown. Despite this, the Reach was the last major region to appear on *Game of Thrones,* only showing up on-screen in the sixth season, when Sam and Gilly travel to Oldtown. The Tyrells rule from the castle of Highgarden, while the macsters of the Seven Kingdoms are trained at the Citadel, in Oldtown—the closest thing the realm has to a university.

Despite not appearing much on the show, the major Houses of the Reach have enough power that they've played important roles on the civil wars wracking Westeros. House Tyrell (words: "Growing Strong") has several influential characters, including Lord Mace, Ser Loras, Queen Margaery, and the Queen of Thorns, Olenna Tyrell. One of their most powerful vassals is House Tarly, whose Lord, Randyll, sends his son Samwell to the Wall. Another minor vassal, House Florent, appears on the series in the service of Stannis Baratheon, husband of Selyse Florent.

Prior to the Targaryen conquest, the Kings of the Reach, House Gardener, ruled the region with relative stability. They came to trust the loyalty of House Tyrell, who acted as their stewards and grew in power alongside the Gardeners. After Aegon had conquered the Riverlands and the Stormlands, the Gardeners joined forces with the Lannisters and led a massive army against King's Landing. Aegon and his sisters turned their dragons on the two kings in what became known as the Field of Fire. The Gardener line was destroyed, and Aegon raised the Tyrells—who hadn't joined the attack—to Lords Paramount of the region, and Wardens of the South.

From then on, the Tyrells stayed either loyal to the Targaryens or neutral in the largest civil war, the Dance of the Dragons. They continued their loyalty when Robert Baratheon led the rebellion against the Mad King, and the Tyrells marched east against the Stormlands. Randyll Tarly and Mace Tyrell met Lord Robert at the Battle of Ashford on the border, and Lord Tarly's assault gave Robert his only defeat of the war.

After the battle, the forces of the Reach besieged Storm's End, where Stannis held the fort against them as Robert won the war at the Trident. When the Targaryens were defeated, the Tyrells surrendered and were pardoned by King Robert, although they were kept out of favor in Robert's court.

The Tyrells first appear on-screen in the first season, with the Knight of Flowers, Ser Loras Tyrell, winning the Tournament of the Hand. Loras also tells his lover, Robert's younger brother Renly, that he should be king—and he could count on the Tyrells' support if he did. (In the novels, Renly attempts to save the kingdom by pushing for Robert to divorce Cersei and marry Margaery, but events move too fast for this plot to move beyond the idea stage.)

When Robert dies, the Tyrells make their move. Renly weds Margaery, and the combined armies of the Stormlands and the Reach march against King's Landing, seemingly invincible. Stannis magically assassinates Renly, however, and adds the lords of the Stormlands to his ranks. Before the Tyrells withdraw, Petyr Baelish offers Margaery another chance to be a queen, setting up an alliance between House Tyrell and House Lannister.

This alliance wins the War of the Five Kings. Tyrell and Lannister forces arrive in the nick of time to save King's Landing from Stannis, and Margaery is engaged to Joffrey. Lady Olenna Tyrell, Margaery's grandmother, arrives in King's Landing to negotiate and plan the wedding. She and Margaery befriend Sansa Stark, from whom they learn that Joffrey is an abusive sadist. They also plan to wed Sansa to Ser Loras, who on the show is the heir to Highgarden. (In the novels, there are two other Tyrell children: Willas, in Highgarden, and Ser Garlan.) The Lannisters, however, get to Sansa first, marrying her to Tyrion and planning to wed Cersei to Ser Loras.

Lady Olenna and Littlefinger join forces to poison King Joffrey, leaving the more pliable King Tommen to marry Margaery. (Mace Tyrell also finally appears on the show, although he's played as an ineffectual buffoon compared to his mother and daughter.) With this wedding and Lord Tywin's death, the Tyrells become arguably the most powerful House in the realm.

The political battle for power between Margaery Tyrell and Cersei Lannister dominates King's Landing in the fifth and sixth seasons. Cersei initially gains the upper hand when she empowers the High Sparrow, who imprisons Loras for homosexuality and Margaery for defending him. Olenna, with Littlefinger's aid, strikes back, getting Cersei imprisoned for her incestuous relationship with Lancel Lannister, and accusations of worse.

In the sixth season, the free Lannisters and Tyrells find common cause, with Jaime and Mace preparing to assault the Sparrows until Margaery outmaneuvers them all. She claims to have been converted by the High Sparrow, and brings Tommen along with her, thus gaining her freedom. But she remains a prisoner of the Faith in practice, having to sneak a message of loyalty to her grandmother, who returns to the Reach for safety and power.

Margaery also only won herself time, as the High Sparrow plans a trial for her, Ser Loras, and Queen Mother Cersei. Loras confesses his crimes, and is stripped of his titles, leaving Highgarden without an heir. But before Margaery's trial can begin, she notices that Cersei isn't present, likely due to a trap. The High Sparrow doesn't believe her in time, and Cersei blows up the venue with wildfire, killing Margaery, Loras, and Mace, leaving the Tyrell family, on the show at least, effectively destroyed. The one survivor, Lady Olenna, is seen with the Martells in Dorne, seeking revenge—which Varys offers in the army of Daenerys Targaryen.

Late in the sixth season we also see Sam and Gilly travel to the Reach. First they meet Sam's family at Horn Hill, where Lord Randyll attempts to bully his son once again. Sam and Gilly steal the family sword and flee. They arrive at Oldtown and Sam begins his training to become a maester.

In the novels, Lord Tarly has a significantly larger role, meeting Brienne several times, defeating a Northern army at the Battle of Duskendale, and being considered for Hand after Tywin's death. Several other Houses have notable roles but don't appear on the show, House Rowan, House Redwyne, and House Hightower being some of the most prominent.

The fate of House Tyrell and the Reach may be up in the air as *Game of Thrones* moves forward, but unlike most other realms, we'll also be seeing and learning more about it, thanks to Samwell and Gilly's presence in Oldtown.

44 House Martell and Dorne

Dorne itself is a relatively harsh, arid land, largely surrounded by the Narrow Sea. George R.R. Martin has stated that he built it on Spanish, Palestinian, and Welsh influences. Dorne is also famous for high-quality wine.

House Martell rules Dorne, with the words "Unbowed, Unbent, Unbroken." Alone among major Houses, they don't take the title of Lord, but instead Prince—hence Dorne is ruled by Prince Doran Martell at the start of *Game of Thrones*. They have this custom based on the culture of the Rhoynar, an ethnic group that had previously lived on the banks of the massive river Rhoyne in Essos.

When the Rhoynar were defeated by the Valyrians, a large group of their refugees fled to Westeros, where their warrior queen, Nymeria, married into House Martell, who then conquered Dorne. (Arya Stark, a fan of warrior women, named her direwolf Nymeria.) Dorne was also the only land in the Seven Kingdoms not to immediately submit to the Targaryen conquest, despite being arguably the least powerful in both numbers and economy.

When the dragons came, the Dornish hid; when the Targaryen armies came, they fought guerrilla wars that pushed the would-be conquerors out. It was only by marriage that Dorne was integrated into the Seven Kingdoms, over a century and a half after the initial conquest.

It is marriage again that brings Dorne into the story of *Game of Thrones*. The Targaryens were famous for marrying incestually amongst themselves, but only rarely married lords of the Seven Kingdoms. Prince Rhaegar, however, had no sisters, and no Valyrians of noble birth and the proper age could be found in

Essos, so he wed Elia Martell, sister to Prince Doran and Oberyn Martell.

This kept House Martell loyal to the Targaryens in Robert's Rebellion, and their armies marched with Prince Rhaegar to his defeat at the Trident. In the aftermath of the battle, Tywin Lannister's army sacked King's Landing, and Lord Tywin sent the Mountain to kill Rhaegar's babies in order to prove his loyalty. Ser Gregor also raped and killed Elia Martell in his bloodlust—something the Dornish remembered for years.

Because of their disgust at the end of the rebellion, and Robert's mistrust of the Great Houses who fought against him, like the Tyrells, the Martells stayed out of the politics of King's Landing for a generation. Dorne's mention plays a major role in the second season, when Tyrion, as Hand of the King, attempts to both lay a trap for his sister's spy on the Small Council and arrange an alliance by marrying Princess Myrcella to Prince Trystane of Dorne. His plan works, Pycelle is revealed as the spy, and Myrcella is sent to Dorne, although still no Dornishmen appear. It's only when King Robert dies, and the wedding between Joffrey and Margaery is set in the fourth season, that a Martell returns to King's Landing.

That Martell is Oberyn, the Red Viper, brother to Prince Doran and Princess Elia. He is a famously passionate man in both love and combat, where his use of poison has given him the nickname of the "Red Viper." Oberyn also brings his paramour, Ellaria Sand. Beyond representing Dorne in the capital, Oberyn has another goal: to find and kill those responsible for his sister's death. Despite that, the man believed responsible, Tywin Lannister, still attempts to recruit Oberyn to the Small Council because Tywin knows Daenerys has dragons, and the Dornish had successfully resisted Targaryen dragons before.

Oberyn sees the chance to get information and revenge when Tyrion Lannister demands trial by combat for Joffrey's death, and his opponent is Elia's murderer, Gregor Clegane. Oberyn takes

Tyrion's cause, but instead of merely fighting to kill Clegane, he wants to beat him and force a confession of Tywin's guilt. The Viper's single-minded desire for revenge leaves an opening for Clegane to grab him and crush his skull in front of Ellaria, Tyrion, and the entire court.

After Oberyn's death, Dorne becomes an important location in both the fifth season of the show and the fourth book, *A Feast for Crows.* Unfortunately, Dorne was one of the biggest problems in that novel, with a sudden focus on previously unimportant characters like Arianne Martell, Arys Oakhart, Areo Hotah, and Gerold "Darkstar" Dayne, all fighting over Princess Myrcella. While these characters could be interesting—especially Arianne—in general the whole storyline felt like a distraction from the characters we care about.

So when *Game of Thrones* sent two of those characters that we care about, Jaime Lannister and Bronn of the Blackwater, to Dorne instead of the no-name Kingsguard of the novels, it seemed like an opportunity to remedy the mistakes of the novels. But those hopes were quickly dashed: instead of improving on the books, the Dornish plot of the fifth season is widely regarded as the worst thing *Game of Thrones* ever did.

The premise has promise: Princess Myrcella and her fiancé, Prince Trystane, have a budding romance, overseen by Trystane's father, Doran Martell. But Ellaria Sand and Oberyn's daughters, the Sand Snakes, want revenge, and send a message to Cersei at King's Landing threatening Myrcella. (The Sand Snakes are so named because bastards in Dorne take the surname "Sand" and they are the Red Viper's daughters.) Cersei sends Jaime to rescue Myrcella, and Jaime brings along Bronn, who's switched loyalties to the Lannisters more generally after Tyrion's murder conviction and exile.

So there's a good, *Game of Thrones*–style political conflict of three different factions, with charming leaders at their heads, all wanting control over Princess Myrcella. The problem is that this storyline is largely resolved in a single scene in the Water Palace, home of the Martells: Ellaria and the Sand Snakes attempt to kidnap Myrcella for their schemes at the same time as Bronn and Jaime try to launch their rescue. The two fight, Myrcella doesn't want to go anyway, and Doran's men, led by Areo Hotah, capture everyone involved.

And that's...pretty much it. The storyline just fizzles after that. Jaime and Ellaria are taken to the palace, where they promise Doran that they'll be good, Bronn and the Sand Snakes are in a bad prison where Tyene Sand toys with Bronn's sexual interest, and in the end, Myrcella and Trystane get on a ship with Jaime to return to King's Landing.

As they leave, however, two things happen. Ellaria kisses Myrcella, poisoning her so that the princess dies on the voyage, betraying her promise to Doran. Second, Tyene Sand tells Bronn "You want a good girl, but you need the bad pussy," which is easily the worst line in all of *Game of Thrones*, but it's so awful it ends up also being maybe the best quote from the show.

The core problem with the storyline? There's no real twist. Doran plays his role, Ellaria plays hers, Jaime plays his, and they don't change. Nothing about the Season 5 Dornish storyline is in any way ambiguous, and it ends up being essentially meaningless.

In the novels, the story is quite different. Arianne Martell, Doran's oldest daughter and his heir according to Dornish law, which treats women and men as equal in the succession, discovers a letter where he treats the middle child, Quentyn, as his successor in Dorne. Arianne launches the coup, is defeated by Areo Hotah, and Myrcella is disfigured. But what Arianne discovers from her father is that the reason she was bypassed for Dorne is that Doran had secretly allied with the Targaryen exiles in Essos: Arianne was supposed to wed Viserys Targaryen, and the Dornish armies would be the first to join the reconquest.

In the sixth season, *Game of Thrones* realizes its mistakes with Dorne and simply adopts the simplest possible route to fixing the story: it kills everyone. Ellaria kills Doran and Trystane and apparently takes the throne. And in the sixth season finale, they align with Lord Varys and Lady Olenna in joining Dany's armies for revenge. Even without Arianne and Quentyn, *Game of Thrones* still finds a way to make the Martell-Targaryen alliance happen.

While there are only a couple quick scenes of the Water Palace, there's more Dorne to be seen in the sixth season—although it's not in the present. Bran Stark's visions shows when his father went to Dorne, to find his sister at the Tower of Joy. There, Ned fights the Kingsguard Ser Arthur Dayne, a Dornishman, and there he discovers his dying sister and her newborn son.

45 Beyond-the-Wall and the Wildlings

The final region of Westeros is the only one never included in the Seven Kingdoms: the lands Beyond-the-Wall. This is a wild, untamed region, too far north for regular agriculture, and only rarely politically united by a King-Beyond-the-Wall. The humans who reside in the far North are considered "Wildlings" by those to the south, although they prefer the term "Free Folk."

Beyond-the-Wall is also the last consistent home of magic in the Seven Kingdoms. Human practitioners of magic, particularly wargs, who project their minds into animal bodies, are well-known in the region. It's also the home of direwolves, giants, the last remaining Children of the Forest—and the White Walkers.

There are a few different regions Beyond-the-Wall. Directly facing the Wall itself is the Haunted Forest, where most of the scenes in the show take place—it's where Craster's Keep is located, for example. To the east lies the Shivering Sea, with Storrold's Point jutting out into the ocean. This is the location of Hardhome, where the remnants of Mance's army flee after his defeat, and where Jon goes to negotiate with them.

To the west are the Frostfang Mountains, glacial and foreboding. The Fist of the First Men, a hill with the remnants of an ancient fort, sits between the Haunted Forest and Frostfangs. It's there that the Night's Watch makes their camp, while Jon Snow and Qhorin Halfhand head into the Frostfangs to scout the Wildling Army. They travel via Skirling Pass into the Frostfangs.

And that's really about it for the relevant, known regions Beyond-the-Wall. Beyond the Frostfangs lie the ominously titled Lands of Always Winter, reputed to be the home of the White Walkers. Deep in the Haunted Forest lie the lands of the Thenns, who consider themselves the last true First Men. Most everything else is shrouded in rumor and mystery.

The history of the region is also shrouded in myth and legend. The biggest invasions in Westerosi history all left their mark Beyond-the-Wall, that much is known. The First Men helped push the fantastic creatures and Children of the Forest into the far North.

This led the Children to create the White Walkers, who rampaged across Westeros in the Long Night (see Chapter 48), until the Children and the beginnings of the Night's Watch defeated the White Walkers, and Bran the Builder put up the Wall to ensure that the Seven Kingdoms would have a defense against another Long Night.

It wasn't long after that when the first King-Beyond-the-Wall, Joramun, is said to have risen. He both fought against the southerners and is said to have joined with them in order to defeat the corrupt Lord Commander of the Night's Watch, known as the

Night's King (who may or may not be the same as the villain of *Game of Thrones*).

Several other Kings-Beyond-the-Wall united the tribes and attacked the southlands, and all were turned back either by the Night's Watch or the Starks and the lords of the North. These were rare events, but the last one before Mance was less than a hundred years prior, when Raymun Redbeard managed to cross the Wall and was defeated by the Umbers and Starks, led by Ned's great-grandfather, Lord Willam.

The King-Beyond-the-Wall is not a hereditary position, but one that only comes when a strong enough personality manages to talk and fight his way into the role. Mance Rayder, the latest, holds his army together by sheer force of personality—as well as sheer force, supposedly having defeated the Magnar of the Thenns three times to convince them to join. Jon Snow realizes this, which is why, at the Battle of Castle Black, he believes that assassinating Mance is the only way to stop the invasion.

Jon fails, but Stannis Baratheon shows up in the nick of time, capturing Mance and dispersing his army. Following this, Jon joins with Mance's lieutenant Tormund Giantsbane to attempt to unite the Wildlings, not as King-Beyond-the-Wall, but as Lord Commander of the Night's Watch, offering them land in exchange for an alliance. The difficulty Jon has during the negotiations at Hardhome ought to show just how much work it takes to become King-Beyond-the-Wall.

Mance's death has left Tormund Giantsbane as the most influential Wildling leader left, and the most important on the show. There have been other major Wildling characters, but most are dead.

The first we meet is Osha, a Wildling woman who joins a group of bandits that attempt to kidnap Bran Stark. They're defeated, and Osha is taken prisoner. She does befriend her captors, however, and eventually leads the youngest Stark children to freedom.

Osha also serves as a Cassandra figure, telling everyone of the true threat of the White Walkers while none believe her. She refuses to return Beyond-the-Wall with Bran, instead taking refuge with the Umbers. She's killed when the new lord of House Umber, the Smalljon, decides that his hatred of Wildlings trumps his support of the Starks, and gives her to Ramsay Bolton.

Early in the second season we meet another Wildling woman, Gilly, one of Craster's daughter-wives. While the "Free Folk" often describe their way of life as far preferable to that of the southlands, Gilly's story shows that it's just as or more cruel. Craster rules his women with an iron fist, bedding all of them, then their daughters, then presumably a third generation. The boys, meanwhile, are left in the woods to die—although it becomes clear that it's actually that he's negotiated a treaty with the White Walkers. Gilly escapes when Craster is murdered and spends the rest of the series with Samwell Tarly, slowly becoming acclimated to life in the south

Finally there's Ygritte, still the most important of the Wildlings. It is Ygritte who shows Jon Snow the temptations of freedom that Beyond-the-Wall can offer. Choosing his lord, meeting giants, gender equality, and most importantly for a teen boy, not having vows of celibacy. The extroverted Ygritte is a force of nature for the repressed Jon Snow, very nearly converting him away from his mission to scout Mance's forces.

But their romance comes to an end when they, too, show the limitations of Wildling "freedom." Their raiding party Beyond-the-Wall is supposed to sow terror, which even the good Wildlings, like Tormund and Ygritte, are more than willing to do. Jon, however, cannot, and flees back to the Watch. Ygritte continues, and her role in the destruction of a nearby village ends up dooming her: a surviving boy, Olly, takes up a bow in the Battle of Castle Black and kills her with an arrow.

At the end of the sixth season, Jon Snow has taken back the North with an army that includes all the Wildling fighters he's brought south of the Wall. Although presumably individuals still live Beyond-the-Wall, the destruction of Hardhome has apparently destroyed any political power of Wildling groups in the far North. Whatever their future entails seems to hinge entirely on Jon Snow, Tormund Giantsbane, and the reborn Stark kingdom. But the White Walkers threaten them as well as *Game of Thrones* heads to its conclusion.

46 The Night's Watch

The Night's Watch originally stood to prevent another White Walker invasion, but the White Walkers, with the possible exception of the Night's King early in the Watch's history (see Chapter 48), never appeared again. Instead the Watch has served primarily to fight the Wildlings from Beyond-the-Wall, with their occasional invasions and constant threat of raids.

A simple system, repeated through the show and especially the novels, shows the priority of the Night's Watch. They use a system of horn blows to grab everyone's attention. A single horn blow means that a ranger has returned—it's about maintaining the institution. Two blows mean a Wildling attack, the most common danger the Watch faces. Three blows of the horn means a White Walker attack, and hasn't been heard for generations. Thus when it's heard by the Great Ranging on the Fist of the First Men at the end of the second season, it's an utterly shocking event, and one the Watch is unprepared for.

At the start of *Game of Thrones*, the Night's Watch is deep into a long, slow decline. There were once nineteen castles on the Wall, but now only three are actually manned. This is, perhaps, a fairly expected development for an order that consists entirely of men whose oaths render them, at least officially, celibate.

Thus the Night's Watch tends to have two kinds of recruits. The first are criminals, who've picked the Watch over being punished for their crimes—like rapists picking the Wall over being gelded. The criminals can be highborn—Ser Alliser Thorne, who served the Targaryens in Robert's Rebellion and was sent to the Wall after his side lost, is one. But many are lowborn, like Jon's friends Grenn and Pyp, or their rival in their class, Rast, who eventually murders Jeor Mormont in the third-season mutiny.

The second batch of recruits tends to be nobles seeking honor. These are usually younger sons, like Benjen Stark or Ser Waymar Royce, the knight who dies in the very first scene of *Game of Thrones*. It also occasionally includes lords or knights who seek to serve in the end of their lives, like Jeor Mormont.

Lord Commander of the Night's Watch is the leader of the group. Despite the feudal nature of the rest of Westeros, the Lord Commander is chosen for life by direct democracy: one man, one vote. In the novels this requires a two-thirds majority, but on the show, it's depicted as the most votes winning.

Jeor Mormont is the 997th Lord Commander of the Night's Watch, with Jon Snow, his successor, the 998th. With Jon tossing his cloak to Dolorous Edd to become the 999th Lord Commander, and the White Walker army bearing down on the southlands over the course of the series, it seems like the near-roundness of that number may be important: we may see a massively important 1,000th Lord Commander.

The members of the Night's Watch are divided into three groups. The Rangers are the class that earns the most glory; they are the ones who go Beyond-the-Wall and explore, trade, and fight with the Wildlings. The Builders are responsible for maintenance of the Wall and its castles. The Stewards are responsible for maintaining the people of the Night's Watch. Jon Snow, expecting to be a Ranger, is disappointed when he's named a Steward, until Samwell Tarly explains to him that he was put in that position to train under Jeor Mormont to become his successor.

After Jon's assassination by his own men, he's resurrected by Melisandre. Jon executes his murderers, but, realizing that the Watch is insufficient as an institution to create an army that can fight back against the dead, leaves the Watch. He tosses his commander's cloak to his surviving friend and loyalist Dolorous Edd, and departs.

The focus of *Game of Thrones* shifts away from the Wall to the North itself as Jon and Sansa campaign to retake it and build an army that way. It says a lot about the Night's Watch that even its greatest remaining characters, Sam and Jon, have almost totally left it behind. The handful of characters remaining at the Wall don't even appear in the rest of the season. But certainly they will at some point, for the White Walkers are coming. Whether the Night's Watch can put up a fight against their sworn enemies, however, is still up for debate.

47 The White Walkers

Game of Thrones starts with a promise. The very first scene of the series shows three Night's Watch Rangers traveling out into the wilderness Beyond-the-Wall and uncovering...something. A pile of bodies. A White Walker. A resurrected child. And the idea is born that the walking corpses of the North are the ultimate enemy, the one that everyone needs to pay attention to.

Well, eventually. As *Game of Thrones* got bigger and bigger, telling the stories of people all across the world, the role of the

The flash actually scrambles White Walkers' circuits. (Photo courtesy of Apaydin Alain/ABACA/Newscom)

White Walkers got relatively smaller. There they are, sitting in the North, biding their time until winter comes and they can actually start kicking some ass. Sure, they had a little fun Beyond-the-Wall, like when they attacked the Night's Watch at the end of Season 2. But for a long time it seemed like that early-season promise made by *Game of Thrones* was forgotten.

Then "Hardhome" happened, toward the end of Season 5. What looked to be another difficult political negotiation, with Jon Snow trying and only partially succeeding at convincing the Wildlings to align with him, turns on a dime. The Night's King, surrounded by several White Walker lieutenants, leads an army of wights to attack the Wildling refuge. The battle that ensues is a desperate attempt to save as many people as possible and avoid a total massacre, which Jon Snow barely manages. But at the end of the episode, the Night's King raises his arms, and all the dead in the battle slowly come to their feet, rebuilding the army of the undead.

When Jon Snow returns to the Seven Kingdoms, having seen the awful power of *Game of Thrones'* northern supervillain, he's murdered by his Crow brothers, but resurrected. Over the course of the sixth season, Jon rises to power in the North and becomes the first political leader in the land to actually take the threat of the White Walkers seriously.

But what exactly are the White Walkers, and who is the Night's King? If you read the novels, for one thing, you'll find out that they're not even the White Walkers most of the time. They're given the name "the Others." That got changed in the show because, well, you can't capitalize "others" when you say it, so people couldn't tell that the Others were special—hence the switch to White Walkers, a secondary name for the beings.

As to what they are? Well, that's not entirely clear. There are two forms of undead. The first are wights, which are near-mindless zombies/skeletons who serve as the grunts for the undead army.

Then there are the White Walkers, who seem to be the leaders of the horde. They're tall and icy, with deep blue eyes as well as long white hair and beards. They also have both intelligence and powers—they're shown taking one of Craster's babies and turning him into one of them, for example. And almost every time a White Walker is shown in battle, he (always male, at least visually) crushes his opponents, shattering steel blades and tossing humans around with ease.

We've only seen two exceptions to this near-invincibility. At the end of Season 3, Sam and Gilly are attacked by a White Walker, who easily swipes Sam aside after shattering his sword. In desperation, Sam attacks with the only weapon he has left, a dragonglass (obsidian) knife recovered from a hidden stash in the North. It works: the White Walker shatters almost instantly. Likewise, at Hardhome, Jon Snow duels a Walker who attempts to destroy Jon's sword. But the sword, Longclaw, is made of Valyrian steel, which holds, and with which Jon destroys the White Walker.

What do dragonglass and Valyrian steel have in common? Both are directly associated with dragons, and fire has also been demonstrated to work against the wights. So it's no secret that most fans expect Daenerys' dragons to be the hard counter to the power of the White Walkers—but somehow I can't imagine it'll be easy for her and her allies to defeat the army of the undead.

48 The Night's King and the Long Night

"The true enemy won't wait out the storm. He brings the storm."—Jon Snow

It's unclear exactly how much power and autonomy the White Walkers have, but one thing is clear: they serve a powerful magician, the Night's King. For all we can see, the Night's King is the big bad guy of *Game of Thrones,* the final, greatest threat to all Westeros.

He, too, is shrouded in mystery and confusion, but in the sixth season, we learned far more about him and the origin of the White Walkers. Bran Stark, learning how to fully use his magical Sight, ventures deep into the past, where he sees the origin of the White Walkers.

A group of the elf-like beings called the Children of the Forest stands in a spiral pattern around a chained, hanging man. One of the Children—Bran's friend Leaf—is shown driving a dragonglass shard into the man's chest, turning him into the first White Walker. It's not explicitly stated that this is the Night's King, but the actor who portrays the imprisoned man is the same as the Night's King. The spiral formation that the Children utilize is also the same pattern as the collection of corpses in the very first scene of *Game of Thrones,* which is both an interesting long-term plan by the show and a neat callback.

Leaf defends the decision by saying that the Children were desperate, and being slaughtered, so they had to do something. She's referring to the original invasion of Westeros by the First Men, who crossed the Narrow Sea from Essos and eventually began to battle the previous inhabitants of Westeros, the Children.

This is a fairly common human-elf narrative in fantasy, going back at least to Tolkien: the arrival of Man, with his technology and warfare, disrupts and destroyed the more powerful and natural, but less plentiful, elves. But these Children fought back with a curse that eventually backfired. For Leaf's part, the decision costs her her life thousands of years later, when the Night's King attacks the Three-Eyed Raven's home and she sacrifices herself to allow Bran to get away.

That backfiring becomes known as the "Long Night," a legendary apocalypse in the history of Westeros, from before even the Andal invasion. The details of this are unclear, but the core of the story is simple: in the worst winter in all of Westeros, the White Walkers invaded, destroying everyone they could find, both human and Children.

But when they found that obsidian weapons could defeat the White Walkers, the Children and a group of humans allied and defeated the undead at the "Battle for the Dawn." This ended the Long Night and created an alliance between the Children and the new Night's Watch, but as the Children faded away, so did the alliance. The Watch was supposed to guard against the White Walkers, but with one exception, the Others never came.

That exception is part of the confusion of the role and name of the Night's King. In the novels, the name "Night's King" is used to refer to a very specific individual: the thirteenth Lord Commander of the Night's Watch, who falls in love with an icy sorceress, declares himself king, and makes sacrifices to the White Walkers. Only a joint alliance between the Starks and the King-Beyond-the-Wall finally defeats that Night's King.

But is this same figure from the books the being leading the White Walkers on the show? That seems unclear. His first appearance, corrupting Craster's baby in the fourth season, is the first time his name appeared on the show as the Night's King in accidentally released documents. In the fifth season, the showrunners started calling him the "Night King," a term that came into use in the show in the sixth season.

It's possible that the producers of *Game of Thrones* just liked the name, and gave a variation of it to a different character. Alternately, they may have diverged wildly from the novels and created a totally different origin for their lead villain. Or maybe everyone's just making it up as they go along.

Another point of mystery—or confusion—is the origin of the ranger "Coldhands," who helps Bran and Meera survive after the fall of the Three-Eyed Raven. Apart from the Night's King, Coldhands is the only one of the undead to demonstrate free will and personality. He's also the former Benjen Stark, killed by a White Walker and brought back by the Children of the Forest shoving a dragonglass dagger into his chest, just like the Night's King. But why is Coldhands still given human motivation, while the Night's King isn't?

Coldhands' role is also much bigger in the books, where he meets Samwell Tarly and then joins Bran on his journey to the Three-Eyed Raven. His mysterious nature and importance led many fans to speculate that he was Benjen, a theory that became roughly as widely believed as R+L=J—right up until someone found a copy of George

R.R. Martin's drafts where an editor asks if he's Benjen and Martin replies with a firm "No!" So are there multiple Coldhands? Is the show just taking a convenient shortcut? Or is there some strange, longer game tying the White Walkers, Coldhands, the Children of the Forest, and the Night's King together?

Regardless of the current mysteries, the Night's King—or Night King—stands as the greatest threat to Westeros, and Jon Snow is the only leader to realize this. It isn't just winter coming: it's a new Long Night.

49 Essos and the Rest of the World

Although most of *Game of Thrones'* action takes place in Westeros, we've had six seasons of Daenerys in Essos, and more and more characters visiting the continent in later seasons. If Westeros serves as a medieval Western Europe analogue, Essos is the Mediterranean and Asia. It's worth taking a look at the general geography of the continent and beyond.

While Westeros is a north-south rectangle generally, Essos is primarily shaped along an east-west axis. Essos is huge—and much of it plays no significant role in Game of Thrones, so this is by no means a comprehensive survey of the continent. For *Game of Thrones*, only the western and southern coasts of the continent, plus the Dothraki Sea, have been essential.

Essos is bound by the Shivering Sea to the north and the Summer Sea to the south. The Narrow Sea separates it from Westeros, and far, far, far to the east lies the Jade Sea.

The Free Cities face the southeastern part of Westeros. These are Mediterranean-style independent commercial hubs, each filled with merchants and bankers. Thanks to their proximity to Westeros, they've been influential in the politics of the Seven Kingdoms, for example, allying with one side in the Targaryen civil war called the Dance of the Dragons, or serving as a home for exiles like Daenerys and Viserys Targaryen.

There are nine Free Cities. Braavos has been portrayed on *Game of Thrones* the most, serving as home to both the Iron Bank and the Faceless Men, and as such appeared regularly in Seasons 4–6.

Two other Free Cities that appear are Pentos, home of Illyrio Mopatis, who hosted Daenerys in the premiere as well as Tyrion and Varys in Season 5. There's also Volantis, home of Talisa Maegyr, and the furthest southeast of the Free Cities. It appeared in a couple of scenes as a brothel in later seasons where Westerosi seeking Daenerys ended up: Tyrion was kidnapped by Jorah in Volantis, and Theon and Yara stayed there on their journey to Slaver's Bay in Season 6. Volantis is also a slave city, closest of the Free Cities to Slaver's Bay, and helped fund the Sons of the Harpy.

Two other of the Free Cities sit near Westeros, and are mentioned in *Game of Thrones*. Myr is the home of the red priest Thoros of Myr, and also where Varys was castrated. Lys is Varys' birthplace, according to Oberyn Martell's reading of the Spider's accent. It's famous for its pleasure houses—Dany's handmaiden Doreah, who taught her the art of seduction, came from Lys.

The city of Tyrosh, on the far southwest edge of Essos, is barely mentioned on *Game of Thrones*, although it is the home of Daario Naharis. Tyrosh is closest to Westeros, and connected to it via a set of islands in the Narrow Sea called the Stepstones. In the War of the Ninepenny Kings, the last of the Blackfyre Rebellions, a Blackfyre pretender named Maelys the Monstrous took over Tyrosh and many of the Stepstones, threatening an invasion of Westeros. A Targaryen army invaded, and Barristan the Bold killed Maelys in single combat.

The last three free Cities are Lorath, Norvos, and Qohor. These are all deeper in Essos, and play no significant part in either the show, novels, or the history of the Seven Kingdoms.

The inland part of the Free Cities region is dominated by the Rhoyne, the largest river in the known world. Branches of it reach out almost as far as Braavos in the far northwest, draining into the Summer Sea at Volantis. This is the massive river that Talisa describes to Robb Stark in explaining how a healer saved her brother's life when all the children of Volantis would play in it. In the fifth novel, much of Tyrion's journey to Slaver's Bay takes place on a ship headed down the Rhoyne, although this isn't shown on *Game of Thrones*. Dornish culture is, in part, so different from the rest of the Seven Kingdoms because it was settled by Rhoynar refugees fleeing Valyrian conquest.

The Rhoyne largely divides the Free Cities from the rest of the continent. The central section of Essos is the plains known as the Dothraki Sea, where hordes of Mongol-like Dothraki khalasars move and occasionally raid the rich cities around them. The Dothraki Sea is massive—like the steppes of Asia combined with Russia, dominating the entire central, northern, and eastern parts of Essos apart from the southern coasts. The Dothraki's only city, their religious capital of Vaes Dothrak, lies far to the east of the Sea.

Just east of Volantis and south of the Dothraki sea is Valyria—or what was Valyria. A huge peninsula, jutting into the Summer Sea, Valyria forms the western boundary to Slaver's Bay.

Valyria is in many ways the Rome of *Game of Thrones*, the home of a nearly world-spanning empire whose culture everyone else's is derived from—before it collapsed. The chief reason for its power is its dragons, which were found by Valyrians and eventually became the backbone of the world power called the Valyrian Freehold. The Valyrians founded the Free Cities as colonies and conquered much of the rest of the continent, even reaching Dragonstone in Westeros. Their conquests also led to major refugees, including

Queen Nymeria leading her people to Dorne, and possibly also the Andal invasion of Westeros.

And then, roughly 400 years before *Game of Thrones*, Valyria collapsed. The Doom of Valyria, a massive, possibly magical seismic event of volcanos and earthquakes, destroyed the entire peninsula, empire, Valyrians, and their dragons in a single day. The only exceptions were the Targaryens, who, based on a prophetic dream, had fled years before to Dragonstone with a handful of dragons.

Exactly what caused the Doom of Valyria is unclear. No magic in *Game of Thrones* seems to be anywhere near having that much power, and in the novels it's treated as a historical event more than a mystery to be solved. Which isn't to say that the end of *Game of Thrones* might not have that revelation, just that it doesn't seem necessary.

Valyria, or what's left of it, does appear on *Game of Thrones*, after Jorah captures Tyrion. He sails with the Imp through the Doom in order to avoid pirates, but the Stone Men, exiled to no man's land, attack. Jorah contracts the disease greyscale, but the two do survive.

They reach the eastern side of Slaver's Bay, the region of Essos best documented by *Game of Thrones*. The three oldest, richest cities of Essos are there: Astapor, Yunkai, and Meereen. All fall to Daenerys Targaryen in her war of emancipation and she settles down to rule in Meereen. Astapor and Yunkai, however, join with Volantis in resisting her. East of Slaver's Bay and inland a bit is the region of the Lhazarene, the "Lamb People" raided by Khal Drogo's khalasar toward the end of Season 1, leading to Drogo's death.

The culture of Slaver's Bay is "Ghiscari," the remnants of the empire of Ghis, which ruled the area. Along the coast to the southeast of Slaver's Bay, two Ghiscari nations remain: Old Ghis on the mainland, and New Ghis on a large island facing it.

Beyond Ghis is the far southeast boundary of what we've seen in *Game of Thrones*, the city of Qarth. A port city that has become wealthy by connecting western Essos to the lands further to east, Qarth is also protected by the brutal desert known as the Red Waste. Daenerys Targaryen found herself in Qarth in Season 2 and did not much enjoy the experience.

North of Qarth, at the eastern edge of the Dothraki Sea, are the Bone Mountains, which separate the unknown of eastern Essos from the known world of the west. There are two prominent locations farther east. The land of Yi Ti, which appears to be *Game of Thrones'* China, lies east of Qarth, and in some legends was home to many of the battles against the original White Walkers during the Long Night.

And beyond that lies the absolute edge of the known world, the city of Asshai. Asshai is ruled by warlocks and famous for its magic. Its particular practice is called "shadowbinding," the use of light and shadow for power. Unsurprisingly, Melisandre is from Asshai, and demonstrates the use of that power. Mirri Maz Duur trained in Asshai as well. Beyond Asshai is only known as the Shadow Lands, from which Illyrio Mopatis is supposed to have acquired the dragon eggs he gifted Daenerys for her wedding.

There are few other known locations in the world of *Game of Thrones*. To the south of the Free Cities, in the Summer Sea, are the Summer Islands. These are known as the home of black-skinned people in Westeros. Xaro Xhoan Daxos, Missandei, and Grey Worm all say they hail from the Summer Isles originally before arriving in Essos. Two other continents or islands can be seen on maps of the world, called Sothoryos, south of Slaver's Bay, and Ulthos, near Asshai.

50 The Dragons of Valyria

The biggest sign that *Game of Thrones* is fantasy? The dragons. Sure, the ice zombies are cool and all, but nothing in the universe screams "fantasy!" more than a flying, fire-breathing lizard. But dragons aren't common in the world of *Game of Thrones*. Far from it. Daenerys' dragons, hatched at the end of the first season, are the first dragons in 150 years. And for the rest of the world, this is both terrifying and seductive.

It's terrifying because dragons are, essentially, the nuclear bombs of Westeros and Essos. If you have them, and your opponent doesn't, you win. Aegon the Conqueror landed an army of a little over a thousand men on the shores of Westeros, but because he and his sisters rode three dragons, they conquered the Seven Kingdoms (save Dorne) with relative ease. But if both sides have dragons, well, then wars would become epic tragedies, like the Dance of the Dragons, the Targaryen civil war that bled the kingdom dry for decades and led directly to the dragons' extinction.

But it's also seductive because the dragons represent uncontrolled power. In some cases, this is direct: if you can ride a dragon, or control a person who does, you hold immense power. There's more to it than that, though. The rebirth of the dragons is also described by multiple characters as a rebirth of their magic. The warlocks of Qarth, previously viewed as charlatans, had enough power to make an attempt to take control of the city. The pyromancers of King's Landing, at the same time, suddenly found their ability to make wildfire vastly improved, something that could only happen if dragons returned.

The rest of the world is wise to be wary of the dragons' power, as the example of Old Valyria proves. Valyria, a peninsula of Essos, was nondescript in most ways until its residents managed to find the secret to taming the local dragons. From this, they managed to create an empire known as the Valyrian Freehold, burning all who opposed them. (One group of defeated people from the river Rhoyne fled all the way to Westeros led by Queen Nymeria and joined with the Dornish.)

The Valyrian Freehold wasn't a single political entity, but something closer to the Athenian empire of the ancient Mediterranean, where a series of politically independent but economically and culturally joined colonies dominated their region. The Valyrians took over most of Essos, from Slaver's Bay to the Free Cities, and even Dragonstone in Blackwater Bay.

They ruled for thousands of years, with their language, High Valyrian, becoming the most important in world, and their silver-haired, purple-haired scions representing the highest racial class.

The Valyrians also gave their name to the art of forging Valyrian steel, a special metal connected to the dragons. Early in *Game of Thrones*, Valyrian steel seems less like the magic swords of other fantasy stories and more like a prestige metal—stronger and more beautiful but not materially different. But in the fifth season, at "Hardhome," we see that Valyrian steel swords actually are magic. They can stop the White Walkers' ability to shatter steel, as Jon discovers with a single parry, and can kill White Walkers with a single swing, as he does in his follow-up.

There's no reason to doubt that this is because of the Valyrian connection to dragons. The only other material we've seen that can defeat White Walkers with a touch is dragonglass, which, well, is clearly dragon-related. Both materials seem to be imbued with the power of the dragons, and so most believe that the endgame of *Game of Thrones* involves Daenerys' three dragons taking flight to burn the White Walker horde.

But there's still danger, as the history of Valyria shows. Roughly 400 years before *Game of Thrones*, Valyria just...disappears. Okay, it's more violent than that. Massive seismic activity causes earthquakes, tidal waves, and volcanoes to essentially destroy the peninsula. What remains is a terrifying wasteland, known as the Doom of Valyria, that no sane person approaches. (Jorah Mormont, on the other hand, does try to sail through in the fifth season, and gets greyscale for his troubles.)

What exactly happened to Valyria is one of the great mysteries of the world of *Game of Thrones*. It's entirely possible that we won't get any answer to how the Doom was created, although given the importance of dragons to the overall plot, I'd say it's pretty likely. What is well-known is that a "century of blood" followed in Essos, where the collapse of the Freehold led to international anarchy.

51 The World of Ice and Fire

A big new hardcover book with George R.R. Martin's name appeared in bookshops in late 2014...but it wasn't *The Winds of Winter*, the long-anticipated sixth volume in the series. It was called *The World of Ice and Fire*, an illustrated reference book for Martin's series. Martin alone didn't write it, though his name was obviously the marquee one in the book's branding. He also worked with Elio Garcia and Linda Antonssen, heads of the central *Ice and Fire* site Westeros.org.

The World of Ice and Fire serves as both a reference book and an art book, filled with gorgeous drawings of some of the most important events, people, and places in Westeros. My favorite is the inside cover, a giant illustration of the gothic fortress of Dragonstone in the fog. Over two dozen artists contributed to the book, so there's variety as well as quantity.

Some of the art is deliberately designed to look different from the show, as the book is technically a reference for Martin's novels, not the show. Hence a picture of the Iron Throne by Marc Simonetti shows the Iron Throne as a massive, asymmetrical structure with dozens of steps leading up to the seat of the throne itself. (You can see this art on the Iron Throne's Wikipedia page.)

But while the art may have a different impulse guiding it than the show does, the bulk of the reference information in the book serves both the show and the books. *Game of Thrones* may have simplified the story of Martin's novels, but the history is essentially the same for both the show and the books—although there are a few exceptions, like Maester Aemon calling the Mad King his nephew on the show, instead of his great-nephew as the books have it. (King Jaeherys II is skipped for convenience.)

The World of Ice and Fire is, amusingly, written in the style of a book of Westeros itself, supposedly put together by a maester of the realm. As such, it's filled with historical debates and arguments, with the author, for example, noting multiple theories of where the Ironborn and their Drowned God came from. Because the book uses this form, it doesn't have to describe the true history of everything in Westeros, but can take a more playful tone that also leaves room for Martin or *Game of Thrones* to surprise us (as the show did when it depicted the Children of the Forest creating the White Walkers).

The historical tone does leave it somewhat wanting as a story, however. This isn't like J.R.R. Tolkien's *Silmarillion*, a book that tells the narrative history of Middle-Earth, with rising and falling empires and grand themes. It's a reference book that goes through the biography of each king, the geography of each land, and so on. This isn't a knock on *The World of Ice and Fire*, though. As a reference to the history and makeup of Westeros, it's extremely useful (especially for writing several chapters of this book). And it's a beautiful coffee table book to boot.

52 Jaime Lannister

"Stark? You think the honorable Ned Stark wanted to hear my side? He judged me guilty the moment he set eyes on me."—Jaime Lannister

It's hard to get more irredeemable than child-killing—after all, this is what finally made it impossible for Anakin Skywalker to come back from the Dark Side, and he's the greatest villain of pop culture history. And yet *Game of Thrones* has done its best to do it with Jaime Lannister. How has it tried to achieve that trick?

The process is actually fairly simple: *Game of Thrones* takes a two-dimensional character and makes him complex. When we first meet Jaime, he's vain, powerful, cruel, and sneering. The Kingslayer is also set up as the anti-Ned Stark; when Robert offers Ned the office of Hand, he threatens to pin the symbol on Jaime Lannister (not, say, Tywin) if Ned doesn't accept. And Jaime fills this role for the first half dozen episodes or so, culminating when he kills Ned's captain of the guard, Jory Cassel, and attempts to duel the Stark lord.

After the fight, Jaime flees the city, and here's where it starts getting complicated. As described in the books, and as played almost perfectly by Danish actor Nikolaj Coster-Waldau, Jaime Lannister is a certain kind of physical perfection. He's tall, handsome, and strong, with blond hair that falls into perfect placement. He is the ideal of knightly masculinity, at least in looks. These traits appear to be genetic; Joffrey certainly looks the part of the perfect prince, especially in Sansa's romance story-addled eyes.

But they're also genetic for the previous generation. Jaime is the embodiment of knightly masculinity, but his father Tywin is the ideal patriarch: tall, handsome, and imposing—his power is in his control of a situation and the people around him. Tywin uses this control against Jaime when Jaime meets him in the Lannister camp. The Kingslayer walks in, the perfect sneering knight, and is promptly dressed down by his dad and turned into a frightened boy. Jaime Lannister, for all his strength, is also the product of a clearly *terrible* family life.

The Kingslayer has a smaller part to play in the next season or so, largely because his physical power is taken away when Robb Stark captures him in battle. Jaime spends almost the entirety of Season 2 chained to a post, with only his barbed tongue giving him any kind of power. In his best scene of the season, Jaime attempts an escape by befriending, then murdering, a distant Lannister cousin who was unfortunately tossed into the Kingslayer's cage. It's another shocking and vicious act, like pushing Bran out the window, but this time it's tinged with understanding. Coster-Waldau totally sells the desperation of a man who's been chained to a post for months, and the willingness to do anything to escape the predicament.

Despite being recaptured, he gets the chance again shortly after when Lady Catelyn Stark, hearing the news of her sons' apparent deaths at Winterfell, secretly frees Jaime in exchange for his promise to send her daughters Sansa and Arya back to her. To this end, Catelyn sends her sworn protector, the woman warrior Brienne of Tarth, to escort and protect the Kingslayer and then bring back the Stark girls.

What ensues is probably the best friendship narrative in all of *Game of Thrones*. Jaime is sullen and snide, cruel about Brienne's looks and role as a woman warrior. She's withdrawn, excessively conscientious and trying to avoid giving this man, whom she believes betrayed the knighthood that she as a woman cannot achieve, any sort of benefit of the doubt. Coster-Waldau and Brienne's actress, Gwendoline Christie, are fantastic in the roles, with both physical and verbal chemistry as they spar and then come to a grudging respect.

The true turning point for Jaime comes after that sparring—with metal swords, on a bridge in the open—catches the attention of Bolton men, led by Locke, seeking the Kingslayer for the North. The men are crass and cruel, making no secret of their intent to rape Brienne that night. Initially Jaime tries to steel her for the coming horror, but when it's about to begin, he moves to stop it more deliberately by convincing Locke that Brienne, from the Sapphire Isle, actually has a father who can ransom her with sapphires.

This move stops the rape, but Jaime's continued attempts to weasel his way into Locke's good graces backfire. The resentful Locke decides to punish the privileged Lannister with the sudden, shocking removal of the Kingslayer's sword hand. The best swordsman in the Seven Kingdoms is instantly removed from the source of his power.

Brienne helps keep Jaime alive on the way to Harrenhal. There Jaime and Brienne engage in one of the show's single best scenes. In the castle's baths, they sit, naked, across from one another and Jaime finally tells the story of how he became the Kingslayer. While most of the world believes he betrayed his sacred oath to protect the king simply to aid his father in the conquest of the capital, there's more complexity to the story. The Mad King had laced the entire city with wildfire and threatened to burn the entire city and all its population in his final moments. To save the city, Jaime killed the king, and then never told anyone why.

At Harrenhal, the ex-Maester Qyburn manages to save Jaime's life and the rest of his arm, ingratiating himself with the Lannisters. Roose Bolton decides to send Jaime back to King's Landing, also making friends with House Lannister, a move that would swiftly lead to the Red Wedding. Jaime, jokingly, tells Roose that "the Lannisters send their regards" to the wedding, which Roose repeats to Robb when he murders his king—a bit of unexpected influence from one Kingslayer to the next.

Westeros' happiest couple, Jaime and Cersei Lannister. (Photo courtesy of HBO / Photofest)

Jaime arrives in King's Landing just in time to witness the royal wedding, and his son's death by poison, supposedly at the hands of his brother Tyrion. This leads to one of the show's most controversial scenes, when, next to the body of their son, Jaime and Cersei have a violent sexual encounter. Most viewers read its depiction on the show as rape, which threatened to undo all of the redemption Jaime had undergone when he used his wits and power to prevent Brienne from being sexually assaulted. Adding to the confusion, the scene is based on a chapter in the novels where the sex is described as consensual, and the director claimed that it was part of the siblings' power thing. But it was hard for many to see the encounter as anything but rape, thus sullying the redemption narrative.

Perhaps fortunately, Jaime somewhat faded into the background following Joffrey's death. He did attempt to behave honorably and kindly, giving Brienne a Valyrian steel sword and sending her to find Arya and Sansa, both having escaped King's Landing. He also attempts to negotiate the complicated relationship with his siblings, loving both (in very different ways) even as Cersei attempts to have Tyrion tried and killed.

That negotiation comes to a screeching halt when Tyrion's champion, Oberyn Martell—who Jaime is clearly rooting for—is killed in the trial by combat. Forced to make a choice, Jaime frees Tyrion from his cell, and allows him to seek vengeance on their father Tywin, then escape. Jaime doesn't take the blame for the escape—it falls on Varys—and he continues in his role at King's Landing.

In the fifth season, following Tywin's death, Cersei sends Jaime on a pretty major detour from his narrative. He goes to Dorne to rescue their daughter Myrcella from the threat of the Sand Snakes. It's one of the weakest storylines on the show, and largely goes nowhere until its last episode. There, with Myrcella's return to King's Landing arranged, Jaime confesses to her that he is her true father, a fact she embraces. In a certain sense, the moment could act as a reward for Jaime's supposed redemption, except for the part where Myrcella, poisoned, immediately collapses and dies.

Jaime again fills a complicated role in the sixth season, where he joins with Cersei and eventually the Tyrells in attempting to negate the power of the High Sparrow. Their attempt to bully the Sparrows is undercut by Margaery Tyrell and King Tommen negotiating their release themselves, and Jaime takes the fall, having to leave King's Landing. He goes to pacify the Riverlands, still volatile after the Red Wedding.

This section of the story is odd because the Riverlands, with their Freys and Tullys, haven't been seen since Season 3, whereas in the novels they're a constant presence and Jaime heads there almost immediately after Tywin's death. So the scenes that should be a demonstration of his continued redemption are a bit out of order. For example, in the novels it's quite clear that his oath to Catelyn Stark not to lift his sword against the Stark armies still guides his thinking: instead of attacking, he negotiates the surrender of multiple castles, including the Tully stronghold of Riverrun, which the show depicts.

But the books' Jaime also slowly turns against his sister during this time, with the climax of his story in the fourth book being the burning of her letter asking him to be her champion in her upcoming trial by combat. Yet on the show he demonstrates his continued burning love for her, convincing Edmure Tully to have Riverrun surrender by telling Edmure that he cares about "only Cersei" and will do literally anything to get back to her.

The turn in Jaime's thinking about his sister occurs when he does finally return to King's Landing. By some marvelous coincidence, the Kingslayer, who once murdered his monarch for threatening to detonate wildfire under the city, arrives just in time to see his sister and lover crowned as queen, having detonated wildfire underneath King's Landing, murdering hundreds if not thousands.

Jaime's expression as he views the crowning isn't easy to parse, but he certainly doesn't look happy about his sister's brutal rise to power. The redemption of Jaime Lannister seems almost certain to be tested during the reign of Queen Cersei and the seventh season of *Game of Thrones*.

53 Stannis Baratheon

Stannis Baratheon is a hero in the first season of *Game of Thrones*. Stannis Baratheon also doesn't appear in the first season of *Game of Thrones*. This is Stannis' problem in a nutshell: he's both exactly right and exactly wrong at the same time. Stannis is dissonant—there's always something off about him.

After all, we're talking about the heroic true king of Westeros—who gains power by assassinating his brother with black magic. He's the best battle commander in the Seven Kingdoms, but he manages to lose two of the three major battles he fights. He's famously honorable and just, but burns people alive for disagreeing with him. And most famously, he's prophesied to sit on the Iron Throne, but dies pathetically in a minor battle deep in the North.

What went so very wrong for King Stannis that he fell to that point?

Stannis Baratheon is the middle Baratheon brother, sandwiched between King Robert and Lord Renly. Stannis was famously humorless and driven; in the novels, a former Baratheon retainer describes the three as such: "Robert, he was true steel. Stannis is iron, hard and brittle, he'll break before he bends. Renly, that one, he is copper, shiny but not worth much."

When Robert's Rebellion kicked off, Stannis was in the Stormlands, and came to command Storm's End, the capital of the region. Wedged between three loyalist lands—Dorne, the Reach, and the Crownlands—the Stormlands were always on the defensive, and Stannis is most famed for holding Storm's End against Mace Tyrell's siege for nearly a year. In that time, Stannis found his most loyal retainer, Davos Seaworth, a smuggler who brought onions into Storm's End to help the men survive.

What Stannis did for Davos is, perhaps, the defining story of his character: for saving the keep, Stannis knights the smuggler, who takes the name "Seaworth" and the onion as his heraldry. But for his crimes of smuggling, Stannis personally chops off the tips of Davos' fingers on one hand. This was Stannis' justice.

After Robert became king, Stannis gained power but his complicated relationship with his brother made him increasingly bitter. Stannis was given the former Targaryen island castle of Dragonstone, while his baby brother Renly got the traditional Baratheon keep of Storm's End. Stannis also sat on the Small Council as the Master of Ships—meaning that when King Robert sailed to the Iron Islands to put down Balon Greyjoy's rebellion, it was Stannis who planned the victory that smashed the Greyjoy fleet. (So he did deserve the reputation of being a great commander at one point!)

Stannis also married the daughter of a minor house, Selyse Florent, and with her had one child who survived infancy, Shireen Baratheon. But Shireen contracted greyscale, and Stannis, though not the world's most demonstrably loving father, spared no expense in having her treated. Shireen's greyscale was arrested, but she remained disfigured by it.

But as *Game of Thrones* starts, Stannis is nowhere to be found. His presence increasingly hangs over the first season as Ned tries to solve the mystery of Jon Arryn's death. Stannis was apparently present when Lord Arryn sought out King Robert's bastards, but departed the city when he learned what Lord Arryn learned. Ned thinks this is a cause, not realizing that Stannis may also have been bitter about Robert naming Ned as Hand instead of the thoroughly deserving Stannis.

But as Ned discovers that Cersei's children aren't Robert's, he plans to have the crown passed to Stannis. This even causes Lord Stark to reject Renly's offer of aid in exchange for crowning the much more likable Renly. (Ned Stark even, in the novels, has a ship set up to sail with his daughters to Dragonstone—which would have created a very different story had he gotten away.) But Ned, of course, fails—leaving Stannis essentially alone on Dragonstone to take the throne that is his by right.

By virtue of Ned's faith in Stannis' worth as a king, and the sheer awfulness of King Joffrey Lannister-Baratheon, *Game of Thrones* makes it seems like Stannis should play a heroic role in the wars to come. But when the show finally comes to Dragonstone at the start of the second season, it's clear that Stannis' role is far more complicated.

Dragonstone is a place of gothic horror. It's dark and dreary, covered in old Targaryen dragon statues. The first scene to take place there heightens the creepiness, as the ethereally beautiful priestess Melisandre burns the statues of the seven gods of Westeros—it's a scene designed to instill feelings of unease with a fanatic, destructive religion. Meanwhile, Ramin Djawadi's music reinforces just how ominous Stannis, Dragonstone, and the religion of the Red God should be to viewers. He uses a "minor second," taking a bigger step between notes than normal, to make it sound slightly dissonant—the *Jaws* theme, famously, uses this same tactic to create tension. It also picks up in tempo, making it seem like doom is approaching.

Stephen Dillane plays Stannis with a quiet intensity that rarely suggests a good man. Stannis, in Dillane's portrayal, is rigid and humorless—but that creates humor of its own, as when Stannis, on two separate occasions, corrects people who say "less" instead of "fewer"!

When Melisandre, with Stannis' tacit support, has Maester Cressen killed at Stannis' council chamber, it becomes clear: King Stannis is not the heroic heir that we might have hoped for. And yet he's constantly being told he is the chosen hero: Azor Ahai, the Prince who was Promised, the true king of the Iron Throne. It's another form of dissonance: Jon and Dany are going through the stories of chosen heroes, but here is one of Westeros' few humans able to wield the supernatural, Melisandre, saying that it's a pedantic, middle-aged man with no apparent charisma.

But with Melisandre at his side, Stannis becomes a power in the War of the Five Kings. Out of nothing, apparently, except the stubborn belief that he is the true liege lord of the Stormlands, he sails his tiny army there to confront his brother, King Renly. After a disastrous parley, where Stannis' demands fall on the more powerful king's deaf ears, the two sides set for battle—when Stannis sends Melisandre and Davos on a secret mission late at night. Melisandre, who's slept with Stannis on the promise to bear him a son, suddenly births a shadow with Stannis' face. The shadow sneaks into Renly's camp and murders the youngest Baratheon, with only Cat Stark and Brienne of Tarth there to witness the truth.

With Renly dead, Stannis takes the Baratheon half of his army. The Tyrell half, without the marriage alliance between Renly and Margaery, heads home—though they would come back to haunt Stannis. Now with a huge fleet and one of the largest armies in the Seven Kingdoms, Stannis sets sail against the virtually undefended King's Landing.

Throughout the series, he has an angel and a devil on his shoulders. The devil is Melisandre, offering him ruthless shortcuts to gain power, and with the angel is Davos, giving him good, solid, honest, but usually losing, advice. Ser Davos convinces Stannis to leave Melisandre and her fire magic at Dragonstone.

It's fire that defeats Stannis at the Battle of Blackwater, however, as Tyrion Lannister, acting Hand of the King, springs a trap on Stannis' fleet with a massive wildfire explosion. Stannis still has an overwhelming force even after his initial offensive is blunted, but Tyrion does just enough to blunt his offensive to delay the capture of King's Landing for the combined Lannister and Tyrell armies to attack from behind, shattering Stannis' armies. At the end of the second season, Stannis is back where he started: with a tiny force at Dragonstone, while the Lannisters are significantly stronger.

In the third season, Stannis is a broken man. Melisandre's magic to "create a son" has weakened him, and she refuses to help him create another, as it would kill him. He's also burning dissidents for the Red God. When Davos, lost after the battle, finds his way home, he tries to put a stop to this—but gets arrested by the increasingly fanatic King Stannis.

However, Stannis' daughter Shireen still loves the Onion Knight, and begins the process of softening the king. Eventually Stannis comes to free Davos when Melisandre captures Robert's bastard son Gendry, and prepares to execute him for the power of a king's blood. The King has finally recovered enough of his humanity to find his better angels. Together they convince Melisandre to only demonstrate what king's blood can do. She uses three leeches to draw Gendry's blood, naming them each after Stannis' royal rivals, and burning them. King Robb, King Joffrey, and King Balon all go into the fire. Shortly thereafter, both Robb and Joffrey die. (Although Balon lasts until the sixth season of the show, he dies in the third book.)

With Melisandre's power demonstrated, Stannis seems to drift back toward her ruthlessness, causing Davos to smuggle Gendry out of Dragonstone. In desperate defense as Stannis prepares to jail him again, Davos reads a letter from the Night's Watch, which says that the White Walkers have returned, and Mance Rayder's army threatens the Wall. Even Melisandre is swayed by this—it is the darkness she and the Red God are dedicated to fighting.

Stannis doesn't do much in the fourth season, largely rebuilding his fleet and his army. Davos proves his worth at the Iron Bank of Braavos, convincing them that Stannis is the best commander and potential king in Westeros, and worthy of their gold. He arrives in the nick of time. At the Battle of Castle Black, Mance Rayder's forces are on the verge of overwhelming the remnants of the Watch, when Stannis' knights surprise and rout the Wildlings, capturing the King-Beyond-the-Wall.

The fifth season sees Stannis take center stage again—I'd even argue that he's the main character of the season. Stannis at the Wall is the most human we've seen. He's still rigid, executing Mance Rayder for not kneeling and joining, but Stannis also treats Jon and Sam with respect, having known their famous fathers. He even offers Jon the opportunity to come south as the legitimized heir to Winterfell, to help bring the loyal lords in the North to his side, although Jon declines.

But it's his scene with Sam that indicates that Stannis might finally be filling his heroic role. Sam's father, Randyll Tarly, bullied the boy and threatened him with death if he didn't join the Night's Watch. Stannis clearly has respect for Randyll Tarly, and his background as a commander would seem to make him a similar man. But rather than bully Sam, Stannis encourages him: he sees Sam's strengths are in research not war, and tells him to continue it, for knowledge will be essential against the White Walkers. It is a remarkably genuine moment—it's still Stannis, searching for victory, but also acting like a leader of men. He even takes some time to bond with his daughter.

It's all a mirage, however. The dissonance of Stannis Baratheon is still present, it just manifests over the course of the season instead of in a single scene or episode. Stannis' army marches south from the Wall to attack the Boltons at Winterfell and bring the North under Baratheon command. Melisandre promises him victory, that he will sit on the Iron Throne, and that she has seen the Bolton banners taken off the walls of Winterfell.

Yet Stannis' offensive becomes the first casualty of the long-promised winter, when an early snowstorm traps his army before it arrives. Stannis sends his better angel, Davos, back to Castle Black for help. But the devil on his shoulder convinces him, after some resistance, that there's only one way to victory: he has to let

Melisandre burn his daughter, Shireen. In one of the most shocking and devastating scenes of all *Game of Thrones*, Stannis burns his daughter in front of his whole army to end the penultimate episode of Season 5.

It works—and it doesn't. The snows melt the next morning. But Stannis' mercenaries desert, taking his horses, Melisandre flees in the night, and Queen Selyse, whose belief brought Melisandre to her husband's court, commits suicide. With his now-tiny army, the king makes a final march to Winterfell, where his pathetic force is swiftly surrounded and destroyed by Bolton cavalry.

The king himself manages to fight his way into the woods near Winterfell, where, despite his wounds, he kills Bolton attackers. But as he collapses, Brienne of Tarth, originally in Winterfell for Sansa Stark, finds the broken king. She asks if he killed Renly with blood magic, and Stannis, acknowledging the severity of his crimes, admits that he did, and for this, he is promptly executed by Brienne.

With Stannis dead, the War of the Five Kings comes to its conclusion. It's also the end of the complicated politics of Westeros: Stannis is neither good nor bad for most of the series—he makes ruthless decisions in desperate situations, but they're always to defeat a greater evil...until they're not, and his sacrifice of his daughter ends up being meaningless and destructive. With Stannis' death, the story—and his lieutenants, Melisandre and Davos—both move on to a more straightforward character, Jon Snow. Stannis didn't live to see the battle of good against evil, but he helped make it possible.

54 "Blackwater"

"Those are brave men knocking at our door. Let's go kill them!"—Tyrion Lannister

It can be hard to pick out the most memorable episodes of *Game of Thrones*, since its particular form of serialization, dancing from place to place across the world of Westeros, can make it difficult to remember which scenes happened in the same episodes. But this format makes it all the more special when *Thrones* deviates from it—particularly in the battle episodes, which have occurred in four of the six seasons so far. These are Season 4's "The Watchers on the Wall," 5's "Hardhome," 6's "The Battle of the Bastards"—and the one that started the trend, the ninth episode of Season 2, "Blackwater."

"Blackwater" is the climax of the second season, and the most important battle in the War of the Five Kings. In it, Stannis Baratheon, having taken much of his brother Renly's support, leads an overwhelmingly powerful army against King's Landing, defended by Tyrion Lannister, the Acting Hand of the King.

It was the first episode of the series to take place in a single area, but King's Landing in the early seasons was one of the few locations with enough major characters that this wouldn't be a disappointment. Stannis and Davos lead the attack; Tyrion, Joffrey, the Hound, Lancel, Bronn, and Podrick fight in the defenses, while Sansa, Cersei, Shae, Pycelle, Varys, and Tommen await in the Red Keep.

This structure allows for "Blackwater" to go back and forth between characters and tones. It builds up tension with preparation scenes at first: Cersei acquires a potentially poisonous potion from

Pycelle; Tyrion gets a map of the secret passages of King's Landing from Varys; and Davos is promised the role of Hand when Stannis takes the city.

In one of the most memorable preparation scenes, Bronn and some Lannister soldiers drink in a tavern, singing "The Rains of Castamere," the Lannister anthem, for the first time on the show. Bronn is sitting with a prostitute, who becomes progressively more nude across the course of the scene. The Hound shows up and almost gets in a fight with the sellsword, before both are called away by the start of the battle.

The battle is joined when Stannis' ships approach the city. King's Landing's bells start ringing, and Davos says "They wanna play music with us, let's play. Drums!" The call for the drums kicks the music, and the editing, and the direction, and the battle overall, into high gear.

With the first act of the battle, Tyrion Lannister plays his trump card: wildfire. In the course of the second season, Tyrion has befriended the pyromancers of King's Landing, the guild with the power to create the pseudo-magical weapon of mass destruction called wildfire. It is the key to Tyrion's plans: a single ship, leading wildfire, is launched into Stannis' fleet. At Tyrion's signal, Bronn lights an arrow on fire and sends it into the ships. It kills Mathos Seaworth, knocks his father Davos out of the fight, and destroys Stannis' initial vanguard into the fight.

With this move, *Game of Thrones* positions Tyrion as the heir to two culturally important, real-world historical concepts. "Greek fire" was the secret weapon of the Byzantine Empire's navy, a still-mysterious process where ships equipped with it could spray it onto water or onto ships, where the fire was inextinguishable. It became a core part of the discursive legends of Eastern Rome, saving it from the Persians, Arabs, and civil wars, before it fell into disuse and its secrets were lost. As such, it's imbued culturally with the idea that it protected Western Christendom from the hordes of the East—a complicated history, but one which fits in with Varys telling Tyrion that he had to save the city from the overzealous follower of the Red God, Stannis Baratheon.

Another cultural marker the wildfire hits: the Battle of Chi Bi, or Red Cliff, from the Chinese epic of the Three Kingdoms. In this semi-legendary story, China has fallen into civil war. The warlord Cao Cao has united the northern part of the empire, captured the emperor and the capital, and attacks the lords of the south with an apparently invincible force. Cao Cao's army approaches on a fleet on the Yangtze river, but the legendarily genius strategists of the allied forces opposing him, Zhou Yu and Zhuge Liang, create a brilliant strategy to burn most of Cao Cao's army, and the southern forces defeat the weakened northern army. It's both the ultimate underdog story—Cao Cao hadn't lost a major battle before this—and proof that a single genius could turn an entire war around. Tyrion Lannister, with the wildfire attack, is treated as that genius strategist—something that Lord Varys recognizes both before and after the battle.

The wildfire attack is remarkably effective, but it only blunts the tip of Stannis' attack. He still has enough ships to launch an army at King's Landing's walls, and everyone knows it, including the king himself, who sees that even with his direct assault ruined, his army is still strong enough that it can take thousands of casualties on the way to the walls and win anyway.

As Stannis attacks, and the battle moves into the hand-to-hand combat, director Neil Marshall keeps things fresh by changing the tone, most notably by interweaving scenes from inside the Red Keep with the war outside. There, Cersei, Sansa, Shae, and assorted ladies hide, waiting for the siege to end. Cersei is convinced the battle is a lost cause, and in addition to her poison, has Ser Ilyn Payne there to kill the women to save to them from the depredations of Stannis' victorious soldiers.

But the real battle inside is not one of soldiers, but a conflict of wits between Sansa and Cersei. Cersei is still convinced the city will fall, and everyone is doomed. But she also recognizes a slight chance of victory, and so continues to attempt to groom Sansa to be the sort of queen who can deal with Joffrey. While getting waaaaaaasteeeedddd. The scenes between Sansa and Cersei demonstrate the growth of both Sophie Turner and Lena Headey as actresses, building the battle's tensions with Sansa's determination to play the part of the good queen, as Cersei increasingly gives up on it. When Cersei shocks the room and deserts it, it's Sansa, demonstrating a Stark family leadership that she's otherwise lacked, who leads the terrified women in singing a hymn to calm them.

Outside the Red Keep, Cersei isn't the only Lannister who bails on the battle. First, Lancel Lannister, seeing Stannis' troops assault the gate, returns to inform Cersei what's happening. She demands that Joffrey return. When confronted, the king wavers on what to do—he knows his duty is to stand and fight, and be a banner for the Lannister forces to follow. But Joffrey is, at heart, a pathetic little bully, and uses any excuse he can to desert the losing battle.

This leaves Tyrion as the only leader left to rally the troops. In a desperate speech, he appeals not to patriotism or loyalty to the crown, but simple survival: if Stannis wins, they and the people they care about are going to die. As a last-ditch effort, Tyrion leads the city's defenders through the tunnels he knows about from Varys' map, to attack Stannis' siege units from behind. The gamble works: they delay the attack for just long enough to win.

Victory, though, comes from a surprising source. Tyrion watches the battle unfold from the ground, after the Kingsguard Ser Mandon Moore suddenly attacks him, brutally scarring his face. Tyrion collapses in the mud outside the gates of King's Landing, and hazily witnesses the battle's turn: an external force attacks Stannis' troops, routing them, and the city is saved.

Cersei, in the throne room, on the verge of poisoning herself and her son Tommen, sees the truth: the force that won the battle is Tywin Lannister's, joined by the Tyrell armies thanks to Littlefinger's successful negotiation of a marriage between Margaery Tyrell and Joffrey Lannister-Baratheon (putting an ironic exclamation point on Cersei's advice to Sansa on how to become a good queen, no less, as it leaves Sans without a marriage alliance).

The aftermath of the Battle of Blackwater seems clear: the Lannisters have won a total victory. Stannis, previously an existential terror to the Iron Throne, now holds a decimated military force at Dragonstone and comprises no strategic threat against the crown. The Lannisters, for the second season, have won, leaving Joffrey holding the throne with no major competition. On the other hand, this is true thanks only to their alliance with House Tyrell, whose ambitions are certainly not limited to being the second most powerful house in the Seven Kingdoms. Finally, it leaves Robb Stark and the armies of the North as the only counter to the Lannisters still in the field—setting up the third season attempting to resolve that war.

But for *Game of Thrones* as a television show, "Blackwater" was a far more positive success. Here was the proof that the show could, when it needed to, focus on the most important events, and turn them into the very best episodes the series had to offer. It also provided a model for the climactic hours of future seasons, like "The Watchers on the Wall," "Hardhome," and "The Battle of the Bastards," some of the most-acclaimed television episodes of all time.

55 Tywin Lannister

"It's a rare enough thing, a man who lives up to his reputation."—
Olenna Tyrell

It takes seven episodes for Lord Tywin Lannister to appear on *Game of Thrones*, but boy is it ever worth the wait. Jaime Lannister, the man who's been treated as the lead villain through the first half of the first season, strides into his father's tent, handsome and sneering and dismissive of their enemies. Tywin cuts him down to size almost immediately: "Attacking [Ned Stark] was stupid. Lannisters do not act like fools." Over the course of less than five minutes, Tywin reduces Jaime to the role of a speechless child while simultaneously skinning and gutting a stag (symbol of House Baratheon). And that's how you introduce your true villain.

For most of the first two seasons, Tywin remains somewhat in the background. The Lannisters in King's Landing are led by his daughter Cersei, younger son Tyrion, and grandson Joffrey. The Lannister armies in the field who face Robb Stark and lose are led by Jaime and Tywin's brother Kevan. Tywin himself doesn't directly face Robb—initially because Robb is wary of him, and later because Tywin is wary of Robb's battle prowess.

But in third and fourth seasons, Tywin returns to King's Landing, takes up the title of Hand of the King, and becomes the dominant political force in Westeros. By this point, he is the primary antagonist of *Game of Thrones*, and his relationship with the other powerbrokers of King's Landing becomes the show's focus.

The key to Tywin's power on *Game of Thrones* isn't necessarily his power, nor the wealth of the Lannisters. It's his *presence*. Some of this is reputational. Tywin isn't just a powerful lord, he's also a ruthless one. This is true both historically, as when he destroyed House Reyne of Castamere for threatening his father's primacy, or when he sacked King's Landing to prove his loyalty to King Robert. It's also seen in the show when he starts a war with the Riverlands to get his son Tyrion back after his arrest, or negotiates the murder of Robb Stark at the end of Season 3.

It's also Tywin's physical presence, though. Played by Charles Dance, arguably the best-respected actor in an extremely well-respected cast, Tywin dominates every scene he's in. One of my favorites occurs in "The Bear and the Maiden Fair," a mid-third season episode. King Joffrey summons Lord Tywin to the throne room in order to reassert his power over his grandfather. But Tywin calmly and slowly mounts the stairs to the Iron Throne, and explains his position to Joffrey.

Dance, with director Michelle MacLaren, keeps the whole scene focused on Tywin's physical location. When he needs to be most condescending, he looms over Joffrey, demonstrating the full extent of his poise and power, and sarcastically telling Joffrey that he'll be informed about the things he needs to know about. Joffrey, cowed, acquiesces.

Indeed, there are only a handful of characters that Tywin cannot stare down. The first is Arya Stark, in one of the show's best deviations from the novels. Instead of becoming Roose Bolton's servant at Harrenhal as in the books, Arya becomes Tywin's, and this helps flesh out the increasingly important Lannister lord. The two have a consistently fascinating relationship: Tywin suspects that she's more than she seems, but not so much that he does anything more than question her. Arya knows he's her family's greatest enemy, but respects him too much to make a move.

Tywin's arrival in King's Landing gives him some adult characters to spar with, however. He attempts to impose his will on his children, but all three of them, in different ways, chafe under his gaze and lash out. In one of *Game of Thrones'* best scenes, Tywin's reintroduction to the Small Council in early Season 3, we see how much the world revolves around him. All of the Small Councilors: Varys, Littlefinger, Cersei, and Pycelle, attempt to sit next to the new ruler of the realm. Tyrion counters them by sitting at the opposite end of the table—but still defined by his father.

The only two characters in King's Landing to face Tywin and defy him are the embodiments of House Tyrell and House Martell, two Great Houses that the Lannisters need in order to survive. Tywin, oddly, never has a major scene with Margaery Tyrell. But her grandmother Olenna, who consistently negotiates with Tywin the Tyrells' behalf, takes Tywin on directly. Her flighty persona can fluster him at times, but at others, as when they negotiate a marriage between Loras and Cersei, he gains the upper hand.

Oberyn Martell has an entirely different relationship with Tywin than most. He arrives in King's Landing in order to seek justice for the death of his sister, which he believes occurred on Tywin's orders. Yet Tywin still seeks to recruit him—to serve as a judge in Tyrion's trial, and then to sit on the Small Council as an advisor regarding dragons. The Dornish had resisted an invasion of dragons while the rest of Westeros fell, so Tywin feels he needs Oberyn to represent them. For this, Tywin promises a "conversation" between Oberyn and the man who killed Elia Martell, the Mountain that Rides, Gregor Clegane.

But when Tyrion demands trial by combat and the Lannisters pick the Mountain to represent them, Oberyn takes a different path: he acts as Tyrion's champion, fighting and seemingly defeating, then technically losing to the Mountain. While a theoretical victory for Tywin, it leads directly to his defeat. Tyrion is set free in an act of rebellion by Jaime Lannister, and finally free of any fear of his father, seeks him out and murders him in his privy—a sadly disgusting death for the greatest power in the Seven Kingdoms.

56 Ned Stark

Look, an epic fantasy series on television is a hard sell. Before *Game of Thrones* you'd probably have to argue that it was an impossible sell. Nothing else that wasn't pure camp had remotely succeeded, and now HBO, home of *The Sopranos* and *The Wire* wants to sell a story of dragons and ice zombies? Get outta here!

Except...except if they got one of the very few actors who could possibly invest the show with the purest of fantasy authenticity: an appearance in *Lord of the Rings*. Except if they got an actor who could invest the show with enough star power to convince casual TV viewers it would be worth viewing, like the villain of *Goldeneye* and *Patriot Games*. Except if Sean Bean, Boromir himself, showed up and became the main character, the focus of all the first season's advertising. Only then could *Game of Thrones* possibly have worked.

Well...*Game of Thrones* worked. And while there are a huge number of reasons that it did, Sean Bean's essential role as Ned Stark, star of the first season, was a huge reason why. The show was pitched, both privately and publicly, as "*The Sopranos* in Middle-Earth," and while that title may have been deeply wrong in a literal sense, in a figurative sense, it worked. This was, at least for the first season, the story of a man trying to wrestle with the straightforward task of keeping his family from breaking apart even as he wrestled with a massive, impossible-to-fix, morally ambiguous political dilemma.

So there were multiple episodes where the resolution seemed to be "Ned struggles to fix his daughters' relationships while he struggles to maintain his role on the Small Council." It's a good pitch. But it's not actually what *Game of Thrones* is about in the

The costuming, actor, and location shooting gave early Game of Thrones *an instant veneer of authenticity.* (Photo courtesy of Nick Briggs/HBO/dapd/AP Images)

long run, and that's a remarkable twist. The story that *GoT* seems to be, of an essentially moral man trying to hold onto his soul in an essentially amoral universe, is a lie.

The story that *Game of Thrones* actually tells, in that crucial first season, is something different: the essentially moral man trying to hold onto his soul in an essentially amoral universe is doomed. Ned's attempts to both play the game of thrones and keep his honor always fail him. Ned Stark, for example, attempts to bribe Janos Slynt—an amoral act!—to dethrone the illegitimate Joffrey in favor of Robert's true heir, Stannis—a moral act! But the act that might have won for Ned was offered just before, when

Renly presented himself as a potential king, with the support of his knights and Loras Tyrell (and through him House Tyrell).

Now compare this to Ned's successor, Tyrion Lannister. Tyrion is equally as moral as Ned, but he's less tragic because he's willing to sell his honor for the right outcomes. Early on, Tyrion meets with the slippery Janos Slynt, and apparently befriends him instead of merely bribing him. But knowing the Slynt is a snake, Tyrion instead simply arrests him and has him sent to the Wall. No honor in it, but no inevitable betrayal.

Ned's inevitable betrayal, however, ends up leading the realm into civil war. Because he hasn't created a firm base of support, literally everything that can go wrong for Ned does. Instead of keeping Joffrey from the throne, Ned strengthens his claim by presenting a treacherous enemy. Instead of preventing war, Ned triggers a five-sided civil war between Joffrey, Stannis, Renly, Ned's son Robb, and Balon Greyjoy. And when he confesses, instead of saving himself and allowing a redemption alongside his supposed bastard Jon Snow at the Wall...Ned misjudges Joffrey's cruelty and his advisors' ability to restrain him.

In the end, pathetically, Ned Stark confesses all his crimes in the hopes of a half-pardon that he's never granted. Joffrey demands his head, and all of Ned's mistakes come back to damn him. Yet he still manages to instill some hope: all of Lord Eddard Stark's children know what became of their father, and work to do still better than the great man who was cast out of his depth as a player in the game of thrones.

And Sean Bean died at the beginning of the story once again, just like *Lord of the Rings*, but in a totally different fashion. The very deliberate fantasy authenticity that *Game of Thrones* used at its start became ironic by the end of its first season—but worked for turning the show into a hit.

57 Bran Stark

"You will never walk again. But you will fly."—The Three-Eyed Raven

Wanna learn how magic works in Westeros? Follow Bran Stark around—that's what he's here for! It's an essential role: part of the overall story of *Game of Thrones* is that magic is returning to the political world of the Seven Kingdoms. And Bran, as the Three-Eyed Raven in training, meets with the supernatural quite a bit, making him theoretically an essentially character. But...Bran hasn't quite been, especially compared to his siblings.

There's an easy case to be made that *Game of Thrones* is the story of the Stark children. They comprise half of the point-of-view characters of the first novel—only Robb and Rickon are left out, and see where that got them. And on the show, the stories of Arya, Sansa, and Jon have obviously all been essential components of every single season.

And then there's Bran Stark. On the page, he's easily the equal of his three siblings. On the screen? He's the most important character to simply get skipped for an entire season. Chances are he still has a major part to play—but why has the show downplayed him?

Some of this was an inevitable result of the transition from page to screen: much of Bran's journey takes place in his head, after Jaime Lannister's attempted murder leaves Bran paralyzed from the waist down. The TV series switches from the subjective point-of-view chapters, filled with thoughts, memories, speculation, and, in Bran's case, visions, to a straightforward, objective presentation of the action—action Bran can't really participate in.

The series also made a deliberate choice to focus on the present. Before the fifth season, there are no flashbacks, and visions, dreams, and prophecies are kept to a minimum. It's essential to Bran's storyline that a few are shown, particularly his warging into his direwolf, Summer, but as a whole, the role of magic is downplayed in the show compared to the books.

But beyond structural issues, *Game of Thrones* made deliberate choices in adapting the story to focus on other characters instead of Brandon Stark. Particularly in the second season, Bran is the point-of-view character who serves as our gateway into the politics of the North, meeting lords like Wyman Manderly (who finally showed up in the sixth season), but particularly introducing the dangerous Bastard of Bolton, and the increasingly untrustworthy Freys. Instead, *Game of Thrones* fleshed out the stories of two more active characters, Robb and Dany. It was possibly a good move at the time, but it limited the fourth Stark child a great deal compared to his siblings.

So what is Bran Stark's major part to play? His apprenticeship with the mysterious Three-Eyed Raven, as well as Jojen Reed's ominous declarations of Bran's importance, answer the question: Bran's use of magic will play a critical role in the upcoming war. It already has, at least conceptually, as Bran saw the long-lost secret of Jon Snow's true parentage—now he just has to make it back to civilization and tell someone.

But there's also the Raven's promise to Bran: "You will fly." Now, we've seen a warg who can take control of birds before, with Orell, the Wildling who was killed by Jon in the third season. This is nothing special, especially on its own, and certainly doesn't appear to be a major advance in Bran's studies beyond warging into Summer, let alone Hodor. But birds aren't the only things that can fly—there are three dragons, and only two known Targaryens who can ride them the conventional way.

(In an interesting aside, the Three-Eyed Raven, Max von Sydow, gives many clues in the novels that he himself is a Targaryen, once the Hand of the King and Lord Commander of the Night's Watch, the legitimized bastard Brynden Rivers. The show doesn't include this, and von Sydow is not made up to look like a Targaryen.)

How has Bran gotten to this point? Like all the Stark children, he's had a dangerous journey, leading increasingly into the realm of the fantastic. When the show begins, Bran, played by Isaac Hempstead Wright, is a cheerful, adventurous boy who can't be stopped from climbing the walls of Winterfell. Isaac Hempstead Wright is another great example of *Game of Thrones'* remarkable success in casting children. Although he never has the huge dramatic opportunities of Maisie Williams or Sophie Turner, Wright does everything he needs to, and does it well.

After the king arrives to name Ned Stark his Hand, Bran is climbing an abandoned tower when he comes across Queen Cersei having sex with her brother, Ser Jaime Lannister. "The things I do for love," Jaime says, shoving Bran out the window, a shocking murder to end the first episode.

But Bran doesn't die here, though he does end up paralyzed. A second attempt on his life comes when a cutthroat breaks into his room wielding a dagger of Valyrian steel. This assassination attempt makes it clear to the Starks that Bran's fall wasn't an accident—and so Catelyn Stark begins the investigation into the dagger that leads to her arresting Tyrion Lannister and beginning the War of the Five Kings. Bran is attacked by a group of Wildlings, but he's saved by Robb and Theon Greyjoy.

One of the Wildlings, a woman named Osha, surrenders, and becomes a servant at Winterfell. She also tells Bran tales of magic from Beyond the Wall, seeing in him abilities beyond those of a normal human. Bran's main role in the show, in many ways, is to be the character through which viewers learn how magic works in

Westeros. Osha, and the occasional appearance of Old Nan, give the story-craving Stark boy all the magical stories that prep viewers for the show's transition from political thriller to magical epic fantasy.

When the war starts, Bran and his brother Rickon remain in Winterfell, with Bran thrust into a position of more responsibility, as his brother's heir, first to Winterfell, then as King in the North. Winterfell's Maester, Luwin, attempts to train Bran, which is a bit of a struggle, though not as much as his brother Rickon, who's practically feral without his parents, smashing walnuts being pretty much his only hobby. But Bran does show some skill at ruling, such as when he sends two orphan boys to be adopted by a local miller who needs help and companionship.

Bran's training is disrupted by the sudden betrayal of Theon Greyjoy, who spends the entire second season making the worst decisions possible. Theon believes, correctly, that a small group of Ironborn could strike Winterfell and take it while the Starks are distracted. But he also rather foolishly believes that he can hold the castle. Theon goes wild, killing the Master-at-Arms and scaring Bran into fleeing with Osha and Hodor. Theon gives chase, but when he can't find them, he kills the miller's boys, burns their bodies, and tells the castle Bran and Rickon Stark are dead.

Theon's comeuppance occurs when the Bastard of Bolton attacks Winterfell, and his own men sell him out, letting Ramsay Snow sack the castle. Bran, Rickon, Osha, and Hodor emerge from the crypts where they'd been hiding, see the wreckage, and flee north to Jon Snow at the Wall.

On the road, the party meets the Reed siblings, Meera and Jojen. Jojen has the greensight, the ability to see the future, across the world, or the past—and he says Bran has it too. Jojen becomes yet another character who explains the magic of the world to Bran. Meera is the muscle of the two, a trained fighter who manages to surprise Osha. Jojen convinces Bran that he has a magical destiny

Beyond the Wall, someplace Osha—whose husband turned into a wight—is unwilling to go. Bran, too, is unwilling to risk his brother Rickon, so Osha takes the boy to the Stark bannermen of House Umber.

Before this, however, Bran has one of the closest encounters with a fellow Stark since the first season, in one of the cleverest sequences of the story. He's warged into Summer when he sees Jon Snow arguing with Tormund's Wildling raiding party. Jon turns to fight the Free Folk, and Bran helps his brother in the direwolf's body. They then meet Samwell Tarly, fleeing Craster's Keep with Gilly. Sam recognizes Bran and offers to take him to his brother, but Bran, committed to his journey, continues on.

In the fourth season, Bran has another close call with his foster brother. Sam tells Jon about Bran, but Locke, the Bolton's agent at the Wall, overhears them and plans to kill the Stark boy for his true masters. Jon, with Locke, attacks Craster's Keep, just after the mutineers have captured Bran's party. Locke diverts from the attack, finding Bran—but Bran wargs into Hodor and snaps the traitor's neck. Although he wants to talk directly to Jon, Jojen Reed, the world's biggest wet blanket, convinces Bran that he'll never get his training if he goes to Jon, thus delaying a Stark child reunion by another two seasons.

Jojen gets his soon enough. The party manages to make it to the Three-Eyed Raven's cave when they're suddenly attacked by Ray Harryhausen-esque skeletons in one of the oddest scenes of show. Meera, Hodor, and Summer manage to fight off most of the wights, but one of them stabs the Reed boy to death. They're saved by the first appearance of the Children of the Forest, the elf-like people who inhabited Westeros before the humans, but were driven into hiding by the First Men's genocide. There the Children introduce Bran to the Three-Eyed Raven (before von Sydow was cast), a man wrapped in weirwood roots who promises to train Bran.

And then Bran disappears for a full season. There are some good reasons for the lack of the Stark lad in Season 5, to be fair. His story, like Brienne's, was largely ahead of his place in the books—at the end of *A Storm of Swords* he's just met Sam, while his meeting with the Three-Eyed Raven only occurs deep in *A Dance with Dragons*.

Perhaps more pressingly, Isaac Hempstead Wright, over the course of the series, hit several growth spurts. The gleeful child of the pilot episode was increasingly a grown-up teenager, and large enough that Hodor's actor, Kristian Nairn, struggled to actually carry Wright—hence the reliance on the sled, instead of Nairn's arms. By taking a season off, and implying that Bran's spent an indeterminate amount of time studying under the Raven, *Game of Thrones* does a sly reboot of Brandon Stark as a serious young adult—check out Hempstead Wright's poise when following von Sydow around in the flashbacks.

And the flashbacks do come, in Season 6. Bran Stark's training for his Sight leads him to see the truth behind three of the greatest mysteries in Westeros: the origin of the White Walkers, Jon Snow's true parentage, and, uh, how Hodor got his name.

The former comes first when Bran, under the Raven's tutelage, stretches further the glimpses of his family that he'd seen, and goes back centuries or millennia, to witness the Children of the Forest plunging an obsidian dagger into the chest of a bound human, whose body swallows it. His eyes turn blue and he becomes the first White Walker. Bran turns to the Child, named Leaf, who was the one who pushed the dagger in. She says they were desperate in the face of human genocide, and made a mistake.

Bran, too, makes a mistake, trying to use the vision without the Raven. He brushes the Night's King, who is standing outside the cave with an army. The wights attack and all present fight to allow Bran the chance to escape. One by one they fall—the Children, the Three-Eyed Raven, Leaf, Summer, and eventually Hodor. In the last case, Bran has warged into the servant's body and forces him to "hold the door" against the horde. The magic is so powerful that it causes the teenaged Hodor, previously seen in Bran's vision, to have a seizure, saying "Hold the door" over and over until all he can say is "Hodor."

Meera carries Bran into the woods of the North, but she isn't strong enough to outrun the wights. There, Bran accidentally solves another great mystery of the story: what happened to his uncle Benjen Stark, First Ranger of the Night's Watch, missing since the first season? Bran and Meera are saved by Coldhands, the name Benjen took after becoming undead. He had been mortally wounded by a White Walker, but the Children of the Forest shoved a dagger in his chest—just like Bran's vision—and he retains his memory and ability to do good. Coldhands takes Bran and Meera to the Wall—though he cannot pass, thanks to its magic conflicting with what animates him.

As Bran's final act of the season, he uses his vision himself to see the resolution of a scene he'd originally only caught part of: Ned Stark at the Tower of Joy. First he saw Ned and Howland Reed defeat the Kingsguard Arthur Dayne (in a fantastically choreographed fight scene, no less). Now Bran sees what Dayne was guarding: Lyanna Stark, dying in childbirth, offering her son with Rhaegar Targaryen to Ned Stark to raise as his own.

With Bran Stark headed into the North, where Jon now rules, and Stark child reunions becoming inevitable, both Bran's news, and his magic, still clearly have a major role in the final act of *Game of Thrones.*

58 Brienne of Tarth

Are there any good guys in *Game of Thrones?*

Well, there's Brienne of Tarth, the woman who cannot be a knight, cannot be a Ser, and yet embodies their ideals and the ideals of viewers more than arguably any other character on *Game of Thrones*. Has Brienne made mistakes? At an individual level, most certainly—particularly leaving her vigil for rescuing Sansa in order to get revenge against Stannis. But has she made those mistakes for the best of reasons, and still ended up alive and on the side of the best people remaining in Westeros? This is an unambiguous yes, and part of why Brienne is so important in the overall narrative of *Game of Thrones*.

It's especially notable that Brienne fills this role. She's a woman, in a man's world, filling a man's position, and still kicking ass. Okay, let's show how much ass she's kicking: at the Tournament of the Hand, the flower of Westerosi knighthood shows up to battle for a week to prove themselves to the King and the Hand. The winner? Sandor Clegane, a worthy victor. He wins somewhat by technicality, though, after saving the life of Ser Loras from his rampaging brother; but would you bet against the Hound in a duel?

And yet Brienne faces the Hound in single combat and, in one of the most brutal duels in all of *Game of Thrones*, beats him, kicking him off a cliff to his apparent death. It could, perhaps, be argued that it was a fluke, that he was infected and ill from a previous battle. And yet Brienne had also defeated Ser Loras Tyrell, another of the very best knights of the Seven Kingdoms and the runner-up in the Hand's tourney, in a melee in front of King Renly. Brienne the Beauty has a legitimate claim to being the very best fighter in the Seven Kingdoms.

For *Game of Thrones* it's terrifically important that Brienne be such an amazing fighter and important character. So much of the series is about the crimes committed against women by a patriarchal society that it's amazing from a purely gut, emotional level to have a woman who can fight back. She can fight back according to normal chivalric norms, or she can bite the Hound's goddamn ear off if she has to win.

An argument can be made that this is the key transition point for Brienne's character, occurring between the end of Season 2 and the start of Season 4. Between those points, the Maid of Tarth is almost entirely focused on her relationship with Jaime Lannister, who she has sworn to Cat that she will deliver to King's Landing in exchange for the Stark daughters.

The Brienne-Jaime relationship is arguably the single greatest friendship in all of *Game of Thrones*. The actors are utterly superb. Nikolaj Coster-Waldau is one of *Thrones'* best in any scene he's in, but the grudging respect and friendship he gains for Brienne is his greatest performance. Meanwhile Gwendoline Christie is more than up for the task of pushing Jaime to be a better person, despite every inclination of his upbringing and personality.

Their best scene occurs in the baths at Harrenhal, where Jaime imposes himself on the withdrawn Brienne just enough that he feels comfortable in confessing his sins to her. Ironically his sins aren't actually sins—he's the Kingslayer because he wanted to help people in King's Landing to live, not simply aid his father's ambition—but to the chivalric Brienne, the lie is shocking in all directions. Her friendship helps redeem Jaime, who, by the time he returns to the capital, becomes almost as much a force for justice as his brother Tyrion.

It's for these reasons that Brienne is the heart of arguably the most uplifting scene in all of *Game of Thrones*. At the start of the sixth season, Sansa and Theon have escaped Winterfell without her promised help. Bolton men and hounds—it's debatable which is worse—have surrounded them, leaving the escapees hopeless and ready for death. Just then, Brienne arrives, alongside her squire Podrick (another candidate for *Thrones'* most moral character) and saves the day.

After, she kneels and swears loyalty to Sansa. It is a direct homage to one of the second season's most moving scenes, where Brienne swears to Sansa's mother Catelyn. But then, Catelyn was merely returning to her son's armies, becoming a key advisor to one of the most powerful men in the realm. When Brienne swears to Sansa, however, Sansa has almost nothing. She even forgets the words, but manages to complete the ceremony with Podrick's help.

This ceremony binding Brienne to Sansa also creates, well, the party of hope for *Game of Thrones*. For so long the villains have run rampant, with the only checks to their power being morally ambiguous characters like Stannis or Margaery. But here we see a new alliance of broken misfits: Sansa, the former foolish teen, now a power in her own right. Theon the villain, redeemed by the pain he's suffered and his ability to break free of Ramsay's conditioning. And Brienne and Podrick, the best characters remaining, granting them what little physical power they have.

Depending on how wide you want to cast your net, this party becomes the source of hope across most of the land. At the Wall, they add Jon, Davos, and Melisandre. Theon adds his sister Yara, and they negotiate an alliance with Daenerys. Brienne and Pod head south, potentially bringing the Blackfish into the fold—although he declines—while the Brotherhood without Banners announces their willingness to head north. All this starts with Brienne, in the snow, telling Sansa that she has power. Brienne of Tarth, once a laughingstock, has inadvertently become a hero for the resistance.

59 Catelyn Stark

Many of *Game of Thrones'* greatest characters are complicated versions of common archetypes. Tyrion? The trickster. Brienne? The woman warrior. Catelyn Stark? At initial glance, Cat doesn't seem to fit those archetypes. She's the prickly but fundamentally good mother of the Stark family, and seems to make decisions according to her and her family's needs…at least in the first season.

But in the second and third seasons, Cat's archetype becomes clearer: she's a Cassandra figure. In Greek mythology, Cassandra is a princess of Troy, cursed by the gods to always tell the truth, especially about the future, but never have anyone listen to her. In the great tragedy of the *Orestia*, Cassandra predicts Agamemnon's murder by his wife Clytemnestra but cannot stop him from returning home, and both die in the same explosion of violence. Such is the case with Catelyn Stark, whose wisdom in the War of the Five Kings goes unheeded by three of those kings, with tragic results for them and, in the end, for her.

But first it's worth noting that the War of the Five Kings is a war that Catelyn starts in the first season. When her son Bran is paralyzed following a bizarre fall, and especially after he's attacked by a mysterious assassin, Catelyn Stark leads the investigation into his vulnerability. What she finds, and what she learns from a letter from her sister, is that the Lannisters seem to be the prime culprits, particularly Tyrion Lannister. When she meets Tyrion at the Inn at the Crossroads, she has him arrested—the act that begins the war.

While Cat takes Tyrion to the Eyrie for trial, the Imp's father Tywin invades her family's—House Tully's—domain in the Riverlands. It's unclear if Cat could have predicted that her act would lead the realm into war, although she did know enough to throw Lannister agents off the trail and have them look at Winterfell, instead of the Vale. But regardless, it does indeed lead to war, with both her blood family and her marriage family taking the brunt of the aggression from the crown and the Lannisters.

Her accusation against Tyrion doesn't hold up either. The Imp, over the course of their time together, seems to convince her that she should at least partially doubt the story of his guilt. And when she arrives at the Vale to discover her sister Lysa descending into madness and vindictiveness, Cat seems to give up on getting justice out of Tyrion—rightfully so, as he wins a trial by combat and walks free.

Game of Thrones never goes into why Cat's motivations seem to switch from the first season to the second. She goes from player of the game who fails in her most important maneuver to an advisor to one of the biggest players, her son Robb, soon to be crowned King in the North. At the end of the first season, she makes another potential mistake, albeit this time one that doesn't seem to have had a better alternative: in order to gain access to the Kingsroad via the Twins, Cat negotiates a marriage for her son to a daughter of House Frey, who join his army. But Robb, of course, is a teenaged boy, and teenaged boys can have very different ideas than their parents about the women they want to be with.

It's in the second season that Cat's cursed gift of prophecy arises. Very early on, she warns Robb not to trust Theon Greyjoy with his message for his father, Balon. Robb's potential alliance with Balon is smart, logical, and has the right messenger for anyone except the Ironborn with their ridiculous sense of honor. Rather than wisely join with Robb, Balon prefers instead to "pay the iron price" for his freedom: to win it in battle by declaring war on their rivals in the North, who put down Balon's first rebellion a decade before.

This would be bad enough but Robb's messenger compounds the error. Theon Greyjoy has been raised alongside Robb almost as a brother, and fought with him at the great victory of Whispering Wood. But Theon, taken hostage by the Starks, is susceptible to the lure of Greyjoy honor, and joins with his father.

Cat continues to warn Robb against the bad decisions that would cost him the war, but after Theon's attack, Robb is largely helpless. She warns him not to trust the Boltons or the Freys, the two houses who end up killing him, but what can he do? He's trapped with a too-small army in hostile territory, doing the very best he can.

The Freys and Boltons murder both Robb and Catelyn at the Red Wedding, and once again Cat is the first person to realize that something's gone horribly wrong. She reaches for Lord Bolton only to discover that he's wearing chain mail, anticipating the violence of the betrayal. But it comes too late, as he calmly shrugs off her attacks. The doors are shut. The armies are drunk. The Freys and Boltons murder the entire Stark host, and the King in the North.

With her last gasp, Catelyn Stark makes one final attempt to save her family. She kidnaps Lord Frey's newest wife and threatens to murder her if Robb isn't allowed to leave. As with most of her advice, though, it's the right idea but without the leverage to make it work. Walder Frey doesn't care enough about the girl to stop his ambition from being carried out. Lord Bolton finishes Robb off, Catelyn holds true to her word and kills Lady Frey, and dies herself. In the very end, Catelyn Stark remained true to her word, her wisdom, and her family—and it wasn't enough.

60 Who the Hell Is Lady Stoneheart?

If you've just watched *Game of Thrones* but you've spoken to people who've read the books and the subject of changes comes up, chances are pretty high you've heard the words "Lady Stoneheart." Readers have been expecting her to show up for years, since possibly the end of the third season, and she never, ever has—and as of the sixth season, it seems pretty much certain that she never will. So who is this lady, and why is her stone heart such a big deal?

(Book spoilers follow, obviously!)

There's no way to really dance around who Lady Stoneheart is, so here it is: she is the resurrected Catelyn Stark, found by the Brotherhood without Banners following the Red Wedding, and given the same kind of life Beric Dondarrion was given. She becomes the leader of the Brotherhood, and turns them toward a single-minded goal: revenge against the Freys, Boltons, and Lannisters. She's first seen in the epilogue of *A Storm of Swords*, judging a random Frey as guilty and having him hanged.

Although Stoneheart is Catelyn Stark in many ways, they're also totally different characters in ways that illustrate major differences in storytelling style between the show and books. For three novels, Cat is one of the books' point-of-view characters, primarily describing Robb's part of the war through Cat's eyes. After the resurrection, Stoneheart becomes a figure of terror and rumor, only occasionally glimpsed, and thanks to her throat having been slit, barely even able to speak. Even the nature of her resurrection is unclear for a while—eventually it's revealed that Beric gave Cat his "gift," sacrificing himself instead of Thoros saying the words.

And so much of *A Feast for Crows*, with major sections taking place in the Riverlands, involves the Brotherhood and their new leader acting as terrifying figures of legend. Stoneheart is relentless in her pursuit of revenge—the act of Red God resurrection more clearly removes pieces of humanity from their subject, leaving only a single core motivation behind. This drive ends up splitting the Brotherhood—Thoros can't support it, and quits. It also threatens the life of some beloved characters (which may end up still happening on the show).

But regardless of Stoneheart's changes from being Cat Stark, she fills what seems to be an absolutely essential role in the story: she dispenses justice. For three seasons, and the better part of three books, the Lannisters win and win and continue to win, while good characters, especially the Starks, keep dying. Although there are counters like Joffrey's assassination, and moments of hope like Jon Snow becoming Lord Commander, the Starks aren't the ones to take revenge. Except then there's Stoneheart, who murders the hell out of all the bastards who murdered the hell out of our heroes.

The lack of thematic counter to Lannister victories embodied by Lady Stoneheart is the main reason fans were desperate to see her—remember the end of Season 3, after the Red Wedding, and only note of hope is...Daenerys, after the fall of Yunkai. And Season 4, while it had some rise of the Starks happening again, seemed to shift focus to the complications of Meereen, the machinations of the Lannisters, Tyrells, and Martells in King's Landing, and almost nothing at the political level from *Game of Thrones'* premiere family.

So where was Lady Stoneheart given this thematic importance? Why was she missing? The simplest explanation is that she's complicated—*Game of Thrones* as a TV series simply doesn't do rumor and myth in the same way that the novels do, so making her work would be difficult. The showrunners also have seemed to want to avoid too many magical resurrections: "Dead is dead" said the showrunners after Jon Snow's death, and that was the party line up until it wasn't anymore (Beric Dondarrion's resurrection was similarly ignored). So perhaps they wanted to keep the magic like this on the down-low in order to make Jon's eventual return more surprising.

But there may be an even more straightforward explanation for Stoneheart's absence: Michelle Fairley was one of the show's lead actors for three seasons, and she's been consistent about saying she's not returning to *Game of Thrones*. Going from a top player in the credits to someone who only appears in shadows and with horrific wounds (and the makeup time that goes along with them) cannot be appealing to an actress whose career is peaking.

For some time I believed the lack of Lady Stoneheart was a pretty major mistake for the series, especially her not appearing in the Season 3 finale when a counter to Lannister victory was most needed. But instead, *Game of Thrones* has played a much longer game.

The Season 4 premiere ends on one of the show's best scenes, with Arya Stark and the Hound taking violent revenge on a set of Lannister soldiers. It wasn't exactly hopeful (a teenager engaging in the premeditated murder of several men is usually considered a bad thing), but it was a thrilling piece of justice. By the end of the season, the other Stark daughter, Sansa, has taken power for herself, putting on a black raven-feathered gown that implies a darker tone for her future.

And although both Stark girls have a bit of a detour in the grim fifth season, the sixth season is Revenge of the Starks—and Cat's daughters are essential parts of it. By the end of the season, two of the men who did the greatest damage to the Stark family, Ramsay Bolton and Walder Frey, are mercilessly killed by Sansa and Arya. Lady Stoneheart may not have made it into *Game of Thrones*—but her daughters have picked up her mantle. Whether their drive for revenge leads them down as dark a path as their mother in the novels remains to be seen.

61 George R.R. Martin's Original Pitch

"All three books will feature a complex mosaic of intercutting points-of-view among various of my large and diverse cast of players. The cast will not always remain the same."—George R.R. Martin

I've mentioned more than a few times how *Game of Thrones'* story is supposed to be both a celebration and subversion of the normal tropes of heroic fantasy, but based just on the text and show itself, it can be hard to see how much of that is intentional. At least, it was until early 2015, when a British bookseller posted a copy of George R.R. Martin's 1993 original pitch letter for the *Song of Ice & Fire*, ah, trilogy. The tweets were taken down relatively quickly, but not before they were passed around the Internet (and can still be found with an Internet search for "song of ice and fire original pitch").

The key difference between the pitch and the final product is that the pitch is, well, simple. It's a fairly straightforward heroic fantasy series, based on the Lannister-Stark civil war early on, while Dany gathers her forces across the seas and a darker threat rises from the North. Many aspects of the story are quite recognizable: all the initial main characters are present, and several of them die over the course of the story in the pitch (particularly Ned and Robb).

But there are two huge differences between the story in the original pitch and the story we've come to know and love. First, it's simple. The dominant characters throughout the civil war, which is given by far the most detail in Martin's letter, are essentially all Starks and Lannisters, good versus evil (with Tyrion straddling both sides). There's no sign of the other major, morally ambiguous Great Houses and rivals. No Stannis, no Littlefinger, no Margaery, not even Lord Tywin—not even Queen Cersei, although that one's more complicated.

The second major difference is that, well, Martin thought he was writing a trilogy. The first book, *A Game of Thrones*, was meant to cover the entire civil war. The second, *A Dance with Dragons*, was supposed to be about Daenerys Targaryen's invasion with the Dothraki horde she collects in the first volume. And the third, *The Winds of Winter*, would cover the undead invasion.

You'll notice that all three of these are novels in the series—the first, fifth, and sixth books, to be precise. What happened to Martin's plan is what happened to the missing books: he started writing a much more complex story.

Those three missing books represent the point where Martin dramatically expanded the scope of his story to include the entire political narrative of the Seven Kingdoms. Unhappy with just presenting a traditional, if bloody, fantasy story, Martin went full-bore into intrigue and moral ambiguity. Along the way, the simmering stories of Dany and the White Walkers got taken off the burner, forced to wait for the resolution of the civil war that shifted from one book into three.

It was actually fairly well-known that most of the first three novels, which were all published relatively quickly from 1996–2000, were initially all part of the same book that grew out of control. The same thing seems to have happened with Martin's next books in the series, but unfortunately for ol' George, he had a demanding fanbase, and eventually a TV show, applying more and more pressure.

There are a few other fascinating bits of trivia in the pitch. Remember that nice relationship with Arya that Jon Snow had in the first couple episodes? That was originally supposed to have been the start of a romance, with Tyrion Lannister, of all people, making it a love triangle.

Cersei's disappearance from the pitch is also fascinating, while Jaime becomes the primary villain of the piece. A clue as to what happened to Cersei can be seen in one line late in the pitch, which says that Jaime succeeds to the throne "by the simple expedient of killing everyone ahead of him in the line of succession...." In other words, Martin took his initial plan for Jaime, split the Kingslayer in half, and gave his twin sister the ruthless political ambition!

You can actually see the original pitch, if you read the first hundred or so pages of *A Game of Thrones* (covering roughly the first two episodes). There's very little in the initial section of the story that counters that initial plan. But once Ned Stark rides into King's Landing, and Martin realizes that his politics are far more fun than his heroic fantasy, *A Game of Thrones* the novel becomes, well, *Game of Thrones,* the epic narrative of page and screen.

62 A Feast with Dragons

When *Game of Thrones* hit its middle seasons, it reached the peaks of its popularity—and various controversies and backlashes. In this it mirrored the books it was based on, *A Feast for Crows* and *A Dance with Dragons*—ironic, since many of the show's controversies were based on the changes from the books. But the middle of the story has proven difficult for both variations, it's worth looking at why.

Part of the problem, for readers, is simple: it took too long between books. The increasing complications of the story led George R.R. Martin to cut the story into two halves (*A Feast for Crows* focused on the south and the Free Cities; *A Dance with Dragons* focused on the North and the rest of Essos), but it also meant that the novels were significantly delayed. Books 1–3 came out every other year from 1996–2000, but the next two came in 2005 and 2011.

So fans had a ton of expectations for each. And those...those were often not met. Especially in *Feast*, Martin spent a lot of time focusing on brand-new characters in new or rarely used locations. Both Dorne and the Iron Islands received multiple point-of-view characters who'd barely or never appeared before, getting into the internal politics of these previously fairly minor regions. Meanwhile, fan favorite characters like Tyrion, Dany, and Jon Snow didn't even appear in *Feast,* only in *Dance*, meaning that one book feels like a collection of *Ice & Fire* spinoff stories, while *Dance* is almost too jam-packed to move.

The solution? Some fans put together a project called "A Feast with Dragons," which is a reading list of the chapters of both novels so that they remain in chronological order, but with the narratives of all the characters in the world mixed in. This helps prevent, say, Cersei from totally dominating the story, which she does in *A Feast for Crows*, and makes characters like the Martells of Dorne and Greyjoys of Pyke feel more integrated into the story.

It also helps resolve an excess of cliffhangers, which was not a trend for the series before these books. In *Feast*, Cersei hears a rumor that Ser Davos has been killed. Readers at the time had to wait five years to find out how and why she thought this, whereas readers of the combined novel will see his point-of-view chapter shortly after.

"A Feast with Dragons" isn't perfect, though much of that has to do with the source material. The combined books have nearly two dozen different POV characters, meaning it can get head-spinning to travel all over the world from chapter to chapter, and many of the newer characters still feel kinda pointless. But it's still probably the best way to read these two novels.

If you're looking for the list, just do an Internet search for "A Feast with Dragons." There are also various ebook editions that can be found, though those are of dubious legality. Some fans have even cut out and repasted the chapters from one book into the next, but that's perhaps an excessive level of dedication. Still, it's something to do while waiting for *The Winds of Winter*.

63 The Wars of the Roses

"Now is the winter of our discontent / Made glorious summer by this sun of York"—William Shakespeare, Richard III

If you take a quick look at a map of Westeros, it kinda looks like England. You've got a big ol' wall directly severing the top third of the continent—like Hadrian's Wall in England, built to keep out the Scots and Picts, though a wee bit smaller in height (16 feet, instead of 600). The capital's in the wider, denser southeast part, just like London, and there's a narrowing as the landmass goes north.

But if you add in the bases of the two most important families in Westeros—the Starks and the Lannisters—the map begins to look like a very specific era in English history: the Wars of the Roses, a series of civil wars pitting the Yorks of northern England against the Lancasters of the south, with their control of the crown. The names and the locations are so similar that it's clear the Wars of the Roses were a major influence on *Game of Thrones'* developing story.

The history goes like this: at the end of the 14th century, King Henry IV violently deposed Richard II, creating a crisis of legitimacy in the royal Plantagenet line. His son, Henry V, died early, leaving a baby to inherit as Henry VI—who would also grow up to be mentally unfit to rule. One of the most powerful nobles serving the realm during Henry VI's reign was Richard, Duke of York, who had a claim to the throne related to Richard II's deposed line. York became Lord Protector of the realm—Hand of the King, basically—but eventually attempted to seize the throne for himself. His chief opposition was Henry VI's queen, Margaret of Anjou.

The Lancastrians and Yorkists traded victories back and forth for decades (1455–1471, specifically) with the king, the crown, and London being held by one side or the other on multiple occasions. Eventually the Yorkists won, crowning Edward IV, who stabilized the country before his early death, when his famously nasty brother Richard III took over. Richard's acts caused civil war, which allowed a distant Lancastrian relative, Henry Tudor, to invade. In 1485, Henry won, became Henry VII, married Richard of York's daughter, and unified England—or so the story goes.

See, the thing with the Wars of the Roses is that we know and understand primarily through the English stories and legends around them, especially William Shakespeare's eight-part history plays (*Richard II, Henry IV parts 1–2, Henry V, Henry VI parts 1–3, Richard III*). In Shakespeare's typical dramatic style, he paints a sordid portrait of the collapse of Plantagenet rule, with larger-than-life personalities like Margaret; Neville, the Earl of Warwick (the Kingmaker); and especially the monstrous Richard III. Shakespeare's Richard III is one of the great historical villains, who deceives his way to the throne and caps it off with the murder of his young nephews, the "Princes in the Tower."

Shakespeare's story is one of the canonical works of civil war literature in the English language, and is an influence on everything, including George R.R. Martin's books. But Shakespeare is also propaganda—his queen, Elizabeth I, was the granddaughter of Henry VII, and his story naturally has a pro-Tudor, anti-Yorkist vibe. Martin's *A Game of Thrones*, however, takes the opposite tack: the militaristic northern Starks are the good guys, and the decadent evil queen holding the crown is the villain.

It's an interesting twist on the historical narrative of the Wars of the Roses, but Martin has largely taken the story in a different direction. In his original pitch (see chapter 61), the parallels were much more explicit: Jaime Lannister, who murders his way to the throne, fills the role of the horrific Richard III.

Jaime's brother Tyrion, meanwhile, was originally supposed to lead the Lannister armies to capture Winterfell and ruin Robb Stark's chances, before switching sides, and helping the Starks fight back. In this respect the Imp was supposed to be like Neville, the Earl of Warwick, also known as the Kingmaker. Warwick was a powerful, ambitious lord who attached himself to the Yorkist cause early, but once they took the throne found himself pushed out and switched sides to help the Lancasters before being captured and executed.

Both of those direct parallels didn't make it into the final story—and it's a good thing, too, as it helps *Game of Thrones* be its own story. But the grand Shakespearean tragedy of wars and betrayals and larger-than-life characters making foolish decisions out of their own ambition is part of the core of *Game of Thrones*— and that comes from the Wars of the Roses and their portrayals in culture.

64 The Accursed Kings

"This is the original Game of Thrones. *"—George R.R. Martin*

Chances are pretty decent you haven't heard of *The Accursed Kings*, a seven-novel series about the end of the Capetian dynasty of the French throne in the 14th century. There's a simple reason for this: the books, written by French author Maurice Druon, weren't in print in English for decades.

The series has proved incredibly popular in France, lending itself to *two* television adaptations, but didn't make much of a splash in English, with one major exception: George R.R. Martin read them and became a fan. Thanks to his recommendation, the series has been republished in English, with the quote at the top plastered dramatically above the books' titles.

The history of the period is ripe for dramatic, pulpy fiction: the novels start at the end of the reign of Philip the Fair, a ruthless, powerful king who has just imprisoned the leaders of the Knights Templar. When he has them executed, they curse him, hence the title of the series. Whether the curse is real or not, a string of conspiracies and bad luck destroys his dynasty, tears the kingdom in half, and leads the kingdom to the disastrous Hundred Years War against England.

This particular span of years is ripe for a *Game of Thrones*–like story. After the public executions, the Capetian dynasty is torn apart by an absurd sex scandal. Philip's three sons had married three daughters of the Duke of Burgundy. The three princesses arranged affairs for two of them, which were exposed. The young gentlemen involved were brutally executed, and the three women imprisoned for life—making it impossible for their husbands to produce heirs.

With sex, violence, corruption, autocracy, and eventually war, all the ingredients that made *Game of Thrones* (except dragons); it's easy to see how Martin was inspired by this—in his foreword, he says, "*The Accursed Kings* has it all. Iron kings and strangled queens, battles and betrayals, lies and lust, deception, family rivalries, the curse of the Templars...."

But there are some major differences beyond the presence of monsters. Martin's books are *dense,* where every random knight has a possible backstory that may never be important to anyone except for a wiki editor, but it's there. *The Accursed Kings* has plenty of characters, but everyone seems to have a specific role to play.

The other thing is that...*The Accursed Kings* isn't all that good. Perhaps that's unfair—it's written in a fashion that feels disorienting to a contemporary English-language reader. Its point-of-view is only partially attached, sometimes rigidly following a single character around for several chapters, sometimes omnisciently describing both characters' feelings in a scene. It occasionally deliberately nods at the modernity of its readers, something our books just don't do (imagine if *A Game of Thrones* described ravens as being like a telegraph, for example).

Still, once you get into the rhythms of how Druon's prose and Humphrey Hare's translation work, the story moves. Much like Martin's first book in his series, the first book of Druon's—*The Iron King*—really starts working when it gets into the government's advisors, such as the Varys-like councilor Nogaret. If you're jonesin' for some bloody, sexy political backstabbing, or you just wanna see *Thrones'* influences, *The Accursed Kings* is worth a look.

65 The Lord of the Rings

"One does not simply behead Eddard Stark."—Sean Bean Internet meme

George R.R. Martin's *A Song of Ice and Fire* novels are, in many ways, a rebellion against Tolkien's *Lord of the Rings*, which provided a model of fantasy that dominated the genre for decades. But *Game of Thrones* as a show couldn't possibly exist without the success of *Lord of the Rings* as a film series just a few years prior.

Before roughly the year 2000, Hollywood did not treat fantasy well, at least in terms of current conventions of fantasy (a totally different world from our own, with pre-industrial technology). This doesn't quite mean there wasn't anything, but most of it was filtered through myths and legend, like *Clash of the Titans* and *Xena: Warrior Princess* for Greek mythology, or *Excalibur* or *The Sword in the Stone* for Arthurian legend.

There was a trend toward the genre in the 1980s in film, with movies like *The Dark Crystal, Willow, Legend, Ladyhawke,* and the genre's closest thing to a classic, *Labyrinth.* While relatively successful, they were largely aimed at younger audiences, and they weren't particularly engaged with fantasy as a literary genre—at that point exploding in popularity.

The most famous work of literary fantasy was J.R.R. Tolkien's *Lord of the Rings* trilogy, initially published in the 1950s, becoming an immensely popular among the counterculture in the 1960s. In the late 1970s, Ralph Bakshi made an animated attempt at bringing it to the screen. It starts promisingly enough, but it's one of the rare sorts of films where you can actually see the budget disappear

297

as it progresses. It only covers half the story, and a sequel was never made.

But Bakshi's film did acquire some fans, including Kiwi director Peter Jackson. As Jackson began to make his name in the 1990s, he started looking to make an ambitious live-action version of the story. New Line Cinema eventually took the monumental gamble of funding three blockbuster films in a trilogy, all filmed at once, which would be released one per year from 2001–2003.

Against all odds—a genre largely dismissed by Hollywood, telling a story that isn't completed in a single trip to the theater, in addition to every other issue any big-budget film has—*Lord of the Rings* was a monumental success. Audiences flocked to them, critics praised them, and fantasy fans, treated so poorly by Hollywood for so long, were vindicated in seeing a genre they loved taken seriously and put on screen successfully. (There were, of course, some holdouts: as with *Game of Thrones*, a vocal contingent of *LOTR* book fans disliked the entire adaptation.)

The *Lord of the Rings* films created the model that *Game of Thrones* would follow in adapting a beloved, serious fantasy novel series. The single most important component of making the adaptation work: full commitment from the people producing it.

This starts with the money, of course. HBO and New Line Cinema both gave their fantasy series buckets of money to look and be the absolute best they could. This involves things like filming in real locations—New Zealand for *Lord of the Rings*, all across Europe for *Game of Thrones*. But it also means hiring great actors, building gorgeous sets, and creating the highest-quality costuming.

It also means full commitment from the people hired with all that money to adapt the story. In one of the "Appendices" (or DVD extras) for *The Two Towers,* the costume designer for the films discusses a dress that Eowyn appears in. She examines the decision-making process that led to its color and its design for this particular scene—then acknowledges that all that went into a dress that only appeared on screen for a couple seconds.

The commitment to having a fully designed work with its own internal logic and connection to the original books creates an overall feeling of *authenticity*, which is essential. It proves to fans of the books that the story they love is being taken seriously by people who might love it as much as they do. And even for people who don't care about the books, the effort to create a quality, consistent product makes the films or shows look great anyway.

Both *Lord of the Rings* and *Game of Thrones* therefore become a great spectacle. They aren't just a fantasy film or a fantasy show, they're a grand *event*, using the fantasy genre to create arguably the best-looking films or shows you can lay your eyes on. And nothing they do breaks that spell: the special effects are best possible, as are the actors, and the sets.

Another crucial element of the spectacle of both *LOTR* and *GoT* is that both have some of the best action sequences around. The fantasy genre offers two big advantages for putting its battles on screen: first, medieval-era weaponry tends to look pretty awesome in a fight. Think of Oberyn twirling his spear, or the focus on Legolas' face he draws his bow. Second, there's magic and monsters, so we can get scenes like Jon Snow dueling a White Walker or Aragon fighting a troll.

But beyond that, both commit to having battles be essential parts of their storytelling and making sure those stories both make sense and are exciting to watch. The climax of *The Two Towers* is a desperate holding action of a small army and band of heroes at Helm's Deep, a battle that has its own narrative of success and failure in holding gates or stopping Orcish plans. Likewise, the Battle of the Bastards in Season 6 of *Game of Thrones* presents both an exciting set of action sequences and tells a coherent story on its own of Jon and his army trying to hold off a flood of Boltons. Both battles end on the same note: a ray of sun bursts through the darkness, and a cavalry charge from unexpected allies rout the seemingly invincible enemies. (The ending similarity is so strong that it's hard not to see the Knights of the Vale's attack as a direct homage to Helm's Deep, honestly.)

The success of *Lord of the Rings* instantly earned it comparisons to another famous speculative fiction trilogy, *Star Wars*. *Star Wars* helped legitimize science fiction, alongside *Star Trek*, leading to consistent production of SF films and, a decade or so later, a boom in space opera television. That hasn't really happened with fantasy and *Lord of the Rings*. Most of the fantasy films that came out after *LOTR's* success tended to be closer to *Harry Potter*, which also achieved screen success at the same time—albeit aimed more specifically at young people. These were films like *Percy Jackson* or *Narnia*—there was no boom in fantasy literature adaptations.

But while it hasn't created a consistent new film genre, *Lord of the Rings* paved the way for successful adult fantasy with mass appeal, which *Game of Thrones* would take advantage of nearly a decade later. Indeed, in casting Sean Bean, previously most famous for his role as Boromir in *Lord of the Rings*, as Ned Stark, and putting him at the center of the show's advertising, *Game of Thrones* specifically moved to appropriate the affection fans had for *Lord of the Rings*.

And then, of course, Joffrey called for Ser Ilyn Payne as his executioner, Sean Bean died again, and *Game of Thrones* made it clear just how different it was from *Lord of the Rings*. But it still owes Peter Jackson's films a major debt—in order to have expectations subverted by *Game of Thrones*, *Lord of the Rings* had to create those expectations.

66 Know Your Direwolves

In the pilot episode of *Game of Thrones*, a group of Stark men and boys come across a dead direwolf in the forest. It's an inauspicious omen, as direwolves rarely come south of the Wall, and she's died of a wound from a stag's horn—the symbol of House Stark being killed by the symbol of House Baratheon.

She also has several pups, who, deprived of their mother, are likely to die. While some of the Stark men suggest killing them, Jon Snow realizes that there are five pups, for the five legitimate Stark heirs. He sacrifices his own membership in the family to suggest that the children adopt the beasts—only for a sixth, albino outcast pup to be found, for him.

Much like the Starks, the direwolves have not had a good time of it on *Game of Thrones*. But unlike the Stark children, most of the wolves are dead. Here's what happened to them.

Grey Wind—Robb's direwolf is well-trained and joins Robb in battle, often serving as the first line of attack, as in the battle that Robb wins at the start of the second season. Robb is so associated with Grey Wind that he becomes known as the "Young Wolf" and is rumored to transform into the beast himself.

At the Red Wedding, Grey Wind is kenneled, and threatens to break free once the massacre begins. Frey crossbowmen manage to kill the wolf, and later sew its head onto Robb's body.

Lady—Sansa's wolf Lady is the best-behaved of the six wolves, supposedly sharing her mistress's sweet temperament. Lady is the first to die, however, as Cersei has the pup killed as revenge for Arya's wolf attacking Prince Joffrey. Sansa having "lost her wolf" is treated as an explanation for her passivity in the court early on, but eventually, Sansa finds her strength without the pup.

Nymeria—Arya's wolf is named for the warrior queen of Dorne (a name shared by one of the Sand Snakes as well). Nymeria is wild like her owner, and when the conflict between the children at the Trident occurs, Nymeria attacks Joffrey. With the prince threatening revenge, Arya realizes that Nymeria won't survive a return to camp, and she throws rocks until the direwolf flees into the wilderness.

On the show, this is the last we've seen or heard of Nymeria. In the novels, however, there are rumors of massive wolfpacks roaming the Riverlands led by a giant queen wolf, and Arya has warg-like dreams that seem to connect her to Nymeria. We may not have seen the last of her.

Summer—Bran Stark's wolf, Summer, is possibly the most important of the direwolves. He saves Bran's life from an assassin meant to silence the boy, for one. But Summer also becomes the focus of Bran's awakening powers as a warg, which Bran uses to find a way to run and be free despite his injury. Bran also wargs into Summer to save Jon Snow's life when Jon is attacked by the Wildlings in Season 3.

Summer continues to help Bran travel north to meet the Three-Eyed Raven. But, like many of the Stark boy's allies, Summer is killed when the forces of the Night's King attack the Three-Eyed Raven's home.

Shaggydog—Rickon's wolf is, like the boy himself, left virtually feral with most of the Stark adults leaving for the civil war. Shaggydog does stick with his master and Summer, though, without causing too many problems. And when the Stark boys split up, Shaggydog goes with Rickon and Osha to House Umber.

When the Smalljon Umber takes over, however, he betrays the Starks, capturing Rickon and taking him to Ramsay Bolton. As proof that Rickon is who Umber says he is, the Smalljon offers Shaggydog's head, a trick he later repeats for Jon Snow's benefit prior to the battle.

Ghost—The only direwolf to make it, alongside his master, through the entirety of the series, with a few detours. The sneaky albino Ghost is Jon's companion, although he's free to roam around Castle Black. Ghost finds the body of the first wight to be confirmed by the Night's Watch in the first season, and he travels with the Watch on their Ranging. Ghost bails on Jon when he joins Qhorin's party, strangely, though it's discovered that he returns to help Sam—the only other character in all of *Game of Thrones* who seems to fully win one of the wolves' trust.

Ghost is also present for the mutiny at Craster's Keep, and while Sam and Gilly flee, he's captured by the mutineers. In the battle at Craster's in Season 4, Bran frees both Ghost and Summer from the mutineers' trap, and Ghost eventually kills Rast, the mutineer who'd been tormenting him during his captivity. He reunites with Jon and plays a key role in saving Castle Black from Mance's attack.

The albino direwolf has a smaller role in the next couple of seasons, saving Sam and Gilly from would-be rapists in the Watch, and watching over Jon's corpse after his murder. Ghost is oddly not present at the Battle of the Bastards, but he is still alive, and we'll almost certainly see more of him, the last (known) Stark direwolf.

67 In the Credits

Here's a quick guide to all the locations in *Game of Thrones'* opening credits, from north to south in Westeros. The credits mandate that four locations always be shown: the Wall, Winterfell, King's Landing, and wherever Dany is. Apart from that, they're usually the locations that appear in the episode.

The Wall: Between the North and Beyond-the-Wall. Castle Black specifically, headquarters of the Night's Watch.

Winterfell: The North. Home of House Stark.

The Dreadfort: The North. Home of House Bolton.

Moat Cailin: The North. A ruined keep, only manned during wartime.

The Twins: The Riverlands. Home of House Frey.

Pyke: The Iron Islands. Home of House Greyjoy.

Riverrun: The Riverlands. Home of House Tully.

The Eyrie: The Vale. Home of House Arryn.

Dragonstone: The Crownlands. Traditional home of House Targaryen, currently seat of Stannis Baratheon.

Harrenhal: The Riverlands. Castle of King Harren the Black, burnt by dragons.

King's Landing: The Crownlands. Capital of the Seven Kingdoms.

Dorne: The only location named after the entire region, which is, of course, Dorne. Home of House Martell.

And in Essos, from west to east:

Braavos: A Free City. Home of the Iron Bank and the House of Black and White.

Pentos: A Free City. Home of Targaryen ally Illyrio Mopatis.

Meereen: Slaver's Bay. Daenerys' home in Seasons 4–6.

Yunkai: Slaver's Bay. The city sacked by Daenerys at the end of Season 3.

Astapor: Slaver's Bay. The city where Daenerys acquires her Unsullied army.

Vaes Dothrak: The only Dothraki city, representing the entire Dothraki Sea.

Qarth: A rich merchant city on the edge of the known world.

68 Who Sent the Assassin After Bran?

Events move fast on *Game of Thrones*. Although it's a show with mysteries in its backstory, they don't define what people do: their personal and political motivation do that. And once they start down a path, its consequences take over from their initial motivations. The story keeps moving.

That is a somewhat longwinded way of asking this question: Do you know who sent the assassin after Bran Stark with the Valyrian steel dagger? This was a critically important question in the early episodes, and Catelyn Stark's answer, given to her by Littlefinger, is that Tyrion Lannister did it. She kidnaps Tyrion, starting the War of the Five Kings. Tyrion wins trial by combat and goes free...and then the show never actually answers the question.

There are plenty of reason to not believe that it was Tyrion. First, and probably most importantly, the Imp is one of the most likable characters in the entire story, and one who always tries to fight for good. Assassinating a paralyzed boy doesn't fit with his character at all, and he denies it vehemently. Also, the information comes from Littlefinger, whose trustworthiness is, shall we say, somewhat lacking.

But by the time Tyrion is freed from the Eyrie, and especially when Littlefinger's betrayal of the Starks is revealed, events had moved well beyond the need to find a resolution for the dagger storyline. There's a war on, and *CSI: Winterfell* has to take a back seat. But it is still strange that such an important question was never resolved.

In the novels, this question takes a back seat as well, although Tyrion does investigate how he'd been set up when he's free in King's Landing. King Joffrey provides several clues that it was him

305

who did the deed, and Tyrion later puts the pieces together. The problem is, Joffrey's motivation doesn't work at all on the show: he's slightly younger on the page and is going through a phase where he tries to emulate his supposed father, Robert. Joffrey overhears King Robert complaining about Bran's injury, saying that it would be better if the boy died. So the sadistic prince, attempting to be like his dad, steals the dagger and gives it to a cutthroat to do the deed.

But on the show, Joffrey never shows any kind of respect toward his father. He orders Robert's bastards killed at the start of the second season (an order given by Cersei in the novels), so any kind of filial duty is off the table.

The only possible clue given by the series is a conversation between Jaime and Cersei, where Cersei insists that Jaime didn't have to try to kill Bran. While the conversation is almost certainly about the initial shove out the window, it is perhaps ambiguous enough to comprise the second assassination attempt as well. Six seasons in, it's clear that *Game of Thrones* has no interest in providing a clear resolution, but viewers have moved on, just like the show did.

69 Tyrion, the Secret Targ?

Okay, so most of the fan theories I've discussed so far are or have been somewhat plausible, or at least reveal something interesting about the books or show. But some of them, well, they're pretty out there, even if they do solve some of the mysteries of the show. So it's worth diving into one to explain what it is and why people might believe it. Ready? Here it goes: one fan theory has it that

Tyrion Lannister is the son of the Mad King Aerys II Targaryen, and is therefore, alongside Jon Snow, a "secret Targ."

On the surface this probably sounds immediately implausible. Tyrion's relationship with his father is arguably the most defining characteristic of both men. He certainly embraces the Lannister lifestyle, if not necessarily all the members of his family. And it's more fun to think that Tyrion, like Tommen and Myrcella, somehow has avoided the genetic disposition toward villainy that the rest of his family possesses. So my first reaction to this, and perhaps yours, is "What on earth are they thinking?"

First, as discussed in the Glossary (chapter 23), there is a prophecy of a three-headed dragon: the three riders for Dany's children. Obviously she's one, and Jon Snow is almost certainly the second. Who's third? Why not Tyrion, arguably the third-main character behind them? Second, there's a historical mystery. At a certain point, after being Aerys' friend and Hand for years, Tywin just packed up and left. No explanation. Aerys, a consummate womanizer, did occasionally embarrass Tywin by seemingly making moves on his wife, Joanna Lannister. But what if he did more than just make a move?

There's also some evidence. When Tyrion was born, he was deformed beyond simply being a little person, he was also said to have had a tail. The show doesn't harp on it much, but as the incest-riddled Targaryen line started to decline, many of their babes were stillborn, with tails—much like Dany's cursed son Rhaego, who died in the first season finale.

Meanwhile, Tywin, who famously only ever demonstrated affection for Joanna in his entire life, clearly despises Tyrion. He respects the Imp's intelligence enough to promote him, but never treats him as a full member of the family by, say, giving Tyrion Casterly Rock, which should be his by the laws of succession. And Tywin, of course, orders Tyrion's death in the fourth season.

Is this enough to believe it? Not for me—I believe Bran will be the third head as a warg, and that the "tail" is an indication of incest (Tywin and Joanna were first cousins). But you could view this theory as proof of the creativity of the *Game of Thrones* fanbase in trying to solve difficult mysteries....or as evidence that with half a decade between books, they have *way* too much time on their hands to theorize.

70 The Costumes of *Thrones*

Take a moment and think about this question. What does *Game of Thrones* do better than any other TV show? There are a few good answers to this. Action scenes, special effects, and child actors immediately come to mind. But here's mine: the costuming. How good are the costumes on this show? They pretty much always look great, and they're often smart as well.

Let's take a quick example. The start of the sixth season finale, "The Winds of Winter," depicts several characters getting dressed for the trials to come, juxtaposing Cersei's clothing with her rivals like the High Sparrow. Cersei, who has almost always appeared in the past wearing Lannister red and gold gowns showing off her neck, is instead wearing a high-necked black and silver outfit. It's a fantastic look in and of itself and was an instant hit with live-tweeters, and it also represents Cersei's role changing from being one power source in King's Landing into being the dominant force in the Southlands, and the show's new primary villain.

But here's what makes the outfit even neater: it's an adaptation of her father Tywin's formal look in King's Landing. Same black and silver, same high neck, same garb that looks like high-class leather armor. At a moment when she lives up to her father's legacy, destroying the Tyrells like he destroyed House Reyne of Castamere, Cersei takes up his sartorial legacy as well. Now that's great costuming.

Game of Thrones knows how important its costumes are. Its costume designer has a prime location in the credits, right next to composer Ramin Jawed. For almost all of the show's run, that role has been filled by Michelle Clapton, who has won three Emmys for her work on *Thrones*, as well as a BAFTA for the British mini-series *The Devil's Whore*.

Clapton actually left *Game of Thrones* temporarily for Season 6, replaced by April Ferry. (Clapton worked on Netflix's lush, expensive period drama *The Crown* in this time.) But she was called back for the sixth season's final two episodes, in part to specifically design Cersei's coronation dress.

In an interview with *Vanity Fair* after the episode aired, Clapton described her very intentional thinking for designing the costume. Black, both to indicate mourning and to show how Cersei was internally dead, a creature of ambition. The connections to Tywin were obvious and intentional, but there are also designs on the gown similar to those on Jaime's golden hand, connecting her to the one living person Cersei still cares about in any way.

This dress was obviously incredibly special, but it's a great example of the considerations *Thrones* makes when picking its costumes. Once you start looking for these things, they pop up again and again, and it's almost never in a negative way.

71 Ramin Djawadi, Composer of *Thrones*

Many of the people involved in *Game of Thrones'* production have rocketed to stardom based on their roles in its success, but if anyone has risen to the absolute top, it's composer Ramin Djawadi, who was fairly successful before *Game of Thrones*, but is now probably the most in-demand composer in Hollywood, with credits on HBO's *Westworld*, the acclaimed CBS series *Person of Interest*, the *Warcraft* movie, and *The Great Wall*, amongst many others.

Djawadi comes from the same soundtrack school as influential composer Hans Zimmer, who is most famous for his work with Christopher Nolan on films like *The Dark Knight* and *Inception*. In order to work directly with the film as it's being made, instead of making a soundtrack to be added later, Zimmer works with computers first, before recording a final version later. Thanks to the limitations and strength of artificial sounds, this form of composition prioritizes short, clear sounds: drums, horns, and sharp strings.

So composers from the Zimmer school tend to prioritize rhythmic repetition that can be altered for use in a variety of different scenes. Consider the main theme of *Game of Thrones* with its two circular patterns, one fast, one a little slower. Those brief melodies also get added to the music of the show at certain crucial moments: during the 360 courtyard sequence in the Battle of Castle of Black, for example, the main theme's melody kicks in right as Jon Snow descends from the elevator and enters the fray.

Djawadi is nowhere near Zimmer's level in terms of leaving melody out, but he tends to drop it into key moments to grab the attention. "The Rains of Castamere," the Lannister theme song, for example, uses a slow meandering cello that conveys the dread of utter destruction that the song is supposed to inspire. One of my favorite of Djawadi's tracks, the dragons' theme "Blood of the Dragon," uses a slow, high string sound that manages to convey both the drive to soar through the sky and the danger of the dragons.

His most notable composition for the show, apart from perhaps the theme song, also breaks almost entirely from Zimmer-style composing. Much like costumer Michelle Clapton, his neighbor in the *Game of Thrones* credits, this creative peak occurs at the start of the sixth season finale, during the trial of Loras Tyrell in the Sept of Baelor. The track—called "Light of the Seven"—is unique in the entire musical history of *Game of Thrones*.

First, it's the longest unbroken track in all of *GoT*'s music, at nearly ten minutes. Most every other piece of great music on the show is built on a rhythmic repetition that goes through alterations over time, but this one has a narrative of rising and falling motifs and instruments.

The track also sounds unlike anything else on *Game of Thrones* because it uses totally different instrumentation. Instead of the beating repetition of the show's usual horns and drums, the song uses a modern piano, children's vocals, and an organ, all of which are almost never used on the show. It also uses a cello, which is the primary melodic instrument of *Game of Thrones*, but the cello seems to be fighting with the other instruments as much as it binds the music together.

Indeed, the entire piece seems to be at war with itself. Its rhythms are off: new sections of the song start a half-beat later than expected regularly; it uses dissonant notes and chords (like the just slightly off voices on some of the vocal notes); it never quite does what's expected next. "Light of the Seven" also totally takes over the sound of the show—again, something *Game of Thrones* has almost never done.

The net result of this is a musical track that overlays a relatively mundane set of circumstances on the show—characters getting dressed, the minor character of Loras having his fate decided—and makes it seem special. It creates the feeling that what you're watching may not look like it now, but it is building to something special, and something dreadful—it's not a happy song.

But "Light of the Seven" is also playful. It's audacious, trying new things with new instruments, but coming back to viewers with things like the occasional flare of the main theme's melody on the organ and winking, as if to say "you're right—things are about to get wild." This, too, fits the scene. Like Cersei, it's a moment where *Game of Thrones* swings for the fences, betting everything that it shows the rise of its supervillain just right. It does, and Djawadi deserves as much credit as anyone for it.

It may not be possible to overstate how important Djawadi has been to *Game of Thrones*. The show's music has been one of its highlights from beginning to end, and the composer hasn't ever really put a foot wrong: whenever a character or storyline has needed a boost, like Dany with her dragons, he's found one, and integrated it into the overall plan for the show. Ramin Djawadi has fully deserved becoming arguably the top film and television composer in the world.

72 "The Rains of Castamere"

"And who are you / the proud lord said / that I must bow my head"— *"The Rains of Castamere"*

Fantasy authors usually love songs. It's kind of a thing, ever since Tolkien would take multiple pages for a song in *Lord of the Rings*, in a made-up elven language no less! George R.R. Martin doesn't love his songs that much (his interest is more in the feasting), but he's still got a few scattered throughout the novels. Some, like "The Bear and the Maiden Fair," made it onto the screen. But there's one that's become an integral part of the show: "The Rains of Castamere."

"The Rains of Castamere" makes its first appearance in one of the defining episodes of the series, "Blackwater." As the Lannister soldiers drink and wait, they sing this song. Bronn joins in, leading them to ask how he knows a Lannister song. At the end of the episode, after Tywin announces that the city is saved, the credits roll with his anthem playing, performed by the deep, gravelly voice of Matt Berninger of The National.

But it's in the third season when "The Rains of Castamere" becomes essential. For one thing, its association with Lannister victory turns it into their theme. Despite the family's importance, they didn't have a clear musical association on the show, certainly not in the same way that Stannis or the Starks did.

Second, "The Rains of Castamere" becomes a point of discussion on the show. In the eighth episode of the season, Cersei Lannister attempts to intimidate Margaery Tyrell by explaining the meaning. Tywin Lannister's father, Tytos, was a weak lord, which eventually led the Reyne family of Castamere to rebel. Tywin took it upon himself to brutally suppress the rebellion, destroying the castle of Castamere and every last member of the Reyne family. The Reyne family sigil is a lion, like the Lannisters, but red instead of gold, hence the "long and sharp as yours" claws of the song.

This is not only good background info on Tywin, who in the third and fourth seasons is arguably the lead antagonist of the series, but also sets up the ninth episode of the season, named "The Rains of Castamere." This is the episode of the Red Wedding: the brutal murders of Robb Stark, his mother, his wife, and his armies. The song itself plays a pivotal role in the events. Musicians are in the balconies above the feast hall, playing upbeat songs fit for a wedding. But the Freys shut the doors, and when the musicians turn to "The Rains of Castamere," Catelyn Stark realizes something has gone wrong, too late to stop the bloodbath.

The Red Wedding may have been the peak of mass interest in *Game of Thrones*, which helped turn "The Rains of Castamere" into a cultural phenomenon. I've heard of bars who've taken to playing it after last call, to clear people out for the night, and I've personally heard it played after dinner at a geek-centered corporate event, with one longtime employee making certain everyone got the joke he'd set up.

Composer Ramin Djawadi deserves massive credit for the tune itself. His arrangement of "The Rains of Castamere" manages to be both incredibly catchy and ominous at the same time. It's a perfect combination for some of the most famous and arguably the best music in the entire series.

73 David J. Peterson, Language Inventor

"Anha vidrik khalasares anni jim, finaan nakhoe rhaesheser, majin adothrak hrazef ido yomme Havazzhifi Kazga ven et vo khal avvos."—Khal Drogo

While many people involved in *Game of Thrones*' production have risen to the top of their fields, only one can safely say he's created an entire industry. That's David J. Peterson, creator of Dothraki, High Valyrian, and all the rest of *Thrones*' languages—and someone so successful at it that he's gone on to create languages for TV shows like *Defiance* and *The 100*, and films like *Warcraft* and *Doctor Strange*. The man has been so successful that he makes a career as a language creator, a full-time job that literally didn't exist before Peterson.

Peterson became interested in creating languages when he discovered Esperanto, eventually starting a group called the Language Creation Society. This generic name proved useful when *Game of Thrones'* producers, believing they'd need a solid Dothraki tongue to make that culture feel more authentic, found the group and asked its members to pitch on creating a Dothraki language. Peterson's pitch won, and the show was a hit, thanks in good part to the Dothraki, particularly Jason Momoa as Khal Drogo.

Creating languages, though, is just one of Peterson's skills. He's also a gifted self-promoter. I don't mean this in a bad way, but it seems at times like he's never encountered an interview request he didn't take. The world seems consistently curious about invented languages, and Peterson is more than willing to expound upon how and why he does what he does.

Perhaps we shouldn't be too surprised. After all, the most famous invented language of the late 20th century was based on another piece of famous geek culture: *Star Trek's* Klingon. That language, however, came about in a totally different fashion: the show and movies had used random gibberish words, but before the third film in the franchise, a linguist was asked to turn those into a language. It was at least a monetary success, with a book based on the language selling hundreds of thousands of copies and Trekkies everywhere beginning to study it.

Klingon, though, was clearly cobbled together. Consistent attempts to use it have made it workable by those who speak it, but it lacks the elegance of Peterson's languages. Those on *Game of Thrones* are constructed around the entire cultural history of the people, and are supposed to make sense in those contexts. As a basic example, English, which grew up on an island, has dozens of words about oceans and sailing, but the nomadic, land-locked

Dothraki obviously do not, and so refer to the ocean simply as "poison water."

Peterson has tried to spread his linguistic gifts in ways beyond simply his interviews, though. He's released an app on how to speak Dothraki with a company called Living Language, and also a book on *The Art of Language Invention*. In doing so, he may accidentally inspire his replacement as Hollywood's leading language creator, but, well, *valar morghulis*.

74 The Duels of Game of Thrones

How does *Game of Thrones* manage to make its duels so cool? The chief thing is that it uses space as well as choreography. The place where the fight takes place is as much part of the story as the action itself. Consider the very first major duel: Bronn fighting Ser Vardis in Tyrion's trial by combat in the Eyrie. Ser Vardis dresses in full plate, with a large shield, where Bronn is in leathers and refuses the shield. The sellsword dances around the knight, forcing him to waste his energy on stairs, pillars, people, and candles, so that when the time comes, Bronn can simply move faster and attack stronger. Without the cramped quarters, Vardis' armor wins—but Bronn is smarter and less honorable.

When it needs to be, though, the fight choreography can be fantastic. In the sixth season, Bran Stark flashes back to his father attacking Ser Arthur Dayne, the Sword of Morning, at the Tower of Joy. Two Kingsguard stand against seven Northerners. The key to this fight's choreography is Arthur Dayne's two swords—with them, he can fight off multiple attackers at once. And they all come together—in most many-against-one fight scenes, the many attack one at a time, making the one look awesome for beating them. But on *Game of Thrones*, the Northerners attack in one group, and Dayne fends them off and kills them until he gets Ned Stark alone. Watch the scene repeatedly, and you can see how the choreography works to make Dayne seem too awesome, but in the moment, it's incredibly effective at presenting him as being the ultimate swordsman.

The last thing about *Game of Thrones* duels is that it adapts them for the story purposes. When it calls for a superb display of swordsmanship, like the Sword of Morning should possess, it's a beautiful, intricate dance. When it needs to be something else, it can do that, too.

When Brienne of Tarth meets Sandor Clegane in the fourth season's finale, in the mountains of the Vale, the fight initially plays out as a match between two brutally powerful swordfighters, exchanging massive blows and parries. When swords are clearly not enough, they use their fists as well, and Brienne's punches give her the advantage. The Hound sees that she's unwilling to kill and fights back, disarming the both of them. What was a swordfight disintegrates into a primal struggle for violent dominance, involving punches and kicks to the groin, an ear bitten off, and the final weapon of victory for Brienne: a rock, picked up and used to bash Clegane off a cliff. It's the ugliest fight on the show, but showing Brienne's ability to win ugly against a man like Clegane establishes her as one of the best fighters in the Seven Kingdoms.

What do you get when you add it all up? For my money, the single best fight scene in *Game of Thrones* is the Mountain versus the Viper, Gregor Clegane against Oberyn Martell in Tyrion Lannister's second trial by combat. This scene uses space, choreography, and variety to be, quite simply, one of the best fight scenes ever put on the screen.

Oberyn enters the fight not merely with the goal of winning, but of humiliating Ser Gregor and forcing him to name Lord

Tywin Lannister as complicit in the murder of Oberyn's sister, who was slain by the Mountain during the Lannister sack of the city at the end of Robert's Rebellion. As such, Oberyn engages in a *performance* for the duel. He wants to kill Clegane, yes, but his true target is Tywin Lannister. As such, Oberyn's focus is as much on the VIP section of the audience as Clegane. So he spins and dances and points and shouts in order to have Clegane taken out directly facing Tywin Lannister. Prince Oberyn wants a dance, but Ser Gregor wants a brawl.

While Oberyn used beautiful choreography and the small, circular space of the duel location to his advantage, Clegane is playing a more direct game: he just wants to win. The Viper's monologue when the duel is won, attempting to implicate Tywin, is again a performance. But the Mountain is in a fight, and he switches it into pure, horrific brutality, grabbing Oberyn's ankles, admitting his crimes (but not Tywin's), and jamming his thumbs into Oberyn's eyes until his skull explodes. The glorious choreography turns into horrifying simplicity. That's a perfect narrative for that fight, and a perfect example of just why *Game of Thrones* is so successful in its fights.

75 "The Watchers on the Wall"

"The Watchers on the Wall" is the *Game of Thrones* episode with the highest degree of difficulty of any episode so far. It is the penultimate episode of the fourth season, and like the much-acclaimed "Blackwater" that filled a similar role in Season 2, "Watchers" spends its entire runtime on a single battle. The episode is also directed by Neil Marshall, who did "Blackwater" as well, which gave it an instant pedigree.

So what made "The Watchers on the Wall" so difficult, relatively speaking? Well, consider that "Blackwater" has several of the most famous and popular characters and actors in all of *Game of Thrones* in the same place: Tyrion, Sansa, Cersei, Joffrey, and Stannis, to name an incomplete list. Now, here are the mere five actors whose names appear in the opening credits for "Watchers": Kit Harington, Rose Leslie, Hanna Murray, John Bradley, and Kroistofer Hivju. That's Jon, Ygritte, Gilly, Sam, and Tormund. Good characters and actors, yes, but nowhere near the same pedigree.

See, the key difference between the two episodes is that while "Blackwater" had so many characters in King's Landing for the battle that it could have a fairly normal credits sequence, "Watchers" is virtually deserted; the single oddest credit sequence in the show's history. King's Landing was the most fascinating location in all of *Game of Thrones*; but the Wall had to work to make its characters and stories compelling.

How much "Watchers" succeeds is a matter of some debate: some fans and critics pronounced it one of the show's very best episodes, while others considered it a great technical achievement but lacking emotional power. Still, that it succeeds at all with only Jon Snow present of all the show's major characters shows just how good a job the creators of *Game of Thrones* did with the episode.

The background of the battle also shows the potential struggle of the episode. It depicts the Battle of Castle Black, when Mance Rayder's Wildling army finally showed up at the Wall and directly assaulted the Night's Watch in order to gain access to the southlands. But it's somewhat hard to see what they're fighting about, other than that the Night's Watch is always supposed to stop the Wildlings. Mance and many of the Wildlings we've met are sympathetic figures, and they're fleeing the White Walkers for their own survival. While Blackwater was a battle for direct control of the Iron Throne, it's hard to shake the feeling that everyone at the Battle of Castle Black would have been better off had the Night's Watch simply let the Wildlings through.

But if there had to be a battle, and if it had to be with just a handful of major characters...well, "The Watchers on the Wall" is a remarkable success at showing a big-budget Hollywood-style battle on the small screen.

Director Neil Marshall and the special effects team do a fantastic job of making "Watchers" a grand, unmissable spectacle. There are three moments in particular that stand out as some of the show's very best images. The first is the very beginning of the battle, where Ygritte, having scouted Castle Black, tells Tormund it's time to begin the attack. The camera switches to an overhead view, showing the raiding party streaming toward Castle Black. As the shot continues, it flies up to the top of the Wall, showing the Night's Watch's defenses there, and then it tilts to show the giant fire Mance's army has built.

The second is the introduction of the giants into the fray. From atop the Wall, the Night's Watch can rain arrows and stones onto Mance's army, and we see Wildling archers try and fail to fire back. At least, until a giant shows up with a ten-foot-long bow. It draws, fires, and damages a building. Then it quickly fires again, and the arrow drives straight through a Crow, sending him through the roof and into the air. It's a magnificent "holy shit!" moment, perfectly timed for effect.

And the third great moment is in the pantheon of great television action sequences. As the raid on Castle Black gets out of control, Jon Snow leaves the top of the Wall to join in the hand-to-hand combat. As he gets off the elevator and dives in, the camera, centered in the middle of the courtyard, spins around, so we see the entirety of the battle in the castle in one 360-degree shot.

Jon Snow contemplating his metamorphosis into Action Hero. (Photo courtesy of HBO / Photofest)

Ygritte fires arrows, Tormund appears unstoppable, the Thenn Styr kills some Crows, and Samwell Tarly releases Ghost from his cage to join the fray. All of these bits are effective action sequences on their own, but combined into a single unbroken shot, they're magnificent.

While the episode does lack some emotional resonance, it manages to find it where it needs to, particularly in two crucial scenes for Jon Snow's development. The most obvious is the death of his erstwhile lover Ygritte, who sees him, pauses when firing, and is killed by Olly for her delay. Jon takes her into his arms and tries to soothe her death.

But my favorite of the quiet scenes in "Watchers" happens right before the battle is joined, on the top of the Wall. Jon has a conversation with Acting Commander Ser Alliser Thorne, the cruel bully who had long hated Jon and dismissed his ideas. Thorne, played by Owen Teale, always seemed to get the best out of Kit Harington's Jon, and does so particularly in this conversation. The two rivals seem to come to a respectful understanding, with Thorne admitting that Jon had been right about preparing for Mance's army. It is a great moment where even Jon's biggest detractor admits that he's become a leader in the Night's Watch.

Perhaps the oddest thing about "The Watchers on the Wall" is its ending, or rather lack thereof. Despite being a full episode at 50 minutes, the battle is inconclusive. The Night's Watch has held for the night and defeated the raid on Castle Black, but Mance's massive army is still out there, undefeatable.

The episode ends with Jon having hit on a plan to disperse the army. Go to parlay with Mance Rayder, assassinate him (and likely die), but see the Wildling army disintegrate without its King. It ends with Jon heading Beyond-the-Wall at dawn.

Of course, that's not what happens. Jon loses his nerve at trying to make the attempt on his friend's life, but before anything can come of it, Stannis Baratheon, attempting to become the Prince who was Promised and defeat the darkness, saves the Night's Watch by attacking Mance's army from the side and routing it, capturing its king. The Night's Watch survived just long enough to be saved by King Stannis, who also gives himself a new power-base from which to try to retake his throne. But that's a story for another battle.

76 "Hardhome"

The second half of the fifth season was one of the darkest times for *Game of Thrones*—both as a story, where the villains were winning in almost every part of Westeros and beyond, and as a show, where that relentless march of violent nihilism was pushing fans and critics away.

And then came "Hardhome," an episode that almost single-handedly made everyone realize why they loved *Game of Thrones* in the first place. As well it should—it maintains the grim thematic tone of the fifth season but leaves just enough room for hope.

Unlike the three other major "battle" episodes, "Hardhome" feels like a typical *Game of Thrones* episode. It bounces around most of the world, including King's Landing, Meereen, Braavos, Winterfell, and the Wall. (Only Dorne is missing of the major fifth season locations.) Some of these scenes are largely keeping the wheels of plot moving—Arya's assigned assassination of the Thin Man and Cersei's treatment at the hands of the Sparrows—and some are special—Tyrion finally meeting Daenerys Targaryen and Sansa confronting Theon, who admits that he didn't kill Bran and Rickon.

But as good as these moments are, they're not what made "Hardhome" famous. That would be the ending, as Jon Snow, previously unseen in the episode, arrives at the Wildling village that gives the episode its name to negotiate with the remnants of Mance Rayder's army. Tension rises, falls, builds again, and then suddenly, it all breaks down. The dogs start barking first, and the weather turns. Suddenly the army of the dead is at the gates, and it's a desperate scramble to survive with as many refugees as possible.

There are a bunch of reasons that the climax works so well, but perhaps the most crucial is the performance of Birgitte Hjort Sorenson as the Wildling chieftan Karsi. "Hardhome" has the difficult task of making the season's most epic battle feel important and have emotional weight when the only major character involved is Jon Snow, and only Tormund Giantsbane and Dolorous Edd are familiar faces at all. Thus Karsi's role is to provide that connection to the Wildlings at the village, and make us really feel the tragedy when she dies (as seems inevitable as soon as she tells her daughters that she'll "be right behind them").

Karsi puts a human face on Wildling concerns about Jon's plans, speaking more than any of them in the negotiation. She's ruthlessly pragmatic; although she maintains her grudge against the Crows, she's willing to bend. And she provides humor too, when the new Thenn chieftan speaks against Jon Snow and takes half the chieftans with him in rejecting the deal, she breaks the ice with a "I fucking hate Thenns." Her death is not disgusting or shocking, like so many others in *Game of Thrones*, but instead after fighting off waves of the dead, she gives up when confronted with the risen corpses of children—the first time we've seen that horror. And then the final indignity: her corpse is one raised by the Night's King as a threat to all living beings.

But while Karsi gives "Hardhome" its straightforward emotional story, it's still primarily Jon Snow's story, as the centerpiece of his long-term strategy to save the Seven Kingdoms from the Long Night. He doesn't start well—when the Thenn asks him what happened to Mance, and Jon says "I put an arrow through his heart" without providing any context it might be Peak You Know Nothing Jon Snow, though Tormund eventually backs him up.

Once the battle starts, however, Jon and Kit Harington are on firmer ground. Sapochnik doesn't film the fighting as elegantly as the previous season's war episode, "The Watchers on the Wall." He shouldn't, though—this is a chaotic ambush and desperate attempt to flee, not a pitched siege where both sides know what their goals are. Yet Jon still has some signature moments. He confronts a White Walker in single combat and, thanks to his Valyrian steel sword, manages to kill it. It is not an elegant duel, not like the Mountain and the Viper, but it fits the scene—it's a chaotic mess, and the fact that Jon's sword isn't shattered by the ice spear of the Walker surprises them both.

The final moments of "Hardhome" are terrifying: the Night's King raises his arms and the fresh dead join his army, as Jon flees with just a fraction of the Wildlings he wanted to save. Yet it's also clarifying: at the lowest ebb of a season largely about the damage humans do to one another, there is a straightforward enemy. And only breaking the wheel, and breaking centuries of hatred, has a chance to beat it.

77 "The Battle of the Bastards"

"Let's play a game. Run to your brother. The sooner you make it to him, the sooner you get to see him again. That's it. That's the game."—Ramsay Bolton

The sixth season of *Game of Thrones* came to a climax in one of the most memorable television episodes of all time: "The Battle of the Bastards." The episode set records for number of Emmys won, and fan votes made it one of the highest-rated television episodes of all time on IMDB, only barely falling below a perfect 10 well after airing. It was a stirring celebration of *Game of Thrones'* return to glory in the sixth season, with the heroes winning, the villains dying, and the story moving into its final phase. At least, that's the easy way to look at it.

"The Battle of the Bastards" focuses on two simultaneous battles, each the climax of storylines that had been building since the third season. In the first, the slaver city-states surrounding Meereen, some of which had previously been "liberated" by Daenerys Targaryen, launch their final assault on Meereen. Meanwhile, Jon Snow and a ragged band of Stark loyalists attack Winterfell, seeking to free it from the Boltons who'd ruled the North since the Red Wedding.

And both win! *Game of Thrones* made its name as the show where the good guys almost never achieve victory. Ned and Robb Stark both died before they could solidify their power. Dany's victories over the cities of Slaver's Bay are undercut before she can consolidate them. And the previous season in particular is an exercise in disappointment: Stannis is killed after losing to the Boltons, Jon is murdered by the Night's Watch, Sansa is married off to the abusive Ramsay Bolton, and more. The entire series got the reputation of being cruel and nihilistic.

But *Game of Thrones*, as dark as it could get, was also working toward an endgame. That endgame involves Jon Snow being King in the North, and Daenerys Targaryen finally invading Westeros. These plots had to be resolved, and resolving them at the same time works for the story: the sixth season is the season of heroism, and the heroes are rewarded.

In Meereen, Dany arrives on Drogon at the end of the previous episode, as the night is at its darkest. When the day comes, she counterattacks the besieging armies. Her Unsullied hold the city; the Dothraki sweep in and destroy the Sons of the Harpy, and Dany's dragons, with her on Drogon's back, destroy the slavers' ships. The whole thing ties up quickly—perhaps a little too quickly, with time to spare for Dany and Yara Greyjoy to negotiate an alliance. But it's really the appetizer for the main course: the Battle of the Bastards.

The setup is this: after Stannis' defeat at the Battle of Ice at the end of Season 5, Bolton control of the North seemed assured. But the successful escape of Sansa Stark and the murder and resurrection of Lord Commander Jon Snow changed matters: they gave the Starks the ability and motive to lead a rebellion. Ramsay Snow only reinforces it, sending the "Pink Letter" to Jon, threatening him, the Wildlings, and especially Sansa. Much of the season involves them acquiring allies—a few of the houses of the North, a small army of Wildling survivors of Hardhome. Sansa rejects an alliance offer from Littlefinger and the Vale, but he tells her the Tullys have retaken Riverrun. Brienne attempts to gain Brynden Tully's trust, but fails, and the keep is surrendered to the Lannisters.

So the tiny army, half the size of the Bolton force, heads to Winterfell, which has been reinforced by House Karstark, still angry at the Starks for killing their lord in Season 3, and House Umber, whose lord, the Smalljon, rejects any alliance with Wildlings. The Smalljon also brings Ramsay Bolton, now Warden of the North after killing his father, a present: Rickon Stark, the youngest of the siblings.

Along the way to Winterfell, the Stark army camps in the same spot as Stannis' last camp. Davos, taking a walk, discovers the pyre built by Melisandre to burn Shireen as dawn comes. This revelation doesn't affect the episode itself in plot terms, but it does provide *Game of Thrones* with possibly its single greatest image: Ser Davos realizing what has happened in the snow as the sun rises in the background. Director Miguel Sapochnik has a gift for images, which he puts to use throughout the episode.

Meanwhile Jon and Sansa are arguing, after having had a fruitless parlay with Ramsay Bolton. Sansa believes that Jon isn't taking Ramsay's cunning seriously enough, but Jon says he doesn't have any other option but to press the attack—unless she has any ideas.

Sansa stays silent, which ends up being controversial thanks to her later actions.

As the battle begins, Jon's army—smaller, without as much cavalry—digs in and tries to force the Boltons to attack. The plan is conceptually similar to the battle of Agincourt, much like Blackwater is based on Chi Bi, where the outnumbered force of Henry V forced the French knighthood to attack, and cut them down in a hail of arrows from their elite longbowmen. Indeed this was the plan for the show as well, but budget limitations and the story pushed them in a different direction.

Ramsay springs his trap at the start of the battle: offering Rickon Stark his freedom if he can make it to the Stark lines while being shot at. Rickon sprints ahead at a consistent speed, which seems like the worst path to take, and Jon rides to meet him. Ramsay, clearly toying with the boy, hits him right at the end, leaving Jon stranded between both armies. Davos orders his men to charge, as the rebellion will die without its leader, and the battle is joined.

What ensues isn't a grand tactical narrative like "Blackwater" or "The Watchers on the Wall." Instead it's a bloody spectacle of metaphor, focusing on the simple but occasionally necessary idea that war is hell. We see the battle primarily through Jon's eyes, on the ground, with very little understanding of a grand narrative—although there are enough scenes of Davos and Ramsay to get the idea that the Boltons are winning, and their arrows indiscriminately killing everyone in the fight.

From Jon's view, it's chaos. Some of the most stunning action shots in the series take place through the early section of the battle, especially the moment when Jon draws his sword to take on the Bolton cavalry himself. The chaos in the battlefield is centered around an absurdly long shot, where Jon attempts to survive the cavalry battle raging around him, as horses crash into each other and infantry. He tries to shout orders to a Northerner who's immediately killed by an arrow. And the corpses pile up. This is interspersed with Davos and Ramsay watching, as well as quick, short, music video-style cuts to reinforce the chaos of the moment.

When Davos finally has the remaining Stark men charge into the battle, Ramsay launches the second part of his plan. Bolton shieldbearers surround the Stark army, combining with a wall of corpses and wounded to encircle the Starks. The pace of the battle changes up here, slowing down significantly to show the helplessness of the Stark army. Despite Tormund and the giant Wun Wun attacking the Bolton shieldwall, they continue to press the Starks, eventually forcing them into the wall of corpses.

This isn't shot as a grand action scene, like the first half of the battle. It's a brutal, imposing, repetitive scene, forcing viewers to grapple with the horrors of war, particularly when Jon Snow goes under, threatened with trampling and suffocation as his army tries to escape the Bolton trap.

I'm not a huge fan of this section of the battle, personally. The shield wall, while an effective medieval combat technique, is deployed here primarily to reinforce the narrative of Stark helplessness. Despite having a giant, and iron weapons to break the spears of the shield wall, the Stark army acts shocked that this combat tactic even exists, and essentially lets it slowly overrun them. The momentum of the first half of the battle is lost to imply that things are bad—and things are indeed really, really bad for the Starks!—but it's shown in such a metaphorical fashion that it feels like it's a different battle entirely. Still, I know I'm in a relative minority here; the massive fan support for the battle suggests that most people engaged with the episode incredibly positively.

Jon's darkest moment ends with another of Sapochnik's incredibly memorable shots. He breaks through the corpses and mud and the gore and the retreating men to take a breath, just as the sun breaks through the clouds. And a horn sounds, signaling the arrival of a third force: the Knights of the Vale, led by Petyr Baelish and Sansa Stark. They crush the shield wall; Tormund defeats Lord

Umber in single combat; and Jon, Tormund, and Wun Wun chase Ramsay back behind the gates of Winterfell.

The battle comes to a swift end there. Ramsay's confidence that he can win a siege is quickly punctured by Wun Wun, sacrificing himself to tear down the gate so the Stark forces can enter. Ramsay is brutally beaten by Jon Snow, who only leaves him alive so Sansa Stark can exact revenge against her psychopathic husband, leaving him to be devoured by his dogs.

In the battle's aftermath, the course of Westerosi history is changed. Jon Snow is crowned King in the North. The Boltons are destroyed, the Umbers have lost their lord, and houses like the Glovers and the Manderleys, who'd previously stayed neutral, join the Starks, as do the Lords of the Vale. Littlefinger, however, is playing a different game, exchanging ambiguous looks with Sansa as her brother receives all the acclaim for their joint recovery of the Northern freedom.

For *Game of Thrones*, "The Battle of the Bastards" provides the show with a flagpole episode, one whose massive popularity and award-winning acclaim make it easy for HBO to cite as their biggest show's biggest moment. It also allows the narrative that the good guys can win—something *Game of Thrones* has long had a reputation for avoiding, but one that gives it even more momentum as it heads into its final two seasons.

78 Rhaegar Targaryen

Rhaegar Targaryen is the most important character who hasn't appeared in *Game of Thrones*. Prince Rhaegar Targaryen was the firstborn son and heir of King Aerys II Targaryen, the Mad King.

Rhaegar was, by reputation, everything his father was not: kind, talented, intelligent, strong, and, above all, sane. Some of this comes through on the series, as when Ser Barristan tells Dany stories of how he and Rhaegar used to visit taverns, where Rhaegar would sing among the common people.

These qualities were widely recognized by everyone and, as Aerys grew more and more unstable, led to plans to have him deposed and Rhaegar installed in his place. Plans like these grew at the famous Tourney at Harrenhal, the last flowering of Targaryen pomp, where all major lords and knights attended. The lords conspired behind the scenes, but their plans were ruined by what happened in the joust itself. Prince Rhaegar won the tournament, defeating Ser Barristan the Bold in the final bout, but instead of granting his favor to his wife, Elia Martell, he scandalously chose Lyanna Stark as the tourney's "queen of love and beauty"—a woman both not his wife, and Robert Baratheon's intended.

A year later, Rhaegar would either abduct or elope with Lyanna, triggering the War of the Usurper. The question of whether Lyanna consented is unresolved. Robert's victory in the ensuing war made his and the Stark version of the story the known one: that Lyanna was kidnapped, perhaps raped, and killed by the Targaryen heir, justifying the entire rebellion and the murders of Rhaegar's children at the end of the war.

On the other hand, Ned Stark—the only person who actually spoke to Lyanna after the kidnapping—doesn't have the same hatred for Rhaegar. In one scene in *A Game of Thrones*, he seems to believe Rhaegar was an honorable man, not the sort to frequent brothels, in stark contrast to Robert. Nor, in the Tower of Joy scene in Season 6, do we see Lyanna indicate that her newborn child, Jon Snow, is an unwanted result of her time with Rhaegar. She just wants Ned to promise to keep him safe from Robert.

Yet regardless of whether Rhaegar was a terrible person or not for his flight with Lyanna, it was a terrible decision for the supposedly wiser Targaryen heir to take. It ended up being a disaster for the dynasty. Lyanna's father and older brother went to King's Landing to protest, and Aerys made his maddest decision yet, deciding instead to have them publicly tortured and murdered in front of the whole court. This triggered the full civil war, with Robert Baratheon, both as an aggrieved party and the non-Targaryen with the best claim on the throne, taking the lead of the rebellion.

After several inconclusive battles, Rhaegar Targaryen took command of the loyalist forces. He supposedly had plans to come back and deal with his father's illness after defeating Robert, but it was far too late for him to play the role of hero. At the Battle of the Trident, Rhaegar met Robert in single combat and was defeated, his ruby-ensconced breastplate being smashed in and scattering the jewels in the river.

Rhaegar's wife and children were murdered by Lannister forces in the sack of King's Landing, seeming to end his line, although his brother Viserys and newborn sister Daenerys managed to flee. But the unsatisfying nature of Rhaegar's death—the apparent hero defeated by a random lord—has led to a series of theories and plans about the true meaning of Rhaegar, both inside the story and outside.

In the world, there are two major plots involving Rhaegar's heritage. The first is only in the book—see the next chapter. The second, of course, was revealed in the Season 6 finale: Jon Snow's parentage. Ned Stark, at the behest of his sister Lyanna, keeps her baby's secret safe, even at the consequence of his own honor and relationship with his wife. (To be fair, it hasn't been shown for certain that Jon's father is Rhaegar, but there's no significant evidence in any way that he's not, and plenty in favor.) Jon's heritage could be a crucial component of the story moving forward for a variety of reasons, as discussed in Chapter 17, but it's also a way to keep Rhaegar's flame alive.

This is important because everything we know about Rhaegar suggests his story wasn't done. He was supposed to be a perfect fantasy hero, but died in foolish combat. The lack of satisfaction in his story has led to common fan theories that he's somehow still alive. The focus of the best of these theories: Mance Rayder, the King-Beyond-the-Wall. Almost every character in *A Song of Ice and Fire* has an extensive backstory, but for such an important character, Mance's is shockingly slight—he was a ranger of the Night's Watch, deserted to join the Free Folk, and that's about it. He also, in background that's played up far more in the novels than on the show, is a talented musician, just like Rhaegar.

Obviously this theory took a bit of a hit when Mance was killed on the show (he still may be alive in the novels). But its popularity indicates just how much the world of *Game of Thrones* had invested in Rhaegar. Especially in the novels, Rhaegar wasn't merely the Targaryen heir. Instead, he believed that he was the Prince who was Promised, the chosen hero for the upcoming battle of the light against the darkness. This is the same prince that Melisandre believed Stannis would be—and perhaps came to believe that Jon Snow, Rhaegar's son, truly was. Rhaegar, in coming to believe this, changed his entire life to become a mighty warrior instead of a quiet musician. Perhaps he was wrong—perhaps everyone was wrong—but perhaps his destiny will come true through his heir.

79 Who the Hell Is Young Griff?

Let's face it, for a bunch of fans, the fourth and fifth books of *A Song of Ice and Fire* were disappointing. But there were a few things that made *A Dance with Dragons* more exciting. Chief among them:

the twist involving a character named "Young Griff"—a twist that's been totally removed from the TV show.

(Obviously, this is a major spoiler for the novels!)

It goes like this: when Tyrion flees King's Landing, Varys doesn't travel with him. Instead he arrives at Illyrio's alone, and it's the merchant who starts to convince the Imp to work for the Targaryens. Instead of traveling with Varys, Tyrion goes with retainers of Illyrio's, a man named Griff and his roughly 20-year-old son, "Young Griff." But as Tyrion spends time with them on the voyage, he finds out that Griff is actually Jon Connington, a former Hand of the King for Aerys Targaryen, exiled after losing a battle to the future King Robert—and Young Griff is actually Aegon Targaryen, Rhaegar's long thought dead infant son.

The thing that makes the storyline make sense is that instead of merely confusing the storyline further by adding yet another claimant to the Iron Throne, it reveals the true motives of one of the story's most intriguing characters: Varys the Spider. It was Varys who smuggled Aegon out, replacing him with a poor man's son, sold for wine (the books are rather darker even with their heroes, if Varys even is one).

Through Aegon, Varys would apply his philosophy of power: that a decent young person, thoroughly trained to be a good king, is the only ruler who has a chance to unite and stabilize Westeros. In the philosophical battle between Varys, Littlefinger, and Cersei, Varys takes the ideals of Plato's *Republic*—that there should be a ruling class, and they should be dedicated to being the best possible rulers.

But the rise of Daenerys Targaryen complicates matters. Although Aegon has a better legal claim to the throne thanks to Targaryen precedence, Dany has dragons. That's a pretty damn unbeatable claim to Targaryen legitimacy. So Aegon takes Tyrion's advice and moves to seize power, to present himself as an equal and potential marriage partner to Dany (thanks, Targaryen incest!) by taking the Iron Throne first. *A Dance with Dragons* ends with him invading the Stormlands with Bittersteel's old Golden Company (see Chapter 35)—and a *Winds of Winter* sample chapter has the Dornish princess Arianne Martell seeking Aegon out for an alliance.

That seems pretty damn important, right? So why would *Game of Thrones* skip over Young Griff entirely, and simply have Dany invade at the end of the sixth season?

There's a straightforward reason and there's a complicated reason. The simple explanation is this: while not a whole lot happens in Books 4/5, they're still incredibly dense, and a lot of that complexity had to be removed to fit into hour-long TV episodes. All sorts of storylines were cut out in part—this one, however, was removed in whole.

More confusingly, however...there may be more twists to come, and this isn't even actually Aegon Targaryen. Dacnerys had multiple prophecies back in *A Clash of Kings*, cut from the show, implying that there was a "mummer's dragon" or a "cloth dragon" in her way. This has made the truth about Young Griff one of the most hotly contested theories in fandom.

Regardless of the truth—which, since the show has ignored him, seems to be on the side of "fake"—the addition of Young Griff added a necessary jolt of energy to the story of *A Dance with Dragons*. His removal is probably the single biggest change the show has made from the books, and will likely be debated for years to come.

80 The Meereenese Knot

"How can I rule seven kingdoms if I can't control Slaver's Bay?"—
Daenerys Targaryen

What's the point of Meereen? For many fans, this is one of the most difficult questions in *Game of Thrones,* show or books. Daenerys Targaryen is one of the most important, if not the most important character in the entire story. But she's not in Westeros. She's only interacted with other major characters—Tyrion, Varys, Yara—when they've come to her. From the beginning, her stated goal has been to build an army and take it across the Narrow Sea to Westeros, but she's been in Slaver's Bay since the start of Season 3, and queen in Meereen since early in Season 4. So why has she been there so long?

"The Meereenese Knot" is the name of the discussion of this question (joked about on the show, when Tyrion introduces a contortionist sex worker as one of four in the world who can perform the Meereenese Knot). It's the term that George R.R. Martin used to describe why his fourth and fifth novels took so long to write, five or six years each. Basically, he had to have the right characters show up in Meereen at the right times for the story to progress and have a point-of-view character present to tell that story.

So Tyrion, the army from Yunkai, Victarion Greyjoy (replaced by Yara and Theon), Quentyn Martell (totally deleted from the show), and a few others had to appear. Martin fixed this specific knot by giving Ser Barristan—still alive in the novels—a point-of-view chapter, which allowed Dany to leave the city before several of the others arrived.

But it gets more complicated than that. Even if this all had to happen, remember that Dany's goal from the first season on was to build an army to take over Westeros. The army that she's raised is now primarily Dothraki—which was the army she started with. So what has been the point with the years of wandering and ruling? This is where the Meereenese Knot stands in for all the complicated decisions Martin has made that made the story more difficult.

The biggest of these decisions: after the end of *A Storm of Swords*—pretty much the end of Season 4—Martin had planned to fast-forward five years. For the young characters, the core of the story, this makes sense. Dany is learning to rule in Meereen; Jon is doing the same as the new Lord Commander of the Night's Watch; Sansa is hiding with and learning from Littlefinger; Arya is training with the Faceless Men; Bran is learning how to control his powers from Bloodraven; Sam is about to go become a Maester; Tommen is learning to rule; Myrcella is growing up in Dorne.

Except the story isn't only about them. What's Tyrion doing in hiding for five years? How is Cersei ruling in King's Landing? How is Brienne's quest to find Sansa and Arya going? Is Theon just being tortured constantly this entire time? Stannis just chilling at the Wall? Basically, the story of *Game of Thrones* became less about the children (specifically the Starks) and more about the entire world of Westeros.

So the kids continued their training, while the story focus shifted to Dorne, to the religious revival of King's Landing, to the succession debate in the Iron Islands, and to Stannis' attack on Winterfell. This kept the story moving, but it had the kids, particularly the four Stark children, sidelined while new characters took their place. So as of the end of *A Dance with Dragons*, the previously essential characters Arya, Sansa, and Bran have had almost nothing to do for two full novels—small wonder many fans were unhappy with the two books.

For *Game of Thrones* as a TV series, many of its simplifications in its later seasons have been attempts to avoid these problems. Bear in mind: the first two seasons each adapted the first two books. The third book, *A Storm of Swords*, was so huge and eventful that it was divided into two seasons, 3 and 4. Then most of the fourth and fifth books, *A Feast for Crows* and *A Dance with Dragons*—which take place simultaneously but focus on different characters (i.e., Cersei and Sansa in *Feast*, Dany and Jon in *Dance)* got merged into Season 5. And Season 6 picked up a few of the missing threads, but has largely passed the books (its finale was named "The Winds of Winter" which is also the title of the as-yet unreleased sixth book).

Bran Stark is removed from the fifth season. Brienne's quest for the Stark girls, which takes place across the fourth book, is combined with third-book plots in the fourth season. Sansa, in revealing her true identity in the Vale at the end of the fourth season, blows past anything she did in the books. Jaime goes to Dorne, instead of a pile of new characters in the fifth season. And his story in the Riverlands, causing the Tully armies to surrender, gets shoved into the sixth season, along with the Kingsmoot in the Iron Islands. Arya's story gets her assassination of one of the names on her list moved from a *Winds of Winter* sample chapter into the fifth season finale.

The net effect of this is that both the fifth and sixth seasons are largely stuffed with storylines, making them bigger and more explosive than most previous seasons. And, in accordance with their source material, the fifth season is largely depressing events, and the sixth season, mostly heroic—including Daenerys Targaryen solving the Meereenese Knot and, six years later, finally setting sail for Westeros.

81 Jorah Mormont

For many fans, the sound that defined early *Game of Thrones* was the word "khaleesi," sonorously pronounced by Iain Glen, as Ser Jorah Mormont. Jorah's role alongside Dany is fairly consistent. His queen is naive, headstrong, or both. He provides a voice of caution and reason. Sometimes this is primarily supportive: in the middle of Season 1, as Dany begins to realize that her older brother Viserys is simply a bully and not the "Dragon" he claimed to be, Jorah says that Rhaegar was the "Last Dragon." It's confirmation of what she was thinking, and leads directly to her freeing herself of Viserys' abuse by allowing Drogo to kill him.

But it's also occasionally a brake on her direct, often violent impulses. In the third season, when Dany takes Jorah's advice to acquire an army of Unsullied, she decides to buy that army from a slaver of Astapor with one of her dragons. Jorah, and new advisor Barristan Selmy, are strenuously opposed to this decision, to the point where she dresses both of them down, telling them never to oppose her in public. In this case, of course, the khaleesi's boldness is fully deserved: she betrays the slavers, regains her dragon, and becomes the Breaker of Chains with the two knights as her primary advisors.

Jorah's support of his queen isn't merely vocal, as important as that is, of course. He's also a fine knight, potentially even as good as his father, Jeor Mormont, Lord Commander of the Night's Watch. In the assault on Pyke in Balon Greyjoy's first rebellion, Jorah was second through the breach, behind only Thoros of Myr, earning a knighthood. His physical skills have come in handy multiple times, defeating Daenerys' enemies and fighting his way to her in Daznak's Pit.

Unfortunately for Jorah, behind his grizzled appearance he's also a hopeless romantic. This proved to be his undoing in Westeros, when he wed Lynesse Hightower, a wealthy lady from the Reach, with its big cities and nice weather. On Bear Island, Lynesse was miserable, and Jorah bankrupted himself attempting to keep her happy.

To maintain his finances, he took to slavery, which, when discovered, forced him to flee into exile. His wife took up with a wealthy merchant prince, and Jorah traveled Essos, eventually learning Dothraki and finding his way to the Targaryens. There he offered his services to the new khaleesi, Daenerys, with a hidden motive: report on her movements to the Iron Throne, and win himself a pardon.

But Jorah's romantic nature gets in the way of his plan again. He falls for Daenerys both as a symbol, the true ruler of Westeros, but also as a person. When he reports that she has become pregnant, the Small Council decides to have her killed. But finding this out, Jorah takes action, stopping the wineseller who was to do the deed. This fully commits him to Dany, and the chaos in King's Landing means he's largely forgotten for the next several seasons.

Ser Jorah makes a critical error, and one that's consistent through his history: he doesn't own up to his mistakes. In this case, he never tells Dany that he had once spied on her, a revelation that only becomes more difficult the longer he waits. When Tywin, in Season 4, believes that he's stabilized the Seven Kingdoms, he turns his attention to Dany. He and Varys hatch a plan to destabilize her—issue a pardon to Ser Jorah for his spying, and break apart their alliance. It works: Jorah's long-ago treachery is revealed, and his stammering "khaleesi..." protests won't save him. He's exiled again.

He heads to Volantis, still utterly devoted to his khaleesi. There, Tyrion Lannister, headed to Slaver's Bay, lands in Jorah's lap, offering a new plan: deliver a Lannister son to Dany, and gain the royal pardon he truly wants. Along the way, Jorah contracts greyscale, a potentially fatal, possibly magical, disease. The two men also develop a grudging respect for one another, which proves essential in saving Jorah's life when he returns from his exile-on-pain-of-death, via quick thinking and gladiatorial skills. Tyrion wants to be Dany's ally, and indeed killed his father, the man who ordered the deaths of her family, so his presence alone isn't enough to win Jorah his freedom. But the Imp does say that Jorah is devoted to Daenerys, and so he's sent into exile again.

It doesn't last long. Jorah returns to his last plan: fight in the gladiatorial pits, win, and somehow utilize that to sway Dany to end his exile. The first part of the plan works, albeit with a strong tinge of luck, as Jorah wins the games. The second part seems dubious, with Dany not immediately reacting well to the reveal that he's the one who won—but the Sons of the Harpy attack at that point, and Jorah's reflexes save Dany's life. In this desperate time, he's reintegrated into the inner circle, with her taking his hand to escape the chaos. But it doesn't last long, as Drogon arrives to save his mother, and she rides her dragon away.

Jorah and Daario head out to rescue Dany, only to discover that she's on the verge of rescuing herself. Learning of his greyscale, Daenerys sends Jorah to find a cure, while she heads off to finally defeat the slavers of Essos and launch her invasion of Westeros. What will happen to Jorah, once so important to the narrative of *Game of Thrones,* is unclear. Will he return for the battles against the Lannisters and the White Walkers? Will he cure the incurable magical disease? And most importantly, will he meet his badass baby cousin, Lyanna Mormont?

82 King Joffrey

"The king can do as he likes!"—Joffrey Lannister-Baratheon

Seven hells, is there anyone worse than Joffrey? The crown prince when the story begins, and the king as it continues, has a legitimate claim to being literally the most awful fictional character on television...ever.

The sadistic Joffrey is introduced as part of a couple different bait-and-switches for *Game of Thrones*. The first is built around the sympathy viewers might have for Sansa Stark and her understanding of the chivalric world. Sansa believes that knights are good, and they serve their ladies, who by being virtuous, win the love of the very best knights. Sansa believes that she is good, and so when she's betrothed to Prince Joffrey, who appears every inch the prince and embodiment of teenaged masculinity, it's her dream coming true.

But Joffrey is actually, well, a little shit. We first see this when Tyrion, attempting to get him to say kind words to the Starks after Bran's fall, slaps him over and over (creating many, many cathartic YouTube videos). The viewers, however, get their true view of Joffrey at the end of the second episode, "The Kingsroad," in which he confronts Arya and her friend Mycah, the butcher's boy, playing at swords. Joffrey refuses to back down from a fight, and forces a confrontation in which Arya's wolf, Nymeria, wounds him, and Arya throws his sword into the river. The endlessly petty princeling makes enough of a fuss about this that Mycah is killed, and Sansa's direwolf Lady takes the fall for Arya.

Sansa still manages to hold out some hope for the prince being good, but that's shattered at the end of the season by Joffrey's other chief personality trait along with his cruelty: his insecurity.

And here's the second bait-and-switch: the role of the hero. When Ned Stark attempts to kick Joff off the Iron Throne due to his illegitimacy as a child of incest, Joffrey feels so threatened that he goes against the advice of every single one of his councilors and has Ned killed—if Ned cannot defeat Joffrey, then Ned clearly isn't the hero. But Joffrey is certainly the villain, and even Sansa cannot deny his villainy after that.

For the next few seasons, Joffrey attempts to rampage across the Seven Kingdoms, making his every whim the true state of things. Sansa becomes the target of his rage in King's Landing, although Tyrion attempts to protect her first as Hand, then as her husband.

You may be interested to learn that there's a video on YouTube of Tyrion slapping this face for 10 hours. (Photo courtesy of HBO / Photofest)

But despite most of the Lannisters recognizing Joffrey's unbalanced nature, they still support him. He does embody their family's ambitions, and for that he gets their support, no matter how many riots he causes.

So for the first three seasons of *Game of Thrones*, Joffrey wins. Not because he's wise, or honorable, or even legitimate. But instead because the Lannisters have taken enough power that they can succeed despite his failures, and because their allies are smart or powerful enough (and ignorant of his evils) and he maintains support.

But when Margaery Tyrell, desperate to become queen, is betrothed to Joffrey, that all changes. Margaery and her grandmother Olenna attempt to find the truth of the king from Sansa, who eventually spits out his monstrous nature. While Margaery attempts to manipulate him into doing good, Olenna aligns with another erstwhile Lannister ally, Petyr Baelish, to dispose of the King.

At his wedding to Margaery Tyrell, Joffrey reaches the height of his petty villainy, attempting to turn his uncle Tyrion into his own personal pet. His rampage is ended by a bit of poison from Littlefinger and Olenna. The sadistic king dies pathetically, choking at his own wedding, reaching for his mother like the child he should have been. And with his death the title of *Game of Thrones'* greatest villain headed north, to meet the new Joffrey, Ramsay Snow.

83 Melisandre and the Red God

How much of fantasy is based on the idea of prophecy? The "chosen hero" that undergirds so much heroic fantasy is often an explicit prophecy, and even if not, people who understand the genre can see that, say, a Jon Snow is meant for greater things than he appears. The trope is one of fantasy's strongest: at some point, the hero will encounter a fortune-teller or wizard, and they will tell them that they have a destiny. And it's always true.

Well. It *was* always true, before *Game of Thrones*. That's because most of *Game of Thrones'* prophecies are dispensed by the red priestess, Melisandre, who consistently and filled with certainty guarantees to her patron, Stannis Baratheon, that he *will* sit on the Iron Throne. Everything he does leads him to that end, and, as the chosen hero who will save the world from the darkness, everything that leads him closer to that end is justified.

Therefore Melisandre's assassination of Stannis' brother Renly is justified: it brings Stannis closer to the throne. Therefore her planned sacrifice of Gendry is justified: it brings Stannis closer to the throne. Therefore her execution of Shireen Baratheon is justified: it brings Stannis closer to the throne.

Except...it doesn't. Shireen's death breaks Stannis' army out of their snowed-in camp, but it so demoralizes the troops that half of them desert. Stannis' queen, Selyse, hangs herself. Melisandre bails as well, despite promising to never leave Stannis' cause. And while Stannis himself goes through the motions of his final battle with the Boltons, he's doomed from the start, and dies at the end.

In other words, every prophecy that Melisandre uttered over the previous five seasons was completely, totally wrong. Stannis would never take Winterfell. He would never sit on the Iron

Throne. He was never the Prince who was Promised, who would lead the armies of the Light against the darkness.

And this is *great*. So much fantasy depends on having a flawless prophet, who explains what's supposed to happen, and maybe it takes a while for the characters to get it, and maybe it doesn't, but the end result is fitting the detailed plot into the flowery language of the prophecy. "Ah, so that's what the old man in the cave meant!" Now to be fair, other stories had broken prophecies before—Tad Williams' *Memory, Sorrow, and Thorn* books, written around the same time as the first few *Ice and Fire* novels, hinge on a busted prophecy. But *Game of Thrones* is popular at a level that almost no other fantasy can manage, and that makes this twist potentially influential on a massive scale.

Part of the reason for the success of the twist is that Melisandre belongs to a religion of utter certainty in a world that seems to otherwise lack it. All the other major religions of the world simply present ethical guidelines or places of power. But the religion of R'hllor, the Red God, the Lord of Light, promises a grand battle of good versus evil, with his priests and their chosen one fighting against the Darkness.

This promise ties into myths about the Long Night and the Battle for the Dawn against the White Walkers, and the legendary hero "Azor Ahai," the Prince who was Promised. Azor Ahai is, supposedly, the warrior who wielded a sword of flame against the Darkness, turning it back for thousands of years. The religion of the Red God says that he will return when the Darkness does, in order to beat it back.

So the world of *Game of Thrones* has a certain messianic tinge, at least amongst the believers. Melisandre believes so firmly that Stannis is the Prince who was Promised, Azor Ahai reborn, that she takes over his entire life and pushes him down this path. Other red priestesses, introduced in the sixth season, take a dim view of her certainty—although Stannis' death makes that an easy call to make on their end.

But there's another character, at least in the novels and the supplemental material, who bought into the messianic vibe, albeit without converting: Rhaegar Targaryen, the Last Dragon. By most accounts, Rhaegar was a bookish lad, training to be a musician more than anything else, when in his studies, he came across something that made him believe that he had to be a warrior—that he was the Prince who was Promised. Much like Stannis, this messianic fervor did him no good, and he died in a civil war as well.

In the sixth season, however, we saw another side to Melisandre. After pushing Stannis for so long to fight the fights she wanted, and use the power she possessed, Melisandre loses all that. In one shocking scene, she lets her guard down, and reveals that she's an old woman, glamoured to look young and beautiful. This isn't merely the fervor of a recent convert, making a mistake. It's an ancient sorceress whose confidence is shattered.

That confidence returns, in part, when Melisandre successfully resurrects Jon Snow, using the words that her counterpart Thoros of Myr had done to resurrect his lord, Beric Dondarrion. From there she serves Jon through the season, until the sins of her past certainty come back to haunt her. Davos Seaworth has found proof that she sacrificed Shireen, for nothing, as Stannis died anyway. Jon Snow exiles Melisandre, and she disappears into the distance at the end of Season 6.

There should be no doubt that the red priestess will return, but the question is, in what form? Are the zealous adherents to R'hllor's cause actually on the side of Light against the darkness? Is Jon Snow the Prince who was Promised? Or are these more false prophecies and misdirection, encouraged by a religion no more true or false than any other in Westeros?

84 The High Sparrow

The High Sparrow, more than arguably any other character on the show (save the Queen of Thorns), is attached to the man who portrays him, famed British actor Jonathan Pryce. Pryce is most famous in film for his work with legendary director Terry Gilliam, particularly his starring role in *Brazil*, a 1985 film examining a near-future dystopia. *Brazil* is one of the biggest cult hits in cinema history, and Pryce's everyman charm is a huge part of that success.

While the ruthless fundamentalist High Sparrow is a tremendously different role for Pryce on *Game of Thrones* in many ways, he once again brings that everyman charm to the role. Despite being a fanatic who rises from virtually nothing to bring the traditional powers of King's Landing to their knees across two seasons, the High Sparrow always manages to seem like a normal, comprehensible, down-to-earth guy, one that you might be able to have a beer with and complain about your boss to. This is Pryce's gift, and it transforms a seemingly uncomplicated villain into one of the highlights of the later seasons of the show.

The Sparrows are a group of poor religious fanatics who develop a center of power in King's Landing. While on the show they're depicted as the poor and vulnerable, they're given a much more specific origin in the novels. The Sparrows are primarily refugees fleeing the war in the Riverlands, and turning to a simple, primal form of their religion. This is something historically based in apocalyptic-level parts of history. The Flagellants, for example, were a radical Christian sect during the plague years who dressed in rags and abused themselves to atone for God's punishment of humanity.

Many of these religious cults in times of great stress on society managed to take over cities or even regions for a few years. Perhaps the most successful religious rebellion took place in the 19th century in China, when a bizarre interpretation of Christianity led to the Taiping Rebellion, which, for over a decade, took over huge swaths of southeastern China. Medieval religious rebellions in Europe could take over major cities and states for a brief time, like the Anabaptists taking over Munchen in the 16th century for a year.

The Sparrows take their power when Cersei Lannister, ever willing to sacrifice the long-term health of the realm for her short-term power and survival, forms an alliance with their leader: the High Sparrow. In exchange for her pushing him as High Septon, leader of the Faith of the Seven across all Westeros, he's supposed to support her against the Tyrells. He does initially, arresting Loras for homosexuality, but eventually turns on Cersei herself.

Along the way, Pryce continues to make the High Sparrow seem human and understandable. He describes the need to uphold the laws of the gods, and the importance that had in his life. It all seems to work—he defuses attempts by Olenna or Cersei to counter his increasing power. Only Margaery, who superficially embraces his worldview but maintains her family loyalty, seems to be able to avoid his sway.

Well, only Margaery and her rival Cersei, who, upon being betrayed by the High Sparrow, manages to find her way free after surviving one of the most vicious punishments at his disposal: the Walk of Penance. Cersei is forced to walk from the Sept of Baelor to the Red Keep in the nude, surrounded by Sparrow bodyguards, with a Sparrow septa ringing a bell in her ear and shouting "shame!"

Cersei spends the next season seeking revenge against the High Sparrow and agency for herself, and finally, in the sixth season finale, she achieves it: she nukes the Sept of Baelor with the High Sparrow and most of her enemies, particularly Margaery Tyrell, inside.

It's only at this point that the High Sparrow, who'd seemed so approachable and so reasonable, shows his true colors. While Margaery Tyrell, the smartest person in the room, realizes that Cersei's refusal to show up for her own trial reveals that she has a plan to destroy her enemies, the High Sparrow refuses to believe her. Instead he reverts to being the fundamentalist, so certain in his own patriarchal ways that he refuses to allow Margaery's attempt to evacuate the Sept. And they all pay for his inability to realize he's been outplayed—the Sept of Baelor is destroyed in a wildfire holocaust, killing nearly all of Cersei's enemies.

The High Sparrow's genius ability to ingratiate himself with, then subvert, everyone in King's Landing went up in flames for one simple reason: Cersei Lannister had a bomb, and she didn't care who was in its blast radius. The High Sparrow, for all his savvy and down-to-earth charisma, wasn't prepared to deal with the worst-case scenario. And so he lost, so soon after seeming to have achieved victory.

85 The Faceless Men

"Valar morghulis."—Arya Stark to the Braavosi captain

The Faceless Men of Braavos occupy one of the stranger positions in the world of *Game of Thrones*. They're one of several religions shown in Westeros and beyond, but unlike the Faith of the Seven, the Old Gods, the Drowned God, or R'hllor, they don't have a wide group of worshippers. The entire faith seems to exist in a single building, the House of Black and White.

The Faceless Men themselves are an elite group of assassins for hire. In the novels, the Small Council debates whether to send one of them to kill Daenerys before settling on the wine-seller idea, after they're talked down by Littlefinger who says the Faceless would be far too expensive. Doreah, telling Dany of the sights she's seen, also mentions that she's seen a man change his face.

Jaqen H'ghar is the first Faceless we meet, imprisoned in a cart with the ruthless, brutal criminals Rorge and Biter. While they're unquestionably horrific enough that they need to be in the cart, the soft-spoken, seemingly kind Jaqen doesn't fit the mold. He befriends Arya enough that, when the Lannisters attack, she sets him and the other men free.

For this, Jaqen gives Arya three lives to take, which she uses to get revenge and save her skin in Harrenhal. Jaqen demonstrates his skill in these assassinations, particularly in killing the Tickler and making it look like an accident. The desperate Arya Stark, needing a way to escape, tells Jaqen to kill himself, or help her flee. He eventually chooses the latter, and despite telling her that she lacks honor, gives her the Braavosi coin and tells her how to find the House of Black and White—and changes his face in front of her, to prove his power.

Jaqen returns as the face of Arya's teacher in the House of Black and White, although it's never quite clear if this is the same man, especially when a Jaqen-faced man commits suicide following Arya's murder of Meryn Trant. This is a change from the books, as well—while fans theorized that the "kindly man" who serves as Arya's main teacher in the House may well be Jaqen, it was never shown for certain. (Other theories also hold that Arya's first Braavosi teacher, Syrio Forel, whose death is implied but never shown, may be a Faceless, even Jaqen.)

We also learn more about the Many-Faced God worshiped by the Faceless Men. He is not a totally new god, but instead an amalgamation of every god of death in every culture, including the Stranger of the Seven. The face-changing used by the Faceless is also shown as a pragmatic tool more than a magical spell—the Faceless choose from a selection of faces, somehow carrying them and shifting into them.

What the Faceless Men and the Many-Faced God want overall is also difficult to tell. They give the gift of death to the broken and suffering people of Braavos for free, and treat the bodies well after. But they also carry out assassinations for high prices.

Although only Jaqen and Arya's kills are shown on *Game of Thrones*, the novels have Faceless playing a bigger role. In the prologue of *A Feast for Crows*, a Faceless Man kills a Maester-in-training in order to gain access to the secrets housed in the Citadel. It's also strongly implied that a Faceless Man murders Balon Greyjoy, although likely at the behest of Euron, who did the deed himself on the show.

The Faceless do have specific goals for their servants, however. In order to become a Faceless, the trainees have to give up their identity and their past, to become "no one." Arya Stark, although clearly gifted as a murderer and willing to learn otherwise, struggles with this throughout her time at the House of Black and White. This leads to a rivalry with another student, known as "the Waif."

The Waif bullies Arya, and when Arya finally breaks with the Faceless, it's the Waif who goes to kill her. But Arya learned despite the Waif's bullying, defeats her, and leaves the temple. Oddly, Jaqen tells her "Finally, a girl is no one" after Arya survives the Waif. But Arya reclaims her old identity and returns to Westeros—although now with a stockpile of faces, which she uses to kill Lord Walder Frey.

It's hard to say whether we'll see more of the Faceless in *Game of Thrones'* concluding seasons. Arya will almost certainly continue to utilize their faces, but whether the organization or the Many-Faced God have a larger part to play is, like most things about the Faceless, a mystery.

86 The Brotherhood without Banners

What is the Brotherhood without Banners? They're a group that's created in the first season, named in the second, finally appear in the third, disappear for the fourth and fifth seasons, and finally re-emerge in the sixth. The Brotherhood is proof of how awesome *Game of Thrones* can be and how confusing it can be, both at the same time.

But let's say what they are first. Back in the first season, after Catelyn Stark arrests Tyrion, Tywin Lannister sends the Mountain to burn and pillage her family home, the Riverlands. We don't actually see this destruction, but there's a scene where Ned, as Hand, takes a petition from Riverlands peasants. He sends a hundred men under the command of the young knight Lord Beric Dondarrion to defeat the Mountain. Events quickly spiral out of control for ol' Ned, so we don't really hear what happens to the men he sent.

In Season 2, Arya and her friends in the Night's Watch recruits are captured by Lannisters, Ser Amory Lorch, and taken to the ruined castle of Harrenhal. Each of the prisoners is being interrogated by a brutal man called "the Tickler," who asks them the same few questions, "Where is the Brotherhood?" being chief among them.

Tywin puts a stop to the torture, and Arya uses Jaqen H'ghar to put a stop to the Tickler, so we don't really hear about the Brotherhood again until the next season when Arya, Gendry, and Hot Pie are captured by a group of bandits led by the lapsed priest Thoros of Myr and the archer Anguy—the Brotherhood without Banners, still loyal to King Robert and fighting a guerrilla war against the Lannister armies in the Riverlands.

Soon after, the Brotherhood captures the Hound, who's deserted the Lannisters after the Battle of Blackwater. He recognizes Arya Stark, so they realize they have a valuable hostage. The Brotherhood plans on putting the Hound on trial, but none of them have a specific enough crime—except Arya, who accuses him of the murder of her friend Mycah back in Season 1.

This is sufficient for Beric Dondarrion, who challenges the Hound to trial by combat. After the tough fight, the Hound appears to slay Lord Beric, winning his freedom. Then Thoros of Myr lays his hands on Beric, says the words of the Red God, and Beric returns to life—as he has many times before. The entire Brotherhood has converted to the faith of the Red God, although not as creepily as Stannis and his court at Dragonstone.

Arya and Gendry are both initially impressed by the Brotherhood. They seem like good people, fighting the good fight, taking care of one another. Arya has no major issue with them ransoming her to her family, while Gendry plans to stay on and work as a blacksmith, since they take care of their own. Sometimes it takes several episodes or seasons for a *Game of Thrones* character to have their idealism crushed, but for poor Gendry, it's just almost immediate, as Melisandre arrives in the Brotherhood camp.

The Red Woman has initial disdain for Thoros of Myr, a cynical, failed, and lapsed priest of the Red God. All true, except that Thoros also has the power of resurrection, which shocks Melisandre almost as much as it shocked viewers. Still, she's not there to debate with Thoros: she's there to purchase Gendry for an unknown purpose. The Brotherhood needs gold to continue fighting the good fight, they tell Arya, and their cynicism is necessary for survival. A betrayed Arya Stark flees into the woods, where she's kidnapped by Sandor Clegane—and the Brotherhood without Banners, like the Riverlands, disappears from *Game of Thrones* for nearly three full seasons.

They make their return in the sixth season, when the Hound, previously left for dead, is revealed to be helping a small, new, hopeful community. A group of Brotherhood bandits arrives and makes demands, but is turned back. With the Hound chopping wood, they attack and murder the entire community. Clegane goes to take revenge and discovers that Beric and Thoros are doing so as well, executing the Brotherhood deserters for their crimes.

Beric attempts to recruit the Hound, his former enemy, to join the fight against the darkness in the North come winter, but Clegane refuses. We're left with the implication that Beric and Thoros are traveling north, but whether they do remains to be seen.

The Brotherhood without Banners' sporadic importance through *Game of Thrones* demonstrates some of the biggest differences between the show and the novels, where the Brotherhood has had a fairly consistent presence through all five books. The two major differences between the novels/show, depth and rumor, both change the group's role tremendously.

In the books, we get a lot more history and different random characters running around. One of the first places this occurs is the Tourney of the Hand, which takes place midway through the first season. On the show, only the semifinals of the joust are shown, and it serves as a way to introduce Ser Loras, the Mountain, and the Hound's rivalry with his brother.

In the novels, the tourney introduces way more characters, including the dashing young knight, Beric Dondarrion. Sansa Stark's gossipy best friend, Jeyne Poole, gets a crush on Lord Beric in much the same way as Sansa develops a crush on Ser Loras. A commoner named Anguy wins the archery competition over far more famous nobles, and the melee is won by a red priest named Thoros of Myr with a "ridiculous flaming sword" that scares other contestants' horses. In other words, the three most important members of the Brotherhood are all introduced long before Ned Stark named Beric Dondarrion to command it.

Second, the Brotherhood exists in rumors throughout the Riverlands throughout the story of the second book/season. Characters hear stories of the Mountain killing Lord Beric, or capturing and hanging him, and yet he's somehow still around—clearly the rumors are false, but something's going on. So when Arya meets the Tickler, the idea of the Brotherhood isn't totally new.

The Brotherhood also keeps their importance even after the Red Wedding, unlike the show, thanks in large part to the recruitment of Lady Stoneheart (see chapter 60). They also play a pivotal role in Brienne's search for the Stark daughters, which is aired far earlier on the show than happened in the books. The combining of storylines therefore left the Brotherhood pretty much irrelevant in Seasons 4 and 5 of the show.

In both cases, however, the Brotherhood fulfills its most important role: showing that devotees of the Red God can, in certain remarkable circumstances, resurrect the dead. For Lord Beric, it's unclear exactly what those might be, but seasons later, as the chosen hero Jon Snow died with a red priestess nearby, it provided a certain level of comfort for fans that he might not be dead.

Moreover, the Brotherhood serves to illustrate just how apocalyptic the war has been for the Riverlands and the Crownlands. The brutal calculations they make—including explicitly attacking Northern soldiers in the books, and selling Gendry on the show—in the service of a war both pointless and necessary simultaneously shows the hell that everyone in the region is going through. Through the Brotherhood, *Game of Thrones* shows just how nasty, complicated, and inglorious war really is.

87 Dunk and Egg, the *Game of Thrones* Spinoff

"Dunk the lunk, thick as a castle wall."—Duncan the Tall's inner monologue

What's next for *Game of Thrones* after its eighth season in 2018? It may not surprise you to learn that many people want a spinoff. Fans like the show, and HBO likes money, so it seems like a natural. But what to spin off?

The most obvious example is the story of Westeros that George R.R. Martin has written about the most apart from the *Game of Thrones* novels: the *Tales of Dunk and Egg.* Martin himself has said that they're most natural spinoff, and one he wants to see on television.

Dunk and Egg are the nicknames of Ser Duncan the Tall, a legendary knight of the Kingsguard, and his squire, the eventual King Aegon V (and brother of Maester Aemon of the Night's Watch), taking place a little less than a century before the events of *Game of Thrones.* Their stories are told through three novellas: "The Hedge Knight," "The Sworn Sword," and "The Mystery Knight." Martin has apparently mentioned that he wants to continue writing stories to take these characters through their entire lives, but the fourth and fifth installations are somewhat on hold while he finishes *The Winds of Winter.*

While these stories are set in Westeros, and many of the ancestors of the Great Houses are present (including a four-year-old Walder Frey), their tone and structure are very different from *Game of Thrones.* They fit more into the genre of sword-and-sorcery than heroic fantasy, with roaming knights having exotic, episodic adventures. There's no grand good versus evil narrative, and because it's after the time of dragons, no significant magic to be found either—just the stories of an honorable if kinda dense knight, and his royal, clever squire, wandering the Seven Kingdoms.

That said, there's still plenty of reasons for fans of *Game of Thrones* to check the stories out. They take place at a fascinating juncture of the history of the Iron Throne: they're decades after the last of the dragons have died out, and a generation or two after legendary Targaryens like Daeron the Young Dragon, Baelor the Blessed, Maegor the Unworthy, and Aemon the Dragonknight. The characters in *Dunk and Egg* are trying to fill their legendary forebears' shoes, much in the same way that Robert's Rebellion hangs over the characters of *Game of Thrones* at its beginning.

Dunk and Egg also presents the start of the great Targaryen decline. The antagonist of the first novella, "The Hedge Knight," is Prince Aerion Targaryen, a cruel and insane man who seems like a prelude to the Mad King and Viserys. Aerion, believing himself a dragon, attacks a puppeteer friend of Dunk's for "treachery" when his performance depicts a knight slaying a dragon. He would eventually die of drinking wildfire, another parallel to Aerys. The Targaryen madness and infighting, as well as the civil wars with the Blackfyres in the same era, would eventually lead to the line almost totally collapsing by the time of *Game of Thrones*.

There's also a sly connection between the hero of these stories and arguably the most heroic character in *Game of Thrones*. Dunk is tall, powerful, and a little dense but honorable enough to do the right thing. There are also strong hints that he is the grandfather of Brienne of Tarth, another strong, tall, honorable, and maybe a little dense character. In *A Feast for Crows*, Martin has Brienne grab a shield from her armory—that used to belong to Duncan the Tall. Martin also mentioned prior to that book that he'd be revealing who has Duncan's ancestry, so it's widely accepted that Brienne shares the previous hero's blood.

Whether the *Dunk and Egg* novellas (also adapted quite beautifully as graphic novels) ever make it to the screen is dubious. Showrunners David Benioff and D.B. Weiss have said they're unlikely to do any spinoffs, and HBO executives seem unwilling to go forward without the men who've brought them such success. But even if the *Tales of Dunk and Egg* never make it to the screen, on the page they're still a fun glimpse into the history of the Seven Kingdoms, and well worth a read.

88 POV Characters

A Song of Ice and Fire is told through a third-person limited perspective, though using many characters, meaning it jumps from character POV to character POV, chapter to chapter. Here is a list of the far-ranging and ever-growing cast of perspectives.

Ned Stark (Book 1)—Ned has the most chapters in *A Game of Thrones*, making his death all the more shocking.

Catelyn Stark (Books 1–3)—Cat is our primary eyes for Robb's war and also Renly's camp and his assassination.

Arya Stark (Books 1–4)—Arya's journey through the Riverlands to Braavos has much the same form.

Sansa Stark (Books 1–4)—Sansa is our eyes for much of King's Landings' politics.

Jon Snow (Books 1–3, 5)—Jon actually appears in Book 4, but in Sam's chapters as a non-POV character.

Bran Stark (Books 1–3, 5)—Bran provides an essential look into Northern politics before the sack of Winterfell.

Tyrion Lannister (Books 1–3, 5)—The greatest traveler in the books, from the Wall to the Eyrie to King's Landing to Slaver's Bay.

Daenerys Targaryen (Books 1–3, 5)—Dany, interestingly, is the only major war-leader to have her story told from her point of view.

Theon Greyjoy (Books 2, 5)—It's unclear if Theon is even alive after the Boltons take Winterfell, meaning his torture is mostly off-screen in the books.

Davos Seaworth (Books 2–3, 5)--Almost everything we know about Stannis before he reaches the Wall comes from Davos' POV.

Jaime Lannister (Books 3–5)—Jaime's road to redemption—without being sidetracked to Dorne—is still one of the story's best.

Samwell Tarly (Books 3–4)—Before his trip to Oldtown, Sam tells the story of the Night's Watch that Jon isn't around for.

Cersei Lannister (Books 4–5)—Cersei's desperate attempts to maintain power after Tywin's death also humanize the villainess.

Brienne of Tarth (Book 4)—Brienne's quest to find the Stark daughters leads us through the post-apocalyptic Riverlands.

Arianne Martell (Books 4–5)—Arianne's role in the story has mostly been given to Ellaria Sand.

Asha Greyjoy (Books 4–5)—Yara on the show. She ends up with Stannis' army during his march on Winterfell.

Victarion Greyjoy (Books 4–5)—Balon's brother has been removed from the show, but he's leading a group of warlike Ironborn into Slaver's Bay.

Quentyn Martell (Book 5)—Another removed Martell. His primary role is an attempt to free the dragons in Meereen, which is given to Tyrion in the show.

Barristan Selmy (Book 5)—In order to unravel the Meereenese Knot (see Chapter 80), Barristan, still alive, becomes the POV character in Meereen after Dany flees on Drogon.

In the fourth and fifth books, a handful of other characters have had fewer than four chapters.

Aeron Greyjoy—Another brother of King Balon, Aeron is the priest who "baptizes" Theon, calls the Kingsmoot, and later crowns Euron.

Areo Hotah—Doran Martell's bodyguard helps tell the story of Dorne.

Arys Oakhart—The Kingsguard assigned to Myrcella in Dorne, he's totally removed for the show.

Griff—See Chapter 79.

Melisandre—A single chapter that shows the fragility and manipulations of the seemingly powerful sorceress.

Kevan Lannister—Kevan shows up in order to die in the epilogue of *A Dance with Dragons*—although in an entirely different fashion than on the show, with the same effect of consolidating power for Cersei.

89 Sit on the Iron Throne

Around the time the second season of *Game of Thrones* ended, a strange new item appeared at the HBO store: a life-sized replica of the Iron Throne. This pleasant piece of furniture that could fit into any living room easily weighed 350 pounds, cost a mere $30,000, and required another $1,800 in shipping—a perfect acquisition for the extraordinarily wealthy *Game of Thrones* fan.

The Iron Throne is the symbol of power on *Game of Thrones*, the grand prize that most of the characters have been fighting for for six seasons now. The imposing structure—even more imposing in the novels, if you check out the art for it in *The World of Ice and Fire*—was built from the swords of the defeated forces at the Field of Fire. This was the biggest battle of the Targaryen conquest, where Aegon and his sisters rode their dragons and torched a combined Lannister-Gardener army. The melted swords were then turned into Aegon's throne.

As you can imagine, sitting on the Iron Throne in Westeros may not be the most pleasant experience. One of the signs of the Mad King's decline was that he was constantly cutting himself on the throne, hands covered in scabs.

In a Craigslist ad that went viral in 2013, one *Game of Thrones* fan offered a more pleasant experience on the Iron Throne. Looking for "a Stark in the streets but a Wildling in the sheets," she said she'd dress as Daenerys and needed a Robb Stark lookalike for one purpose: "on the Iron Throne I've so recently won, I make wild and passionate love with him, repeatedly." It's unclear if this was the official HBO replica throne, whether she actually succeeded, or if the whole thing was a prank.

There are a few easier ways to sit on the Iron Throne than winning a civil war, being named Hand, or having a skeezy casual encounter. HBO often sets one up for their public exhibitions, with show costumes, sets, and VR experiences in addition to having a fancy chair. These tend to be temporary setups in major cities, like London and New York City, or in *GoT*-associated cities like Belfast. There's also an Iron Throne at the venues of the *Game of Thrones* Concert Experience, which toured North America in early 2017, for example.

HBO knows how symbolically important the Iron Throne is, and does their best to make it possible—though perhaps not likely—for fans to sit on it. You probably can't wear Cersei's outfit from the sixth season finale (unless you're fantastic at cosplay) but you'll have a very special photo regardless.

90 Take a *Game of Thrones* Tour!

The heart of *Game of Thrones*' shooting and tourism industry is the city of Dubrovnik, Croatia. Dubrovnik has been used as the setting for King's Landing since the start of the second season (Malta was used in the first), and has also stood in for the Free Cities of Braavos and Pentos.

Dubrovnik has several major advantages for filming. The old medieval core of the city, with narrow, winding streets, old walls, and several forts seems perfect for *Game of Thrones*. The coast of the Adriatic is also a famous vacation and holiday locale. Locations like Illyrio's mansion (Villa Sheherezade) are Eastern European resorts. And Croatia has become understandably proud of their role on the hit series, sending their culture minister to filming dates in the city.

The other major filming location where tours can be found is Northern Ireland, particularly around Belfast. Most of the indoor sets for *Game of Thrones* are in Belfast, although clearly these are off-limits. Around the city, however, are several outdoor locations used for the North, the Riverlands, and the Crownlands.

One of the most famous of these are the "Dark Hedges," a road flanked by two rows of trees that give it both an elegant and ominous look. This path is used by the show to represent the Kingsroad just outside of King's Landing, with both Arya (Season 2) and Brienne (Season 4) traveling down it. While many of the sets in Belfast are off-limits, enough like the Dark Hedges are available that you can find *Game of Thrones* tours in Belfast.

From the fifth season, on a new country became an essential part of *Thrones* filming, and is possibly worth looking into as a tourist. That's Spain, which was used in Season 5 to represent Dorne, but has also started to be used for major set pieces. The

Water Gardens of Dorne, where most of that kingdom's plot has taken place, are filmed in the Alcazar de Sevilla, a palace that's already a major tourist attraction on its own.

A few other key scenes have been filmed in Spain: the sixth season's Tower of Joy, also in Dorne, is the castle of Zafra in Spain, while the great bullring outside of Osuna became the location for the battle at Daznak's Pit at the end of Season 5. Major battle scenes in Season 7 are also being filmed in Spain.

There are a few other countries that have played host to *Game of Thrones* for filming, but may be less effective for tourism purposes. Iceland has been used for the North and especially for the Beyond-the-Wall scenes of Season 2, but it's hard to get excited about walking along a largely blank glacier. Slaver's Bay was initially filmed in Morocco in Season 3, but shifted to Croatia for future seasons.

If you're in Europe, or thinking of visiting, checking out *Game of Thrones* locations may not be a full vacation in and of itself. But so many of these locales are connected to fascinating regions with impressive history that they're a great supplement to a European tour, and worth researching further.

91 Tommen and Myrcella

Game of Thrones is a show about huge personalities in powerful roles, and few are bigger than the kings and queens. Think of how memorable Robert, Joffrey, and now Cersei have been on the Iron Throne. Or the rebels and exiles, like Daenerys, Robb, Jon, Renly, and Stannis. They're all huge presences, dominating their factions politically and their scenes as actors and characters.

And then there's King Tommen. Poor, doomed, weak-willed King Tommen.

This isn't a criticism of the writing of Tommen, nor of Dean-Charles Chapman, his actor. There are weak kings all throughout history. One of *Game of Thrones'* chief historical influences, the Wars of the Roses (see Chapter 63) is largely centered on the sickly, pathetic King Henry VI. Henry ruled for forty years, but increasing bouts of insanity led to conflict between his would-be regents. Tommen didn't last this long, but was in a similar vein: less a leader than a football passed back and forth between factions, primarily the Lannisters and Tyrells.

Tommen's sister Myrcella is cut from the same cloth. Like her brother, she's a fundamentally decent person, but also like her brother, she cannot play the game at any level. She's a prop—used by Tyrion to both negotiate a marriage alliance with Dorne and uncover which of the Small Council members is a spy, and then potentially as a hostage when the Sand Snakes make their move. The two children are victims of the game, not its players, not like the Stark children grow into.

This is their role through the first two seasons: they're the good Lannisters, showing up occasionally to remind the world they exist. In the second season, Myrcella gets the spotlight briefly as a pawn in Tyrion's marriage alliance game, before being engaged to Prince Trystane of Dorne. Tommen, too, shows up in a critical episode. He's taken by Cersei to sit on the Iron Throne and await the results of the Battle of Blackwater—to be poisoned alongside her, should Stannis win.

Neither of the children appear in the third season, and Myrcella is gone from the fourth as well. Both are recast with older, more established actors: Tommen is changed from Callum Wharry to Dean-Charles Chapman (who had played a Lannister cousin in Season 3), and Myrcella is recast from Aimee Richardson to Nell

Tiger Free. Richardson, amusingly, posted to her social media that she was a "Princess for Hire" after the recast.

Tommen takes a much larger role than his sister, becoming a main cast member from the fourth through the sixth seasons, as the King of the Seven Kingdoms. Or at least, he's present. In the fourth season, he's utterly dominated by his grandfather and Hand, Tywin Lannister. After Tywin's death, his mother Cersei and wife Margaery battle for control over him, with Cersei calling in the High Sparrow to gain an initial victory before herself being imprisoned by the fanatics.

King Tommen is helpless through this crisis, too weak to figure out and act upon the right course of action. Margaery Tyrell, however, manages to figure out a way to free herself: by converting the king to the Sparrows' form of the faith, and turning Tommen against Cersei by declaring trial by combat illegal.

But instead it just pushes Cersei into a corner. With almost everyone save Qyburn against her, Cersei launches a decapitation strike that kills Margaery, the High Sparrow, and hundreds of other nobles. Ser Gregor prevents Tommen from being one of those present during the attack, but when he fully realizes what his mother has done, he quietly sets aside his crown and jumps to his death.

Myrcella's death the previous season is only slightly less pathetic. In Dorne, she's fallen in love with her fiancé, Prince Trystane, and is living like a Disney princess. But the death of Oberyn Martell has his paramour and daughters, the Sand Snakes, looking for revenge. They send a threat to King's Landing, and Cersei sends Jaime to bring their daughter back. Jaime arrives right as the Sand Snakes launch their coup, both attempting to kidnap Myrcella and both failing.

Jaime manages to negotiate his way home with Myrcella, and they even have a moment of father-daughter bonding where he admits that he is her father, and she accepts him. Then she promptly dies, murdered by Ellaria Sand's slow-acting poison. Both of the Lannister children, far too sweet to survive the world of King's Landing, end up dead almost as soon as they become players of the game.

Who Is the Heir to the Iron Throne?

"...Lannister will follow Joffrey on the throne of the Seven Kingdoms by the simple expedient of killing everyone ahead of [them] in the line of succession...."—George R.R. Martin's original pitch

Sitting on the Iron Throne isn't all it's cracked up to be, with four different kings in the last 20 years—three of the four murdered, the other a suicide. So it's worth asking: when King Tommen kicked the bucket, who, legally, should have taken his place? We all know Cersei took the throne for herself, but was that anywhere near legal?

To the latter question: no, Cersei's seizure of the throne was thoroughly illegal for everyone who should have cared. On the other hand, Westeros is in a thoroughly illegal place right now, so we're seeing lords declaring independence in the North, or seeking a former heir across the Narrow Sea in Daenerys Targaryen. (Both Dany's possible inability to reproduce and Jon Snow's true parentage complicate matters as well, but both are as yet not public.)

But who, according to the laws of the Seven Kingdoms, should have been the real heir? There are a couple legal answers. During Robert's Rebellion, the Baratheons had the strongest legal claim because his grandmother was Rhaelle Targaryen, aunt to King Aerys Targaryen. When the revolt started, he was the closest relative who wasn't a direct relation of the Mad King. But every one of Rhaelle's legal descendants—House Baratheon—are dead with Tommen's passing, so that doesn't help.

Meanwhile, the incest-loving Targaryens only rarely married outside of their family. So the question of the legal heir is this: who was the last Targaryen before Rhaelle to marry outside his or her family, and do they still have descendants in the Seven Kingdoms?

The answer, it turns out, is Elaena Targaryen, who, nearly a century and a half before the events of *Game of Thrones*, married several lords. The first one with whom she had legal children was Lord Ossifer Plumm. The Plumms aren't on the show at all, but they are in the books as a minor house in the Westerlands under the Lannisters. (One younger Plumm brother has a larger role as a mercenary during the battles in Slaver's Bay). Lord Philip Plumm is encountered briefly by Jaime Lannister, who thinks Plumm is an all right dude. So the Lannisters could have propped him up, if Cersei didn't just seize the throne for herself.

Does it matter? Probably not: if Tommen's legal heir was ever going to play a role in the story, he or she would probably have been introduced by now (although there's always Gendry). For the sake of narrative convenience, it's easy to see why *Game of Thrones* simply had Cersei seize the throne instead of a protracted debate about succession and a new major character being introduced. But if you were ever curious about who the law said had the right, it was Lord Philip Plumm.

93 Margaery Tyrell

"Forget about the bloody gods and listen to what I'm telling you."—
Margaery Tyrell

Of all the new characters introduced in the second season of *Game of Thrones*, the most exciting might have been Margaery Tyrell. While initially she's just seen as a quiet queen by Renly Baratheon's side, embodiment of his alliance with the Tyrells, that changes in a hurry. *Game of Thrones* cast rising star Natalie Dormer, previously known for playing Anne Boleyn on *The Tudors*, and she was not someone they could hide in the background.

As played by Dormer, Margaery Tyrell is as clever as she is beautiful, moral but pragmatic. She's a near-perfect player of the game of thrones. She has a simple goal—become queen—and she takes whatever's available in order to achieve that goal. For viewers, Margaery's impressive ambition is depicted soon after her appearance, when, trying to convince King Renly to impregnate her and legitimize their marriage and his claim to the throne, she offered to let him bring in her brother, Renly's lover Ser Loras. There've been a lot of daring moves to seize the crown in the game of thrones, but nothing else quite like that.

The cool thing about Margaery is that the book version of her is nothing like this. Or rather—the book version of Margaery is the woman at the melee, sitting next to her king, the perfect instrument for winning an alliance with one of Westeros' most powerful families. Margaery is a cypher, someone everyone else projects their views onto. Sansa views her as a potential friend and ally, where Cersei views the younger queen as a conniving, backstabbing rival. This is interesting too—there's a major character whose motives are totally obfuscated!—but it's nowhere near as fun as seeing Dormer's sly smile as she verbally twists the knife in Queen Cersei.

Unlike most of the major players in the game, Margaery appears to be a fundamentally decent person. She and her grandmother Olenna are two of the very few people in King's Landing who treat Sansa Stark with kindness and respect. She also gives

In the 1960s, Diana Rigg was the best, sexiest actress on television. In the 2010s, she may have found her successor in the superb Natalie Dormer.
(Photo courtesy of HBO / Photofest)

charity to the poor of King's Landing, an idea that seems to baffle and terrify the Lannisters. And Margaery's downfall begins with her arrest by the Sparrows for lying to protect her brother.

All of this makes it a little odd to think that Margaery Tyrell's primary focus, her burning ambition, is to become queen. Not a queen like Daenerys or Cersei, who would rule from the Iron Throne, weak men be damned, but the queen who marries the king. So Margaery marries Renly, who would have won the War of the Five Kings but for his brother Stannis' "secret sorceress" cheat code. Then she marries Joffrey, or at least she tries to, before her grandmother has that king murdered thanks to Sansa's honesty about Joff's crimes. And she finally ends up with poor, sweet, dense Tommen. (In the novels there's even another king she makes a play for: she's first mentioned early in *A Game of Thrones* by Renly as a proposed marriage partner for King Robert if Cersei can be divorced.)

In the end, her single-minded ambition may have been what doomed her. Characters like Cersei and Olenna do what they do to protect their family, while Jon and Dany try to make the world a better place. Margaery? She tried to be queen and protect her family and be a decent person. So when the Sept of Baelor went up in flames, Margaery Tyrell—clever and beautiful, moral and pragmatic—was the only person to see that everyone there was in danger. She just didn't have the power to do anything about it. It's usually sad when a favorite character dies on *Game of Thrones*, but Margaery's intelligence shining through in the end, even if she couldn't do anything about it, made her a hero at the last.

94 Robb Stark

"That's not the kind of king I want to be."
"What kind of king do you want to be?"
"I don't know. The good kind?"—Robb Stark and Talisa Maegyr

Robb Stark seems like the hero of *Game of Thrones* in its second and third seasons. After the chaos of his father's death, it's Robb who steps up and provides a stable, powerful, moral resistance to Lannister dominance. His rebellion gives even the best characters trapped by the Lannisters, particularly his sisters (and *Game of Thrones* fans) hope.

Then, of course, in the most stunning episode of the series, Robb, much of his family, his armies, and his rebellion are destroyed by a Lannister-Bolton-Frey conspiracy at the Red Wedding, seeming to end any hope of a straightforward, good resolution to the civil war tearing Westeros apart. Because Robb Stark, just like his father, is a powerful, honorable man, which makes him easy to betray.

Robb's obvious mistake, of course, was marrying Talisa Maegyr for love, instead of maintaining his marriage alliance with the Freys. Without the Frey armies, he couldn't stay on the offensive. After winning multiple battles against the Lannisters, Robb was invincible in the field, but not strong enough to take on King's Landing directly without them. Hence the tragic set of events leading to the Red Wedding. But was that Robb's real mistake?

Perhaps his biggest error came in the middle of Season 1, before Ned was even executed. As Robb calls his banners and marches south, leaving Bran in charge of Winterfell, the Wildling Osha tells the younger Stark boy that Robb should have turned his army north, not south. The real threat, to her, came from the White Walkers. Now, Robb couldn't know this for certain, and it's unfair on one hand to expect him to see the true threat for what it is. On the other hand, this short-sighted focus on the temporary political battle is a mistake everyone has made, and despite his tactical genius and moral clarity, Robb makes it just like everyone else.

Robb's second major mistake: investing undeserving lieutenants with his full trust. Much like the previous mistake, this was to some extent inevitable. Roose Bolton led arguably the second-most powerful house in the North, and was an effective battle commander. Of course Robb would have to invest his trust in Lord Bolton—without him, the war effort was likely doomed anyway. Even still, his mother Catelyn warned him not to trust Roose too much, and she ended up more than correct on that count.

A more pressing example of Robb's trust in the wrong people, and Cat's correct warnings, came with Theon Greyjoy's defection. Against his mother's advice, Robb allowed Theon to deliver his offer of alliance to Balon Greyjoy. And the weak-willed Theon fell under his culture's sway, defected, and aided in their assault on the North, capturing Winterfell in a bold, if doomed, raid. Regardless of the inevitability of Theon's failure, the sacking of Winterfell crippled Robb's war effort.

Robb's third mistake: continuing to prosecute the war, even after his father was killed, his castle taken, and, eventually, his army started to fall apart. On the show, he tells Talisa that he has to keep fighting now, because if he marches back and retakes the North from the Ironborn, his men will go home for the winter, and he can't possibly win. This is, to a certain extent, true—but it's not like the Lannisters would be in a position to invade.

The bigger problem for Robb is that his allies in the Riverlands would be doomed if he deserted them. The war started, after all, when the Lannisters attacked House Tully in exchange for one of its daughters, Robb's mother, arresting Tyrion Lannister. And

Robb's first great victory came when he defeated and captured Jaime Lannister in front of Riverrun, breaking its siege. Without Robb, though, how could his allies and family defend themselves? Robb was honor-bound to keep up the fight.

In the novels, Robb's honor is the more direct cause of his death, just like his father. There, he marries the daughter of a minor Lannister vassal house, Jeyne Westerling. After capturing their castle, he's wounded, and while nursing him back to health, he hooks up with Jeyne. Robb feels honor-bound to wed the woman he's slept with, leading to his death. The showrunners of *Game of Thrones*, however, thought that that was a bit too repetitive, and instead had Robb wed for love.

The marriage to Talisa also allowed *Game of Thrones* to humanize Robb Stark far more than the novels did. Apart from the near-infant Rickon, Robb was the only Stark not to be a point-of-view character in the novels. He was certainly heroic, and through his mother's eyes, we got to see some depth. But it was far harder to actually like the Robb of the novels compared to the one on the show. The interplay between Richard Madden (who's gone on to star in several films) and Oona Chaplin (yes, like Charlie—her grandfather), especially once they married in the third season, built the grand tragedy of the Red Wedding even bigger.

Still, while Robb made several major mistakes, none necessarily should have led to his death. Dany's story, for example, is a litany of mistakes. They hurt her cause, of course, but they don't kill her and destroy her armies. That's because Dany isn't merely the leader of a faction in the struggles for Westeros and beyond: she's the leader of a movement, an attempt to make the world better by freeing slaves and "breaking the wheel."

The Stark lords, Ned and Robb, are essentially conservative: they want to maintain and reform the current order, putting better people in charge but not working toward freedom like Dany, or trying to end ancient rivalries for the greater good like Jon. This makes Robb Stark expendable, and so he expires.

95 Oberyn Martell

"It is rare to meet a Lannister who shares my enthusiasm for dead Lannisters."—Oberyn Martell

He's only in one season of *Game of Thrones*, but Oberyn Martell is one of the show's most notable characters. From the moment he shows up in a pansexual orgy with Littlefinger's brother, he upsets the natural order of King's Landing. Add in one of the most spectacular deaths in the series, in definitely the best duel in all of *Game of Thrones*, and it's easy to see why he's so memorable.

This makes it stranger since Oberyn is also, in many ways, a collection of clichés. First, he's the fiery Latin lover, voracious in his sexual appetites—and his appetite for revenge. Second, he's a sort of deliberate counter to the idea that trial by combat is a cheat code in Westeros. Tyrion already used it successfully once in the first season—it might feel cheap if he did it again in Season 4, but he needed a champion to try and die for him.

Third, Oberyn is actually sort of a joke by George R.R. Martin. The author thought it would be interesting to create an Inigo Montoya–style character—the guy in *The Princess Bride* who repeats the same revenge-seeking phrase over and over in his big, climactic duel. Martin wanted to do exactly that, only to have the guy die in the end. In other words, Oberyn was initially supposed to be a one-dimensional joke...it's just that that joke turned into a real character thanks to Martin's writing and Pedro Pascal's performance.

The most important part of Oberyn's biography isn't even his, it's his sister's. Elia Martell, decades before the start of *Game of Thrones'* story, was married to Rhaegar Targaryen, the dashing young heir to the Iron Throne. This was a marriage of alliance more than love, as Rhaegar eventually ran away with Lyanna Stark, leaving Elia and their two babies in King's Landing. Still, Dornish troops supported the Targaryens during Robert's Rebellion. After Rhaegar's defeat and death, Lannister troops sacked King's Landing, with Ser Gregor Clegane, the Mountain that Rides, raping and killing Elia, and murdering her babies as well—possibly on the direct orders of Tywin Lannister.

Oberyn wanted revenge for the act as soon as he found out. In the novels, he wanted to keep the fight going for Viserys, but the new Hand, Jon Arryn, convinced him and his brother Lord Doran Martell to keep Dorne peaceful. The two men would still conspire to aid a Targaryen restoration, signing a pact with Viserys' protector for him to wed Doran's daughter Arianne—who was later removed from the series, along with this plotline.

The younger Martell brother was always a passionate lover. At sixteen, Oberyn was caught in bed with a minor lord's wife, and the two fought a duel to first blood. Although he only scratched his opponent, the wound eventually became infected, killing the lord, and giving Oberyn Martell his nickname: "the Red Viper." An informal exile to Essos followed, where Oberyn learned about the Unsullied, and fought in the fighting pits of Meereen.

Robert Baratheon's death apparently thaws relations between Dorne and the Iron Throne enough that Oberyn travels to King's Landing as the official representative of what has, on *Game of Thrones*, been the quietest of the Seven Kingdoms up until then. This wouldn't last—Oberyn disrupts everything he can in King's

Landing from the moment he arrives, skipping Tyrion's official welcome to the city and heading straight to the brothel.

His directness tends to show different sides of existing characters. The always-composed Tywin Lannister is forced into discomfort when the Hand himself is forced to find Oberyn in a brothel. A conversation about their daughters reveals a very human side to both the Viper and Cersei Lannister. And in perhaps the most revealing moment, he knocks even the unflappable Lord Varys when the Viper manages to recognize the Spider's accent as being from Lys—something apparently no one else can even hear.

Although he's direct in manner, Oberyn is indirect about his true goals in King's Landing—avenging Elia—until Tyrion's trial presents an opportunity. When Tyrion demands trial by combat, the Lannister champion is inevitably Gregor Clegane, so Oberyn offers his services to Tyrion.

Oberyn has two goals in the combat: to kill Gregor, but also to defeat him so cruelly that the knight would finger Tywin as the man who gave the order to have Elia and her children killed. Against all apparent odds, the Red Viper succeeds at the first, dancing around Clegane until he can find an opening and knock the Mountain to the ground. But in performatively interrogating Clegane, Oberyn lets his guard down just enough that the Mountain can grab him and crush his skull, all while admitting his own—though not Tywin's—guilt.

It was a horrifying moment for all Oberyn's new fans made across the course of the season, nearly matching the Red Wedding in shocked fan reaction. It was still a fitting end, however: one of *Game of Thrones'* hottest-burning stars had to have a truly explosive finish. And Oberyn's legacy would live on, in part, with his paramour Ellaria Sand leading his daughters in cutting a bloody swath of revenge through Dorne, then aligning with Daenerys Targaryen to seek revenge against the Lannisters.

96 Telltale's *Game of Thrones*

There are a few different kinds of *Game of Thrones*–inspired games, and they're often both really good and really interesting. There are the officially licensed games, discussed here, but there are also strategy games and roleplaying games without the license, but with the spirit of the story.

Before it became an international mega-hit, the *Game of Thrones* license went to the medium-sized French publisher Cyanide, which released two games with it. They weren't terribly exciting games—Cyanide is a publisher that does interesting experiments and ambitious, janky attempts at big-budget games. So their two *Game of Thrones* games didn't make too much of a splash.

The first, *Game of Thrones: Genesis* was a largely uninspiring real-time strategy game involving the history of Westeros that was not well-received, as it lacked most of what made *Game of Thrones* interesting.

The second, called simply *Game of Thrones*, was a role-playing game where you played a brother of the Night's Watch plus a Thoros-like red priest in the southlands. It was an interesting experiment, but its reach exceeded its grasp, especially compared to other cinematic RPGs released in the same time period, like *Mass Effect* or *The Witcher 2*. Still, you could play as a "Water Dancer"—Syrio Forel's combat style—and that alone means it's got some value.

But the most exciting *Game of Thrones* video game dropped a couple years later, when Telltale got the license. Telltale is an adventure game company that gained massive prominence in 2012 when it released *The Walking Dead,* a game that put you in the role of a survivor of the zombie apocalypse, running parallel, but only barely connected to, the TV series and comics.

Instead of focusing on puzzles, the traditional heart of adventure games, *The Walking Dead* focused on dialogue. With expressive animated faces and top-tier voice actors, Telltale had the technical foundation for a character-based story. They added in complex moral choices, like deciding whether to leave an incompetent but well-meaning survivor to his death. It was a hit, and Telltale adapted the model to the new licenses they got: the *Fables* comic books, the *Borderlands* video games...and in late 2014, *Game of Thrones*.

The premise of Telltale's *Game of Thrones* is this: you play the various members of House Forrester, a minor Northern house that is mentioned, without specifics, in the novels. Telltale constructed House Forrester to be a minor parallel to House Stark, with several different characters taking roles very similar to those of the Starks. Mira Forrester, for example, ends up a Northern girl in King's Landing during the Lannister ascendance just like Sansa Stark, while Gared Tuttle, the son of a key Forrester retainer, finds himself on the way to the Wall just like Jon Stark.

Telltale uses these Stark-like premises well, but it also takes advantage of the *Game of Thrones* license in really interesting ways. For one thing, it utilizes several actors and characters from the show. Iwan Rheon as Ramsay Bolton, for example, is a chaotic evil nightmare who may destroy what you hold dear in a second if he gets the whim, no matter how well you think you've planned for him.

But the best example comes in the first episode, when the Sansa-like Mira is sent to an audience with Queen Cersei. Cersei grills Mira, pushing the girl to either swear full loyalty to the Lannister-controlled crown, betraying her friend Margaery Tyrell, or reveal herself a Northern loyalist. The neat thing about this scene is that, if you've played video games with choices like these—including Telltale's *The Walking Dead*—the answer is simple: be non-committal. Say nice platitudes, and assuage both Cersei and Margaery.

Except that this is Cersei brotherfuckin' Lannister, and she will not put up with your half-assed shit. Try to deflect her probing questions, and she just gets meaner. The fact that she is Cersei, she has the Lannister smirk, and she's voiced by Lena Headey all make it quite understandable that in Telltale's *Game of Thrones* you can't do what other video games let you do. You have to make a hard choice in front of Cersei, Margaery, and the court.

While Telltale's *Game of Thrones* continues in this mode, and quite well, that's not to say that it's perfect. It seems oddly low-budget in certain ways, particularly in outdoor scenes with cheap-looking backgrounds. Perhaps more importantly, it was released before and during the fifth season of *Game of Thrones*, when the show was at its grimmest, and the game adopts that tone as well. Fundamentally decent characters are slaughtered at a moment's notice, and the choices you make still lead inexorably to a dark finish.

But if you're looking to play the game of thrones in a character-focused sense, there's nothing better than *Game of Thrones: A Telltale Games Series*.

97 Crusader Kings 2, the Strategy *Game of Thrones*

If you want to play the game of thrones, there are story-based forms, like Telltale's *Game of Thrones* in the previous chapter. But there are also strategy-based games, Littlefinger simulators, where you can play as a lord or a king, and try to control the Iron Throne that way.

The best of these isn't even officially a *Game of Thrones* game—it's called *Crusader Kings 2*, by Swedish developer Paradox Interactive, and available on Steam. There are two relevant forms of *CK2* for *Game of Thrones* fans: the base game, a medieval European political simulator; and the *Game of Thrones* user modification (a "mod") for the game, which turns *Crusader Kings 2* into Westeros and lets you fight Robert's Rebellion or the Clash of Kings. Both are great for *GoT* fans, for oddly different reasons.

Crusader Kings 2 is built around the idea that you control a specific dynasty in medieval Europe. That dynasty can be focused on, from smallest to largest: a count, duke, king, or emperor. Sometimes you're a small part of a huge empire, sometimes half of a breaking kingdom, and sometimes a world power.

The thing that makes *CK2* really work as a *Game of Thrones* simulator, though, is the building sense of history. You may start as count in, say, the southwest part of France, but as time goes on, you might find yourself in a rivalry with the Duke of Burgundy, one which eventually leads to civil war. Like *Game of Thrones*, you could find yourself, like Tywin Lannister, attempting to assassinate a rival like Robb Stark.

Now, before we get too far, I wanna say this: *Crusader Kings 2* is a complicated game where, as a medieval lord or lady and head of a family, you have a ton of different choices as to how to change laws, declare holy war, build your infrastructure, appoint a small council, marry your children off, find new hobbies, assassinate your childhood rival, hold a nation-wide tournament of knights, and more. This is complex, and if you're a first-time player just diving in, it can definitely be overwhelming. But there are a few ways around this. Obviously, looking up tutorials online can help, as can focusing on role-playing a specific character.

But the best way to learn how to play *Crusader Kings 2?* It's probably to play the *Game of Thrones* mod, where you know how the politics around the Iron Throne work, and can learn how the rest of the game works from there. Want to take control of King Robert as he starts and wins his rebellion against Targaryens? You'll also have to figure out how to keep the realm under control via marriage, like marrying Cersei Lannister.

The *Game of Thrones* mod is also based around specific scenarios, which makes it a great way to get into Westerosi history and geography. Aegon's Conquest, Robert's Rebellion, the Clash of Kings (Season 2), and the Feast for Crows (Season 5) are all potential starting points, as well as minor points in the history of the Seven Kingdoms, like the first Greyjoy rebellion or the Faith Militant uprising shortly after the Targaryen conquest. This is also based more on the books than the show, which is actually part of its appeal: the density of characterization in the novels works great in a game where you can play as literally any house in Westeros, from the Baratheons to the Mormonts.

98 Ramsay Snow

Over the course of his time on the show, Ramsay became the most-hated character for fans and critics, as his one-note cruelty became increasingly repetitive. Ramsay did have his charms; Iwan Rheon played him with a sly, nasty enthusiasm that worked especially well when he wasn't fully in charge in a situation, usually with his father, Roose Bolton. But those were too rare. How was it Ramsay Snow became the symbol of *Game of Thrones* at its grimmest?

The answer to this lies in the difficulty of adapting a TV series from a series of novels. See, here's the thing with Ramsay in the novels: he only appears in *A Clash of Kings* and *A Dance with Dragons*, the second and fifth books. Yet he doesn't appear at all in

Season 2—the *Clash of Kings* season—and then does consistently after that.

The primary reason for this is simple: Alfie Allen was really good at portraying Theon in Season 2. So in order to be sure they could maintain him, and not have to recast like the Mountain or Daario, HBO needed something for Theon to do. But what does he do in that time span in the books? He gets tortured and converted into Reek by Ramsay Snow. Likewise, Iwan Rheon, fresh off a star turn in the cult TV series *Misfits,* was a great piece of casting, and worth keeping around for when he became important.

Why wasn't Ramsay in Season 2? That's a more difficult question, and one with far-reaching effects on the show as a whole. In *A Clash of Kings*, the North is a politically complex place, with Bran Stark as acting Lord of Winterfell learning to deal with the lords. One of those is Ramsay Snow, who murders some innocents, gets captured, and then wins Theon's ear when the Greyjoy takes over. It's Ramsay who suddenly kills Rodrik Cassell, and it's clear he's the one who sacks Winterfell, proving the Boltons are not to be trusted long before the Red Wedding.

Not including this political complexity in the North also causes *Game of Thrones* some trouble in later seasons, as Ramsay becomes more integrated into the main story. Following the third season, where Ramsay's true parentage is revealed right around the same time his father puts a knife in Robb Stark's heart, the Boltons become the dominant house in the North—even given the title Wardens of the North by the Lannisters.

But they have to take the North from their enemies, which pushes Ramsay outside of his simple torture of Theon and into the wider world. The first group of enemies are the Ironborn, who still hold most of the castles on the west coast of the North, including Moat Cailin, which prevents Roose Bolton from returning to his home. Using the abused Theon Greyjoy, Ramsay convinces the defenders of that stronghold to surrender, opening the road to the north to his father's armies.

For this, Ramsay is given his greatest honor: he's legitimized by Roose Bolton, and made the heir to what's now the most powerful house in the North. For many people this might be enough, but for the cruel and paranoid Ramsay, it most certainly isn't. Roose is equally cruel, and enjoys twisting the knife in his son, playing on his insecurities. One of those is that he might be deposed, and when Roose's new wife, Walda Frey, becomes pregnant, Ramsay's position in his own mind is under threat.

Throughout this all, the Bastard of Bolton's cruelty continues. His preferred weapon is his collection of dogs, who he orders to kill and eat his enemies, lovers, or anyone he feels like. This includes Tansy, his secondary lover who makes his main squeeze Myranda jealous. Later, it includes his stepmother and newborn stepbrother.

The focus of the psychological battles between father and son becomes Ramsay's bride, Sansa Stark. Ramsay successfully plays the part of the good son in winning the betrothal from Littlefinger, but as Sansa becomes more and more within his grasp, he can't help toying with her, by, for example, showing Theon Greyjoy, who supposedly killed her brothers, to her at a dinner. The pragmatic Roose recognizes that Ramsay is putting his cruelty ahead of any other considerations and so attempts to rein in his son—not because he disagrees, but because he understands the importance of appearances. For Ramsay, though, such a milquetoast criticism isn't enough to stop him.

Ramsay Bolton abuses his new wife, raping and imprisoning her, setting his lover Myranda to psychologically torture Sansa as well. Sansa attempts to recruit her comrade in abuse, Theon Greyjoy, to her cause, but initially fails.

The impending attack of Stannis Baratheon changes all the decisions of House Bolton, however. While the pragmatic Roose wants to hole up and win a siege, the ruthless Ramsay has a better

idea: launch a raid and destroy Stannis' supplies. This works—
Stannis is forced into desperately sacrificing his daughter, causing
half his army to retreat and making them easy pickings for the
Boltons. But while this is happening, Theon finally finds himself
and flees alongside Sansa.

When the sixth season begins, Roose Bolton cannot help twisting the knife against his son again, threatening to have him replaced
as heir if Ramsay cannot find his wife again to make heirs. Yet
Ramsay is different now: perhaps his marriage, perhaps his military
success, or perhaps his paranoia at being supplanted make him
change his mind.

Roose has said that despite being a bastard and a product of
rape, Ramsay is a true Bolton and son. Roose seems to believe that
this is some kind of father-son bonding attempt. But for Ramsay,
being a true Bolton means betrayal: he kills his father and seizes the
North for himself.

Sansa, however, has escaped his forces, and joined with Jon
Snow at Castle Black. There they raise a new army, and a new threat
to House Bolton. Ramsay has allies this time, however. The heir to
House Karstark, still hating the Starks for Robb's execution of his
father, joins the Boltons. So too does the head of House Umber,
the Smalljon, who despises Jon's alliance with the Wildlings and
therefore sells Rickon Stark to Ramsay for an alliance.

Unfortunately this is another case where the simplicity of
Northern politics damages the show. In the novels, the impending arrival of winter and Stannis' army turns the Bolton camp at
Winterfell into a place of gothic horror, with betrayal, murder,
accidental cannibalism, and uncertainty about who's on whose
side, leading to the "Battle of Ice." The show, however, made
the first "Battle of Ice" between Stannis and the Boltons a simple
victory. Any sort of intrigue is left for the sixth season "Battle of
the Bastards." But because it hasn't laid the groundwork for, say,
Lord Manderly preparing to betray the Boltons, it doesn't follow

through. Everyone in the battle is on exactly the same side as they say they are.

Ramsay's cleverness begins to win him the day, pulling Jon's army from their defensive positions into a trap. But as his men surround the Stark army, the Knights of the Vale, allied with his ex-wife Sansa Stark, attack and destroy his men. Ramsay, ever-confident, flees into Winterfell to wait out a winter siege—only to see his gates smashed by Jon's giant, Wun Wun.

The Bastard of Bolton kills Wun Wun as his last free act, but is attacked and brutally beaten by Jon, who only spares his life so that Sansa can do as she pleases with him. For the man who abused her, destroyed the North, and killed her brother Rickon, she has a simple punishment: she leaves him in the kennels with his starving dogs. Ramsay Snow, in the end, is devoured by the instruments of his greatest cruelties.

99 Have a Beer with Brewery Ommegang

"It's not easy being drunk all the time. Everyone would do it if it were easy."—*Tyrion Lannister*

If you're a beer drinker and a *Game of Thrones* fan, it's worth taking a look at the *Thrones*-inspired offerings from New York-based Brewery Ommegang, who, since 2013, have been releasing officially licensed, limited-edition *Game of Thrones* brews with names like "Iron Throne" and "Valar Morghulis."

Ommegang does Belgian-style ale, which tends to be light and smooth but with complex flavors. (Chimay or Fin du Monde are decent comparison points—there really isn't a mass-produced beer that comes close, although Samuel Adams has similar lightness and complexity, but it's a lager, not an ale.)

Seven different types have been released as of this writing, at a rough pace of two new models per year. Those seven are:

Iron Throne, a smooth golden ale inspired by the Lannister wearers of the crown.

Take the Black Stout, a smooth, malty dark beer obviously inspired by the Night's Watch.

Fire and Blood, a spicier red ale based on House Targaryen's words and Daenerys' dragons.

Valar Morghulis, a light dubbel ale with a spicy little kick in the aftertaste inspired by Arya's quest for revenge (and easily my favorite of the five I tried).

Three-Eyed Raven, an interesting combination of a dark ale and a pale, fruity saison, built on Bran Stark's quest.

Seven Kingdoms, a hoppy and fruity light ale.

Valar Dohaeris, another complex light ale inspired by Arya's quests.

As Ommegang has continued with this project, their beers have become more complex, experimental, and thematically intertwined with the show (and, having had the first five, they've become better over that time as well, with Iron Throne and Take the Black being good but nothing special, while Valar Morhulis and Three-Eyed Raven had tastes I hadn't really encountered before).

It's pretty easy to scoff at corporate tie-ins for *Game of Thrones*—as one of the most popular franchises in the world, everyone wants a piece of the action. But Brewery Ommegang shows how to do this kind of tie-in right: a company that wants to flex its creative muscles in association with a show they clearly love, and a final product with a quality that matches *Game of Thrones'* production values.

If you want to find one of Brewery Ommegang's *Thrones*-inspired beers, they're not the cheapest things in the world—recommended $10 price tag for a 750ml bottle. They also tend to be only at specialty liquor stores, so it's worth checking out their website (ommegang.com) to see where they've been delivered.

 **Hodor?**

"Hodor."—Hodor

Hodor! Hodor Hodor Hodor. Hodor.

Hodorhodorhodorhodor.

Hodor, Hodor Hodor Hodor Hodor, Hodor. Hodor! Hodor Hodor Hodor Hodor Hodor, Hodor Hodor Hodor Hodor.

Hodor?

Hodor!